PERSONAL TAXATION

Finance Act 2008

Study Text

In this edition

- Plenty of exam focus points to ensure you focus on the exams you will be facing in 2009

- A question and answer bank including preparatory and exam standard short and long form questions and pilot paper questions for this syllabus. Marking schemes have been added to some of the answers so that you can gauge how well you are doing

- A general index

- **Icons** which highlight relevant chapters for study in the ATT's law manual 'Essential Law for the Taxation Technician'.

- Thorough and reliable updating for the Finance Act 2008 with changes highlighted in the text

FOR EXAMS IN MAY AND NOVEMBER 2009

Tax Qualification Training

Contents

3rd edition August 2008
Printed text ISBN 9780 7517 5549 7
e text ISBN 9780 7517 5460 5

British Library Cataloguing-in-Publication Data

A catalogue record for this book
is available from the British Library

Published by

BPP Learning Media Ltd
BPP House, Aldine Place
London W12 8AA

www.bpp.com/learningmedia

Printed in Great Britain by WM Print Limited

Page

Introduction

Chapters

Part A: Personal Income Tax

Part B: Capital Gains Tax

Part C: Administration

Question and Answer bank

Index

Review form

Using your ATT texts

The ATT texts aim to ensure your success in the 2009 exams.

Key features of this text include:

- **Exam focus points** to help ensure you focus your efforts on the exams you will be facing in 2009.

- **Finance Act 2008** changes highlighted throughout the text. This enables you to identify material that may have changed since your previous studies.

- **Relevant legislative references** provided throughout the text. As you are permitted to take your legislation into the examination room, it is important that you develop the habit of looking up references in the legislation as you study. Publications taken into the examination must be bound copies. They can be **underlined, sidelined and highlighted. Annotating, use of 'post-its' and tagging is NOT allowed.**

- **Icons** highlight when to study areas of the ATT's law manual 'Essential Law for the Taxation Technician.

- **Worked examples** throughout the text.

- **Chapter roundups** at the end of each chapter summarising the key points covered in the chapter.

- **Quizzes** at the end of each chapter designed to test your grasp of the principles explained. Solutions to the quiz follow immediately.

- **A separate short form and long form Question and Answer section**. At the end of every chapter there are short form and long form questions that you should attempt. Some of the long form questions are preparatory questions and others are exam standard. Some of the answers contain marking schemes which will help you gauge how well you are doing.

- A **general** index is included at the back of the text.

TQT
Tax Qualification Training

The Examination Papers

Overview of the examination structure

The examination

The ATT examination offers a choice from seven free-standing Certificates of Competency in a modular structure. It is possible to take an examination in one topic only. This will lead to the award of a Certificate of Competency in that topic.

The certificate papers are:

1   Personal Taxation
2   Business Taxation & Accounting Principles
3   Business Taxation: Higher Skills
4   IHT, Trusts & Estates
5   VAT
6   Business Compliance
7   Practice Administration & Ethics

Relevant law and accounting issues will be examined in each paper.

The papers may be sat on a modular basis, ie they may be sat as and when the candidate decides.

Certificates of Competency

A certificate will be valid for a three-year period but will be renewable for any number of further three-year periods.

Members

Membership can be applied for by those who have passed the examination requirement in four Certificates of Competency which must include Personal Taxation, Business Taxation & Accounting Principles and Practice Administration & Ethics and who can demonstrate at least two years acceptable current practical experience in UK taxation.

Examination pass mark

To pass a Certificate paper a candidate is required to achieve 50% of the total marks available.

Those who fail a paper will be permitted to re-sit any subsequent examination, provided that they submit an examination entry form and fee at each attempt and are registered as a student at the time of re-sitting.

Reference works and calculators for the examination

Pocket calculators (except those with an alpha-numeric keyboard) may be brought into the examination. Candidates are also allowed to bring into the examination room:

- Tolley's Yellow Tax Handbook and Orange Tax Handbook: or
- CCH Editions Ltd Lax Statutes and Instruments; or
- HMSO copies of taxing statutes.

Publications brought into the examination must be bound copies. They can be underlined, sidelined and highlighted. Annotating, use of 'post its' and tagging is **not** allowed.

No other written material or calculation aid will be permitted.

Candidates will be provided with a sheet giving the tax rates and tables required for the examination.

Format and syllabus of certificate papers

Each certificate paper is three hours in length.

Questions will not be set which require knowledge of:

- any statute receiving Royal Assent or any statutory instrument made less than 5 months before the examination date,

- with the exception of Inheritance Tax, any legislation repealed or suspended more than 5 months before the examination date,
- any case reported less than 3 months before the examination date.

Questions may be set:

- on prospective legislation passed more than 5 months before the examination date even if it is not in force,
- on matters which are not specifically listed in the syllabus but which are related to topics within the syllabus (for example, accountancy principles for the computations of business income),
- on matters which require a knowledge of taxes which are not specifically within the syllabus of a particular paper but are within the syllabus as a whole.

Certificate papers will be a mixture of computational and written questions and no question choice. The short-form questions will carry marks of between 2 and 4 marks each and in total will account for 40% of the available marks. There will therefore be between 10 and 20 such questions in each paper. The remaining available marks will be accounted for by between 3 and 5 longer questions carrying from 10 to 20 marks each. Questions requiring a knowledge of law will normally attract between 10% and 15% of the available marks in each of the technical papers (either as an element of questions or as a stand alone question).

The overall and specific objectives of each of the papers are as follows.

Paper 1: Personal Taxation

Overall objectives

- To prepare the information of income and capital gains to be included in the SA personal tax return
- To prepare any associated computations in relation to the above
- To be able to submit the return and computations under UK self assessment
- To be able to complete a client's claim for tax credits

Specific objectives

- To be able to identify all relevant forms of income and to prepare the income tax computations for an individual
- To be able to identify capital gains transactions and calculate the computations and liability
- To be able to prepare the appropriate entries on tax returns for both income tax and capital gains
- To understand both the differences and similarities between the self assessment and tax credit systems
- To show awareness of professional ethics issues
- To deal with the administration process of SA returns
- To demonstrate understanding of relevant legal issues/implications when dealing with the tax affairs of individuals
- To be able to communicate with clients in a professional manner in written correspondence

Paper 2: Business Taxation & Accounting Principles

Overall objectives

- To prepare the information to be included in SA tax returns for sole traders or partners
- To prepare the information to be included in the SA partnership tax return
- To prepare the information to be included in CTSA returns for companies
- To prepare any associated computations in relation to the above
- To be able to submit returns and computations under self assessment and CTSA

Specific objectives

- To prepare the income tax computations for trades and professions for all aspects of the business life-cycle
- To prepare corporation tax computations for individual companies
- To be able to identify those transactions which have a capital gains impact and compute the liabilities
- To be able to complete the appropriate entries on tax returns
- To demonstrate an understanding of accounts which form the basis for tax computations
- To be able to prepare basic accounts
- To show awareness of professional ethics issues
- To deal with the administration process of SA and CTSA returns
- To demonstrate understanding of legal issues/implications when dealing with the tax affairs of the self-employed and companies
- To be able to communicate with clients in a professional manner in written correspondence

Paper 3: Business Taxation: Higher Skills

Overall objectives

- To be able to deal with all aspects of the Paper 2 syllabus in more complex situations

Specific objectives

- To be able to identify the tax implications of setting up, or disposing of, a business including the consideration of alternative mediums
- To be able to advise on the tax implications of the incorporation of a business
- To demonstrate understanding of legal issues/implications when dealing with the incorporation of companies
- To be able to advise on the tax implications of changes in the membership of a partnership
- To demonstrate understanding of the tax treatment of Limited Liability Partnerships
- To be able to advise on the tax implications of the legislation relating to personal service companies
- To be able to advise on the tax implications of family owned companies
- To be able to advise on the taxation treatment of groups of companies
- To show awareness of professional ethics issues
- To be able to communicate with clients in a professional manner in written correspondence

Paper 4: Inheritance Tax, Trusts & Estates

Overall objectives

- To prepare the information to be included in the SA Trust & Estate Tax Return
- To prepare any associated computations in relation to the above
- To be able to submit the return and computations under UK self assessment

Specific objectives

- To demonstrate understanding of the distinction between types of trusts to complete the appropriate entries on tax returns
- To be able to distinguish between the entries required on all relevant forms
- To be able to prepare all relevant computations to complete the above
- To be able to calculate the tax liability on income arising to the estate of a deceased person

TQT
Tax Qualification Training

- To be able to compute the capital gains tax for trustees, executors and beneficiaries

- To be able to identify the IHT implications of lifetime gifts for individuals

- To be able to prepare basic computations of the inheritance tax liability arising on a death

- To show awareness of professional ethics issues

- To deal with the administration process of SA returns

- To demonstrate understanding of legal issues/implications when dealing with trusts

- To be able to communicate with clients in a professional manner in written correspondence

Paper 5: Value Added Tax

Overall Objectives

- To prepare the information to be included in the VAT Return for a taxable trader

- To be able to compute any annual or periodic adjustments to be included within a VAT return

- To be aware of any special schemes available for taxable traders generally, and to be able to complete returns where such schemes apply

Specific Objectives

- To understand the accounting and other documents and records required to be maintained for VAT

- To identify traders requiring registration or able to deregister for VAT

- To define a taxable person; supply; time of supply and place of supply

- To be aware of the basis of valuation of supplies

- To be able to identify different types of supplies

- To be able to prepare a computation involving partial exemption using the standard method, and to be able to compute annual adjustments

- To be aware of the VAT treatment of imports and exports including international services

- To be able to determine deductible input tax

- To understand the provisions relating to transfers of a going concern

- To be able to compute the adjustments necessary for the capital goods scheme

- To be able to identify the VAT implications of land transactions

- To be able to prepare a VAT return where a special scheme applies

- To be able to explain the rules relating to groups of companies and group registration

- To understand the regime of penalties and interest on late payment and the implications of other irregularities for VAT

- To show awareness of professional ethics issues

- To demonstrate understanding of relevant legal issues/implications affecting VAT transactions

- To be able to communicate with clients in a professional manner in written correspondence

Paper 6: Business Compliance

Overall objectives

- To be able to deal with employer obligations under PAYE, NIC and related matters under the tax system
- To be able to complete and submit VAT returns

Specific objectives

- To compute PAYE and NIC deductions and ERNIC liabilities
- To be able to identify the correct treatment of non-cash items, travel expenses and lump sum payments
- To prepare computations on benefits in kind
- To be able to identify and distinguish the various forms of share options and the related tax and NIC liabilities
- To be able to complete all relevant forms in relation to PAYE and NIC on the above
- To be able to deal with all aspects of payroll administration, including all deductions and credits.
- To be able to demonstrate knowledge of UK VAT and related calculations
- To be able to prepare a basic VAT return   •
- To deal with the VAT administration process
- To show awareness of professional ethics issues
- To be able to communicate with clients in a professional manner in written correspondence

Paper 7: Practice Administration & Ethics

Content

The paper will cover the following areas:

- Administration of taxation
- The legal framework in which the tax adviser operates
- Ethical rules and practice guidelines

Administration of taxation

Candidates will be expected to have a thorough understanding of the processes by which the taxpayer notifies that they are within the charge, through to returns, assessments/self assessments, and enquiries. Detailed knowledge of the process of pursuing an appeal through to the commissioners and beyond would not be required.

Much of the administration is generic and will apply as much to corporate as to personal tax.

Some basic knowledge of the way VAT, IHT and PAYE is administered will also feature. Even if a candidate does not sit the specific paper on these topics it is not unreasonable to require a prospective member to be able to relay to a client at least the very basics of compliance in these areas.

Candidates will also be required to deal, at a fairly basic level, with questions of what should be disclosed and why, and also how to deal with errors, both by HMRC and by the adviser.

Tax administration is not an area on which students generally spend enough time studying; they will avoid it as much as possible in examinations. Given that the whole tax system is built on providing information to HMRC, it is essential that prospective members give this area the attention it deserves.

The legal framework in which the tax agent operates

This involves not only the relationship between the agent and HMRC, but also some of the basic framework which exists between a client and an adviser. Candidates will be expected to understand something of the nature of the duty of care owed to a client and the normal contractual arrangements regulating an engagement.

The majority of the Association's members will be employees and therefore candidates need to understand something of the quadripartite relationship between client, tax authority, adviser and employee.

Ethical rules and practice guidelines

The Association's publication: *Professional Rules and Practice Guidelines* will form the basis of the syllabus. Some of this material is covered in the discussion of the legal framework above, but there is much which does not fit into this category. All of that publication which relates to the activities likely to be carried on by an Association member is potentially examinable.

TQT
Tax Qualification Training

Detailed syllabus

The tables on the following pages show the subjects which are within the syllabuses of the seven certificate papers. The tables also show the specific areas and specialised matters which are specifically excluded from the syllabus.

For each paper, the required depth of knowledge is indicated:

P = Principles

Candidates will be expected to have an awareness that a provision exists and its main thrust, without necessarily knowing the details of the provision. For example, they will be expected to be aware of the concept of domicile and how domicile status can affect liability to tax, but they would not be required to advise on the steps which would be required to acquire a domicile of choice.

C = Computational

Candidates will be expected to calculate a liability from data already provided. They might, for example, be provided with data about the exercise of a Revenue approved share option and asked to calculate the resulting liability. They would not, at this level, be expected to comment on the detailed requirements for that option to receive Revenue approval.

D = Detail

Candidates will be expected to know the detail of legislative provisions and be able to explain them to others, whether clients, colleagues or the authorities.

Income tax

	Personal Taxation	Business Taxation & Accounting Principles	Business Taxation: Higher Skills	IHT Trusts & Estates	VAT	Business Compliance	Practice Adminis -tration & Ethics	Excluded
Accrued income scheme	C			C				
Adjustment income			C					
Administration	D	D	D	D		P	D	
Allowances and rates	D	D	D	D		P		
Annual payments	D	D	D					
Appeals	P	P	P	P			D	
Approved share schemes – employee's tax position								
– Company share option plans	C	.				D		
– Enterprise management incentives	C					D		
– Profit-sharing schemes	C					D		
– Savings-related schemes	C					D		
– Share incentive plans	C					D		
Basis periods		D	D					
Benefits and expenses	D		P			D		
Capital allowances – P&M, IBA		D			P			
Charities – Gift Aid, Gifts of assets and payroll giving	D					D		
Computation of profits		D	D					
Construction Industry Scheme						D		
Deceased person's estate								
– Tax position of beneficiaries	C			D				
– Tax position of estate				D				
Domicile	P			P		P		
Double taxation relief	C						P	X
Employee trusts								
Employment income and expenses	D					D		
Employment related securities	C					D		
Enterprise Investment Scheme – reliefs for individuals	D							
Entertainers and sportsmen								X
Farmers								
– ABA			D					
– Averaging			D					
– Herd basis			P					
Foreign income	D							
FURBS								X
Incorporation of a business			D					
Individual Savings Accounts – tax position of individuals	D							
Interest on late payment of tax	D	D	D	D		P	D	
Interest paid	D							
IR35 – Provision of services through an intermediary		P	D			D		

Income Tax continued

	Personal Taxation	Business Taxation & Accounting Principles	Business Taxation: Higher Skills	IHT Trusts & Estates	VAT	Business Compliance	Practice Administration & Ethics	Excluded
Life policies – tax position of individual investor	C							
Lloyds underwriters								X
Marriage, separation and divorce and civil partnerships	D							
Married couples – income from jointly owned businesses			D					
Miscellaneous income taxable on individuals								
Non-domiciles individuals – UK tax position	D			D				
Non-UK resident entertainers								X
Notification of Avoidance Schemes								X
Occupational pension schemes – tax relief from employee contributions	C					D		
Offshore funds								X
Overseas employment and expenses						C		
Partnerships (excluding LLP's)		D						
Partnerships (including LLP's)								
PAYE including penalties						D	D	
Payment of tax	D	D	D	D			D	
Payments to employees for restrictive covenants	D							
Penalties	D	D	D	D			D	
Pension income	D							
Pensions – relief for individual contributions	D							
Pre owned assets	C			D				
Pre trading expenditure		P						
Profits of trades and professions		D			P			
Property incomer	D							
Post cessation receipts and expenses		P						
Real estate investment trusts -tax position of investor	C							
Remittance basis	D							
Residence, ordinary residence	P			P		P		
Revenue enquiries under SA	P	P	P	P			D	
Savings income	D							
Self employed/employee		P	D			D		
Self-assessment	D	D	D	D	P		D	
Share Schemes – Employer liability						D		
Small Self administered Pension Schemes								X
Social security benefits – tax position of individuals	C							

Income Tax continued

	Personal Taxation	Business Taxation & Accounting Principles	Business Taxation: Higher Skills	IHT Trusts & Estates	VAT	Business Compliance	Practice Adminis -tration & Ethics	Excluded
Sole traders – current year basis		D	D					
Student loans – administration						D		
Tax credits (including Working Tax Credits and Child Tax Credits)	D							
Taxation of earnings						P		
Termination payments	D		D			D		
Trading losses		D	D					
Transactions in land – Anti Avoidance Provisions								X
Transactions in securities (other than taxation of accrued income of individuals)								X
Transfer of assets abroad				P				
True and fair accounting		P	P					
Trusts								
– tax position of beneficiaries	C			D				
– tax position pf UK trusts				D				
Venture capital trusts – reliefs for individuals	D							
Withdrawal of EIS relief – impact on individual	D							

TQT
Tax Qualification Training

Capital Gains Tax/
Corporation tax on Capital gains

	Personal Taxation	Business Taxation & Accounting Principles	Business Taxation: Higher Skills	IHT Trusts & Estates	VAT	Business Compliance	Practice Administration & Ethics	Excluded
Administration	D	D	D	D			D	
Amalgamations and takeovers	C							
Anti-avoidance								X
Capital sums derived from assets	D							
Chargeable assets	D	C	C	C				
Chargeable persons	D	C	C	D				
Chattels/wasting assets	D	C	D	P				
Companies (disposals by)		C	C					
Compensation	D							
Compulsory acquisition of land								X
Connected persons	D		P	D				
Debts	D		P					
Demergers								X
Double taxation relief	C							
Enterprise investment scheme – reinvestment relief	D	P	P					
Entrepreneurs' relief		D	D					
Estates				D				
Gifts/holdover relief	D	C	C	D				
Gifts and QCBs	D							
Groups of companies		P	D					
Incorporation			D					
Indexation		C	C					
Insurance companies								X
Interest on late payment of tax	D	D	D	D			D	
Land								
– general	D	C	C	P	P			
– grant of short lease form short lease	C							
– part disposals	D	C	C					
Lloyds underwriters								X
Losses on unquoted shares	D							
Miscellaneous case within TCGA 1992 Part IV Ch IV								X
Negligible value claims	D							
No gain/no loss disposals	D	P	D	P				
Non resident companies								X
Occasion of charge	D	C	C	D				
Offshore trusts								X
Oil and Mining industries								X
Options								X
Overseas elements eg remittance basis/temporary no residence	D			D				

TQT
Tax Qualification Training

Capital Gains Tax/Corporation tax on Capital gains continued

	Personal Taxation	Business Taxation & Accounting Principles	Business Taxation: Higher Skills	IHT Trusts & Estates	VAT	Business Compliance	Practice Adminis-tration & Ethics	Excluded
Partnership matters								X
Payment of tax	D	D	D	D			D	
Penalties	D	D	D	D			D	
Personal representatives				D				
Principal private residence	D			D				
Principles of computation	D			D				
Reorganisations and Reconstructions (share for share/share for QCB on takeover)	C	C	C	D				
Rollover relief (excluding degrouping charges		P	C					
Series of transactions	P							
Share and securities	D			P				
Substantial shareholdings (Companies)			P					
UK Trusts				D				
Valuation	D		P	C				
Value shifting								X

Corporation tax

	Personal Taxation	Business Taxation & Accounting Principles	Business Taxation: Higher Skills	IHT Trusts & Estates	VAT	Business Compliance	Practice Administration & Ethics	Excluded
Accounting period		C	C					
Administration		D	D				D	
Anti-avoidance relating to change of ownership			P					
Anti-avoidance – sale and leaseback								X
Capital allowances – P&M, IBA		D	D		P			
Close companies		P	D					
Company residence			P					
Computation of profits		C	C					
Controlled foreign companies								X
Corporate Venturing scheme - relief for investor			P					
CT Self-assessment		D	D				D	
Distributions			P					
Double tax relief			P					
Double tax treaties – OECD model								X
Financial instruments								X
FOREX								X
Group of companies, consortia – definition		P	C					
Group reconstructions and charges			P					
Group relief		P	C					
Income tax re company		P	C					
Insurance companies								X
Intellectual property								
- Goodwill			P					
- Other								X
Interest on late payment of tax		D	D				D	
Interest/Loan relationships		C	D					
Investment companies			P					
IR35 – provision of services through an intermediary		P	C			C		
Liquidation/receivership								X
Losses (apart from surplus franked investment income)		D	D					
Notification of Avoidance Schemes							D	X
Penalties		D	D					
Property income		P	D					
Purchase of own shares								X
Quarterly accounting		P	D					
Research and development			P					
Small companies relief		C	C					
Transfer pricing								X
Unit/investment trusts								X

Inheritance tax

	Personal Taxation	Business Taxation & Accounting Principles	Business Taxation: Higher Skills	IHT Trusts & Estates	VAT	Business Compliance	Practice Adminis-tration & Ethics	Excluded
A&M Trusts				D				
Accounts/returns				D				
Administration				D			D	
Agricultural property relief				C				
Annual exemption				D				
Anti-avoidance								X
Business property relief				C				
Chargeable transfers				D				
Computation at death								
– on estate				C				
– recalculation for lifetime gifts				D				
Computation of lifetime transfers				D				
Debts				D				
Deeds of variation				D				
Discretionary trusts – post 1974				D				
Discretionary trusts – pre 1974								X
Dispositions				D				
Domicile and excluded property				D				
Double taxation relief				P				
Excluded property				D				
Exemptions				D				
Gifts at marriage				D				
Gifts of residue				D				
Gifts to charities				D				
Gifts with reservation of benefit				D				
Grossing up				C				
Heritage property				P				
Increase in thresholds				D				
Inter-spouse transfer				D				
Interest of late payment of tax				D			D	
Interest in possession trusts				D				
Intestacy				D				
Lex situs				P				
Liabilities				D				
Lifetime transfers				D				
Normal expenditure out of income				D				
Payment of tax				D			D	
Penalties				D			D	
Post-mortem reliefs				D				
Potentially exempt transfers				D				
Protective trusts				P				
Quick succession relief				C				

Tax Qualification Training

Inheritance tax continued

	Personal Taxation	Business Taxation & Accounting Principles	Business Taxation: Higher Skills	IHT Trusts & Estates	VAT	Business Compliance	Practice Adminis -tration & Ethics	Excluded
Rates				C				
Related property				D				
Seven year accumulation period				D				
Small gifts exemption				D				
Taper relief for recalculate of lifetime gifts				D				
Transfer of value				D				
Trusts								
- immediate post-death trusts				D				
- relevant property trusts				D				
- trusts for the disabled				D				
- bare trusts				D				
Valuation				C				
Woodlands								X

VAT

	Personal Taxation	Business Taxation & Accounting Principles	Business Taxation: Higher Skills	IHT Trusts & Estates	VAT	Business Compliance	Practice Adminis-tration & Ethics	Excluded
Accounting and records		P	P		D	D	P	
Administration					D	D	D	
Agency								X
Annual accounting					D	D		
Anti-avoidance/blocking orders					P			
Bad debt relief					D	D		
Business/non-business – definition					D	P		
Capital goods scheme					C			
Cash accounting		▸			D	D		
Charities					P			
Construction services								
- definition					D			
- relevant residential/charitable purposes					D			
- conversions and alterations					D			
European law					P			
Exempt, reduced rate and zero-rated supplies		P	P		D	D		
Farmers flat rate scheme					P			
Flat rate scheme					D	C		
Government departments, local authorities and similar bodies								X
Groups of companies and group registration					P	P		
Imports and exports (EU and non-EU)					D	P		
Input tax		C	C		D	D		
Interest of late payment of VAT					D	P	D	
International services					D	P		
Investigations								X
Land transactions								
- election to waive exemption					D			
- grants of an interest in land					D			
- standard rated supplies					D			
Liquidations								X
Notification of Avoidance Schemes								X
Partial exemption – override provisions								X
Partial exemption – standard method					D	C		
Penalties/Defaults					D	C	D	
Place of supply		P	P		D	P		
Refunds under 8th and 13th directives					P			
Registration/deregistration		C	C		D	D	D	
Retail schemes					C	C		
Returns					D	D	P	
Self supply					P			
Supplies					D	D		

VAT continued

	Personal Taxation	Business Taxation & Accounting Principles	Business Taxation: Higher Skills	IHT Trusts & Estates	VAT	Business Compliance	Practice Administration & Ethics	Excluded
Taxable person		P	P		D	D		
Time of supply		P	P		D	D		
Tour operators' margin scheme								X
Transfer of going concern					D	D		
Value of supplies		C	C		D	C		
VAT Tribunal specific decisions					P			

National Insurance Contributions

	Personal Taxation	Business Taxation & Accounting Principles	Business Taxation: Higher Skills	IHT Trusts & Estates	VAT	Business Compliance	Practice Adminis -tration & Ethics	Excluded
Administration						D	D	
Benefits and expenses		C	C			D		
Classes of NIC		P	P			D		
Contracting out provisions						P		
Directors						D		
Employed/Self-employed		P	C			C		
Married women's reduced rate						P		
Maximum contributions and deferral		C	C			P		
Overseas Aspects		▸						X
Share Options						D		
SSP and SMP rules						P		

TQT
Tax Qualification Training

Other topics

	Personal Taxation	Business Taxation & Accounting Principles	Business Taxation: Higher Skills	IHT Trusts & Estates	VAT	Business Compliance	Practice Adminis -tration & Ethics	Excluded
ATT practice guidelines	P	P	P	P	P	P	D	
ATT professional rules and statements	P	P	P	P	P	P	D	
Money Laundering Regulations	P	P	P	P	P	P	D	
ATT 'Essential Accounting for Taxation Technicians' manual								
- All chapters		D	D					
- Chapter on: Accounting for taxation						D		
- Chapter on; Accounting for taxation - VAT					D			
Company accounting profit/taxable profit reconciliation			D					
Customs duties								X
Insurance Premium Tax								X
Petroleum Revenue Tax								X
Stamp duty and SDLT								X

Law

Law is also an integral part of this exam paper.

The syllabus for the law element of the paper is set out in the ATT manual entitled *Essential Law for the Taxation Technician*.

This book can be purchased directly from the ATT. TQT strongly recommend that you purchase this book

HOME STUDY PLANNER

1 Introduction

This TQT Home Study Programme will guide you through this 2008 edition of the TQT Study Text. This Home Study planner is intended for use by students who are studying on their own. If you are attending a taught course, your course provider may provide you with a different programme of studies.

2 Using the Home Study Programme

This Home Study Programme is made up of 20 **Study Periods**.

The tax and law in each study Period should take about 3 hours. In addition you are directed to read various parts of the ATT's professional rules and practice guidelines and the ATT's Professional Conduct in relation to tax. Experience shows that the best way of studying these documents is to approach them little and often.

Exams

To gain the greatest benefit from the exams, you must set aside a period of three hours and fifteen minutes during which you will have no interruptions.

By sitting these exams, you will increase your chances of passing the real exams by 30%.

Please note, these exams are available only as part of the home study package. If you are attending a taught course, your provider may provide you with other exams to sit at different times during your studies.

3 Getting ready to Study

To get off to the best possible start to your study, you should take time to read the following guidance.

Before you begin your studies, you may want to spend some time thinking about how to approach them. Consider the following.

(a)   **The study environment.** Studying while working is very different from studying full time. Time management is crucial.

(b)   **Types of subject.** You need to think about the form the exam will take and the skills it will draw on. For example, does it test knowledge, numerical skills, application of knowledge or application of theory?

(c)   **What is your learning style?** Your learning preferences should affect the way you approach this study material.

(d)   You need to think about **how to work through the text**, how to take notes and how to do examples.

(e)   How will you approach your **revision**?

(f)   You need a technique for dealing with **common types of question**.

(g)   You must approach the exam in a **methodical manner**.

Approaching Personal Taxation

This guidance describes what the paper seeks to achieve, the skills you are expected to demonstrate and how you can improve your chances of passing the paper.

Paper 1, Personal taxation seeks to test the liability of individuals to:

- Income tax, and

- Capital gains tax

The exam may also contain questions on the ethical considerations of being in practice, and certain areas of legal knowledge:

- Property Law
- Land Law
- Working relationships

We have indicated where you should also study from the 'Essential law for the Tax Technician text book and the ATT guidelines on Professional Rules and Practice, Money Laundering guidelines and ATT Professional Conduct guidelines.

Because you are not expected to have any previous knowledge of these subjects, we will be introducing them to you from first principles. If you have any previous knowledge of personal taxation, perhaps as a result of work experience, you can modify the amounts of time you send on each topic, to take account of your knowledge.

The examination

The examination is made up of two parts:

Part one – which is made up of a number of short form questions (SFQs), with mark allocations ranging from 2 to 4 marks. The total marks for Part one of the exam are 40 marks. As you work through the study text you will encounter SFQs at the end of each chapter. By practising this kind of question you can help prepare for the real exam as you go along. SFQs can be on any syllabus area and Part 1 of the exam typically includes a cross section of questions taken from all areas of the syllabus.

Topics covered in Real Past Papers are set out below;

	May 2007	November 2007	May 2008
1	IT: Age allowance	IT: Calculation of IT liability	IT: Calculation of IT liability
2	CGT: Chattels	Self-assessment: Penalties, interest and HMRC enquiries	CGT: Married couples
3	CGT: Shares	Law: Property law	Accrued income scheme and CGT on loan stock
4	Self-assessment: Penalties, interest and surcharges	Tax credits: CTC & WTC	CGT: 31 March 1982 asset and taper relief
5	Tax credits: CTC & WTC	CGT: Shares and taper relief	Self-assessment: Penalties, interest and surcharges
6	CGT: Lease premiums	CGT: EIS deferral relief	CGT: Overseas issues
7	CGT: Connected parties	CGT: Negligible value claim	Life assurance policies
8	CGT: March 1982 asset	CGT: Loss on unquoted shares	Self- assessment: Determinations
9	Self- assessment: Short tax returns	IT: Accrued income scheme	CGT: Chargeable disposals
10	IT: Married couple's allowance	CGT computation	IT: Pre owned assets
11	IT: Residency status	Furnished holiday accommodation	IT: Employment benefits
12	Ethics: Money laundering	Law: Contract of employment	Ethics: Fee arrangements
13	IT: Social security benefits	Discovery assessments	
14	CGT: Damaged assets		
15	Law: Property law		

Part two of the exam is made up of between three to five long form questions with total marks amounting to 60. The marks will be allocated between the questions, but may not be allocated evenly.

On the prior papers the marks were allocated as follows:

	May 2007	November 2007	May 2008
Question 1	17 marks	19 marks	20 marks
Question 2	19 marks	10 marks	20 marks
Question 3	12 marks	16 marks	20 marks
Question 4	12 marks	15 marks	

You need to be prepared to answer long form questions too and practising the questions at the end of each Study Period and in the Course Exams, will help with this.

Make sure you consider how long a question is supposed to take. Where a question has a mark allocation this will be an indication of the time it is expected to take. As a rough guide, the exam is 3 hours long, and so each mark should take, on average, 1.8 minutes of your time. Therefore, a 20-mark question should take around 36 minutes to answer and a 10-mark question around 18 minutes to answer. This is only a rough guide, but it helps you to allocate your time in the exam, so that you do not spend more time on a question than it requires to gain the available marks, as this might make your answers to later questions weaker.

Topics covered in Real Past Papers

	May 2007	November 2007	May 2008
Question 1	IT computation and joint income election.	IT and CGT computations including overseas issues and furnished holiday lettings.	Tax credits: CTC & WTC. IT payable calculation. Law: Employment law.
Question 2	Property: PPR relief, IT income. Law: Joint ownership.	CGT disposals including share pool, VCT shares, company share option scheme and chattels.	CGT disposals including land, chattels, compensation. Loss relief for unquoted shares.
Question 3	CGT shares: Takeovers.	Overseas issues: Residency rules, IT and CGT basis of assessment and PPR relief.	EIS: IT and CGT implications.
Question 4	Employment income including benefits. Law: Employee dismissal.	Employment income including benefits. Ethics: Client non-disclosure.	

Please note that all the questions set in the Sample Paper issued by the ATT have been included within the Question Bank.

Detailed Home Study Planner

Use this planner and your exam timetable to plan the dates on which you will complete each Study Period.

At the end of each Study Period you will be advised to study a section from a separate publication issued by the ATT called the Professional Rules and Practice Guidelines. Students often say they find studying from this ATT publication very hard going. We find that by studying a little and often you will find the task a little less daunting

Study Period	Guidance through Study text	Attempt Questions
1 **Taxable income**	The understanding of income tax is underpinned by an understanding of the basic income tax computation.	SFQ 1.1 – 1.18
	Subsequent study periods will deal with the calculation of the different types of income subject to income tax. This study period introduces the basic knowledge of how an income tax computation is put together and how income tax is calculated.	
	This knowledge will be tested throughout the exam. The last three exams have included an income tax computation as part of a long form question.	
	Tax credits are also a popular exam topic, covered in the short form questions in the sample, May 2007 exam and November 2007 exam papers and in Part 2 of the sample paper and the May 2008 exam.	
Examined: May 2007 November 2007 May 2008	Please read Chapter 1 after reading the guidance here. Read through Section 1 to gain background knowledge about the UK tax system. This knowledge may not be examined but will aid your understanding. Read through Section 2 to familiarise yourself with who pays income tax in the U.K.	
	Read through Sections 3 to 9 in detail, making notes, and working the examples. Take particular note of the step by step approach to building up an income tax computation in the right order. In step 1 we consider the income that an individual will be taxed on. Make sure that you know the deductions that can be made at step 2, the personal allowances that can be deducted from taxable income at step 3 and the tax reducers available at step 6. Work through Illustrations 1 and 2 and example 3 carefully, they illustrate the rates of tax applicable to income. It is important that you understand the order in which income is taxed and the rates of tax applicable to income. Illustration 3 in section 9 shows the complete computation. Make sure you learn the format of the income tax computation.	
	Section 10 deals with social security benefits and tax credits. Child and working tax credits are examined frequently. Work through examples 5, 6 and 7, to understand the eligibility for and calculation of these tax credits. Sections 11 and 12 cover the taxation of income from jointly owned property and the tax arising on both the deceased and beneficiaries of an estate on death. Both these topics are important background knowledge. Section 13 lists the sources of income that are exempt from income tax. You need to be able to identify them in exam questions.	
Professional Rules and Practice Guidelines	Now revise Chapters 1 and 2 of your ATT Professional Rules and Practice Guidelines • Introduction • Professional Rules	

TQT
Tax Qualification Training

2 **Savings income**	You are likely to be asked to calculate income tax for individuals in both the short form and the long form questions.	SFQ 2.1 – 2.8 LFQ 2.1 – 2.6
	For income tax computation purposes the rates of tax differ depending on whether the income being taxed is savings or non-savings income and different types of savings income are taxed at different rates. You will be expected to be able to identify the different types of income and calculate tax at the appropriate rate.	
Examined: Sample Paper May 2007 November 2007 May 2008	Please read Chapter 2 after reading the guidance below: • Read through the introduction to understand the meaning of savings income and understand that it is mainly made up of interest and dividends. • Read through sections 2 and 3 and note that interest is received both gross and net (of 20% tax) and that dividends are received net (of 10% tax).	
	Make sure you understand that interest and dividends are included gross in the income tax computation.	
	Read through Section 4 and make notes on how savings and non-savings income are taxed, the order in which income is taxed and the rates of tax used. Pay particular attention to the three column format of the computation. Attempt examples 1 to 3 to check you have understood this section. Review the illustration in section 5 to check you understand the taxation of savings and non savings income and how this fits into the income computation you learnt abut in study period 1 and then attempt example 4.	
	Note the way that income from non-discretionary and discretionary trusts is taxed and the associated tax credits, from section 6.	
	Refer to the rates and allowances sheet at the front of the Study text as you go along to ensure that you are aware of the rates and allowances that will be given to you in the exam.	
Professional Rules and Practice Guidelines	Now revise Chapter 3 or your ATT Professional Rules and Practice Guidelines • Practice Governance	

3 **Income from UK land and buildings**	This Study Period considers how to calculate the amount of taxable income arising from UK land and buildings and the legal aspects of property law.	SFQ 3.1 – 3.10 LFQ 3.1 & 3.2
	In the exam, calculations of the property income taxable on individuals can be included in both the short form and the long form questions. An example of these can be found on Part 1 of the sample paper, question 12 and Part 2 of the May 2007 exam paper, question 2. You may also be asked factual questions, such as the conditions for rent a room relief to apply.	
	Questions may combine the income tax and capital gains tax aspects of owning and disposing of land and buildings (capital gains tax will be covered in later Study Periods) and the legal aspects of property law.	
Examined: Sample Paper May 2007 November 2007	Please read through Chapter 3 of the Study Text, after reading the guidance here. Read through Sections 1-8 of the Chapter, which deal with how to compute property income for an individual. You need to be able to calculate:	
	• Property income net of capital allowances and allowable expenses	
	• Property losses	
	• The portion of a lease premium received on a short lease or sublease, which will be subject to income tax on the landlord (please attempt example 1).	
	You need to be able to state:	
	• The uses of property losses.	
	• The conditions for a letting to be classed as a furnished holiday letting and the tax implications of being a furnished holiday letting.	
	• The conditions that need to be satisfied for rent-a-room relief to apply and the tax implications of these rules applying to rental income.	
	• The tax implications of receiving rental income from a Real Estate Investment Trust (although less likely to be examined than the others)	
	Read through the topics, Property Law and Land Law in the ATT manual Essential Law for the Taxation Technician.	
Professional Rules and Practice Guidelines	Now revise Chapter 4 of your Professional Rules and Practice Guidelines	
	• New clients	

4 **Tax efficient investments**	You will be expected to be able to identify the main forms of tax efficient investment scheme and understand the tax implications of investing in such a scheme. Questions could consider the conditions for qualifying for a particular scheme, the tax implications of investing or calculating the tax position of an individual making such an investment.	SFQ 4.1 – 4.4 LFQ 4.1
	The EIS scheme was examined in detail in Part 2 of the May 2008 exam. In May 2007, Part 2, Question 1 included interest received from an ISA and candidates would need to have been aware of the tax implications arising from receiving interest from an ISA.	
Examined: May 2007 May 2008	Please read Chapter 4 of the Study Text after reading the guidance below:	
	Read through Section 1 of the Chapter and note the main sources of tax free investment. You need to be able to identify these in questions so that the income arising from them is treated as tax free.	
	Read through Section 2 on ISAs. Make notes on the conditions applying to ISAs – who can invest, how much can be invested etc. Understand the tax exemption granted for a qualifying ISA and also the tax implications of the exemption being withdrawn.	
	Read through Section 3 on the enterprise investment scheme and make notes on the conditions for both the investor and the investee company to qualify for the scheme, the maximum investment possible under the scheme and the tax implications of a qualifying investment. You also need to be aware of the circumstances in which relief will be withdrawn and the tax consequences of relief being withdrawn. Make sure you use your legislation to look up these rules under sections 156-234 ITA 2007. Attempt example 1.	
	Read through Section 4 on venture capital trusts and make notes on the conditions which must be satisfied to qualify for relief. You also need to be aware of the amount of investment that can qualify for relief and the tax implications of the relief being granted. Again make sure that you use your legislation to look up the sections relating to venture capital trusts so that you are aware of the information available to you in the exam.	
	Section 5 is of less importance. Please read through this section and make sure you are aware of the broad issues contained within this section.	
Professional Rules and Practice Guidelines	Now revise Chapter 5 of your Professional Rules and Practice Guidelines • Client Service	

5 **The employed** **earner** Examined: Sample Paper May 2007 November 2007 May 2008	This Study Period considers the calculation of the income for an employed earner, for inclusion in the income tax computation Questions can focus on many different aspects of the employed earner: Understanding the basis of assessment for employment income. Identifying and calculating taxable employment income, including the tax value of benefits received and identifying tax free benefits (Sample Part 2 Question 1, Question 4; May 2007 Part 2 Question 4; November 2007 Part 2 Question 4; May 2008 Part 1 Question 11) Understanding the taxation of termination payments (Sample SFQ 9) Please read Chapter 5 of the Study Text, after reading the guidance below. • Read through Section 1 to understand the types of employment income that are subject to income tax and the receipts basis, which determines the tax year in which employment income will be taxed. Work through example 1. • Read through Section 2 and make notes on how to calculate the tax value of the benefits that are taxable on all employees, regardless of their income level. Work examples 2, 3 and 4. • Read through Section 3 and make notes on how to calculate the tax value of the benefits taxable on directors and employees earning £8,500 p.a. or more. Work examples 5 to 10. • Read through Section 4 and make sure you can identify the benefits that can be received tax free. • Read through Section 5 and ensure you understand the items that can be deducted from employment income. Work example 11. • Read through Section 6 and make notes on the tax implications of the various different types of payment that can be made to an employee on termination of employment. Make sure you can identify which payments are taxable and which are exempt from tax. Work example 12.	SFQ 5.1 – 5.23 LFQ 5.1 & 5.6
Professional Rules and Practice Guidelines	Now revise Chapter 6 of your Professional Rules and Practice Guidelines • Conflicts of Interest	

6 **Tax efficient** **remuneration**	In addition to calculating taxable employment income, as in Study Period 6, you may also be examined on:	SFQ 6.1 – 6.3 LFQ 6.1
	• Understanding the rules applying to tax efficient remuneration schemes, applying these rules to individuals and determining how such remuneration is treated for tax purposes. (Sample paper SFQ 8; November 2007 Part 2 Question 2)	
	• Employment Law (May 2007 Part 2 Question 4; November 2007 Part 1 Question 12; May 2008 Part 2 Question 1)	
Examined: Sample Paper May 2007 November 2007 May 2008	Read through Chapter 6 from your Study Text after reading the guidance below read through Section 1 and make sure you understand the difference between granting shares directly to employees and granting share options to employees and the tax implications of unapproved share option schemes and work example 1.	
	Read through the information on the four main approved share schemes and make notes ensuring that you know how each scheme works, the conditions for approval and the tax implications of each scheme.	
	Read through the topic, working relationships in the ATT Manual Essential Law for the Taxation Technician, after reading the guidance below:	
	• Read through the sections which introduce the subject of employment law, and the tests that may be used to determine whether an individual is employed or self employed.	
	• Read through the section on contracts of employment. and make notes on the format of employment contracts, including express and implied terms.	
	• Read through the sections on termination of employment to understand the law surrounding this topic.	
Professional Rules and Practice Guidelines	Now revise Chapter 7 of your Professional Rules and Practice Guidelines	
	• Other client handling issues	

7 **Pensions**	You may be asked to calculate the amount of pension contributions that an individual can make to either an occupational or a personal pension scheme and to explain the tax implications of making contributions to a scheme, the timing of the contributions and on drawing the pension once retirement has taken place (Sample Paper Part 2 Question 1 (occupational scheme), May 2007 Part 2 Question 1 (personal pension scheme).	SFQ 7.1 – 7.6 LFQ 7.1 – 7.3
Examined: Sample Paper May 2007	Read through Chapter 7 of the Study Text after reading the following guidance. Read through section 1 of the Chapter to gain background knowledge and understand the distinction between occupational and personal pension schemes. Read through Sections 2 and 3 of the Chapter and make notes making sure you understand for both occupational and personal pension schemes: • Whether payments are made net or gross of tax. • How tax relief is given for pension contributions made and make sure you can se how this fits in with the income tax computation you studied in Study Periods 1 and 2. Work example 1. Read through Section 4 of the Study Text and understand how pension income is taxed on retirement.	
Professional Rules and Practice Guidelines	Now revise Chapter 8 of your Professional Rules and Practice Guidelines • Charging for services	

8 **Overseas matters**	So far all the individuals we have considered have been UK resident. You may also be examined on:	SFQ 8.1 – 8.4 LFQ 8.1
	• Determining the status of an individual, to decide if they are liable to UK income tax (November 2007 LFQ3)	
	• Understanding the tax implications of individuals coming to and leaving the UK (Sample Paper SFQ Question 13, May 2007 SFQ Question 11)	
	• Deciding when overseas income will be subject to UK income tax	
	• Calculating the amount of double tax relief available on foreign income.	
Examined: Sample Paper May 2007 November 2007	Read through Chapter 8 of the Study Text after reading the following guidance.	
	Refer back to Section 2.4 of Chapter 1 and make a note of the UK tax implications of residence and domicile status.	
	Read Section 1 of Chapter 8 and make notes on the meaning of residence, ordinary residence and domicile for UK tax purposes. Make sure you understand how they are interpreted where individuals are leaving or coming to the UK. Work example 1.	
	Read Section 2 of Chapter 8 which covers overseas income and in particular overseas savings income.	
	Read Section 3 and make notes on how relief is given against the UK Income tax liability on foreign source income for tax paid overseas. You may be asked to compute double tax relief in the exam. Attempt example 2 to test if you have understood this section.	
Professional Rules and Practice Guidelines	Now revise Chapter 9 of your Professional Rules and Practice Guidelines	
	• Complaints	

9 Administration of income tax	Once income tax has been calculated for an individual we need to be aware of:	SFQ 15.1 – 15.3
	• The self assessment reporting requirements and due dates for reporting. (Sample paper SFQ11, May 2007 SFQ 9)	
	• The due date for payment of any tax due. Relatively easy to learn and easy marks in the exam, if you can remember them. (May 2007 Part 2 Q3)	
	• The penalties, interest or surcharges chargeable for non-compliance with these rules. (May 2007 SFQ 4, November 2007 SFQ1, May 2008 SFQ5)	
	• HMRC's powers with regard to returns and payment of tax	
	These points could be examined as SFQs or as parts of longer questions.	
Examined Sample Paper May 2007 November 2007 May 2008	Read Chapter 15 of the Study Text, after reading the following guidance.	
	Chapter 15 considers the tax administration aspects of both income tax and capital gains tax. As you have not yet studied capital gains tax study the income tax aspects only of this chapter at this stage and leave the administration of capital gains tax until later.	
	In each case make sure you note down any deadlines or due dates, so that you can memorise them for use in the exam. Read Section 2 and note the deadline for notifying HMRC of your liability to income tax.	
	Read Section 3 and note the deadline for submission of paper and electronic self assessment tax returns and the requirements for submitting short form tax returns. You should also be able to state the penalties for the late submission of a tax return. Note the time period for which records must be kept and the penalties for failing to keep records.	
	Read Section 4 which covers amendments to a return and the time limits for making claims for reliefs.	
	Read Section 5 and make a note of the payment dates for income tax and understand how payments on account are calculated (attempt example 1) and reduced, where applicable. Identify the situations when surcharges and interest are charged on overdue tax when a repayment supplement will be paid to a taxpayer.	
Professional Rules and Practice Guidelines	Now revise Chapter 10 of your Professional Rules and Practice Guidelines	
	• Ceasing to act	
10 Course Exam	Once you have completed the above study periods you are ready to sit Course Exam 1 on Income tax.	Course Exam 1 (Income tax)
	To gain the most from this exam, set aside 3 hours and 15 minutes to complete it.	

TQT
Tax Qualification Training

11 **Outline of CGT**	In examining capital gains tax (CGT) for individuals, questions may require a candidate to be able to discriminate between situations where CGT applies and where it does not and to be able to calculate the CGT liability for a tax year. (Sample paper SFQ5, May 2008 SFQ9)	SFQ 9.1 – 9.3 LFQ 9.1 – 9.2
	These background areas are covered in this study period and whilst they are unlikely to be examined in their own right, they are essential to any question involving CGT.	
Examined: Sample Paper May 2008	Read through Chapter 9 after reading the following guidance.	
	Read Sections 1 and 2 of the Chapter, which form essential background knowledge to CGT, and make notes making sure you can identify:	
	• Who pays CGT. • The rate of tax applicable to individuals (attempt example 1). • Chargeable and exempt persons, disposals and assets.	
	Section 3 is very brief, note the date of payment of CGT, this will be dealt with in more detail in Study Period 17, Administration of CGT.	
	Read Section 4 and make sure you understand:	
	• The impact of residence and domicile status on the chargeability of an individual to UK CGT on the disposal of UK and overseas assets (attempt example 2).	
	• How the location of assets (UK or overseas) is determined. • When double tax relief will be available and how it will be calculated (attempt example 3).	
Professional Rules and Practice Guidelines	Now revise Chapter 11 of your Professional Rules and Practice Guidelines	
	• Training and CPD	

12 **Computing gains and losses**	You will be expected to calculate capital gains tax on many different types of disposals. You will need to be able to calculate gains/losses as the basis of most questions on CGT. You may be examined on:	SFQ 10.1 – 10.10 LFQ 10.1 – 10.3
	• The basic gain computation. The use of capital losses.	
	• The computation of a gain for an asset held before 31/3/82 (Sample paper SFQ2, SFQ3, May 2007 SFQ8, May 2008 SFQ4)	
	• Gains on transfers between connected persons , husband and wife, and on part disposals and on debts and loans (sample paper SFQ4 (PD), May 2007 SFQ7 (CP))	
Examined Sample Paper May 2007	Read through Chapter 10 of the Study Text after taking account of the following guidance.	
	Section 1 is important showing the basic computation of a capital gain. Attempt example 1.	
	Section 2 shows how a capital loss can be calculated. You need to be aware of the uses of capital losses and how these uses differ depending on whether it is a current or brought forward loss. Attempt examples 2 to 4. Be aware of the use of losses on death (example 5), the use of trading losses against capital gains (example 6) and share loss relief.	
	Section 3 is important it shows how the computation is modified for Pre 31/3/82 assets. Attempt example 7.	
	Sections 5 and 6 set out the rules for dealing with disposals between connected persons and married couples.	
	Section 7 is important and shows how cost and other deductions are split between different disposal computations if a single asset is disposed in more than one disposal (examples 11 and 12). Read the Exam focus points after example 12 and then attempt example 13 to revise the chapter so far.	
	Section 8 then stands alone as it explains whether debts and loans can have CGT implications. This is less important than other areas of this study period.	
Professional Rules and Practice Guidelines	Now revise Chapter 12 of your Professional Rules and Practice Guidelines • Members in Employment	

13 **Shares and securities**	You may be examined on the special rules for calculating gains on the sale of shares and securities. You need to be able to:	SFQ 11.1 – 11.3 LFQ 11.1 – 11.4
	Match share costs with share disposal proceeds using the matching rules for individuals and be able to construct the share pool holding. (Sample paper SFQ6, May 2007 SFQ3, November 2007 LFQ2)	
	Modify the basic computation of a gain on a share disposal to deal with bonus issues and rights issues of shares (Sample paper part 2 Q2)	
	Share disposal questions can seem complicated as the questions often involve a lot of information. They are a good topic for a long form question.	
Examined: Sample Paper May 2007 November 2007	Read through Chapter 11 of the Study text after reading the following guidance.	
	Section 1 explains the need for special rules for disposals of shares and securities, read this as background knowledge	
	Read through Sections 2 and 3 carefully, attempting examples 1 and 2. At the end of these sections you will be able to deal with calculating a capital gain on the sale of shares. This computation will form the basis of all questions on the disposal of shares. It is important to make sure you understand this part of the chapter well before you progress to the other sections of the chapter.	
	Once you are happy with the basic computation on the sale of shares, you can then look at how the basic rules are modified in different circumstances. In Section 4 you will find information about:	
	Bonus issues (example 3), Rights issues (example 4), Capital distributions (example 5), Re-organisations & takeovers (examples 6 to 8).	
	You need to work through each of these situations. All of these options could be examined, but the most important are bonus issues, rights issues and takeovers. At the end of the chapter Section 5 is a short section to read through on gilts and QCBs. Attempt example 9.	
Professional Rules and Practice Guidelines	Now revise Chapter 13 of your Professional Rules and Practice Guidelines • Legal matters	

14 **Chattels and** **wasting assets**	Again, this chapter deals with the way in which the basic gain computation changes on the disposal of specific types of assets. In this case the disposal of chattels and wasting assets, including leases.	SFQ 12.1 – 10.7 LFQ 12.1 – 12.3
	These calculations have been frequently examined as part of SFQs. (Sample paper SFQ2 and May 2007 SFQs 2, 6 and 7). The types of calculation involved make these calculations really easy to examine as SFQs and also as small parts of long questions, including many different capital disposals (November 2007 LFQ 2, May 2008 LFQ 2).	
Examined: Sample Paper May 2007 November 2007 May 2008	Read through Chapter 12 after taking note of the following guidance.	
	Read through Section 1 about chattels and make sure you can identify a chattel, understand that wasting chattels are exempt and how the basic gain computation would be amended for the sale of a chattel. These calculations often crop up as SFQs and you need to be able to identify them and perform the calculations.	
	Quickly note the general treatment of wasting assets from Section 2, as background knowledge. This is less likely to appear as a separate question in its own right.	
	Read through Section 3 on leases. Make sure you understand the difference between assigning a lease and granting a lease and the definition of a short and a long lease. Then work through the five different situations and work examples 5 to 9. Make notes about how the computation works in each of the five circumstances. There is a lot of detail to take in this section and it can get quite complicated. Don't waste too much time here – just note down the difference between the different types of computations. You will have time to practice these calculations later, which is the best way to revise them.	
Professional Rules and Practice Guidelines	Now revise the remaining sections of your Professional Rules and Practice Guidelines • Advertising Publicity and Promotion • Appendices	

TQT
Tax Qualification Training

15 **Principal private residence relief**	Having computed capital gains, the examiner may then test you on circumstances when those gains may either be exempted from tax or deferred by the operation of CGT reliefs.	SFQ 13.1 – 13.3 LFQ 13.1 – 13.2
	The first relief you may be tested on is Principal Private Residence Relief. This relief exempts gains from tax.	
	Questions will rarely focus on a property that is entirely exempt from tax under this relief. It is more likely that you will be expected to consider situations where a property may be partially exempt, perhaps where there has been a period of absence from the property or where the more than one residence was held at once. For example see Long Form Question 3 on the Sample Paper and long form Question 2 on the May 2007 real exam paper.	
Examined: Sample Paper May 2007 November 2007	Read through Chapter 13 of the Study Text after reading the following guidance:	
	In Section 1.1 establish the basic principle of when the relief applies. The rest of the chapter relies in this understanding. Read and make notes on the periods that are deemed to be occupation of the property for CGT purposes, attempt example 1.	
	Briefly read Section 2 and be aware of the rules where more than one residence is owned.	
	Read through Section 3 and make sure you are aware of the circumstances in which letting relief will be available. This topic can get quite complicated, make sure you don't waste too much time on it and attempt example 2 to make sure you have understood the principles involved.	
	Finally, read Section 4 and attempt example 3 to ensure you are aware of the impact of a period of business use on the exemption.	

TQT
Tax Qualification Training

16 **Other CGT reliefs**	You may also be examined on the other ways in which individuals can gain relief from CGT. Entrepreneurs' relief was introduced in April 2008 and is therefore very topical. Like PPR it exempts part of the gain arising on certain disposals. The other reliefs in this study session are deferrals of tax, rather than exemptions.	SFQ 14.1 – 14.11 LFQ 14.1 – 14.9
	Because use of these reliefs can be tested in calculations they are frequently examined as SFQs. (See Sample paper SFQ3 and SFQ7, May 2007 SFQ14, November 2007 SFQ6) However, they could also feature as part of a long form question on future exams.	
Examined: Sample Paper May 2007 November 2007	Read through Chapter 14 from the Study Text, after reading through the following guidance:	
	Section 1 on entrepreneurs' relief is a very important section. The relief was recently introduced and is a very valuable relief for certain business disposals. Attempt examples 1 to 5 to make sure you fully understand the application of this important relief.	
	Read through Section 2 of the Chapter, to learn about gifts.	
	This is an important area and frequently examined. Make sure you understand the CGT treatment of gifts and the way in which CGT can be deferred on a gift.	
	Attempt examples 6 and 7 to check your understanding. There are then a series of special cases in which the basic gift relief rules are amended. Please read them through. The most important of these is Section 3.5, sales at an undervalue. Please attempt Example 9.	
	Read through Section 4 to learn about EIS deferral relief. Make sure that you understand the amount of relief available but also the qualifying conditions when the deferred gain will crystallise.	
	At the end of the chapter, Section 5 describes the treatment of the receipt of insurance proceeds and compensation. This can be a tricky area and is not always examined. However, it is the kind of area that could be examined in SFQs. Don't get bogged down in this part of the chapter, it is not as important as the rules for gift relief.	
	Make sure you attempt examples 11 and 12 to make sure you have understood the rules.	

17 **Administration of CGT**	Once capital gains tax has been calculated for an individual we need to be aware of :	SFQ 15.3
	• The self assessment reporting requirements and due dates for reporting.	
	• The due date for payment of any tax due. Relatively easy to learn and easy marks in the exam, if you can remember them. (May 2007 Part 2 Q3)	
	• The penalties, interest or surcharges chargeable for non-compliance with these rules	
	• HMRC's powers with regard to returns and payment of tax	
	These points could be examined as SFQs or as parts of longer questions.	
Examined: May 2007	Read Chapter 15 of the Study Text, after reading the following guidance.	
	Chapter 15 considers the tax administration aspects of both income tax and capital gains tax As you have already studied the administration of income tax in Study Period 9 and in most cases the rules are identical, you can simply revise the basic rules from Study Period 9 and learn the points where the administration of CGT differs from the administration of income tax.	
	Read Sections 2, 3 and 4 for revision.	
	Read Section 5 to revise the payment dates for income tax and capital gains tax and understand how payments on account are calculated were there is both income tax and capital gains tax due for a period (attempt example 1). Identify the situations when surcharges and interest are charged on overdue tax and note the rates of surcharge and the method of calculating the interest due. Identify when a repayment supplement will be paid to a taxpayer on repayment of tax and note the method of calculating repayment supplement. Note when CGT may be paid by instalments.	
	Read Section 6 and revise the powers of HMRC to enquire into returns, determine the sum of tax due, and the powers of the taxpayer to appeal against an assessment and postpone all or part of the tax due.	
18, 19, 20 **Revision**	If you are a home study student attempt the course exam in Study Period 18. Then spend the next session and any remaining time you have revising your weak areas.	Course exam 2 (CGT) Pre-Revision Mock Exam
	You should also refer to the law syllabus at the front of the ATT's law manual 'Essential Law for The Taxation Technician' and ensure you have read through all the sections of law that are within this syllabus.	
	Just before you are about to start the 'revision phase' of your studies you should sit the pre-revision mock. This mock is a good indicator of whether you are ready to move on to practising questions in TQT's revision kit.	

Revision Phase

TQT provide you with the following material to assist with your revision phase:

Passcards

TQT's Passcards will be published in January 2009. TQT's Passcards follow the overall structure of the TQT Study Texts, but they are not just a condensed book, each card has been separately designed for clear presentation. Topics are self contained and can be grasped visually. **They are the perfect aid to your revision.**

i-pass CD Rom

TQT's i-Pass CD-Rom will be published in January 2009. This is a useful tool which is designed to test the knowledge which is fundamental to your exam. It enables you to attempt tests, making it an ideal revision tool.

i-Pass has two modes. The first one is 'Test as you learn'. This allows you to test yourself on the areas that you are studying at the time or a combination of different areas. Use the sliders to choose the number of questions to do to fit the time you have available.

The second mode provides exam practice by creating an exam containing questions selected at random from those within 'Test as you learn' for you to answer.

Each mode gives you **comprehensive feedback on the questions and your performance.**

Revision Kit

TQT's Revision Kit is packed full of past examination questions and answers for you to practice. Plenty of question practice is the key to passing this exam. Many of the answers to questions in the Revision Kit have annotated marking schemes attached. This means that you can see where the easy marks are likely to be awarded on your examination and thus learn how to maximise your chances of passing. There are also a number of recap questions covering key areas of the syllabus.

CTA AND ATT EXAMINATIONS
MAY AND NOVEMBER 2009
TAX TABLES

Income Tax rates

	2008-09	2007-08
	%	%
Starting rate	n/a	10
Starting rate for savings income[1]	10	n/a
Basic rate[2]	20	22
Higher rate[2]	40	40
Trust rate	40	40
	£	£
Starting rate band	n/a	1 – 2,230
Savings income starting rate band [1]	1 – 2,320	n/a
Basic rate band	1 – 34,800	2,231 – 34,600
Standard rate band for trusts	1,000	1,000

Notes (1) Savings income is taxed at 10%, 20% or 40%. In 2008-09, if an individual's taxable non-savings income exceeds £2,320, the 10% starting rate for savings will not apply.
(2) Dividend income is taxed at 10% or 32.5%.

Income Tax reliefs

	2008-09	2007-08
	£	£
Personal allowance	6,035	5,225
– age 65–74	9,030	7,550
– age 75 or over	9,180	7,690
Married couple's allowance [1] [2]		
– age under 75	6,535	6,285
– age 75 or over	6,625	6,365
– Maximum income before abatement of relief - £1 for £2	21,800	20,900
– Minimum allowance	2,540	2,440
Blind person's allowance	1,800	1,730
'Rent-a-room' limit	4,250	4,250
Enterprise investment scheme relief limit [3]	500,000	400,000
Venture capital trust relief limit [4]	200,000	200,000
Employer supported childcare	£55 per week	£55 per week

Notes (1) Relief restricted to 10% (2) Only available where at least one partner was born before 6 April 1935
(3) Relief at 20% (4) Relief at 30%

Child Tax Credit

		2008-09	2007-08
		£	£
Family element	(one per family)	545	545
Baby element	(child under one year)	545	545
Child element	(in addition to baby element, paid for each child)	2,085	1,845

Working Tax Credit

		2008-09	2007-08
		£	£
Basic element	(one per single claimant or couple)	1,800	1,730
Couple's and lone parent element	(in addition to basic, one per couple)	1,770	1,700
30 hour element	(in addition to other elements, one per couple)	735	705
Childcare element	(if one child in registered childcare)	£175 pw	£175 pw
maximum eligible cost	(if two children in registered childcare)	£300 pw	£300 pw
% of eligible childcare costs covered		80%	80%

Notes (1) If entitled to only CTC and (combined) income > £15,575 (£14,495 – 2007-08) then the maximum amount of credits will be reduced by 39% (37% – 2007-08) of the excess income.
(2) If entitled to WTC only or both CTC and WTC and (combined) income > £6,420 (£5,220 – 2007-08) then the maximum amount of credits will be reduced by 39% (37% – 2007-08) of the excess income.
(3) Only family (and baby element) of CTC available if (combined) income > £50,000. These elements are reduced by 1/15 of income in excess of £50,000.
(4) Income disregard £25,000. The disregard is the amount by which the claimant's income can increase, compared with the previous year, before their tax credit award is recalculated.

Income tax – Pension contributions

	Annual allowance £	Lifetime allowance £
2006-07	215,000	1,500,000
2007-08	225,000	1,600,000
2008-09	235,000	1,650,000
2009-10	245,000	1,750,000
2010-11	255,000	1,800,000

Basic amount qualifying for tax relief   £3,600

Company cars and fuel

Company cars

Cash equivalent   15% of list price for cars emitting 135g/km (2007-08 140 g/km)
increased by 1% per 5g/km over the limit
Capped at 35% of list price
10% of list price for cars emitting 120g/km or less (2007-08 n/a)
3% supplement on diesel cars
9% of list price for electric cars

Van scale charge

£3,000 (2008-09 and 2007-08)

Fuel scale benefits for private fuel

Cars   For 2008-09 the benefit is £16,900 (2007-08 £14,400) multiplied by the percentage used in calculating the car benefit

Vans   £500 (2008-09 and 2007-08)

Official rate of interest	2008-09	2007-08
	6.25%	6.25%

ITEPA Mileage Rates

Vehicles		2008-09 and 2007-08
Car or van[1]	First 10,000 business miles	40p
	Additional business miles	25p
Motorcycles		24p
Bicycles		20p
Passenger payments		5p

Note   (1)   For NIC purposes, a rate of 40p applies irrespective of mileage.

Value Added Tax

Standard rate		17½%
Annual registration limit	From 1 April 2007	£64,000
	From 1 April 2008	£67,000
De-registration limit	From 1 April 2007	£62,000
	From 1 April 2008	£65,000

Cash accounting

	£
Turnover threshold to join scheme	1,350,000
Turnover threshold to leave scheme	1,600,000

Annual accounting

	£
Turnover threshold to join the scheme	1,350,000
Turnover threshold to leave the scheme	1,600,000

TQT
Tax Qualification Training

Capital allowances
Principal writing down allowance rates[1]

	6.4.08 – 5.4.09	6.4.07 – 5.4.08
Annual investment allowance[2]	100%	-
Plant and machinery, patent rights and know-how	20%	25%
Integral features/long life assets	10%	6%
Industrial buildings and agricultural buildings	3%	4%

First year allowances available to certain businesses/companies [1]

	6.4.06-5.4.08
Small-sized businesses/companies	50%
Medium-sized businesses/companies	40%

Notes   (1) Dates for companies are 1 April - 31 March rather than 6 April - 5 April

            (2) 100% on the first £50,000 of investment in plant and machinery (except cars)

Small and medium sized business/company limits

	Small	Medium
(i) Turnover	£5.6m	£22.8m
(ii) Balance sheet assets	£2.8m	£11.4m
(iii) Employees	50	250

A business/company must meet 2 of the 3 criteria listed in this year and the previous year to qualify as small or medium sized.

100% first year allowances available to all businesses
On new Energy Saving Plant and Water Efficient Plant

On new cars registered between 16 April 2002 and 31 March 2013 if the car either emits not more than 110 g/km (120g/km prior to 1 April 2008) of CO_2 or it is electrically propelled.

On the renovation or conversion of vacant business premises, in any of the disadvantaged areas of the UK designated as Enterprise Areas, for the purpose of bringing those premises back into business use (the Business Premises Renovation Allowance).

On the costs of converting or renovating an empty or under-used space above a commercial property into qualifying residential accommodation (Flat Conversion Allowances).

On capital expenditure incurred by a person on research and development (Research and Development Allowances).

Corporation Tax

Financial year	2008	2007
Full rate	28%	30%
Small companies' rate	21%	20%
Profit limit for small companies' rate	£300,000	£300,000
Profit limit for small companies' marginal relief	£1,500,000	£1,500,000
Marginal relief fraction for profits between £300,000 and £1,500,000	7/400	1/40

Research and Development expenditure

	SMEs	
	From 1.1.05	With EU approval
Employees	250	500
Turnover	€50m	€100m
Balance sheet assets	€43m	€86m

SMEs must meet the employees criteria and *either* the turnover *or* the balance sheet assets criteria.

TQT
Tax Qualification Training

National Insurance contributions

Class 1 contributions	2008-09 Annual	Weekly	2007-08 Annual	Weekly
Lower earnings limit	£4,680	£90	£4,524	£87
Earnings threshold	£5,435	£105	£5,225	£100
Upper earnings limit	£40,040	£770	£34,840	£670

Employee's contributions in 2008-09 (2007-08)

Not contracted out:	11% (11%) on earnings between £105 (£100) and £770 (£670)
	1% (1%) above £770 (£670) per week
Contracted out:	9.4% (9.4%) on earnings between £105 (£100) and £770 (£670)
	1% (1%) on earnings above £770 (£670) per week
	1.6% rebate on earnings between £90 (£87) and £105 (£100)

Employer's contributions in 2008-09 (2007-08)

Not contracted out:	12.8% (12.8%) on earnings in excess of £105 (£100)
Contracted out:	
Salary related:	9.1% (9.1%) on earnings between £105 (£100) and £770 (£670)
	12.8% (12.8%) on earnings in excess of £770 (£670)
	3.7% (3.7%) rebate on earnings between £90 (£87) and £105 (£100)
Money purchase:	11.4% (11.4%) on earnings between £105 (£100) and £770 (£670)
	12.8% (12.8%) on earnings in excess of £770 (£670)
	1.4% (1.4%) rebate on earnings between £90 (£87) and £105 (£100)

	2008-09	2007-08
Class 1A contributions	12.8%	12.8%
Class 1B contributions	12.8%	12.8%
Class 2 contributions		
Normal rate	£2.30	£2.20
Small earnings exception	£4,825 pa	£4,635 pa
Class 3 contributions	£8.10	£7.80
Class 4 contributions		
Annual lower earnings limit	£5,435	£5,225
Annual upper earnings limit	£40,040	£34,840
Percentage rate between limits		
Percentage rate above upper limit		

	2008-09	2007-08
Capital gains tax		
Annual exempt amount	£9,600	£9,200
CGT rates for individuals	18%	10%,20%,40%
CGT rate for trusts	18%	40%

Taper relief: Disposals in 2007-08

Number of whole years in qualifying period	Percentage of gain chargeable Business assets	Non-business assets
Less than 1	100%	100%
1	50%	100%
2	25%	100%
3	25%	95%
4	25%	90%
5	25%	85%
6	25%	80%
7	25%	75%
8	25%	70%
9	25%	65%
10	25%	60%

Entrepreneurs' relief: Disposals in 2008-09

Relevant gains (maximum)	£1,000,000
Reducing fraction	4/9

TQT
Tax Qualification Training

Lease percentage table

Years	Percentage	Years	Percentage	Years	Percentage
50 or more	100.000	33	90.280	16	64.116
49	99.657	32	89.354	15	61.617
48	99.289	31	88.371	14	58.971
47	98.902	30	87.330	13	56.167
46	98.490	29	86.226	12	53.191
45	98.059	28	85.053	11	50.038
44	97.595	27	83.816	10	46.695
43	97.107	26	82.496	9	43.154
42	96.593	25	81.100	8	39.399
41	96.041	24	79.622	7	35.414
40	95.457	23	78.055	6	31.195
39	94.842	22	76.399	5	26.722
38	94.189	21	74.635	4	21.983
37	93.497	20	72.770	3	16.959
36	92.761	19	70.791	2	11.629
35	91.981	18	68.697	1	5.983
34	91.156	17	66.470	0	0.000

Retail Prices Index

Where Retail Price Indices are required, it should be assumed that they are as follows.

	Jan	Feb	Mar	Apr	May	Jun	Jul	Aug	Sep	Oct	Nov	Dec
1982	–	–	79.44	81.04	81.62	81.85	81.88	81.90	81.85	82.26	82.66	82.51
1983	82.61	82.97	83.12	84.28	84.64	84.84	85.30	85.68	86.06	86.36	86.67	86.89
1984	86.84	87.20	87.48	88.64	88.97	89.20	89.10	89.94	90.11	90.67	90.95	90.87
1985	91.20	91.94	92.80	94.78	95.21	95.41	95.23	95.49	95.44	95.59	95.92	96.05
1986	96.25	96.60	96.73	97.67	97.85	97.79	97.52	97.82	98.30	98.45	99.29	99.62
1987	100.0	100.4	100.6	101.8	101.9	101.9	101.8	102.1	102.4	102.9	103.4	103.3
1988	103.3	103.7	104.1	105.8	106.2	106.6	106.7	107.9	108.4	109.5	110.0	110.3
1989	111.0	111.8	112.3	114.3	115.0	115.4	115.5	115.8	116.6	117.5	118.5	118.8
1990	119.5	120.2	121.4	125.1	126.2	126.7	126.8	128.1	129.3	130.3	130.0	129.9
1991	130.2	130.9	131.4	133.1	133.5	134.1	133.8	134.1	134.6	135.1	135.6	135.7
1992	135.6	136.3	136.7	138.8	139.3	139.3	138.8	138.9	139.4	139.9	139.7	139.2
1993	137.9	138.8	139.3	140.6	141.1	141.0	140.7	141.3	141.9	141.8	141.6	141.9
1994	141.3	142.1	142.5	144.2	144.7	144.7	144.0	144.7	145.0	145.2	145.3	146.0
1995	146.0	146.9	147.5	149.0	149.6	149.8	149.1	149.9	150.6	149.8	149.8	150.7
1996	150.2	150.9	151.5	152.6	152.9	153.0	152.4	153.1	153.8	153.8	153.9	154.4
1997	154.4	155.0	155.4	156.3	156.9	157.5	157.5	158.5	159.3	159.5	159.6	160.0
1998	159.5	160.3	160.8	162.6	163.5	163.4	163.0	163.7	164.4	164.5	164.4	164.4
1999	163.4	163.7	164.1	165.2	165.6	165.6	165.1	165.5	166.2	166.5	166.7	167.3
2000	166.6	167.5	168.4	170.1	170.7	171.1	170.5	170.5	171.7	171.6	172.1	172.2
2001	171.1	172.0	172.2	173.1	174.2	174.4	173.3	174.0	174.6	174.3	173.6	173.4
2002	173.3	173.8	174.5	175.7	176.2	176.2	175.9	176.4	177.6	177.9	178.2	178.5
2003	178.4	179.3	179.9	181.2	181.5	181.3	181.3	181.6	182.5	182.6	182.7	183.5
2004	183.1	183.8	184.6	185.7	186.5	186.8	186.8	187.4	188.1	188.6	189.0	189.9
2005	188.9	189.6	190.5	191.6	192.0	192.2	192.2	192.6	193.1	193.3	193.6	194.1
2006	193.4	194.2	195.0	196.5	197.7	198.5	198.5	199.2	200.1	200.4	201.1	202.7
2007	201.6	203.1	204.4	205.4	206.2	207.3	206.1	207.3	208.0	208.9	209.7	210.9
2008*	209.8	211.4	212.1	212.8	213.5	214.2	214.9	215.6	216.3	217.0	217.7	218.4
2009*	219.1	219.8	220.5	221.2	221.9	222.6	223.3	224.0	224.7	225.4	226.1	226.8

* = assumed

Stamp duty   Shares = 0.5%

Stamp duty land tax

Rate (%)	Residential	Non-residential
Zero	Up to £125,000[1]	Up to £150,000
1	Over £125,000[1] – 250,000	Over £150,000 – 250,000
3	Over £250,000 – 500,000	Over £250,000 – 500,000
4	Over £500,000	Over £500,000

Note   (1)   A higher threshold of £150,000 applies to transactions in residential land in disadvantaged areas.

New leases - duty on rent

Rate (%)	Net present value of rent	
	Residential	Non-residential
Zero	Up to £125,000[1]	Up to £150,000[2]
1%	Excess over £125,000	Excess over £150,000

Notes   (1)   A higher threshold of £150,000 applies to transactions in residential land in disadvantaged areas.

           (2)   No nil band on non-residential property (other than in disadvantaged areas) where annual rent is £1,000 or more.

Inheritance Tax

	Nil rate band		Nil rate band
6 April 1996 – 5 April 1997	up to £200,000	6 April 2002 – 5 April 2003	up to £250,000
6 April 1997 – 5 April 1998	up to £215,000	6 April 2003 – 5 April 2004	up to £255,000
6 April 1998 – 5 April 1999	up to £223,000	6 April 2004 – 5 April 2005	up to £263,000
6 April 1999 – 5 April 2000	up to £231,000	6 April 2005 – 5 April 2006	up to £275,000
6 April 2000 – 5 April 2001	up to £234,000	6 April 2006 – 5 April 2007	up to £285,000
6 April 2001 – 5 April 2002	up to £242,000	6 April 2007 – 5 April 2008	up to £300,000
		From 6 April 2008	up to £312,000

		Wedding gifts	
Death rate	40%	Wedding gifts - Child	£5,000
Lifetime rate	20%	- Grandchild or remoter issue	£2,500
Annual exemption	£3,000	- Other party to marriage	£2,500
Small gifts	£250	- Other	£1,000

Taper relief		Quick Succession relief	
Death within 3 years of gift	Nil%	Period between transfers less than one year	100%
Between 3 and 4 years	20%	Between 1 and 2 years	80%
Between 4 and 5 years	40%	Between 2 and 3 years	60%
Between 5 and 6 years	60%	Between 3 and 4 years	40%
Between 6 and 7 years	80%	Between 4 and 5 years	20%

Other Indirect Taxes

		2008-09	2007-08
Insurance Premium Tax[1]	Standard rate	5%	5%
	Higher rate	17.5%	17.5%
Landfill Tax[2]	Per tonne	£32	£24
	Qualifying material	£2.50 per tonne	£2 per tonne
Landfill Communities Fund (LCF)	Relief for 90% of qualifying contributions	6.0% × landfill tax liability	6.6% × landfill tax liability
Aggregates Levy	Per tonne	£1.95	£1.60
Climate Change Levy[3]	Electricity	0.456p per kwh	0.441p per kwh
	Gas	0.159p per kwh	0.154p per kwh
	Liquid hydrocarbons	1.018p per kwh	0.985p per kwh
	Any other taxable commodity	1.242p per kwh	1.201p per kwh

Notes   (1)   Premium is tax inclusive – IPT is 1/21 or 7/47 of the premium

           (2)   Pro rated for part tonnes

           (3)   Where the reduced rate applies it is 20% of the rate shown in the table

Personal Taxation

Part A:
Personal Income Tax

- identify the UK's main taxes and sources of tax law
- identify who pays income tax
- follow the seven steps to calculating income tax
- understand the distinction between gross and net income
- identify which payments are deductible from total income
- identify the allowances available to reduce net income
- explain how tax relief is obtained for charitable donations
- identify and calculate the tax reductions available
- calculate the child and working tax credits
- calculate social security benefits
- understand the tax consequences of owning property jointly
- set out the tax position of beneficiaries of deceased person's estates
- identify the various categories of exempt income

References: ITA 2007 unless otherwise stated

Taxable income

1 Introduction

1.1 Taxes in the UK

The following are examples of the main UK taxes:

(a)   Income tax
(b)   National insurance
(c)   Corporation tax
(d)   Capital gains tax
(e)   Inheritance tax
(f)   Stamp duty
(g)   Value added tax
(h)   Customs duty, tobacco, petrol and other expenditure taxes

Items (a) to (f) are known as direct taxes. Items (g) and (h) are indirect taxes. For direct taxes, Her Majesty's Revenue and Customs (HMRC) collects directly (we count the PAYE system as a form of direct collection) from the taxpayer, whereas for indirect taxes HMRC collects from an intermediary, who attempts to pass on the cost to the final consumer.

There are other classifications which may be helpful. Items (a) (b) and (c) are, in general, taxes on income whereas those under (d), (e) and (f) are known as capital taxes. The indirect taxes in (g) and (h) are often called expenditure taxes.

1.2 Sources of tax law

Tax law is made by statute – although it is interpreted and amplified by case law. The main taxes and their sources are set out below.

Tax	Suffered by	Source
Income tax	Individuals Partnerships Trustees	Income Tax Act 2007 (ITA 2007) Income Tax (Trading and Other Income) Act 2005 (ITTOIA 2005) Income Tax (Earnings and Pensions) Act (ITEPA 2003) as amended
Corporation tax	Companies	ICTA 1988 as amended
Capital gains tax	Individuals Companies (which pay corporation tax on capital gains)	Taxation of Chargeable Gains Act 1992 (TCGA 1992) as amended
Value added tax	Businesses, both incorporated and unincorporated	Value Added Tax Act 1994 (VATA 1994)
Inheritance tax	Individuals	Inheritance Tax Act (IHTA 1984) as amended

1.3 The legislative process

The **tax year**, or **year of assessment** runs from 6 April to 5 April following. **For example, the year of assessment of 2008/09 runs from 6 April 2008 to 5 April 2009**.

Finance Acts make changes which apply mainly to the tax year ahead. For example, the Finance Act 2008 is concerned with the tax year 2008/09 for income tax purposes. This study text sets out the law as it stands in relation to the tax year 2008/09, including the provisions of Finance Act 2008, which students taking exams in May 2009 and November 2009 will be expected to know.

The annual Budget process commences with the Chancellor presenting a pre-Budget report around November/December indicating areas of legislation which will be included in the Budget speech and subsequent Finance Bill. This is followed by the Budget speech in the following March, announcing, amongst other things, the changes to taxation proposed for the coming fiscal year. A Finance Bill is printed and, after Parliamentary debate and various amendments, passes into law (by receiving Royal Assent to become a Finance Act) some time later.

Under the government's long term project to re-write tax legislation in a more user-friendly form, all income tax law previously contained in the Income Taxes Act 1988 (ICTA 1988) has now mainly been rewritten: in the Income Tax Act 2007 (ITA 2007); in the Income Tax (Trading and Other Income) Act 2005 (ITTOIA 2005); in the Income Tax (Earnings and Pensions) Act 2003 (ITEPA 2003); and in the Capital Allowances Act 2001 (CAA 2001).

The Taxes Management Act 1970 (TMA) provides the authority and the framework for administering the income tax system. Other provisions are found in subsequent Finance Acts. The consolidation acts are amended by the annual Finance Act which broadly enacts the Budget proposals.

Statutory Instruments (SI) are used by the government as a convenient way of introducing detailed legislation. They are numbered on a calendar year basis (eg SI 1989/469 is SI No. 469 issued in 1989).

2 Who pays income tax

2.1 General

The following may be liable to income tax.

(a)   Men and women
(b)   Children, however young
(c)   Each partner carrying on a business in the form of a partnership.

2.2 Children

A child is a taxpayer in his own right.

There is an important exception to this rule where investment income of a minor (under 18), unmarried child arises from a gift made by his parent. This income is treated as the parent's income if, in the year, it exceeds £100.

2.3 Husband and wife and civil partners

Married men and women, and same sex couples in a civil partnership, are taxable persons in their own right, each with their own allowances and bands of tax (see 6 and 7 below).

If the husband, wife or civil partner was born before 6 April 1935, a married couple's allowance (MCA), is available to reduce the tax of usually whichever spouse or partner has the higher income (see 8.2 below).

2.4 Residence, ordinary residence and domicile

A taxpayer may be UK:

(a)   resident, and/or
(b)   ordinarily resident, and/or
(c)   domiciled

If he was born in the UK of UK domiciled parents and has never left the UK for any length of time he is likely to be all three. Another individual may be non-resident or non-ordinarily resident or non-domiciled. Various combinations are possible and depend on the facts of each case as well as legislation and HMRC practice.

In Chapter 8 we set out the definitions of residence, ordinary residence and domicile in detail.

Generally, a UK resident person is liable to UK income tax on his UK *and* foreign income whereas a non-resident is liable to UK income tax only on income *arising* in the UK. If non-residents were treated identically to UK residents HMRC would try to collect income tax from French residents on their French income. You can imagine the reaction!

A UK resident, who is not domiciled in the UK, may claim to be liable to UK tax on foreign income on a *remittance basis* ie only to the extent that such income is brought to the UK, subject to paying a minimum £30,000 tax charge on the unremitted income (see Chapter 8).

2.5 Exempt persons

To conclude this section, here is a list of some of the persons or bodies exempt from UK income tax.

(a)   Registered pension funds
(b)   UK registered charities
(c)   Representatives of foreign countries. (diplomats)

3 Calculating income tax

There are seven steps to calculating an individual's income tax liability. [s.23]

Step 1   Identify the amounts of income on which the taxpayer is charged to income tax for the tax year. The sum of those amounts is '**total income**'. Each of those amounts is a 'component' of total income.

Step 2   Subtract allowable deductible payments from total income to arrive at '**net income**'. Deduct any available losses.

Step 3   Deduct the personal allowance (and blind person's allowance where relevant).

Step 4   Calculate tax at each applicable rate on the amounts of the components left after Step 3.

Step 5   Add together the amounts of tax calculated at Step 4.

Step 6   Deduct from the amount of tax calculated at Step 5 any tax reductions to which the taxpayer is entitled for the tax year.

Step 7   Add to the amount of tax left after Step 6 certain amounts of tax listed in s.30. The result is the taxpayer's liability to income tax for the tax year.

Below we look at each of these steps in further detail.

4 Step 1: Calculating total income

4.1 'Components' of total income

The most common types of income are listed below.

Non savings income:	
Trade profits	Profits earned from a trade, profession or vocation
Employment income	Income earned from employment including salaries, bonuses, benefits and pensions
Property income	Rent etc, from all types of land and buildings
Discretionary trust income	Income from a discretionary trust
Savings income:	
Interest income	Interest received either net or gross
Dividend income	Dividends received

Each of these types of income, known as a 'component', is added together to arrive at 'total income'. Each type is considered in detail later in this Study Text.

4.2 Gross and net income

The total income for a tax year (6 April to 5 April) is the *gross* amount (that is, including any tax deducted at source) and is in most cases the income arising in that year.

Some income is received in full ('gross'), with no tax deducted in advance. Other income is received after deduction of tax ('net').

Tax is deducted from employment income by the employer under the PAYE system. The salary figure in the exam will always be the gross amount and you will be given the amount of tax deducted under PAYE separately.

If income is received net of 20% tax, eg bank interest, it must be grossed up by $^{100}/_{80}$ to include the gross amount in the income tax computation.

If income is received net of 10% tax, eg UK dividends, it must be grossed up by $^{100}/_{90}$ to include the gross amount in the income tax computation. Savings and dividend income is considered in detail in Chapter 2.

Where an individual is the beneficiary of a discretionary trust, any income he receives from it is received net of *(40% tax)* **40% tax and must be grossed up by** $^{100}/_{60}$. It is then taxed on the individual recipient at the non-savings rates of 20% or 40%.

If an individual is the beneficiary of an interest in possession trust he is taxed on all income arising in the trust regardless of whether it is paid to him or not. Income from an interest in possession trust is received net of 20% tax (or 10% tax if it is dividend income).

Exam focus point

In the exam you may be given either the net or the gross amount of income: read the question carefully! If you are given the **net** amount, gross up the figure at the appropriate rate. For example, if Jack receives net building society interest of £160 it is equivalent to gross income of £160 × 100/80 = £200 with tax deducted at source of £200 × 20% = £40.

Examiner's report – Personal Taxation

May 07 – Part 2 Question 1

The main problem….was in grossing up the trust income and dividends using the appropriate rates.

---

5 Step 2: Deductible payments and losses

5.1 Introduction

A deduction is available for certain payments from total income to arrive at 'net income'.

The amount of relief available is the gross amount paid in the tax year.

Deductible payments include: [s.24]

(a)   Gifts of shares and land to charity (5.2 below)
(b)   Interest payments (5.3 below)
(c)   Annual payments and patent royalties (5.4 below)

Relief for losses, such as property losses (see Chapter 3) are also deducted at Step 2.

5.2 Gifts of shares and land to charity

Relief is available for gifts of the following shares or securities to charity. [s.432]

(a)   Shares or securities which are listed on a recognised stock exchange or dealt in on a UK designated market (eg AIM shares)
(b)   Units in authorised unit trusts, and
(c)   Shares in open-ended investment companies (OEICs).

Relief is also available for gifts of freehold or leasehold land to charity, provided it is situated in the UK and the charity gives a certificate that:

(a)   Describes the qualifying interest in land
(b)   Specifies the date of the disposal, and
(c)   States that the charity has acquired the qualifying interest in land. [s.433 and s.441]

Relief is given by deducting the **market value of the assets** (<u>less</u> any consideration given by the charity, plus any incidental costs of making the disposal) **from total income**.

5.3 Interest payments

Interest payments are deductible from total income when a loan is used for the following purposes.

(a) **To buy plant or machinery for use in a partnership.** Interest qualifies for three years from the end of the tax year in which the loan was taken out. If the plant is used partly for private purposes, only a proportion of the interest is eligible for relief. [s.388]

(b) **To buy plant or machinery for employment purposes.** Interest qualifies for three years from the end of the tax year in which the loan was taken out. If the plant is used partly for private purposes, only a proportion of the interest is eligible for relief. [s.390]

(c) **To buy an interest in a close company (ordinary shares)** (other than a close investment holding company) or lending money to such a company for the purpose of its business. When the interest is paid the borrower must *either* hold some shares and work full time as a manager or director of the company *or* have a material interest in the close company (ie hold more than 5% of the shares). [s.392]

Relief will not be available if Enterprise Investment Scheme (EIS) (see Chapter 4) relief is claimed on the shares.

A close company is a company controlled by its shareholder-directors or by five or fewer shareholders.

(d) **To buy shares in an employee-controlled company.** The company must be an unquoted trading company resident in the UK with at least 50% of the voting shares held by employees. [s.396]

(e) **To invest in a partnership**, or contribute capital or make a loan. The borrower must be a partner (other than a limited partner), and relief ceases when he ceases to be one. [s.398]

(f) **To buy shares in or lend money to a co-operative.** The borrower must work for the greater part of his time in the co-operative or a subsidiary. [s.401]

(g) **To pay inheritance tax.** Interest paid by the personal representatives qualifies for 12 months [s.403]

(h) The replacement with other loans qualifying under (c) to (f) above.

Clue
*

Exam focus point

If the examiner asks you to give examples of deductible interest payments try looking at s.383(2) ITA 2007 which sets out the eligible loans on which interest is deductible.

If the interest is paid wholly and exclusively for business purposes the taxpayer can instead deduct the interest when computing his trade profits, rather than from total income. The interest need not fall into any of the categories outlined above.

Interest on a loan taken out to buy a letting property will qualify as an expense when computing property income (see Chapter 3.)

Where interest is allowable in the computation of trade profits or property income, the amount *payable* (on an accruals basis) is deducted rather than interest *paid* in the tax year.

5.4 Patent royalties — non-trade related

The only examinable deductible payment that is <u>paid *net*</u> is a non-trade related patent royalty payment ie it is paid net of basic rate income tax (20% × the gross amount). [s.448]

However, <u>as it is always the *gross figure*</u> that is subtracted in the payer's tax computation, the deductible patent royalty payment <u>must be grossed up by</u> $^{100}/_{80}$ in the tax computation. Doing so, however, means that the taxpayer has obtained tax relief twice, so the <u>tax deducted must be collected</u> as part of the <u>taxpayer's self-assessment</u>, even where they may not usually be required to submit a self assessment return.

Note that patent royalties paid for the purposes of the trade are deducted in calculating the individual's trading income and not as a deductible payment.

Example 1

For 2008/09 Brenda has earnings of £4,350 and pays non-trade related patent royalties of £800 (net amount).

What amount can Brenda deduct from her total income and how much tax must she add to her liability?

---

6 Step 3: Personal allowance and blind person's allowance

6.1 Introduction

Two allowances, the personal allowance and the blind person's allowance, are deducted from net income to arrive at 'taxable income'. The amounts given in the following paragraphs are for 2008/09.

Exam focus point

The amount of personal allowance and blind person's allowance is given in the tax tables. Find them!

Clue

6.2 Personal allowance (PA)

All individuals (including children) are entitled to an amount of tax free income, the personal allowance (PA), of £6,035.

An individual aged between 65 and 74 years (at any time in the tax year) is **entitled to an age allowance of £9,030** instead of the ordinary PA of £6,035.

6035

Where net income exceeds £21,800 the age allowance is reduced by one half of the excess of net income over £21,800. The allowance cannot fall below £6,035.

For the purpose of the £21,800 income restriction we consider **'adjusted net income'**, which is net income less a deduction for the gross value of:

(a)   Gift Aid payments (see Section 7.2 below)
(b)   Personal pension scheme contributions (see Chapter 7).

Individuals aged 75 or over (at any time in the tax year) obtain a more generous age allowance of £9,180. The higher age allowance works in the same way as the basic age allowance, with the same net income limit of £21,800.

Someone who dies in the tax year in which they would have had their 65th or 75th birthday is treated as having reached that age during the year.

Example 2

Geoff is 68 and has income of £23,600. What is his personal allowance for 2008/09?

6.3 Blind person's allowance (BPA)

A taxpayer who is registered with a local authority as a blind person is entitled to an allowance of £1,800. This is given in addition to the personal allowance.

6.4 Persons resident abroad

In general, non-residents are liable to tax on income arising in the UK, but are not entitled to allowances. However, certain people are entitled to allowances despite being non-resident. These are: [s.56(3)]

(a) Individuals resident in the Isle of Man or the Channel Islands
(b) Former residents who have left the country for their own or a family member's health reasons
(c) Current or former Crown servants and their widows or widowers
(d) Employees in the service of any territory under Her Majesty's protection
(e) Missionaries — *countries formerly ruled by Britain eg. Australia*
(f) Commonwealth citizens and EEA nationals. [s.278 ICTA 1988]
— *European &*

The rules for non-residents apply both to allowances deducted from net income (the PA and the BPA) and to allowances which reduce tax (see Section 8).

Individuals who claim the remittance basis of taxation on their foreign income (eg a non UK domiciled individual) are not entitled to personal allowances (see Chapter 8).

Exam focus point

Calculation of allowances is often tested in the short form questions. Make sure you are familiar with the rules.

7 Steps 4 & 5: Calculating income tax

7.1 The personal tax computation

We have now considered the fundamental elements of the *personal tax computation*. Here is an example of what that computation might look like so far.

Illustration 1

MRS A: INCOME TAX COMPUTATION 2008/09

	£
Employment income – salary (PAYE of £6,100 deducted)	36,200
Property income – rent from cottage	4,100
Taxed income from discretionary trust £1,620 × 100/60	2,700
Total income	43,000
Less: qualifying interest paid	(1,017)
Net income	41,983
Less: personal allowance	(6,035)
Taxable income	35,948

Income tax is charged on the figure of 'taxable income' according to the type (or component) **of income being taxed**.

From 6 April 2008, the basic rate of tax for non-savings income has been reduced from 22% to 20% and the starting rate for non-savings income has been abolished.

In 2008/2009 the first £34,800 of non-savings income is taxed at the basic rate of 20%. Taxable non-savings income above £34,800 is taxed at a higher rate of 40%.

In the above illustration all of the taxable income is taxed as non-savings income:

(a) **On the first £34,800 at the basic rate (20%)** = £6,960
(b) **On any excess at the higher rate (40%)** ie £1,148 @ 40% = £459

The total tax liability would be £7,419.

The tax bands and rates are provided in the Association's rates and allowances tables in the examination.

Different tax rates apply to savings income and dividends (see Chapter 2).

7.2 Gift Aid

The tax calculation may be affected by cash donations to charity made under the Gift Aid scheme. [s.414]

All cash donations are treated as being paid net, ie after deduction of income tax at the basic rate (20%). So, a net donation of £800 is worth £1,000 (£800 × $^{100}/_{80}$) as the charity can claim £200 (20% × £1,000) from HMRC.

(In addition, in the tax years 2008/09, 2009/10 and 2010/11 charities will be able to claim an extra 2% supplement on donations from the government, in order to compensate them for the reduction in the basic rate from 22% to 20%.)

The donor's basic rate band is also increased by an amount equal to the gross amount of the gift (£1,000 in our example above). This only affects higher rate taxpayers.

In the following illustration the taxpayer has paid a total of £1,920 to charity under Gift Aid.

Illustration 2

MR B: INCOME TAX COMPUTATION 2008/09

		£
Net income		45,050
Less: personal allowance		(6,035)
Taxable income		39,015

Tax liability	£	£
Basic rate:	34,800 @ 20%	6,960
Extended basic rate band: £1,920 × 100/80	2,400 @ 20%	480
Higher rate:	1,815 @ 40%	726
	39,015	8,166

Thus the taxpayer obtains relief at the higher rate of £480 (£2,400 × (40 − 20 = 20%)) as income that would otherwise be taxed at 40% is only taxed at 20%.

The charitable payment must not be repayable to the donor.

Any benefits the donor or any person connected with him receives must not be worth more than: [s.418]

(a)   For gifts ≤ £100:   25% × the donation
(b)   For gifts between £100 and £1,000:   £25
(c)   For gifts > £1,000:   lower of (i) 5% × the donation and (ii) £500

The charity must confirm on a declaration that the appropriate amount of tax has been paid. For a donor who pays insufficient tax it may be necessary to restrict his personal allowance to ensure the tax being recovered has been paid.

All cash payments to charity (other than those made under the Payroll Deduction Scheme – see Chapter 5) are potentially relievable under the Gift Aid scheme. There is no maximum or minimum threshold for Gift Aid payments.

Taxpayers may elect to carry back the Gift Aid payments for one year. [s.426] This may enable them to obtain higher rate tax relief in the previous year if their income in the current year is not sufficient to obtain higher rate relief.

Example 3

Zoë earns £50,000 in 2008/09 and expects to earn £30,000 in 2009/10. She has no other income. In May 2009, she pays £8,000 under the gift aid scheme. Zoë makes a claim for additional tax relief on the gift aid donation for 2008/09. Show Zoë's tax liability in both years assuming that rates and allowances for 2009/10 are the same as for 2008/09.

Tax Qualification Training

A claim for carry back must be made no later than the date on which the taxpayer files his return for the earlier year, and in any event no later than the statutory filing date for that year. A claim to carry back relief from 2008/09 to 2007/08 must be made by 31 January 2009.

Where an individual overpays tax he can tick a box on his tax return to instruct HMRC to send the repayment directly to the charity of his choice.

8 Step 6: Tax reductions

8.1 Introduction

Tax reductions reduce the tax on the income once it has been calculated. The tax reductions are as follows.

	Tax reduction
Venture Capital Trust Scheme (VCT) (see Chapter 4)	30% of investment (maximum investment = £200,000)
Investment under the Enterprise Investment Scheme (EIS) (see Chapter 4)	20% of investment (maximum investment = £500,000 – see below)
Maintenance payments following the breakdown of marriage	10% of payment
Married couple's allowance	10% of allowance

(handwritten margin note: Can only be used to reduce tax down to nil)

The increase in the maximum investment for EIS income tax relief purposes from £400,000 to £500,000 is subject to State Aid approval by the EC. Once this is given, the £500,000 limit will be backdated to 6 April 2008.

Married couple's allowance and relief for maintenance payments are only available where the individuals concerned were born before 6 April 1935 (ie were aged 73 or over at the start of the 2008/09 tax year).

8.2 Married couple's allowance (MCA)

8.2.1 The relief

The MCA is available in respect of both a married couple and a same sex couple within a civil partnership. [s.42]

The MCA is only available if either spouse or partner (or both) was born before 6 April 1935 (ie 73 by 6 April 2008).

If this condition is satisfied a minimum allowance is available of £2,540.

The tax reduction is given at 10% so the minimum tax reduction is 10% × £2,540 = £254.

For couples who are married before 5 December 2005 (the date civil partnerships were introduced), the tax reduction is automatically allocated to the husband.

For marriages and civil partnerships entered into after 5 December 2005, the tax reduction is allocated to whichever partner has the higher income.

The maximum value of the MCA is £6,535 (£6,625 if either partner is over 75 by the end of the tax year) **but is subject to an income restriction**. *(handwritten note: I thought it was at start of tax year)*

When adjusted net income exceeds £21,800, the personal allowance given to an elderly person is reduced by half of the excess, as explained above. Once that has been reduced to £6,035, the married couple's age allowance is then reduced by the excess restriction, but not to below £2,540. For marriages prior to 5 December 2005, the reduction in the married couple's age allowance always depends on the *husband's* adjusted net income.

For marriages and civil partnerships entered into after 5 December 2005, the restriction to the MCA depends on the adjusted net income of the partner with the higher income.

8.2.2 The year of marriage

In the year of marriage/civil partnership, the MCA is reduced by $^1/_{12}$ for each complete tax month (from the 6th of one month to the 5th of the next) that has passed before the wedding/civil partnership.

8.2.3 MCA elections

The wife (or for partnerships/marriages entered into after 5 December 2005, the lower earning partner) can unilaterally elect to have half of the tax reduction from the MCA set against her tax instead of her partner's. The election must be made by the start of the tax year.

Alternatively, the couple can jointly elect, by the start of the tax year, to transfer all of the tax reduction to the wife (or for partnerships/marriages entered into after 5 December 2005, the lower earning partner). An election remains in force until revoked, and any revocation applies from the following 6 April. For the year of marriage/partnership, an election may be made during the year. The elections can only apply in respect of the minimum £2,540 MCA even if a higher value is available.

Any MCA which turns out to be wasted (because either spouse or partner has insufficient tax to reduce) may then be transferred to the other spouse or partner.

8.2.4 The year of death/separation

If a wife (or for partnerships/marriages entered into after 5 December 2005, the lower earning partner) dies during a tax year, her partner receives the personal allowance (PA) and a full MCA for that year. The wife or lower earning partner will have a full PA for the year of death.

When a husband (or for partnerships/marriages entered into after 5 December 2005, the higher earning partner) dies the full PA and MCA (subject to age) are available. Any election relating to the MCA becomes void in the year of death. The widowed spouse or partner obtains the PA for the year, as normal, and is entitled to any MCA that becomes surplus.

In the tax year in which separation takes place, the husband or higher earning partner receives the PA plus a full MCA. However, any MCA election remains valid.

8.3 Maintenance payments

Provided the payer or the recipient (or both) was born before 6 April 1935 a tax reduction is available for payments under court orders or written agreements, or for maintenance assessments by the Child Support Agency. [s.453]

All maintenance payments are made gross (without deduction of tax at source). The recipient is not liable to income tax on maintenance payments made, however large.

Provided that the payment is made to the former spouse/partner for the benefit of the former spouse/partner or of a child of the family, the payer is entitled to claim a tax reduction of 10% of the lower of:

(a)   the payments *due* in the tax year; and
(b)   the minimum value amount of the MCA (£2,540 for 2008/09).

8.4 Giving tax reductions

Investments under the enterprise investment scheme or venture capital trust scheme, married couples' allowance and qualifying maintenance payments must be taken into account in preparing an individual's income tax computation.

The tax reduction must be calculated and it is only given if the individual has enough tax to reduce. For example, if the tax is £130 and the reduction is £200, the tax is only reduced to nil. The individual *cannot* claim a repayment of (£200 − £130 =) £70.

An individual may be entitled to several different tax reductions. They must be applied in a set order as follows.

(a)   Investments under the venture capital trust and then enterprise investment schemes

(b)   Maintenance payments

(c)   The married couple's allowance

Using the MCA last enables any unused amount to be transferred to the other spouse/partner.

Example 4

Peter, a married man aged 74, pays maintenance of £3,000 a year to a former spouse. His current wife has no income and is younger than him. Show his tax position for 2008/09 if his income consists of:

(a)   Trading profits of £27,700 and rental income of £2,000,

(b)   Trading profits of £8,100 and rental income of £2,000.

Exam focus point

Don't confuse how relief is given for allowances and tax reductions. **Allowances** are deducted from **net income**. **Tax reductions** reduce **tax on income**.

---

9 Step 7: Tax liability

The final step in calculating tax liability is to add certain tax charges including: [s.30]

(a)   The pension lifetime allowance charge, and

(b)   The pension annual allowance charge (see Chapter 7).

Any tax already suffered by deduction at source (or already paid on account under self-assessment) can then be deducted from the tax liability to arrive at the tax payable by the tax payer.

We have now completed the steps for calculating the tax liability. Let's look once more at Illustration 1 (Mrs A) for an example of what a full personal tax computation may look like.

Illustration 3 7.4

MRS A: INCOME TAX COMPUTATION 2008/09

	£
Employment income – salary (PAYE of £6,100 deducted)	36,200
Property income – rent from cottage	4,100
Taxed income from discretionary trust £1,620 × 100/60	2,700
Total income	43,000
Less: qualifying interest paid	(1,017)
Net income	41,983
Less: Personal allowance	(6,035)
Taxable income	35,948
Income tax:	
£34,800 @ 20%	6,960
£1,148 @ 40%	459
	7,419
Less: Tax reduction	
– EIS subscription (see Chapter 4) £1,000 @ 20%	(200)
Tax liability	7,219
Less: Tax suffered at source:	
– PAYE	(6,100)
– Discretionary trust income £2,700 × 40%	(1,080)
Tax payable	39

10 Tax credits and social security benefits

10.1 Tax credits

Child Tax Credit (CTC) and Working Tax Credit (WTC) are designed to support single people and couples with children who have low incomes. The Pension Credit is for those aged 60 or over to provide them with a minimum income.

The term 'credits' is a misnomer as they are not tax credits that appear in the individual's tax computation but are non-taxable amounts that are payable directly to the individuals who are entitled to receive them.

The table below lays out who is eligible for the CTC and WTC.

TAX CREDIT	AVAILABLE TO:
CTC	UK resident individual responsible for at least one child/qualifying young person
WTC	Employed/self employed individual on a relatively low income who is either: • $\geq$ 25 years and working $\geq$ 30 hours a week; or • $\geq$ 16 years, responsible for one or more children and working $\geq$ 16 hours a week; or • $\geq$ 16 years, disabled and working $\geq$ 16 hours a week

Single or separated individuals claim tax credits based on their individual circumstances. Married or co-habiting couples must make a claim based on their joint circumstances.

10.1.1 Income levels for CTC and WTC

Tax credits for any tax year are calculated based on the income of the last complete tax year before the year of the claim.

Gross income less registered pension scheme contributions and Gift Aid donations is used to calculate entitlement. Income includes cash remuneration, benefits, taxable interest income, taxable rental income, and foreign income.

The first £300 of interest, dividends, rental and foreign income is excluded with the £300 limit applying to a couple's joint income, not £300 each.

An annual adjustment is carried out at the year end to finalise the tax credit based on current year income if lower than the prior year, or if higher than the prior year by more than £25,000.

If income in the year of claim rises by less than £25,000, it does not affect the level of tax credit awarded ie the claim is still based on the income of the prior year. The increased income will affect the amount awarded for the following year. For example if in 2008/09 income is £12,000, the tax credit is based on the prior year's income of say £10,000. However in 2009/10 the £12,000 of income from 2008/09 will be used to calculate the tax credit.

Where income in the current year is more than £25,000 higher than the prior year, the tax credits will be based on the income of the current year.

Where the income in the current year is lower than the prior year a higher credit may be due. The individual can either:

- inform HMRC immediately, in which case the tax credit will be adjusted accordingly. Though if credits are then overpaid, they will need to be repaid at the year end; or

- wait until the end of the year and receive a one-off credit at the year end.

Entitlement to tax credits is **not** affected by capital (ie savings, investments, property etc.)

10.1.2 Child Tax Credit

Those who receive Income Support or income-based Jobseeker's Allowance will automatically receive the full amount of CTC for which they qualify.

The maximum annual amounts of CTC for 2008/09 are:

Element	Applies	Maximum Annual amount
		£
Family element	(one per family)	545
Family element, baby addition	(per family if at least one child under 1)	545
Child element	(per child including those under 1)	2,085

Ignoring WTC, for joint income up to £15,575 the maximum CTC is payable as detailed above.

For joint income between £15,575 and £50,000, the full family element of £545 is payable plus the £545 baby element, if applicable. However, above the income threshold of £15,575, the 'per child' elements of £2,085 per child are reduced by 39% of the excess income.

Once joint income exceeds £50,000, the per child elements have already been reduced to zero and now the family and any baby elements are also reduced by £1 for every £15 over the £50,000 threshold.

Example 5

Charlie and Helen are married with two children and had joint family income of £16,000 last year. This year, joint income is expected to be £17,000. They are not eligible for WTC. They also have joint interest income of £250. Calculate the CTC that they are entitled to.

Example 6

Megan and Llewelyn are married with four children and had joint family income of £54,600 last year. This year, joint income is the same. They are not eligible for WTC. They also have joint interest income of £700.

CTC is paid to the main carer. Where the claim is made by a couple the CTC can only be paid to the person in that couple who is the main carer for all the children of that couple.

Where there is a dispute as to whom the main carer is, HMRC will determine who, in fact, the main carer is.

CTC should not be confused with Child Benefit which is paid to all parents regardless of their level of income and is tax free.

10.1.3 Working tax credit

The maximum annual amounts of WTC for 2008/09 are:

Element	Applies	Maximum Annual amount
		£
Basic element	(one per single claimant or couple)	1,800
Couple's and lone parent element	(in addition to basic, one per couple)	1,770
30 hour element	(in addition to other elements, one per couple and look at joint hours)	735
Childcare element maximum eligible cost	(if one child in registered childcare)	£175 per week
	(if two children in registered childcare)	£300 per week
	% of eligible childcare costs recovered	80%
50+ return to work payment	16 – 29 hrs	1,235
	30+ hrs	1,840

WTC is payable in addition to CTC. **The childcare element of the WTC is paid direct to the main carer together with any CTC**. To qualify for the childcare element a lone parent or a couple must work at least 16 hours per week in total.

WTC is paid to the person who is working 16 hours or more each week. Couples where both partners qualify must decide who will receive it. WTC cannot be paid to the unemployed.

The amount received depends upon the income of the family. Tax credits are payable in full where the income is less than £6,420. Excess income above £6,420 reduces entitlement to tax credits at the rate of 39%. The WTC is reduced first, then CTC.

Example 7

Sophie and Shaun are married with four children and had joint family income of £13,000 last year. This year, joint income is expected to be £13,500.

Shaun works more than 30 hours per week. Sophie works 18 hours per week. The youngest child is placed with a childminder (cost £75pw).

10.1.4 Claiming the CTC and WTC

Tax credits need to be claimed within three months of entitlement. Therefore claims for 2008/09 should be submitted by 6 July 2008.

Where a claim needs to be backdated, it can only be backdated for a maximum of 3 months. Supposing an individual earns £60,000 salary, he would probably not complete a form as he's above the upper limit to any entitlement. However, if he's made redundant in October the earliest he could backdate his claim to is July. Thus he would lose any entitlement to tax credits for April to June. Clients with children are advised to make a protective claim to CTC even if at the start of the year they have joint income above the level at which entitlement is reduced to nil.

10.1.5 Pension Credit

Pension Credit is available to people aged 60 or over. It guarantees those aged 60 and over a minimum income of at least:

- £124.05 a week for a single person, or
- £189.35 a week for a couple

There is an additional element intended to reward savings which is payable if the claimant (or their partner) is age 65 or over. The maximum additional benefit is £19.71 per week for a single pensioner and £26.13 per week for a couple.

Whether the full benefit is available depends on income, which for this purpose includes earnings and pension benefits (including State pensions) and some other benefits such as Carer's Allowance and Bereavement Benefit. The definition excludes Attendance Allowance, Disability Living Allowance, Housing Benefit and Council Tax Benefit (see below).

10.2 Social security benefits

In certain situations individuals may be able to claim state benefits. We look at various benefits in this section.

10.2.1 Benefits available following a death

Bereavement payment

A bereavement payment is a non-taxable one off lump sum payment of £2,000 (2008/09). It is available to widows and widowers whose **late spouse made sufficient National Insurance (NIC) contributions** or died as a result of their job.

Widowed parent's allowance (WPA)

Widowed parent's allowance is a taxable weekly benefit of £90.70 available to individuals:

- Bringing up a child under 19 (or expecting their late husband's/ civil partner's baby), **and**
- They are under State Pension age (60 for women and 65 for men), **and**
- Their husband, wife or civil partner died and they paid National Insurance contributions (NICs), **or**
- Their husband, wife or civil partner died as a result of their work - even if they didn't pay NICs.

Bereavement allowance

Bereavement allowance is a taxable weekly benefit paid for up to 52 weeks after the death of the claimant's spouse/civil partner. It is available to widows and widowers whose **late spouse made sufficient NIC contributions. The claimant must be aged 45 or over at the death of the spouse, have no dependent children, and not be entitled to WPA.**

A claimant aged 55 or over when widowed gets the full rate of bereavement allowance (£90.70). Those aged between 45 and 54 get a reduced amount based on their age at the date of death of their spouse/civil partner.

10.2.2 Benefits available on illness

Statutory sick pay (SSP)

SSP of £75.40 per week is payable to employees who are:

- Aged between 16 and 65
- Sick for at least four days in a row (weekends and bank holidays are included)
- Earning at least £90 a week on average (the NIC lower earnings limit).

SSP is limited to a maximum period of 28 weeks. Different periods of sickness less than eight weeks apart can be linked for this purpose. If incapacity continues after the end of the 28 week period then incapacity benefit may be claimed (see below).

SSP is subject to tax and NICs as normal earnings.

Incapacity benefit

Individuals who are unable to work due to illness or disability may be entitled to a weekly incapacity benefit.

It is available where for example SSP has ended, or the individual is self employed or unemployed, and the individual has been:

- Paying National Insurance Contributions
- Unable to work due to sickness or disability for at least four days in a row
- Getting special medical treatment and unable to work for two or more days out of seven consecutive days

There are three rates of incapacity benefit:

Weekly rate	Amount	Amount if over State Pension age
Short-term (lower rate – first 28 weeks)	£63.75	£81.10
Short-term (higher rate – weeks 29 to 52)	£75.40	£84.50
Long-term basic rate (from week 53)	£84.50	not eligible

Short-term lower rate incapacity benefit is not taxable. Other incapacity benefit is taxable.

10.2.3 Benefits available to those needing long term care

Disability living allowance (DLA)

DLA is a tax-free benefit for children and adults who need help with personal care or have walking difficulties due to physical or mental disability. Individuals over the age of 65 may be eligible for attendance allowance (see below).

There are two components to the DLA:

- Care component – for those needing help looking after themselves or supervision to keep safe
- Mobility component – for those who cannot walk or need help getting around

There are three different weekly rates of the care component dependent upon the degree of care needed.

- Highest rate   £67.00
- Middle rate   £44.85
- Lowest rate   £17.75

There are two different rates of the mobility component.

- Higher rate   £46.75
- Lower rate   £17.75

Attendance allowance

Attendance allowance is a tax-free benefit for people aged 65 or over who need help with personal care due to physical or mental disability.

There are two weekly rates:

- Higher rate   £67.00
- Lower rate   £44.85

10.2.4 Benefits available to carers

Child benefit

Child benefit is a non-taxable benefit paid to people responsible for at least one child. It does not count as income for Tax Credit purposes (see above).

The following weekly amounts are payable in respect of each qualifying child:

- £18.80 a week for the eldest child
- £12.55 a week for each additional child.

TQT
Tax Qualification Training

The benefit can be claimed by anyone bringing up a child who is:

(a) Under 16.

(b) Under 19 and is studying full time up to A Level, Advanced Vocational Certificate of Education (AVCE) or equivalent.

(c) 16 or 17 and registered with the Careers Service for work or training.

Carer's allowance

This is a taxable benefit for those who spend at least 35 hours a week caring for someone who is in receipt of either attendance allowance or the disability living allowance at the higher or middle rate of the care component (see above).

Carer's allowance is not paid to claimants earning more than £95 per week.

The weekly rate is £50.55, reduced by the amount of certain other benefits, including State Pension, that the claimant receives. It is not payable at all if the claimant's other social security benefits exceed this amount.

10.2.5 Benefits available on retirement

State pension and state second pension (S2P)

Where sufficient NICs have been paid, a full basic State Pension, currently £90.70 per week for a single person and £145.05 a week for a couple, will become payable at State pension age. This is generally 65 for men and 60 for women although all individuals will have a State pension age of 65 by 2020.

A state second pension (S2P) will be earned by those **employees** who satisfy the entitlement conditions by having **paid sufficient NIC** contributions.

The self employed earn no state second pension benefit. **A widow or widower may inherit a state second pension (S2P) from their late spouse.**

Both the State Pension and the S2P are taxable.

11 Joint property

Where a husband and wife, or partners in a civil partnership, jointly own income-generating property (eg joint bank account) it is **assumed that they are entitled to equal shares of the income**.

The presumption of equal shares does not apply:

(a) To earned income eg employment income
(b) To profits from a business partnership
(c) To dividends from jointly owned shares in close companies
(d) Where the couple have separated.

If the couple separate the equal shares rule is discontinued.

The couple can make a joint declaration of their actual interests in an asset held in joint names if their actual entitlements to the asset and its income are unequal. **This will result in the income being assessed on each partner according to their actual share**.

Income will be split on the basis of the declaration from the date of the declaration. A declaration in respect of an asset cannot be withdrawn and remains in force until either the marriage/partnership comes to an end or the interests change.

If the interests do change the 'equal shares' rule applies until a further declaration is made. If an asset ceases to be held in joint names, the partner entitled to all the income from the asset will be assessed on it from the date of the change.

If one partner's marginal rate of tax (the rate on the highest part of his or her income) is higher than the other partner's marginal rate, **it is sensible to transfer income-yielding assets to the partner with the lower rate**. Income might then, for example, be taxed at 20% instead of at 40%. However, **an outright gift of the property (with no strings attached) is required**.

Recently HMRC has shown a clear intention to scrutinise the division of assets and income very closely. Where it feels the split is really tax avoidance, HMRC has the power to reassess the tax liability of both parties for the past six years.

12 Beneficiaries of deceased person's estate

12.1 Introduction

The deceased is liable for income tax on any income *receivable* up to the date of death, regardless of whether it is actually received before or after death.

The 'personal representatives' (PRs) are taxed on any income receivable during the 'administration period.' This starts on the date of the deceased's death and ends when the administration of the estate is completed.

A PR, is defined as a person who acts as executor (named in the deceased's will) or administrator (where the deceased died without having made a will (ie intestate)) of a deceased person's estate.

12.2 Specific gifts

A will may specify that a certain beneficiary (or legatee) should receive a particular asset or a set sum of money. Where the asset bequeathed is an **income producing asset eg shares, the beneficiary is taxable on the income receivable on and after the date of death on an arising basis**.

Where the beneficiary is taxable on the income, the income will have first been taxed on the PRs who will provide the beneficiary with a statement of income (R185 (Estate Income)). This will show the gross income for the beneficiary to report and any tax suffered by the PRs, which the beneficiary can deduct from his own liability.

12.3 Beneficiaries with an absolute interest in the residue

12.3.1 General principle

what is left of an estate after the discharge of debts

A beneficiary has an absolute interest in the residue if he is entitled to both the income and capital of the whole (or part) of residue. **The residuary beneficiary is taxable on the income of the residue after setting off the PR's income expenses.**

In some cases this will include income that arose before death but is received after death.

Expenses are set against dividend income first, then savings income, then non-savings income. For income tax purposes the residuary beneficiary is treated in a similar way to an interest in possession trust beneficiary.

12.3.2 Assessments on the beneficiaries

Where the estate administration is carried on over a number of years, it is usual for the PRs to make interim income payments to beneficiaries. **These interim income payments are assessed on *a receipts* basis.** They are treated as being made from non savings income, then savings income, and then dividend income. The amount of the receipt is grossed up at the appropriate rate for the type of income in question in the year of receipt by the beneficiary, regardless of the tax actually paid by the PRs.

If there is an excess of income left at the end of the administration period, it is treated as income of the year in which the administration ended, regardless of when it is actually paid over to the beneficiary.

Illustration 4

Paul died on 1 November 2008, leaving his entire estate to his wife, Christa. The PRs received a dividend of £6,750, bank interest of £1,600 and rental income of £3,000 in 2008/09.

The PRs had expenses of £540. They made an interim payment of £4,090 to Christa on 1 April 2009. The administration of the estate ended on 31 December 2009.

The assessable amounts and the statement of income given to Christa for 2008/09 will be as follows:

2008/09

The interim payment of £4,090 is treated as coming from non-savings income (ie property income) first, then savings income, then dividend income.

Gross income available for distribution

	Non Savings £	Savings £	Dividends £
Rental income	3,000		
Bank interest £1,600 × $^{100}/_{80}$		2,000	
Dividends £6,750 × $^{100}/_{90}$			7,500
Taxable income	3,000	2,000	7,500
Less: expenses (from dividends first) £540 × $^{100}/_{90}$			(600)
Income available for distribution	3,000	2,000	6,900
Less: distributed to Christa 2008/09 (non savings first, then savings, then divis)			
£2,400 × $^{100}/_{80}$	(3,000)		
£1,600 × $^{100}/_{80}$		(2,000)	
£ 90 × $^{100}/_{90}$			(100)
£4,090			
c/f to 2009/10	Nil	Nil	6,800

Note. The above shows how the income will be distributed to Christa and is NOT an income tax computation.

2008/09 statement of income

	Net £	Tax £	Gross £
Non savings income	2,400	600	3,000
Savings income	1,600	400	2,000
Dividend income	90	10	100

Christa will use the statement of income to report the income received and tax suffered on her income tax return.

12.3.3 Beneficiaries with a limited interest in the residue

A beneficiary has a limited interest in the residue if he is only entitled to the income (and not the capital) of the whole (or part) of residue. He will be taxed on the net income of the estate during the administration period, after the PRs expenses have been deducted. Again, if he is only entitled to part of the income of the estate, he will only be taxed on that part.

The same tax rules used for beneficiaries with absolute interests also apply for those with limited interests.

13 Exempt income

Here is a list of some of the main types of income that are exempt from income tax.

(a)   Scholarship income (in the hands of the scholar; taxable on parent if paid by parent's employer)

(b)   Winnings from betting and gaming (including the lottery)

(c)   Gifts

(d)   Many social security benefits eg child benefit, return to work credit, in-work credit, CTC and WTC.

(e)   Interest or terminal bonus on National Savings & Investments certificates and prizes on premium bonds

(f)   First £30,000 of certain compensation payments received on termination of employment (see Chapter 5)

(g)   Damages (and interest on damages) for personal injuries

(h)   A terminal bonus paid under a 'save as you earn (SAYE) scheme' (see Chapter 6)

(i)   Interest on government stocks held by persons not ordinarily resident in the UK

(j)   Income arising from an Individual Savings Account (ISA) (see Chapter 4)

(k)   Up to £4,250 gross letting income from letting furnished accommodation in the landlord's own main residence (see Chapter 3)

(l)   Dividends on ordinary shares in a Venture Capital Trust (up to the permitted maximum £200,000 investment per year) (see Chapter 4)

(m)   Employment pensions paid to individuals retiring through work-related illness or injury but only the amount in excess of an ordinary ill-health pension.

Note that the exemptions in (b) and (c) do not derive from statute, but from the general principle that income is taxable only if, broadly, it arises from a *source*. Neither gambling winnings nor gifts have a source and hence they are non-taxable.

Chapter roundup

- Income tax is charged on the chargeable income of a chargeable person for a tax year.

- Men, women and children are all liable to income tax on their income.

- All components of an individual's income are brought together in a personal tax computation.

- All figures in the computation must be included gross.

- Certain payments can be deducted from total income. The main deductions are payments to charity in the form of shares or land and interest on certain loans.

- *Net income* is a figure representing the taxpayer's assessable income from all sources, after deductible payments.

- The personal allowance is deducted to arrive at *taxable income*. The personal allowance is available to each individual. It is increased for certain aged individuals (subject to their level of income).

- Cash donations to charity under Gift Aid are made net (saving basic rate tax at source) and also reduce the higher rate tax bill (by extending the basic rate tax band).

- Tax reductions, as their name implies, are deducted in arriving at the tax liability. These include the married couples' allowance (only available to certain aged individuals) and VCT and EIS investments.

- The *tax payable* is the tax liability less tax suffered at source (and payments on account).

- Certain tax credits may be claimed by workers with low incomes and by families with children. The award depends on various factors and is scaled down by reference to income thresholds.

- Various state benefits may be available on death, illness, disability, unemployment and retirement.

- State benefits may also be available to those with children and those who look after the disabled.

- Married couples and civil partners are taxed equally (ie 50:50) on income from assets held jointly (except shares in a close company) unless they have notified HMRC of an actual ownership percentage which is different.

- When someone dies the person they leave their assets to (ie the beneficiaries of their estate) are usually taxable on income arising from the assets they have been left.

- Certain types of income are exempt from income tax.

Quiz

1. A 'tax year' is a 12-month period running from 1 April to the following 31 March. True/False?

2. The income of a minor child (aged under 18) is always treated as income of his parent. True/False?

3. To what extent are the following individuals liable to UK income tax?

    (a) John Smith, resident, ordinarily resident and domiciled in UK, who has both UK and foreign source income.

    (b) Johann Schmidt, who has never been to the UK, but who receives rental income from a property in London in addition to his salary from his German employer. Johann has always lived in Germany.

4. Define 'net income'.

5. Daniel is 35, has trade profits of £43,000 and makes a Gift Aid donation of £500 (net). Calculate Daniel's tax liability.

6. On 31 December 2008 an individual receives income from a discretionary trust of £1,650. Show how much must be included in their income tax computation.

7. Sarah is 67 and has net income of £23,600. She makes a donation via Gift Aid to Oxfam of £560. To what personal allowance is Sarah entitled?

8. Jack (aged 63) is married to Elsie (aged 73). To what allowances and tax reductions is Jack entitled in 2008/09, assuming his net income is £22,600?

9. Maria is a single parent to Josh aged 12. They have no contact with Josh's father. Maria earns £15,000 pa as a secretary and has rental income of £20,000 per annum. Calculate Maria's tax situation for 2008/09 if she paid £3,500 in tax under PAYE and her entitlement to Child Tax Credit.

10. Oberon (age 73) and Titania (age 38) married on 24 December 2008. What allowances and tax reductions are they entitled to in 2008/09 assuming Oberon's income is £11,000 and Titania's income is £16,000?

11. Peter (aged 73) and Rita (age 57) separate on 1 July 2008. Thereafter, Peter pays Rita £250 per month in maintenance. Payments are made on the last day of each month.

    (a) Will Peter make the payments net of income tax or gross?
    (b) What tax reduction is Peter entitled to in 2008/09?

12. James has an investment property. He pays income tax at 40% on the rental income. His wife Jill has insufficient income to utilise her personal allowance so he wishes to transfer the income to her for tax purposes. Which of the following statements are correct?

    (a) He can transfer the property into her name, on condition she hands over the income to him, and the income will be taxed on her.

    (b) He can transfer the property into her name, let her use the income as she chooses but require her to leave the property to him in her will and the income will be taxed on her.

    (c) He can transfer the property into joint names with his wife, retain a 95% beneficial interest, and thereby transfer half the income to her.

    (d) Under (c) he could declare that 95% of the income was hers.

1. False – it runs from 6 April to the following 5 April.

2. False – the income is only treated as the parent's income (broadly) if it is derived from the parent and exceeds £100 in the year of assessment.

3. (a) John Smith is liable to UK income tax on all his income, regardless of where it arises.

   (b) Johann Schmidt, being not resident in the UK, is liable to UK income tax only in respect of income arising in the UK, ie on his UK rental income.

4. Net income: total income (from all sources) less deductible payments (eg qualifying interest).

5.

	£
Net income	43,000
Less: PA	(6,035)
Taxable income	36,965
Tax:	
£35,425 × 20%	7,085
£1,540 × 40%	616
Tax liability	7,701

   (W) Basic rate band extended to £34,800 + (500 × 100/80) = £35,425

6. £2,750 ie £1,650 × 100/60

7.

	£
Personal Age Allowance (PAA)	9,030
Less: ½(23,600 – 700 (W) – 21,800)	(550)
PAA	8,480

   (W) Gross donation to charity is 560 × 100/80 = 700. This is taken as a notional deduction from net income when calculating the restriction to the PAA.

8.

Personal allowance	£6,035
Married couples' allowance (given by reference to age of elder spouse)	£6,535
Less: ½ × (£22,600 – £21,800)	(400)
	£6,135

   Tax relief restricted to 10% (ie £614)

9.

	Non savings £	Tax suffered £
Employment income	15,000	3,500
Property income	20,000	
Net income	35,000	3,500
Less: PA	(6,035)	
Taxable income	28,965	
Income tax	£	
£28,965 @ 20%	5,793	
Less: tax suffered at source	(3,500)	
Tax payable by Maria	2,293	

CTC

Maria's income of £15,000 + £19,700 (excess of rental income over £300) reduces the per child elements to nil. She is, therefore, only entitled to the family element of £545. This will be paid direct to her bank account.

10. **Oberon**:

Personal allowance: £9,030

Titania:

Personal allowance: £6,035

MCA: given as one spouse over 73, apportioned as they married part way through the tax year: £6,535 × 4/12 = £2,178

Tax reduction @ 10% = £218

Note. The marriage took place after 5 December 2005, so the MCA is allocated to the spouse with the higher income, Titania.

11. (a) Gross

    (b) Lower of

        (i) payments due: £250 × 9 = £2,250; and
        (ii) £2,540.

           ie £2,250

           tax reduction £2,250 × 10% = £225

12. (a) and (b) are False as the property must be transferred without 'strings attached'.

    (c) is True as income on jointly held property is deemed to be shared equally.

    (d) is False. A joint declaration can be made to overturn the 50:50 split assumption but it can only change the split to the actual proportions of beneficial ownership.

Solutions to chapter examples

Solution to Example 1

Brenda can deduct the gross patent royalty payment from her total income (£800 × 100/80 =) £1,000

She will need to add the tax retained on the payment (£1,000 × 20% =) £200 on her self assessment return.

Solution to Example 2

	£
Net income	23,600
PAA (> 65)	9,030
Less: ½ × (23,600 – 21,800)	(900)
PAA given	8,130

Solution to Example 3

	2008/09 £	2009/10 £
Salary	50,000	30,000
Less: personal allowance	(6,035)	(6,035)
Taxable income	43,965	23,965
Tax		
£34,800/£23,965 × 20%	6,960	4,793
£9,165 × 20%	1,833	
	8,793	4,793

Income is bèlow the higher rate threshold of £34,800 in 2009/10, so if no claim were made no higher rate relief would be given on the Gift Aid donation in 2009/10.

The claim allows £9,165 of income in 2008/09 to be taxed at 20% rather than 40%, saving tax of £1,833. The basic rate band is extended by £10,000 (£8,000 × $^{100}/_{80}$) in 2008/09.

Solution to Example 4

	(a) £	(b) £
Trade profits	27,700	8,100
Property income	2,000	2,000
Net income	29,700	10,100
Less: personal allowance	(6,035)	(9,030)
	23,665	1,070
Income tax		
£23,665/1,070 × 20%	4,733	214
Tax reductions		
Maintenance payment £2,540 (max) × 10%	(254)	(214)
	4,479	nil
Married couple's allowance £5,580 × 10%	(558)	–
Income tax liability	3,921	nil

Tax reductions cannot lead to repayments of tax, so in (b) the part of the relief for the maintenance payments and the MCA is wasted. If Peter's wife had income of her own, the surplus MCA could have been transferred to her.

Income restriction:

	(a) £
Net income	29,700
Less: income limit	(21,800)
Excess	7,900
Half	3,950
PA	9,030
Reduction (maximum)	(2,995)
	6,035
MCA	6,535
Excess reduction £(3,950 – 2,995)	(955)
	5,580

Solution to Example 5

Their maximum tax credit entitlement is:

* Child tax credit – family element £545 and two child elements of £2,085 each, giving a total of £4,715.

As the interest income is below £300 it can be disregarded as relevant income. As the joint income is expected to rise by less than £25,000 this year, the tax credit awarded will be based on the income of the prior year:

		£
Annual income		16,000
Less: CTC only threshold		(15,575)
Excess income		425
Maximum tax credit		4,715
Less: 39% × 425		(165)
Award		4,550

Solution to Example 6

As the interest income is over £300, the excess of £400 needs to be included as income. As the joint income is the same in both years, the tax credit awarded will be based on £55,000 (54,600 + 400).

As joint income exceeds the £50,000 upper threshold, they are only entitled to the family element. This is tapered by 1/15:

	£
Family element	545
Less: (55,000 − 50,000) × $^{1}/_{15}$	(333)
Award	212

Solution to Example 7

Their maximum tax credit entitlement is:

CTC: family element £545 and four child elements of £2,085 each, giving a total of £8,885.

WTC: basic element £1,800, couple's element £1,770, 30 hour element £735, childcare element (80% of £75 × 52 weeks) £3,120, giving a total of £7,425.

Total tax credits = £16,310

As the income of the current year changes by less than £25,000, the amount awarded will be based on the income of the prior year:

	£
Annual income	13,000
Less: CTC & WTC threshold	(6,420)
Excess income	6,580
Maximum tax credit	16,310
Less: 39% × £6,580	(2,566)
Award	13,744

The family (and baby element if applicable) would not be reduced until income exceeds £50,000. These would then be reduced by $^{1}/_{15}$th of the income over £50,000.

Now try the following questions

Short Form Questions:

1.1 – 1.18 inclusive

Long Form Questions:

1.1	Mr Daphnis
1.2	Mr Rich
1.3	Tax Credits (Pilot Paper)

The purpose of this chapter is to help you to:

- understand what types of income are treated as non-savings and savings income

- identify the types of savings income received net of tax

- understand the non-refundable tax credit received with dividends

- apply the appropriate tax rates to savings and dividend income

- use the three column personal tax computation

- understand how income from trusts is taxed

- identify miscellaneous income

Savings income

1 Savings income and non–savings income

A distinction is made between savings and non–savings income. Savings income comprises mainly:

(a)   Interest (including interest from banks, building societies, gilts, debentures and the National Savings & Investments Bank)

(b)   Dividends

Note that savings income includes all types of interest whether received gross or received net of basic rate tax as well as dividend income.

Patent royalties received, rental income and discretionary trust income are categorised as non-savings income.

2 Savings income

2.1 Introduction

Savings income principally covers interest, whether received net or gross and dividend income. **The income assessed in a tax year is the full amount received in that year** without any deductions for expenses.

Dividends are covered in Section 3.

2.2 Interest received gross

Examples are interest on:

(a) **National Savings and Investments (NS&I) accounts**
(b) UK government (Treasury) stocks (issued after 6 April 1998)
(c) Loans between individuals

2.3 Interest received net of 20% tax

Most building society and bank deposit interest is paid net of 20% tax, but this tax is refundable to individuals if it exceeds their tax liability.

Bank and building society interest must therefore be grossed up by $^{100}/_{80}$ for inclusion in the income tax computation.

Interest received from debentures (ie loans to a company) is also received net of a 20% tax credit.

Individuals who are not liable to income tax (eg. because their allowances cover their income) **can certify their status** (on Form R85) to any bank or building society at which they have an account **and interest will be credited gross.** Should the income later prove to be assessable, it remains taxable as savings income and the individual must declare it in the usual way and tax will be paid under self assessment.

NS&I bank interest is paid gross (see 2.2).

Exam focus point

Examiner's report – Personal Taxation

November 2007 –Part 1 Question 9

Too many candidates went down the route of calculating the taxable interest on an accruals basis, thereby not realising that interest is taxed on a receipts basis.

---

3 Dividends

3.1 Introduction

UK dividends are treated as if received net of a deemed 10% tax credit. This tax credit cannot be repaid to the shareholder although it can be deducted from the tax liability calculated on taxable income.

Dividends are grossed up by $^{100}/_{90}$ for inclusion in the computation.

3.2 Basis of assessment of dividends

The individual is taxed on the gross amount received during the tax year. The date on the dividend voucher is taken as the date of receipt regardless of when the cheque is cashed or when the credit transfer made.

TQT
Tax Qualification Training

4 Taxation of savings income

Savings income is primarily income in the form of UK or foreign interest whether it has been subject to deduction of basic rate tax at source or received gross. One exception to this is foreign interest taxed on a remittance basis which is always treated as non-savings income (see Chapter 8).

In our 3 column computation, we distinguish between 'savings income' (essentially interest) and 'dividend income' as the two are taxed differently.

'Savings income' is taxed after 'non-savings income'. 'Dividend income' is taxed as the ' top slice' of a taxpayer's income.

If savings income falls in the starting rate band up to £2,320 it is taxed at 10%. If it falls in the basic rate band between £2,320 and £34,800 it is taxed at 20%. If the savings income falls in the higher rate band, 40% tax on the gross amount of the savings income is payable.

The tax taken at source on bank/building society interest (20%) is deducted from the tax liability in the income tax computation. This can give rise to a refund of tax.

Dividends falling in the starting rate or basic rate tax bands are taxed at the rate of 10%. Therefore, since a 10% deemed tax credit attaches to such income, no further tax is payable on dividends for starting rate or basic rate taxpayers. Dividends falling into the higher rate tax band are taxed at 32.5%.

The 10% starting rate band for savings/dividend income is only available if the tax payer has taxable non-savings income of less than £2,320. Non-saving income, whilst always being taxed at 20% or 40%, uses the starting rate band in priority to savings/dividend income. Thus if a taxpayer has taxable non-savings income of £5,000 and savings income of £500, the 10% band is not available and the total income of £5,500 is taxed at 20%.

UK dividends and foreign dividends are both taxed in this way (unless taxed on the remittance basis in which case they are taxed as non-savings income).

The 10% tax credit on dividends is deductible from the tax liability. However, since it is not a real tax credit it cannot be repaid to the taxpayer.

As a general principle, personal allowances and other reliefs which are set against an individual's total income may be set off in the way that minimises the individual's tax liability. **Deductible payments, losses and personal allowances should therefore be set against non savings income first then savings income (interest) and finally against dividend income.**

There are two main exceptions to the rule that dividend income is treated as the top slice of a taxpayer's income. Taxable gains on life assurance policies and the taxable part of termination payments are both taxed after dividend income, in that order. Therefore a taxpayer with £20,000 of salary, £15,000 of dividends and a £100,000 termination payment would still have some dividends within the basic rate band (and therefore taxable at only 10%) and the balance within the higher rate band taxed at 32.5%.

Tax Qualification Training

Example 1

Albert has a salary of £11,200, £2,000 (gross) of building society interest and £3,000 (gross) of UK dividends. What is his tax liability?

Example 2

Barry has rental income of £21,185, bank interest (net amount received) of £8,000, and receives UK dividends of £10,800. What is his tax liability?

For the 10% credit to be available, the dividend income has to be chargeable to tax.

For example, if a taxpayer had net income of £42,000 consisting only of gross dividend income, his taxable income would be £35,965 after deducting the PA of £6,035. His tax liability would be £3,858 (34,800 × 10% + 1,165 × 32.5%) but he would be entitled to a tax credit of only £3,596 (£35,965 × 10%) – not the whole £4,200.

This is not the case for other savings income where the full tax credit will be available.

Example 3

Carol has a salary of £5,100 and received building society interest of £12,800 and a UK dividend of £19,800. How much tax is payable by Carol?

Exam focus point

When offsetting the tax deducted at source from the tax liability always deduct the tax credit on dividends first. Remember that the dividend credit cannot give rise to a refund of tax.

TQT
Tax Qualification Training

5 Typical personal tax computation

Here is a typical personal tax computation. Note the way in which it is set out.

Illustration

MR TAXPAYER: INCOME TAX COMPUTATION 2008/09

	Non savings income £	Savings income £	Dividend income £
Employment income	26,990		
Less: occupational company pension scheme contribution	(1,080)		
	25,910		
Rental income	2,000		
Dividends £12,600 × $^{100}/_{90}$			14,000
Bank deposit interest: £1,200 × $^{100}/_{80}$		1,500	
Building society interest: £288 × $^{100}/_{80}$		360	
Less: qualifying interest	(100)		
Net income	27,810	1,860	14,000
Less: personal allowance	(6,035)		
Taxable income	21,775	1,860	14,000

Income tax	£		£
Basic rate band non savings income	21,775 × 20%		4,355
savings income	1,860 × 20%		372
dividend income £(34,800 – 23,635)	11,165 × 10%		1,116
	34,800		
Higher rate £(14,000 – 11,165)	2,835 × 32.5%		921
			6,764
Less: tax reduction: EIS subscription (£2,000 × 20%)			(400)
Tax liability			6,364
Less: tax deducted at source			
Tax credit on dividends £14,000 × 10%	1,400		
PAYE (say)	3,861		
Tax suffered on bank interest £1,500 × 20%	300		
Tax suffered on building society interest £360 × 20%	72		
			(5,633)
Tax payable			731

Remember: the income is split into three parts: non-savings income, savings income and dividend income. Non-savings income is taxed first, savings income (ie interest) second and dividends last.

Also note that the deductible payments and personal allowance have been set against non-savings income in priority to savings income and dividend income.

Example 4

Jackie, has the following income and outgoings.

	£
Salary (tax deducted under PAYE £4,355)	26,240
UK dividend received (net)	2,000
Building society interest received (net)	13,200
Gift Aid donation (net amount paid)	640

What is Jackie's tax payable for 2008/09?

6 Other income

6.1 Income from non-discretionary trusts

As we saw above income from discretionary trusts is always taxed as non-savings income, regardless of the type of income received by the trust.

Income from non-discretionary trusts (ie interest in possession trusts), however, retains its original nature when the beneficiary receives it and is taxed at the rates relevant to the type of income received by the trust, ie at 10%, 20% and 40% or 32½%.

The statement of income from the trustees (Form R185) will show the gross income, tax deducted and net income.

6.2 Miscellaneous income

Income that is not categorised as from a specific source, eg savings, property or earnings, is taxed as miscellaneous income. An example of miscellaneous income is income received by a child but taxed on the parent (see Chapter 1).

Chapter roundup

- Some interest income is received gross and some net. Interest received net (typically bank and building society interest) must be grossed up by 100/80 for inclusion in the income tax computation.

- Dividends from UK companies are deemed to be received net of a 10% tax credit. They must be grossed up by 100/90 for inclusion in the tax computation.

- We categorise income into different types: non-savings, savings and dividends. Each type of income suffers different rates of tax depending on whether the income falls into the starting, basic or higher rate band. Non-savings income is taxed first (at 20% then 40%) then savings income (at 10%, 20% then 40%) and finally dividend income (at 10% and 32.5%).

- The 10 % band for savings/dividend income is only available if taxable non-savings income does not exceed £2,320.

- Income from discretionary trusts is always taxed as non-savings income. Income from interest in possession trusts is taxed at the beneficiary's tax rates, depending on the type of income.

- Some income does not fall into a specific category and is taxed as miscellaneous income.

Quiz

1. How will the following sources of interest be taxed?

    (a)   NS&I Easy Access Savings Account Interest
    (b)   Current account interest from Lloyds Bank
    (c)   Interest on 3½% War Loan
    (d)   Interest on NS&I Certificates

2. Glenda is age 70 and has a state pension (received gross) and a small amount of building society interest each year. What advice would you give her on tax recovery?

3. On 31 December 2008, an individual receives a UK dividend of £832. Compute the amount that will be shown in the income tax computation.

4. Doreen is a single woman aged 30 with the following sources of income in 2008/09.

Income from employment (PAYE suffered £2,323)	£17,000
Income from rented properties	£3,500
Interest received on NS&I Easy Access Savings account	£3,800
UK dividends received	£6,500

    Calculate her tax payable for the year.

Solutions to Quiz

1. (a) Received gross and taxable in full as savings income.
   (b) Bank interest is received net of 20% tax and the gross amount is taxable savings income.
   (c) Interest on 3½% War Loan, as with most UK government stocks, is received gross.
   (d) Exempt.

2. She is clearly a non-taxpayer so should lodge a form R85 with the building society to be paid her interest gross. This is more efficient from a cash-flow perspective than making a claim for repayment of tax which would be required if the interest continued to be paid net.

3. £924 (ie £832 × 100/90)

4.

	Non-savings income £	Savings income £	Dividend income £
Employment income	17,000		
Property income	3,500		
NS&I interest (received gross)		3,800	
Dividends £6,500 × 100/90			7,222
Net income	20,500	3,800	7,222
Less: PA	(6,035)		
Taxable income	14,465	3,800	7,222

Tax:	£
14,465 @ 20%	2,893
3,800 @ 20%	760
7,222 @ 10%	722
Tax liability	4,375
Less: tax suffered at source	
tax credit on dividends	(722)
PAYE	(2,323)
Tax payable	1,330

Solutions to chapter examples

Solution to Example 1

	Non-savings income £	Savings income £	Dividends £
Net income	11,200	2,000	3,000
Less: PA	(6,035)	–	–
Taxable income	5,165	2,000	3,000

Income tax:	£
£	
5,165 × 20% (non-savings income taxed first)	1,033
2,000 × 20% (savings income taxed second)	400
3,000 × 10% (UK dividends taxed last (top slice))	300
10,165	
Tax liability	1,733

The £2,000 savings income falls within the basic rate band so is taxed at 20%. The £3,000 dividend income also falls within the basic rate band and is taxed at 10%.

Note that the non-savings income exceeds the savings income starting rate band of £2,320. All of the savings income therefore taxed at the basic rate.

Albert has tax credits of £700 (£2,000 × 20% + £3,000 × 10%) which can be offset against his tax liability leaving tax payable of £1,033 (1,733 – 700) most of which, if not all, will have been collected under PAYE.

Solution to Example 2

	Non-savings income £	Savings income £	Dividends £
Property income	21,185		
Interest (× 100/80)		10,000	
Dividends (× 100/90)			12,000
Less: PA	(6,035)	–	–
Taxable income	15,150	10,000	12,000

Income tax:

	£	£
15,150 × 20%		3,030
10,000 × 20% (savings income)		2,000
9,650 × 10% (UK dividend income in BR band)		965
34,800		
2,350 × 32.5% (UK dividend income in HR band)		764
37,150		
Tax liability		6,759

UK dividend income in the basic rate band is taxed at 10%. The 32.5% rate applies where it exceeds the higher rate threshold. Barry's tax credits of £3,200 (£10,000 × 20% + £12,000 × 10%) reduce the liability to tax payable of £3,559 (£6,759 – £3,200).

Solution to Example 3

	Non-savings income £	Savings income £	Dividends £
Employment income	5,100		
Interest (× 100/80)		16,000	
Dividends (× 100/90)			22,000
Less: PA	(5,100)	(935)	–
Taxable income	Nil	15,065	22,000

Income tax:

	£	£
2,230 × 10%		232
12,745 × 20%		2,549
19,735 × 10%		1,973
34,800		
2,265 × 32.5%		736
37,065		
Tax liability		5,490
Less: tax deducted at source:		
On dividends (£22,000 @ 10%)		(2,200)
On interest (£16,000 @ 20%)		(3,200)
Tax payable		90

Solution to Example 4

	Non-savings income £	Savings income £	Dividends £
Employment income	26,240		
Building society interest (BSI) £13,200 × 10/0/80		16,500	
UK dividends £2,000 × 100/90			2,222
Net income	26,240	16,500	2,222
Less: PA	(6,035)		
Taxable income	20,205	16,500	2,222

Income tax		£	£
Basic rate band	non-savings income = 20,205 × 20%		4,041
	savings income		
	£(34,800 – 20,205) = £14,595 × 20%		2,919
	£800 × 20% (note)		160
Higher rate	£(16,500 – 14,595 – 800) = £1,105 × 40%		442
	dividends £2,222 × 32.5%		722
Tax liability			8,284
Less: tax suffered on dividends £(2,222 × 10%)		222	
tax suffered – PAYE		4,355	
tax suffered on BSI £(16,500 × 20%)		3,300	(7,877)
Tax payable			407

Note. The basic rate band is extended by the gross amount of the Gift Aid payment ie by £800 (£640 × $^{100}/_{80}$).

Now try the following questions

Short Form Questions:

2.1 – 2.8 inclusive

Long Form Questions:

2.1	Mr Poor
2.2	Jonty
2.3	Fred
2.4	Fiona
2.5	Jane Bradbury
2.6	George and Mildred Roper

Income from UK land and buildings

References: ITTOIA 2005 unless otherwise stated

The purpose of this chapter is to help you to:

- understand the rules for the taxation of income from land and buildings

- set off property losses correctly

- calculate the amount of a short lease premium taxable as income

- identify a furnished holiday letting property

- understand when the rent-a-room scheme applies

- understand the tax position of landlords living outside the UK

- be aware of the rules for Real Estate Investment Trusts (REITs)

1 Introduction

All lettings in the UK by an individual landlord are treated as a single business with the profit or loss computed for a tax year on normal business accounting principles – ie **rents and expenses included <u>on an accruals basis</u>. Profits and losses on individual properties are automatically set-off.**

Exam focus point

This is a core area of the syllabus. It appears within the personal income tax computation and can be set either as a long written or computational question.

A <u>UK resident landlord</u> will be taxable on property income from property within and outside the UK.

In this chapter we consider the rules for taxing UK property income.

Now look at the following topics in the ATT Manual 'Essential Law for the Taxation Technician'.

- Property Law
- Land Law in England, Wales and Northern Ireland
- Land Law in Scotland (This is a Scots Law supplement which is available from the ATT).

You need only study Land Law in Scotland if you are intending to answer the paper under Scots law.

2 UK property income

2.1 Calculating property income

The property income taxable on individuals is based on the annual profits arising from the business including:

(a)   Rent charges
(b)   Part of the premium on the grant of a short lease (see below)

A person receiving rental income is taxed on the full amount of the profits accrued in the tax year. **Property income is always non-savings income.**

2.2 Allowable property expenses

Expenses are deductible if they are wholly and exclusively incurred for the 'business' of letting. Expenses such as advertising, accountancy and insurance are allowed but depreciation is not (capital allowances or 'wear & tear' allowances (see below) are given instead).

Capital expenditure on properties let eg cost of building an extension **is not deductible** when computing the assessable property income.

Bad debts are allowed on business principles, so if a rent payment appears unlikely, the landlord can provide for it in his letting accounts at the end of the tax year.

Capital allowances are not allowed on furniture used in a residential dwelling. Instead, HMRC gives relief for such capital expenditure on a renewals basis. The original cost and the cost of any improvements are not relieved <u>but</u> the cost of replacing furniture to the same standard <u>is allowed</u> as an expense.

As this can be cumbersome to administer **for furnished lettings there is a concession whereby a 'wear and tear allowance' is given instead**. This allowance is equal to:

> **10% × [rents – (water rates & council tax if paid by the landlord)]**

and is allowed as a deduction in place of claiming relief for the replacement of furniture.

The cost of repairing or maintaining furniture and fittings is also allowed whether the renewals basis or the 10% relief is claimed.

Where there is a business of letting, the landlord can set-off the running expenses incurred on empty properties (eg properties under repair between lets), against property income generally.

If property normally let furnished is occupied at some time by the owner, the allowable deduction for repairs, insurance, council tax and so on is restricted to a proportion based on the period that the property is available for letting. For example, if HMRC accepted that letting took place throughout the year and was occupied by the owner for 4 weeks and by tenants for 30 weeks, 48/52 of the expenses would be allowed. Expenses specific to the letting such as advertising would, however, be allowed in full.

Both loan (ie mortgage) interest and overdraft interest are deductible in computing property income, provided the related borrowing was applied wholly and exclusively for the purposes of the letting business.

2.3 Capital allowances

plant & machinery

Capital allowances (ie the tax equivalent of accounting depreciation) may be claimed on P&M used for the maintenance or repair of the properties or plant let as part of the building (eg lawn mowers).

As explained above, capital allowances are not available in respect of furniture and instead the renewals basis or the wear and tear allowance is available.

The Landlord's Energy Savings Allowance is also available to landlords who incur capital expenditure on energy savings items eg insulation and draught proofing in a dwelling house. The allowance is an amount of up to £1,500 per property.

3 Property losses

Energy Saving's Allowance = £1,500 PER EACH PROPERTY!

Where there is an overall loss:

(a) The loss is carried forward and set against the UK property income for the following year and subsequent years

(b) Losses resulting from capital allowances can be set against the taxpayer's general income for the year of the loss and the next following tax year. [s.120(2) ITA 2007]

The loss relief at (a) above is automatic and no claim is required. Losses under (b) above must be claimed within 12 months from the self assessment filing date for the year of the loss.

Where a property is let under non-commercial terms (eg to a relative at a nominal or 'peppercorn' rent), and a loss arises in respect of that property, this is not pooled with profits/losses on other rental properties. It may only be offset against future rental profits on that same lease to that same tenant. As such, it is unlikely that this loss will ever be fully relieved.

4 Premiums on leases

4.1 Basic principle

A 'lease' is a right to use an asset (in this case a property) for a specified period of time. Any amount paid up-front by the lessee (the tenant) to the lessor (landlord) for the use of a property is referred to as a *premium* and is treated as a capital receipt. There are usually therefore no income tax implications for a premium.

However, when a premium is received on the *grant* (that is, by a landlord from a tenant) of a short lease (50 years or less), part of the premium is treated as rent and is taxed as property income in the year of grant.

4.2 Amount taxed as income

The premium taxed as property income: is the whole premium less 2% of the premium for each complete year of the lease, except the first year. This is expressed as the formula:

Premium	£A
Less: 2% (n – 1) × A	(a)
Taxable as property income	£X

Where n = number of years on the lease.

This rule does not apply on the _assignment_ (ie sale) of a lease (one tenant selling his interest in the property to another).

The capital element (2% × (n-1) × A) will be subject to capital gains tax (see Chapter 12).

4.3 Premiums paid by traders

Where a trader pays a premium for a lease, he may deduct an amount from his taxable profits in each year of the lease. The amount deductible is the figure assessed as rent on the landlord divided by the number of years of the lease.

Illustration 1

Brown, a trader, pays Green a premium of £30,000 for a ten year lease on a small shop.

Green is assessed on property income of £30,000 – (£30,000 × (10 – 1) × 2%) = £24,600.

Brown can deduct £24,600/10 = £2,460 in each of his accounts for the next ten years.

He starts with the accounts year in which the lease starts and apportions the relief to the nearest month eg if the lease was taken out 8 months into his accounting period then only 4/12 of £2,460 could be deducted from that period's profit.

4.4 Premiums for granting subleases

A tenant may sublet the property and charge a premium on the grant of the lease to the subtenant. This premium is taxed as property income in the normal way, except that where the tenant originally paid a premium for his own original or head lease, relief is given, computed as:

$$\text{Taxable premium for head lease} \times \frac{\text{duration of sub-lease}}{\text{duration of head lease}}$$

Example 1

Clive granted a lease to Derek on 1 March 1994 for a period of 40 years. Derek paid a premium of £16,000. On 1 June 2008 Derek granted a sublease to Eric for a period of ten years. Eric paid a premium of £30,000. Calculate the amount assessable as property income for 2008/09 in respect of the premium received by Derek.

---

5 Furnished holiday lettings

Income from holiday lettings is assessed as property income but, provided certain conditions are satisfied, is treated as normal trade profits so that:

(a) **Relief for losses is available as if they were trading losses**, including the facility to set losses against general income.

(b) The profits are treated as earned income so the **income qualifies as relevant earnings** for pension purposes (see Chapter 7).

(c) **Capital allowances are available as for traders**. This applies to furnishings etc used in a dwelling. This replaces the wear and tear allowance.

(d) Capital gains tax entrepreneurs' relief, rollover relief, and relief for gifts of business assets, are available.

The letting must be of furnished accommodation made on a commercial basis with a view to the realisation of profit. The property must satisfy the following conditions: [s.325]

(a) It is **available for commercial letting to the public for not less than 140 days** in a year and is so **let for at least 70 days** in that 140 day period. If two or more properties each pass the 140 day test separately, then they need only pass the 70 day test on average.

A landlord may choose to leave particular properties out of the averaging computation if they would pull the average down to below 70 days.

(b) Not more than 155 days may fall during periods of longer term occupation. Longer term occupation is a continuous period of more than 31 days during which the accommodation is in the same occupation.

Where the taxpayer also has other letting income, he is treated as running a 'business of letting' and a 'business of furnished holiday letting' and the two are computed separately.

Exam focus point

Examiner's report – Personal Taxation (old syllabus)

November 2006 – Question 5

The main areas where marks were lost were in the explanation of income tax and capital gains tax in connection with the holiday home. Several candidates did not mention the beneficial treatment as a business and simply described the taxation of rental property.

---

6 The rent a room scheme

If an individual lets a room or rooms in his main residence (ie to a lodger), then a special exemption may apply.

If gross rents (ie before deducting expenses) **are less than the limit of £4,250 per property a year, the rents are wholly exempt from income tax** and expenses and capital allowances are ignored. However, the taxpayer may claim to ignore the exemption, for example to generate a loss by taking into account both rent and expenses.

This limit is halved if any other person (including the owner's spouse) also received income from renting accommodation in the property while the property was the owner's main residence.

If gross rents exceed the limit, the taxpayer will be taxed in the ordinary way, ignoring the rent a room scheme, unless he elects for the 'alternative basis'. **If he so elects, he will be taxable on gross receipts less £4,250** (or £2,125 if the limit is halved), with no deductions for expenses or capital allowances.

An election to ignore the exemption or an election for the alternative basis must be made on or before the anniversary of 31 January following the end of the year of assessment concerned. An election to ignore the exemption applies only for the year for which it is made, but an election for the alternative basis remains in force until it is withdrawn or until a year in which gross rents do not exceed the limit.

7 Deduction of tax from payments to non-residents

Regulations provide for tax to be deducted at source from income paid to non-residents from property in the UK. [s.971 ITA 2007]

Under the Non Resident Landlord Scheme (NRLS) the agent for the property or (where there is no agent the tenant) must deduct basic rate tax at source. Any further tax is dealt with by the non-resident landlord under self-assessment.

Rent can be paid gross to the non-resident landlord by agreement with HMRC under the NRLS, as long as the landlord's tax affairs are up to date and he undertakes to include tax from property income in the payments on account which he makes under self-assessment.

8 Real Estate Investment Trusts (REITs)

Since January 2007 property companies have been able to operate as **Real Estate Investment Trusts** (REITs).

A REIT is a listed company (AIM does *not* count for this purpose) owning, managing and earning rental income from commercial or residential property.

REITs can elect for their property income (and gains) to be exempt from corporation tax and must withhold basic rate (20%) tax from distributions paid to shareholders (who cannot own more than 10% of a REIT's shares) out of these profits. These distributions are taxed as property income, not as dividends.

Distributions by REITs out of other income (ie not property income or gains) are taxed as dividends in the normal way.

Illustration 2

Sue has a holding of shares in The Property Business which is a REIT. During 2008/09 she received a dividend from her investment of £6,400. She also has a salary of £31,000 and interest income (gross) of £1,000 in the year.

Sue's tax liability for 2008/09 is as follows:

2008/09	Non-savings income £	Savings income £	Total £
Salary	31,000		
Dividend from REIT – Property income £6,400 × 100/80	8,000		
Interest		1,000	
Net income	39,000	1,000	40,000
PA	(6,035)		(6,035)
	32,965	1,000	33,965
Non-savings income			
£32,965 @ 20%			6,593
Savings income			
£1,000 @ 20%			200
Tax liability			6,793

Note. Dividends from REITs are taxed as property income not as company dividends. Basic rate tax (20%) is deducted at source from such distributions.

- UK property income is calculated as accrued rental income less accrued revenue expenses for each property.

- Profits and losses of individual properties are pooled to arrive at the UK property income assessment for the individual

- A wear and tear allowance is available on furnished properties.

- Losses on UK properties must be carried forward and set against future UK property profits.

- An element of the premium received by a landlord on the grant of a short lease is taxable as UK property income.

- If a property meets various conditions it may be classified as a Furnished Holiday Let (FHL).

- Income/losses from FHLs will be treated as trading income/losses.

- If an individual rents out a room in their main residence and charges their tenant less than £4,250 pa, this amount will not be taxable.

- Dividends from REITs are taxed as property income not as company dividends. Basic rate tax (20%) is deducted at source from such distributions.

Quiz

1. David buys a property for letting on 1 August 2008 and grants a tenancy to Ethel from 1 December 2008 at £3,600 pa. payable quarterly in advance. How much is assessable in 2008/09?

2. Catherine rents out a furnished property for £16,000 pa. and pays the water rates of £320 and council tax of £780 on the property. How will relief for wear and tear of furnishings be given?

3. John pays buildings insurance premiums for 12 months in advance on 1 October each year to cover all his letting properties. He pays £4,800 in 2007 and £5,200 in 2008. How much is deductible from his property income in 2008/09?

4. Debbie lets a flat to her widowed mother for £600 pa. when a market rent would be £3,600 pa. Debbie pays all the letting expenses which amount to £1,800 for 2008/09. Explain what relief is available for the loss incurred.

5. Paul grants a lease for 10 years to Graham for a premium of £20,000. How much is assessable as property income and when will it be assessed?

6. Fred has let three holiday bungalows during 2008/09 making a net loss. Explain briefly the difference in the treatment of this loss if the lettings meet the conditions required for furnished holiday lettings.

7. What is the main income tax advantage of a profitable 'furnished holiday letting' business?

8. What is the income threshold for 'rent a room relief'?

Solutions to Quiz

1. Rent accrued 1.12.08 – 5.4.09 ie $^4/_{12} \times £3,600 = £1,200$.

2. Wear and tear allowance against rents:

   $10\% \times £(16,000 - 320 - 780) = £1,490$

3. Insurance premiums accrued in 2008/09

	£
$^6/_{12} \times £4,800$	2,400
$^6/_{12} \times £5,200$	2,600
	5,000

4. A loss of £1,200 would arise (£600 – £1,800). This can only be offset against profits made on the same property with the same tenant.

5.

	£
Premium	20,000
Less: £20,000 × 2% × (10 – 1)	(3,600)
Property income	16,400

   Assessable in the year the lease is granted.

6. Losses on UK properties are generally carried forward against UK property income. However if they arise from a FHL they are allowed as if they were trading losses and can be set off against other income.

7. FHL income qualifies as relevant earnings which gives scope to make higher pension contributions.

8. £4,250 a year.

Solution to chapter example

Solution to Example 1

	£
Premium received by Derek	30,000
Less: 2% × (10 – 1) × £30,000	(5,400)
	24,600
Less: allowance for premium paid	
(£16,000 – (2% × 39 × £16,000)) × 10/40	(880)
Amount assessable	23,720

Now try the following questions

Short Form Questions:

3.1 – 3.10 inclusive

Long Form Questions:

3.1	Randall
3.2	Corelli

chapter

4

The purpose of this chapter is to help you to:

- identify specific tax free investments

- set out and apply the rules for Individual Savings
  Accounts, the Enterprise Investment Scheme and
  Venture Capital Trusts

- identify when the accrued income scheme rules apply

- describe the tax treatment of both qualifying and non-
  qualifying life assurance policies

- apply the rules for pre-owned assets

References: ITA 2007 unless otherwise stated

Tax efficient investments

1 Introduction

1.1 Tax-free investments

The following investments are tax free:

(a)   NS&I Savings Certificates (including indexed-linked issues) (see below)
(b)   Save As You Earn (SAYE) (building society, bank, or NS&I) schemes
(c)   Premium Bond winnings
(d)   Income from Individual Savings Accounts (ISAs) (see below)
(e)   Dividends from Venture Capital Trusts (VCTs) (see below)

1.2 NS&I Savings Certificates

These are attractive particularly to higher rate taxpayers as the accumulated interest paid at the end of the period of investment is totally free from income tax and CGT. There is a maximum holding permitted of £10,000. NS&I Index-Linked Certificates are also popular as they provide protection from inflation. The maximum holding is again £10,000. In both instances, the limits apply to each spouse/partner in a civil partnership.

2 Individual Savings Accounts (ISAs)

2.1 Introduction

ISAs are available to individuals **aged over 18** who are **resident and ordinarily resident in the UK. Investment is permitted in cash and shares**.

The main features of ISAs are as follows.

(a) There is an annual subscription limit for each individual of £7,200, of which no more than £3,600 can be in cash

(b) There is no statutory lock-in period or minimum subscription

(c) There is no lifetime limit

(d) The account is completely free of tax on both income and capital growth

(e) ISAs are offered and operated by HMRC approved account managers who must agree to operate accounts in accordance with the ISA regulations.

Individuals under 18 but over 16 are allowed to subscribe up to £3,600 pa into a cash only ISA account.

Once the maximum amount has been subscribed for in any type of ISA for a year, it is not possible to make further investments even after a withdrawal is subsequently made.

2.2 Types of ISA

There are two types of ISA account:

(a) **Cash**, including all the kinds of bank and building society accounts as well as NS&I products, supermarket savings accounts and similar;

(b) **Stocks and shares**, including shares obtained from approved profit sharing or savings-related share option schemes (transferred into the shares component at market value) but not shares acquired on a public offer or a demutualisation.

2.3 Tax exemption

Total exemption from income and capital gains tax is provided for investments within an ISA.

There is no statutory minimum period for which an ISA must be held. A full or partial withdrawal may be made from an ISA at any time without loss of tax exemption. However providers of ISAs are not prohibited from setting conditions on accounts that require a specified notice period or the maintenance of minimum balances to obtain particular rates of return.

Where an investor ceases to qualify by becoming non-resident or not ordinarily resident the benefits, including tax reliefs, of any ISAs held up to that time may be retained but no further subscriptions may thereafter be made (unless appropriate residence status is regained).

3 The Enterprise Investment Scheme (EIS)

3.1 Introduction

The EIS is intended to encourage investment in the **ordinary shares** of **unquoted trading companies**. When an individual subscribes for eligible shares in a qualifying company, the **amount subscribed is a tax reduction, saving income tax at 20%**. [s.158]

If an investment is less than £500 no relief is available (unless subscription is made by an approved EIS fund, which pools the contributions of several investors).

Relief is usually given on an actual basis: a 2008/09 investment will attract relief against the tax liability for 2008/09. **However, a taxpayer can claim to treat up to half of his EIS investments made between 6 April and 5 October in a tax year as made in the previous tax year, subject to a maximum carryback of £50,000 from any one year**.

Relief must be claimed within 12 months of HMRC authorising the company to issue a certificate to the investor that the share issue qualifies for relief.

Dividends from EIS shares are taxable under the normal rules.

3.2 Withdrawal of relief

If an individual disposes of shares (by sale or gift other than a gift to a spouse or civil partner) **within three years of their issue, the tax reduction obtained may be wholly or partly withdrawn**. [s.209 and s.210]

If the shares are given away (other than to the investor's spouse or civil partner) **within the three years, all of the tax reduction is withdrawn**.

On a sale within the three years, the tax reduction to be withdrawn is:

$$\text{Consideration obtained} \times \frac{\text{Tax reduction obtained on issue}}{\text{Issue price of shares}}$$

However, the withdrawal cannot exceed the tax reduction originally obtained.

A transfer of shares between spouses/civil partners does not give rise to a withdrawal of the tax reduction. The reduction obtained remains associated with the shares, and if the recipient partner disposes of the shares outside the marriage/ civil partnership within three years of their issue, it is withdrawn by an assessment on the recipient spouse/ partner.

The death of a shareholder is not treated as a disposal.

If shares are disposed of after three years from issue, the following consequences ensue:

(a)   **The tax reduction is not withdrawn**

(b)   **If there is a gain for CGT purposes, it is exempt**

(c)   **Any loss for CGT purposes is restricted by reducing the issue price, ie the cost, by the tax relief not withdrawn (but not so as to create a gain).**

When shares issued under the EIS are sold at arm's length at a loss at any time (within or outside the first three years), and the EIS relief is not wholly withdrawn, the loss may be relieved in the same way as a trading loss, ie set against general income of the current and/ or previous year. [s.131]

Example 1

In May 2008, David subscribes £34,000 for shares in an EIS company. David's tax liability for 2008/09 the year (before tax reductions) is £5,000, reduced to nil by EIS relief.

In May 2010, David sells half of the shares for £12,000. The other half are sold for £25,000 in June 2011, giving rise to a gain of £3,270.

(a)   How much tax relief is withdrawn on the first sale?
(b)   How is the gain on the second sale treated?

3.3 The conditions for relief

The legislation should primarily be relied on in this area but an outline of the conditions is given below.

3.3.1 Qualifying individual

A **qualifying individual is one who is not connected with the company** at any time in the period from two years before the issue (or from incorporation if later) to three years after the issue. An individual is connected with the company in any of the following circumstances. [s.166-170]

(a)   He (either alone or with his associates) holds **more than 30%** of the ordinary shares or can exercise more than 30% of the voting rights in the company or any subsidiary

(b)   On a winding up of the company or any subsidiary, he (either alone or with his associates) would be entitled to more than 30% of the assets

(c)   He is a **partner** of the company or of any subsidiary

(d)   He is an **employee or a non-qualifying director** of the company or of a subsidiary, or of a partner of the company or of a subsidiary. **A qualifying director who is also an employee is not treated as connected under this rule**.

Associates include partners, spouses, partners in a civil partnership, parents or remoter forebears and children or remoter issue.

A **qualifying director, broadly, is one who only receives reasonable remuneration (including any benefits) from the company**. [s.169]

3.3.2 General requirements

The shares must be newly issued, fully paid up ordinary shares which carry no preferential rights to dividends, assets or redemption in the three years from the date of issue. [s.173]

They must be issued in order to raise money for the purpose of a **qualifying business activity**, which can be to carry on a qualifying trade *or* carry out research and development intended to lead to such a trade *or* to hold shares and securities in companies carrying out qualifying trades or research and development. [s.174]

The company must use 80% of the cash raised from the share issue for a business purpose within 12 months of the share issue. Any amount remaining must be employed within the following 12 month period. [s.175]

3.3.3 Qualifying company

A **qualifying company** is a company which satisfies all of the following conditions: [s.180]

(a)   It exists wholly to carry on one or more qualifying trades

(b)   At any time in the 3-year period when trade or research and development is being carried on, it is carried on **wholly or mainly in the UK**

(c)   The company must be **unquoted** at the time the EIS shares are issued and no arrangements must exist at that time for the company to cease to be unquoted

(d)   **It does not control any other company** (except for qualifying 90% subsidiaries) **and it is not under the control of another company**

(e)   The **assets of the company** must not exceed £7 million immediately before and £8 million immediately after the issue

(f)   The company must have **fewer than 50 full-time employees** and must have **raised less than £2 million** in venture capital funds in the previous 12 months

A **qualifying trade is one carried on commercially with a view to profit**. The following activities are excluded. [s.192]

(a)   Dealing in commodities, futures, shares, securities, other financial instruments or land

(b)   Dealing in goods other than in an ordinary trade of wholesale or retail distribution

(c)   Financial activities such as banking, hire purchase and insurance

(d)   Leasing, apart from chartering of ships (other than oil rigs and pleasure craft) for up to 12 months at a time

(e)   The receipt of royalties or licence fees, except in respect of a company's research and development or by a film production company

(f)   The provision of legal and accountancy services

(g)   Property development

(h)   Farming or market gardening

(i)   Holding or managing woodlands or any forestry activity

(j)   Operating or managing hotels

(k)   Operating or managing residential care homes or nursing homes

(l)   Providing certain services for another business [s.199]

(m)   Shipbuilding

(n)   Coal and steel production

Exam focus point

Most of the information above on EIS is contained in the legislation sections 156-234 ITA 2007. There is no need for you to learn things that can easily be looked up. Just learn where to find it!

---

4 Venture Capital Trusts (VCTs)

4.1 Tax reduction on investment

An **individual** who is at **least 18 years of age** who subscribes for **new eligible shares in a Venture Capital Trust** (VCT) is entitled to claim income tax relief in respect of his investment. The amount of income tax relief available to such an individual is the lower of: [s.263]

(a)   **30% of the amount subscribed for eligible shares in VCTs in the year up to a maximum of £200,000** per tax year, and

(b)   The individual's income tax liability for the year.

4.2 Relief on distributions

Distributions (ie dividends) received by an individual in respect of ordinary shares in a VCT are exempt from income tax, provided:

(a)   The company was a VCT when the individual acquired his shares, and

(b)   The dividend is paid out of profits, etc which accrued to the company in an accounting period ending after its approval as a VCT, and

(c)   **The shares in respect of which the dividend is paid were not acquired by the investor in excess of the permitted maximum £200,000** investment for any year of assessment. [s.709 ITTOIA 2005]

This relief is available to individuals who acquired VCT shares by purchase on the Stock Exchange (or by gift, or in any other manner). **It is not necessary for the individual to have subscribed for new VCT shares.**

The relief on dividends is given on the first £200,000 of ordinary shares **acquired** in each tax year at a time when the company was a VCT. **The 30% relief on investment** is given on the first £200,000 of new VCT ordinary shares **subscribed** for in each tax year. [s.261]

Illustration 1

Miss Davis bought existing ordinary shares in VCT1 with a value of £30,000 on 1 May 2008. On 1 December 2008 she subscribed £400,000 for new ordinary shares in VCT2.

1. The VCT1 shares will qualify for relief on distributions only as she did not subscribe for these shares and therefore they do not qualify.

2. The first £200,000 of the £400,000 invested in VCT2 shares will qualify for the 30% relief on investment as these shares were subscribed for. Only £170,000 of the investment will qualify for relief on distributions.

4.3 Withdrawal of relief

VCT income tax relief is withdrawn if the investor disposes of his shares in the VCT within five years of their issue. A disposal by gift or sale at a profit results in a withdrawal of the full relief.

A disposal by sale for less than the cost of the shares results in a clawback of relief equal to the consideration received multiplied by the lower rate of income tax for the tax year in which the relief was given. The death of the investor or a disposal to a spouse/civil partner does not result in any withdrawal of relief.

VCT income tax relief is also withdrawn if the VCT loses its approved status within five years after issuing eligible shares to the investor. In such circumstances the investor's full income tax relief is withdrawn. [s.266]

Withdrawals of VCT income tax relief are made by way of an assessment for the year in which the relief was originally given. [s.270]

Investors are required to give notice to an officer of HMRC within 60 days if an event occurs which gives rise to withdrawal of relief. Similarly, an officer of HMRC may serve a notice requiring such information where he has reason to believe that an individual has not given notice. [s.271]

Exam focus point

Again it is worth highlighting the relevant sections of the legislation on VCTs. Also note the similarities and differences between EIS and VCT investments.

4.4 Conditions for relief

VCTs are companies, that are not close companies, that are approved by HMRC. The legislation should primarily be relied on in this area but an outline of the conditions is given below. [s.274]

(a) **Its ordinary shares are quoted on the Stock Exchange**

(b) Its **income has been derived wholly or mainly from shares** or securities

(c) It **has not retained more than 15% of the income it derived from shares and securities**; ie it must distribute an amount equal to 85% of its income from shares and securities and 100% of any other income. However, this distribution requirement is waived if the amount required to satisfy the 15% rule is less than £10,000 per 12 month accounting period

(d) **No holding in any company** – other than in another VCT or a company which would qualify as a VCT if it were quoted – has at any time in the period **represented more than 15% of its total investments**

(e) **At least 70% of its investments are in shares in qualifying holdings** which are (broadly) holdings in unquoted companies carrying on qualifying trades in the UK. However, funds realised from the disposal of a qualifying holding that was held for at least six months will be ignored for a period of six months for the purpose of this 70% test.

(f) **At least 30% of the company's qualifying holdings has been or will be represented by holdings of eligible shares**

(g) The company must have **fewer than 50 full-time employees** and must have **raised less than £2 million** in venture capital funds in the previous 12 months

HMRC will specify the date from which a VCT is approved. This cannot be earlier than the date on which application for approval was made by the company.

Approval may be withdrawn where a VCT ceases to satisfy the above conditions or fails to satisfy such conditions within the above time periods. A notice of withdrawal of approval normally has effect from the time it is given.

At least 80% of the money received by the VCT from the issue of shares must be used wholly for the purposes of its qualifying trade within 12 months. Any amount remaining must be similarly employed within the following 12 month period. [s.293]

The value of the relevant company's assets must not exceed £7 million immediately before the share issue and £8 million immediately afterwards. [s.297]

4.5 Qualifying trades

All trades (including research and development from which it is intended that a trade will be derived) **are qualifying trades except for the following prohibited activities**. [s.303]

(a) Dealing in land, in commodities, shares, securities or other financial instruments
(b) Dealing in goods, otherwise than in the course of an ordinary trade of wholesale or retail distribution
(c) Banking, insurance, money-lending, debt-factoring, hire-purchase financing or other financial activities
(d) Leasing
(e) Receiving royalties or licence fees
(f) Providing legal or accountancy services
(g) Property development
(h) Farming or market gardening
(i) Holding or managing woodlands or any forestry activity
(j) Operating or managing hotels
(k) Operating or managing residential care homes or nursing homes
(l) Providing certain services for another business [s.310]
(m) Shipbuilding
(n) Coal and steel production

5 Anti-avoidance

5.1 Accrued income profits

When interest-bearing securities (Treasury stock (gilts) and company loan stock) are transferred from one person to another the sale agreement specifies who receives the next interest payment. **In cum-dividend sales the buyer receives the next interest payment**, and the proceeds will be higher to reflect the value of that payment. **In ex-dividend sales the next interest payment will be paid to the seller** and the proceeds will be lower to take that into account.

The Accrued Income Scheme (AIS) determines the tax treatment of interest for the period spanning the date of sale. **The AIS allocates the interest on a straight-line time basis** between buyer and seller so that the seller is taxed on the income from interest that has accrued up to the date of transfer, and the buyer is taxed on the income accruing from the date of transfer.

Consequently, one party is treated as receiving an amount taxable as **miscellaneous income**, and the other party is entitled to relief on the same amount (as a reduction in the amount of actual interest on which they are taxed).

The rules do not apply in a number of situations, principally where an individual has not held securities exceeding £5,000 (nominal value) in the current or preceding year.

Illustration 2

Ralph purchases £10,000 5% Treasury Stock cum interest on 1 February 2008 and sells it cum interest on 1 April 2009. Interest is paid on the stock on 1 May and 1 November each year.

The assessable interest income for Ralph for 2008/09 is:

		£
1.5.08	Interest: 5% × £10,000 × ½	250
	Less: accrued income relief (1 Nov 07 – 1 Feb 08)	
	£250 × $^{92}/_{182}$	(126)
		124
1.11.08	Interest	250
		374

The accrued income profit taxable as miscellaneous income in 2009/10 is:

		£
1.5.09	Accrued income (1 Nov 08 – 1 Apr 09)	
	£250 × $^{151}/_{181}$	209

5.2 Life assurance policies

5.2.1 Qualifying policies

There is no income tax charge on the maturity or encashment of a qualifying life assurance policy.

A policy is qualifying if:

(a) The policy secures a capital sum on death, earlier disability, or a date not before the tenth anniversary of taking out the policy

(b) The premiums are reasonably even and are payable annually or at shorter intervals

(c) At least a certain capital sum is assured, broadly 75% of the premiums payable.

Gifts worth up to £30, such as are commonly offered to induce people to take out policies, do not render policies non-qualifying.

Any profit (the excess of proceeds over total premiums paid) **on maturity or encashment of the policy is free of tax so long as premiums have been paid for a minimum of one of the following.**

(a) **Life of the assured**
(b) **10 years and**
(c) **3/4 of the term.**

TQT
Tax Qualification Training

5.2.2 Non-qualifying policies

Non-qualifying policies include **single premium bonds, investment bonds** or **property bonds**. A lump sum is invested in a life fund, a small part of which buys life cover and the balance is invested. During the term of the policy any investment gains and income are taxed only in the hands of the insurance company.

The overall gain on the policy on a **chargeable event** (eg encashment, sale or death of the investor) is taxed as savings income and comes with a basic rate tax credit (20%). Top slicing relief (see below) is available to mitigate the tax.

Partial encashments up to 5% of the premium per year (on a cumulative basis) **are allowed with no immediate tax liability.** So, in 2008/09 an investor who purchased a £30,000 single premium bond in 2002 can effect a partial surrender for £9,000 (6 years × 5% × £30,000) tax free.

When the policy is finally encashed, any tax free withdrawals are added to the amount received on encashment to determine the overall tax liability. There is no starting rate or basic rate liability. In addition, any tax at the higher rate is determined using the following *top slicing* rules.

Step 1 Calculate the overall profit from the policy.

(proceeds on encashment *plus* early withdrawals *less* initial premium).

Step 2 Divide the overall profit by the number of complete years since the policy was taken out

Step 3 Calculate the increase in the taxpayer's total tax liability that arises from adding the slice found in Step 2 to his other sources of income. This slice is taxed as the top slice of income above all other income, *including savings income and termination payments*. Remember that the slice is only liable to tax at the higher rate.

Step 4 Multiply the increase found in Step 3 by the number of years used in Step 2 to find the tax payable.

If, before final encashment, withdrawals exceed the permitted limit, the excess is taxable immediately at the higher rate. Again, top slicing applies. The slice is found by dividing the excess by the number of years since the policy was taken out (or, if appropriate, since the last excess occurred). In calculating the tax on final encashment, the excess(es) are excluded from the calculation of the overall profit since they have been taxed already.

Example 2

An investor took out a single premium policy on 31 October 2002 for £15,000. He withdrew 4% of the premium in each of the next five years and he encashed the policy on 30 June 2008 receiving £20,000. In 2008/09 his other income (all non savings) was £33,900 after deducting his personal allowance.

Calculate the amount of tax payable in respect of the bond.

5.3 Pre-owned assets

5.3.1 Introduction

An **income tax charge** may apply where a person disposes of property and subsequently benefits from that property **in circumstances where the IHT gift with reservation rules do not apply**. This mainly targets IHT mitigation schemes, but may also catch genuine transactions.

This anti-avoidance rule applies to land (including buildings) and chattels. There is no charge if the total taxable amount does not exceed £5,000.

5.3.2 Land

The rules apply where an individual occupies land and he had either:

(a)   Previously owned the land but had disposed of it, or

(b)   Provided consideration used by another person in acquiring the land.

The charge is the **annual value of the land** less any amount paid by the individual for the use of the land. Payment of full rent will reduce the charge to nil.

5.3.3 Chattels

The rules apply where an individual possesses a chattel and he had either:

(a)   Previously owned the chattel but had disposed of it, or

(b)   Provided consideration used by another person in acquiring the chattel.

The charge is the **value of the chattel multiplied by the prescribed rate of interest**, which will be given in the exam, less any amount paid by the individual for the use of the chattel.

5.3.4 Exclusions

The rules do **not** apply to:

(a)   Arm's length disposals to an unconnected person

(b)   Disposals to connected persons made as if at arm's length (the definition of connected persons is extended by including as 'relatives' uncles, aunts, nephews and nieces)

No charge will be made if the land or chattel is treated as a gift with reservation for IHT purposes.

5.3.5 IHT election

An individual caught by the rules can elect to disapply this income tax charge, usually by 31 January following the tax year in which the charge arises. The property will then be treated as subject to a reservation, so falling within the individual's estate for IHT purposes.

Example 3

Joe gifted £400,000 to his son, Tony, in June 2003. Tony bought a house with the money in September 2006. Joe moved into the property, which has an annual rental value of £6,000, shortly after. What is the pre-owned asset tax charge for Joe, who is a higher rate taxpayer?

Example 4

Joe also gifted £400,000 to his daughter, Caroline, in June 2003. Caroline bought a picture worth £250,000 with the money. The picture hangs in Joe's reception room. What is the pre-owned asset tax charge for Joe, assuming a notional interest rate of 6.25%?

Chapter roundup

- Certain investments (eg NS&I certificates) are completely tax free.

- ISAs are available to individuals over 18 (over 16 for cash investments) who are resident and ordinarily resident in the UK.

- ISAs can exist as cash or shares accounts.

- There is no income tax on interest or dividends, nor capital gains tax on disposal of shares from the ISA.

- Certain income tax and capital gains tax advantages are available to individuals who invest in EIS and VCTs.

- EIS relief applies where an individual subscribes for new ordinary shares in a qualifying company. Qualifying companies are in general unquoted trading companies where the trade is not a 'secure' one ('secure' being dealing in land, finance etc).

- EIS relief allows 20% of the investment as a tax reduction. The maximum investment qualifying for relief is £500,000 (subject to EC approval).

- Under certain specific circumstances EIS relief can be clawed back (ie withdrawn) by HMRC.

- A VCT company must meet a number of conditions for approval for VCT relief to be available including that the VCT must be a listed company whose income must derive wholly or mainly from shares and securities.

- The VCT investor will receive a tax reduction for 30% of the amount subscribed up to £200,000 of new VCT ordinary shares subscribed for in each tax year. This relief is withdrawn if the investor disposes of his shares in the VCT within five years of their issue.

- VCT dividends on the first £200,000 of VCT ordinary shares acquired (by subscription or purchase) are ignored for higher rate income tax purposes.

- Various anti-avoidance rules apply in connection with certain investments such as investments in securities and life assurance policies.

Quiz

1. Mr and Mrs Daniels have two sons, Jason aged 17 and Paul aged 19. Who may invest in an ISA?

2. Which of the following individuals cannot obtain EIS income tax relief?

   (a) An individual who, together with his associates, controls 26% of the voting power in the company
   (b) An unpaid (non-executive) director of the company
   (c) The managing director's secretary.

Solutions to Quiz

1. All of them but Jason may only subscribe to a cash account as he is under 18.

2. (a) Is fine because he owns ≤ 30%.
    (b) Is fine as a 'qualifying director'.
    (c) Employees are not entitled to relief.

Solutions to chapter examples

Solution to Example 1

(a) The tax reduction obtained on the shares sold after two years was £5,000/2 = £2,500. The issue price was £34,000/2 = £17,000. The amount of relief withdrawn is £12,000 × £2,500/£17,000 = £1,765

(b) The full gain of £3,270 is exempt

Solution to Example 2

	£
Proceeds on encashment	20,000
Early withdrawals 5 × 4% × £15,000 (within 5% limit)	3,000
	23,000
Less: initial premium	(15,000)
Overall profit	8,000

Number of complete years = 5. One slice = £8,000/5 = £1,600
Tax liability in respect of the bond:

	£
Total income: £33,900 + £1,600	35,500
Less: basic rate band	(34,800)
	700
Tax @ 20% (40% – 20% credit)	140
£140 × 5 years	700

Solution to Example 3

Income tax charge: £6,000 @ 40%	£2,400

Solution to Example 4

Notional interest: £250,000 @ 6.25%	£15,625
Income tax charge: £15,625 @ 40%	£6,250

Now try the following questions

Short Form Questions:

4.1 – 4.4 inclusive

Long Form Question:

4.1	Enterprise Investment Scheme

The purpose of this chapter is to help you to:

- explain the scope of the charge to income tax on employment income

- identify and calculate the benefits taxable on all employees

- calculate the benefits taxable only on employees paid £8,500 or more pa and directors

- identify tax-free benefits available to all employees

- identify the payments and expenses that can be deducted from employment income

- apply the special provisions taxing payments on termination of employment

References: ITEPA 2003 unless otherwise stated

The employed earner

1 Basis of employment income

1.1 Assessable income

Remuneration from an office or employment is taxed as employment income. Employment income is divided into:

(a)   General earnings; and — *salary, benefits* (handwritten)
(b)   Specific employment income — *termination payments, employee share dividend, pension income from non-approved pension* (handwritten)

General earnings include:

(a)   Any salary, wages or fee
(b)   Any benefits

Specific employment income includes:

(a)   Payments made on termination of employment
(b)   Income from acquisition of shares derived from employment
(c)   Pension income received from non-approved pensions.

Pensions and annuities paid in the UK, whether provided by the State, an occupational pension scheme or a personal pension scheme are taxed simply as 'pension income'.

Various social security benefits are taxed as 'Social Security income' (see Chapter 1).

1.2 The receipts basis

General earnings are assessed as income for the year in which they are received. The date of receipt is the earliest of:

(a)   the date of payment (or payment on account), or

(b)   the date when a person becomes entitled to the payment, or

(c)   in the case of directors only, the earliest of:

      (i)   the date the earnings are credited in the company's records or accounts, or

      (ii)   the end of a period of account if earnings for that period are determined before the period ends, or

      (iii)   the date earnings are determined if the amount is not determined until after the period ends.

Taxable benefits are generally treated as received when they are provided to the employee. If an employer provides a benefit to an employee's family member, the benefit will be taxable on that employee.

Example 1

A director of a company is entitled under his employment contract to a salary of £24,000 pa. payable monthly on the last day of each month in equal amounts. Additionally he is entitled to a performance-related bonus calculated on each half year's profits. The company prepares accounts to 31 December each year. His bonus for the six months to 30 June 2007 of £8,000 is determined on 1 November 2007, credited to his account on 1 January 2008 and paid to him with his January salary. His bonus of £11,500 for the six months to 31 December 2007 is not determined until agreed by the shareholders at the AGM on 30 April 2008. It is then entered into the company's records and paid with his May salary.

You are required to calculate his taxable employment income for 2007/08 and 2008/09.

If remuneration is received after the employee has ceased to work for that employer it is still taxable, regardless of whether the office or employment is still held at the date of receipt.

Pensions and any taxable social security benefits are not assessed on the receipts basis but on the basis of the amount accruing in the tax year.

LAW   **Now look at the topic, working relationships, in the ATT Manual 'Essential Law for the Taxation Technician'.**

2 Taxable benefits assessable on all employees

[handwritten: If can be converted into cash]

2.1 The general rules

The general rule for benefits received by excluded employees (ie paid less than £8,500 pa) is that they are **only taxable** if they can be turned into money. The value of such benefits can be thought of as the **'second-hand value'**.

The general rule for non-excluded employees is that the taxable value of the benefit is the cost to the employer of providing the benefit. *[handwritten: paid over 8,500]*

For both excluded and non-excluded employees there are now many specific rules, which override the general rules.

[handwritten: paid less than 8,500]

The following specific rules which apply to the provision of vouchers, living accommodation and mileage allowances apply to *all* employees regardless of the level of their earnings.

Certain benefits are only taxed on employees earning £8,500 or more and directors (i.e. non-excluded employees). The specific rules for how to calculate these taxable benefits are set out in section 3.

Exam focus point

'Benefits' are a core area of the syllabus. Spend time, making sure you understand how to calculate the cash value of benefits.

2.2 Vouchers

If an employee receives

(a) Non-cash vouchers (eg book tokens), or
(b) Credit tokens (eg a credit card)

he will be assessable on the *cost to the employer of providing* the benefit, unless the benefit itself is exempt (see section 4).

If an employee receives a cash voucher, he is assessable on the sum of money for which the voucher is capable of being exchanged. He is assessed in the year he receives the voucher.

2.3 Accommodation [s.104-s.107]

2.3.1 Basic charge

The value of the accommodation benefit provided to any employee (including employees paid £8,500+ and directors) **is the annual value of that property** (given in the exam). If the premises are rented rather than owned by the company, then the benefit to the employee is the higher of the rent actually paid by the employer and the annual value.

The amount taxable on the employee will be reduced by any contribution he makes for the use of the property and any element of business use.

Example 2

Tony is provided with a company flat.

Annual value	£300
Rent paid by the company	£3,380
Amount paid by Tony to the company for the use of the flat	(£520)

You are required to show Tony's assessable benefit.

3,160

2.3.2 Job-related accommodation

The employee will not be taxable if the accommodation is provided in one of the following circumstances.

(a) Residence in the accommodation is **necessary** for the proper performance of the employee's duties (eg a caretaker); or

(b) Accommodation is provided for the better performance of the employee's duties and the employment is of a kind in which it is **customary** for accommodation to be provided (eg a vicar or policeman); or

(c) The accommodation is provided as part of special **security** arrangements in force because of a special threat to the employee's security (eg the Prime Minister).

2.3.3 Expensive accommodation

Where the cost of the living accommodation exceeds £75,000, an additional benefit will be chargeable which is found by applying the following formula: [s.104]

official
rate of
interest

cost

a total of the amount formed from separate units

$$ORI \times (C - £75,000)$$

ORI is the official rate of interest at the start of the tax year, C is the 'cost of providing' the living accommodation. The cost is the aggregate of the cost of purchase and the cost of any improvements made before the relevant tax year. It is therefore *not* possible to avoid the charge by purchasing a property requiring substantial repairs and 'doing it up'. The cost is the net cost, after taking account of any amounts paid by the employee.

If the accommodation was acquired by the employer more than six years before it was first provided to the employee and its original cost, plus improvements, exceeded £75,000, the 'cost of providing' is increased (or reduced if appropriate) to its market value when first provided to that employee. Note that regardless of current market value, an additional charge cannot apply if the *original* cost plus improvements is under £75,000.

Where any contribution paid by the employee exceeds the annual value of the property, the excess may be deducted from the further benefit.

Example 3

Simon is provided with a house by his employer (not job-related accommodation). It was originally made available to him on 1 July 2005, although the company had acquired the house at a cost of £125,000 on 1 April 2002.

On 1 September 2005, £8,000 was spent on extending the property.

For 2008/09, the annual value of the house is £1,400. Simon pays £3,000 for the use of the house to his employer.

You are required to calculate his total benefit for 2008/09 in respect of the house. The official rate of interest is 6.25%.

2.4 Mileage allowances

Where employers pay mileage allowances to their employees to use their own cars for business travel the employees are taxed on any amounts in excess of the HMRC authorised mileage rates.

The tax-free limits are 40p a mile for the first 10,000 business miles and 25p a mile thereafter and are shown in the Association's tables available in the exam.

Any amount paid in excess of the limit is taxable on the employee. If the employer pays less than the authorised rates the employee can claim a deduction from their employment income for the shortfall.

The rates take into account depreciation, running expenses etc and the employee cannot claim a deduction for any loan taken out to purchase the car or any capital allowances for the cost of the car.

Any amount paid to the employee for mileage other than on the employer's business (eg for home to office mileage) is always taxable in full.

Example 4

Owen drives 14,000 business miles in his own car. Calculate the taxable benefit or allowable deduction assuming:

(a)   He is reimbursed 40p a mile
(b)   He is reimbursed 25p a mile
(c)   No reimbursement is made.

The employer is only required to report the taxable profit (if any) and the employee will only claim for the shortfall (if any).

Employers can pay employees using their own cars up to 5p a mile tax free for taking fellow employees as passengers on business journeys. There is no tax relief where employees receive either no payment from the employer or less than 5p a mile.

Employers can also pay a tax free mileage allowance to employees using motor cycles and bicycles in the course of their employment as follows:

Motorcycles	24p
Bicycles	20p

These generous rates are intended to encourage the use of more environmental friendly transport. There is no reduction in the rates for over 10,000 miles (although, in the case of bicycles, this is not likely to be a practical point!)

TQT
Tax Qualification Training

3 Benefits assessable on employees paid £8,500 or more and directors

3.1 Employees paid £8,500 or more and directors

'Emoluments', or earnings, for the £8,500 pa. test include salary, commissions, fees, reimbursed expenses and also
benefits assessable on employees paid £8,500+ pa./directors. In other words, one must *initially assume* that a particular
employee is paid £8,500 pa. or more in order to determine whether or not he really is in that category.

You may find it useful to learn the following pro-forma:

	£
Employment income (net of occupational pension contributions)	X
Reimbursed expenses	X
Benefits as if were paid £8,500 pa. or more	X
TEST HERE	X
Less: allowable deductions	(X)
Assessment if the taxpayer is paid £8,500 pa. or more	X

The £8,500 is pro-rated where the employment is held for less than the full tax year.   *— apportioned for whole year*

The term 'director' refers to any person who acts as a director or any person in accordance with whose instructions the
directors are accustomed to act (other than a professional advisor).

A full-time working director, or a director of a non-profit making company or charity, and who, with associates, controls
not more than 5% of the voting rights of the company is excluded unless he earns £8,500 pa. or more.

3.2 The general rule

The value of a benefit is the cost to the employer *of providing* that benefit. So, for example, private medical insurance
is caught, even though there is no resale value. There are, however, special rules for a number of specific benefits.

A **benefit arises if it is provided 'by reason of the employment' so there is no need for the employer to provide it
directly**. In addition the rules apply if benefits are provided to members of individual's family or household.

Where **in-house benefits** are provided, the case of *Pepper v Hart (1992)* established that the cost of **providing the
benefit is the marginal (ie additional) cost** and not the average cost. This case involved employees of a public school
paying reduced fees for their own children, calculated to cover the extra cost to the school eg food and laundry for the
employee's child. They successfully argued that there was no cost to the employer as they had reimbursed the marginal
costs. HMRC had wanted to value the benefit by averaging the total school costs over the total number of pupils.

This marginal cost basis is relevant to a wide range of employments and can apply, for example, where employees of
transport undertakings (eg British Airways) are allowed to take up unsold seats free or at below the full price.

3.3 Expenses connected with living accommodation

The following expenses are only assessable on higher paid employees, or directors.

(a) Heating, lighting or cleaning the premises
(b) Repairing, maintaining or decorating them
(c) Providing furniture etc normal for domestic occupation (annual value taken as 20% of cost – see 3.7 below).

Unless the accommodation qualifies as 'job-related' (see 2.3.2 above) the full cost of additional services (excluding structural repairs) is assessable. If the accommodation is 'job-related', however, the value of additional services is restricted to a maximum of 10% of 'net earnings'. For this purpose, net earnings are all amounts taxable as employment income (*excluding* the additional benefits (a) – (c) above) less any allowable expenses. [s.315]

If the employer pays the council tax due in respect of the property this will also be assessable unless the employee is in job-related accommodation.

Example 5

Mr Quinton is employed as a security guard earning £12,000 in 2008/09. In order to carry out his duties properly he is required to live in a house adjacent to his employer's premises and this is accepted by HMRC as job-related accommodation. The house cost £70,000 two years ago. The annual value of the house is £650. In the year the company pays an electricity bill of £250, a gas bill of £200, a gardener's bill of £150 and redecoration costs of £1,000. Mr Quinton makes a monthly contribution of £50 for his accommodation. He drives a company car on which the assessable benefit is £2,990 (see 3.4 below).

You are required to calculate the amount assessable as employment income for 2008/09.

12,000
2,990
(50)
14,950

3.4 The car benefit rules

Special rules apply for taxing car benefits enjoyed by employees paid £8,500 pa or more and directors. [s.121]

(a) The tax charge arises whether the car is provided by the employer or by some other person.

(b) **The taxable benefit is a percentage, determined by the level of the car's carbon dioxide (CO_2) emissions** (see (g) below), × **the car's list price**.

(c) The **list price** of the car is the sum of the following items:

(i) The list price of the car for a single retail sale in the UK at the time of first registration, including delivery charges and the cost of standard accessories. **Discounts are not taken into account.**

(ii) The price (including fitting) of all optional accessories added when the car was first provided to the employee, excluding mobile telephones, equipment needed by a disabled employee, and equipment for the car to run on road fuel gas.

(iii) The price (including fitting) of all optional accessories fitted later and costing at least £100 each, with exclusions as in (ii). Such accessories affect the taxable benefit from and including the year of assessment in which they are fitted. Accessories that merely replace existing accessories and are not superior to the ones replaced are ignored.

(d) There is a special rule for classic cars. If the car is at least 15 years old (from the time of first registration) at the *end* of the tax year, and its market value at the end of the year is over £15,000 and greater than the price found under (c), that market value (including accessories) is used instead of the price.

(e) **If the employee makes a capital contribution** towards the cost of the car or accessories this is **deducted from the list price** for calculating the benefit, subject to a **maximum deduction of £5,000**.

(f) **The maximum list price after deducting the employee's capital contribution is £80,000.**

(g) The basic percentage is 15% for cars that emit up to 135 grams of CO_2 per kilometre (g/km) and increases by one percent for every additional 5 g/km up to a maximum of 35%.

From 6 April 2008 a base percentage of just 10% applies to cars that emit 120 g/km or less. The base percentage of 15% then applies to cars that emit up to 135 g/km.

There is a 3% supplement for diesel cars (maximum is still 35%).

Exam focus point

Examiner's report – Personal Taxation (old syllabus)

Nov 2006 – Question 1

Some candidates lost a mark in the car benefit calculation as they deducted the employee's contribution from the cost price of the car.

need to deduct from List price not cost

Example 6

+ 3% supplement

Nigel Issan is provided with a diesel car which had a list price of £22,000 when it was first registered. The car has CO_2 emissions of 198g/km.

You are required to calculate Nigel's car benefit for 2008/09.

(h) **The benefit is reduced on a time basis where a car is first made available or ceases to be made available during the year** or is incapable of being used for a continuous period of not less than 30 days (for example because it is being repaired). If a car is unavailable for less than 30 days and a replacement car of similar quality is provided, the replacement car is ignored and treated as being the usual car.

Exam focus point

Note that where benefits are only available for part of the tax year, the taxable benefit must be time apportioned. Look carefully at the dates given in the question.

(i) **The benefit is reduced by any payment the user is required to make for the private use of the car** (as distinct from a capital contribution to the cost of the car). However, the benefit cannot become negative to create a deduction from the employee's income. Payments for insuring the car do not count.

List price

Example 7

[handwritten: 3 monts] *[handwritten: no diesel supplement]*

[handwritten left margin: deduct from list price]

Vicky Olvo starts her employment on 6 January 2009 and is immediately provided with a new petrol car with a list price of £25,000. The car was more expensive than her employer would have provided and she therefore made a capital contribution of £6,200. The employer was able to buy the car at a discount and paid only £23,000. Vicky contributed £100 a month for being able to use the car privately. CO₂ emissions are 262g/km per the car's registration document.

[handwritten: 1 x 3] You are required to calculate her car benefit for 2008/09. *[handwritten: do not count]*

(j)　**Pool cars are exempt**. A car only qualifies as a pool car if *all* the following conditions are satisfied.

　　(i)　It is used by more than one director or employee and is not ordinarily used by any one of them to the exclusion of the others.

　　(ii)　Any private use is merely incidental to business use.

　　(iii)　It is not normally kept overnight at or near the residence of an employee.

(k)　Where an employee has sacrificed salary to obtain private use of a car, the taxable benefit will be the higher of salary foregone and the benefit calculated above.

(l)　Employers must make quarterly returns of any changes in cars provided to employees on form P46 (car). These returns are made for income tax quarters (ending on 5 July, 5 October, 5 January and 5 April), and must be made within 28 days of the end of each quarter.

(m)　**The benefit calculated above covers all expenditure by the employer on repairs, servicing, insurance, road fund licence and cleaning**. It does not cover the cost of a chauffeur. Where a chauffeur is provided for both business and private mileage, an agreed proportion of the employer's associated costs would be assessable on the employee.

(n)　Car telephones are exempt (see 4(h) below).

(o)　No benefit arises on the provision of a car parking space at or near work (see 4(b) below).

3.5 The fuel benefit rules

Where fuel for private motoring is provided to an employee paid £8,500 pa. or more or a director with a company car, he will be assessed on a fuel benefit in addition to the car benefit above.

The fuel benefit charge is based on the same percentage as is used to calculate the car benefit × the base figure. The base figure for 2008/09 is £16,900 and is shown in the Association's tax tables. [s.150]

There is no taxable benefit if either all the fuel was provided for business travel or the employee reimburses all of the cost of private fuel. *[handwritten: the employer]*

Any reduction for non-availability of a company car also applies to the fuel benefit. If the car is available for *x* months but fuel is only supplied for private use for *y* months (*y* < *x*) the fuel charge is still *x*/12 of the full charge.

The taxable fuel benefit only applies to company cars. If fuel is provided for an employee's own car, the normal rule of 'cost of providing' applies.

Example 8

An employee was provided with a new petrol car costing £15,000 (the list price) on 1 June 2008. During 2008/09 the employer spent £900 on insurance, repairs and vehicle licence. The firm paid for all petrol (£2,300) without reimbursement. The employee was required to pay the firm £25 per month for the private use of the car.

The car has CO_2 emissions of 135g/km.

You are required to calculate the total assessable benefit for 2008/09 in respect of the car and fuel.

Exam focus point

Examiner's report – Personal Taxation (old syllabus)

May 2002 – Question 3

... The majority covered the car benefit adequately although not all mentioned that the benefit is based on list price not cost. In respect of the fuel benefit, around half of the answers stated that the £50 contribution from the employee could be deducted....

3.6 Company vans

An annual scale charge of £3,000 applies for unrestricted private use of company vans. A further £500 charge applies for the provision of private fuel. [s.157]

This charge only applies to employees who use a company van for significant private journeys other than journeys between home and work.

The charge is pro-rated if the van is only provided for part of the year or if it is incapable of being used for 30 or more consecutive days. The charge is also reduced by any employee contributions.

3.7 Private use of employer's assets

The taxable value of the private use of an employer's assets (other than cars, vans and accommodation) **is:**

20% × the market value of the asset when first used by the employee. [s.205]

If the asset is leased by the employer and the lease charge is greater than the 20% benefit, that lease charge will be the taxable benefit.

If that asset is subsequently acquired by the employee, the assessable benefit on the acquisition is the greater of:

(a)   **the current market value of the asset**, and

(b)   **market value when first provided less any amounts already assessed as a benefit (at 20%) in respect of use of the asset**.

This rule prevents tax free benefits arising on fast depreciating items by the employee purchasing them at a much reduced second-hand value.

Illustration

A suit costing £200 is bought by an employer for use by an employee on 6 April 2007. On 6 April 2008 the suit is purchased by the employee for £15, its market value then being £25.

			£
The benefit assessable in 2007/08 will be 20% × £200			40

The benefit assessable in 2008/09 will be the greater of:

		£	£
(a)	Market value at acquisition by employee	25	
(b)	Original market value	200	
	Less: assessed in respect of use	(40)	
		160	
	ie		160
	Less: price paid by employee		(15)
	Benefit		145

If the employee does not buy the asset he will continue to be assessed on 20% × the original value each year (even if use continues for more than five years). However, it remains tax efficient for assets like suits, which need replacing every two or three years, to be purchased by the employer rather than by the employee out of net income.

As the provision of a bicycle for home to work travel is a tax free benefit (see 4(b) below) if an employee buys a bicycle that they have previously used, the tax charge is always based on the market value when they buy it.

For computers lent to employees before 6 April 2006 there is no taxable benefit where the computer cost less than £2,500 (ie where the benefit is £500 (20% × £2,500) or less). The normal rules apply on the value of the benefit in excess of £500 and the exemption will not apply if the equipment is confined to directors. The tax charge if the employee subsequently buys the computer is based only on the market value at the date they buy it.

Exam focus point

Examiner's report – Personal Taxation (old syllabus)

May 2002 – Question 3

Most of the answers stated that the computer was not taxable due to the exemption but very few mentioned the related expenses rule, stating that either the internet access was not a benefit (business use) or that it was chargeable in full.

3.8 Taxable cheap loans

3.8.1 Basic rule

Loans to employees, directors and their families give rise to a benefit equal to:

(a) **Any amounts written off, and**

(b) **The excess of the interest based on the official rate over any interest actually charged.** [s.175]

There is no taxable benefit if the total balance on all loans to the employee did not exceed £5,000 at any time in the year. If the £5,000 threshold is exceeded, a benefit arises on interest on the whole loan, not just on the excess of the loan over £5,000. [s.180]

When a loan is written off there is no £5,000 threshold so writing off a loan of £1 would give rise to a £1 benefit.

TQT
Tax Qualification Training

Exam focus point

Examiner's report – Personal Taxation (old syllabus)

May 2006 – Question 5

The main errors were ... assuming that the loan written off was exempt.

3.8.2 Calculating the interest benefit

There are two methods of calculating the amount of the benefit.

(a) **The normal 'averaging method'** takes the average of the amount of loan outstanding at the beginning and end of the tax year (or the dates on which the loan was made and discharged in the tax year) and applies the official rate of interest to it. [s.182]

(b) **The alternative method calculates interest on a daily basis on the actual amount outstanding**. [s.183]

The normal 'averaging' method applies automatically unless an election is made by the taxpayer or HMRC who normally only make the election where it appears that the 'averaging' method is being deliberately exploited.

Different loans to the same employee are usually treated separately.

Example 9

Handwritten: $30,000 + 10,000 \div 2 = 20,000 \times 6.25\%, \ 1,250$ (250) $1,000$

At 6 April 2008 a cheap loan of £30,000 was outstanding to a director, who repaid £20,000 on 6 December 2008. The remaining balance of £10,000 was outstanding at 5 April 2009. Interest paid during the year was £250.

What is the benefit under both methods for 2008/09, assuming that the official rate of interest was 6.25% throughout 2008/09.

3.8.3 Exceptions

Handwritten: $30,000 \times 6.25\% = 1875 \times 8 / 12 = 1,250$

Handwritten: $10,000 \times 6.25\% = 625 \times 4 / 12 = 208$

The following categories of cheap loan can be ignored.

(a) Loans made on **ordinary commercial terms** [s.176]

(b) Loans **qualifying for tax relief** (eg loan to buy shares in a close company or to buy a property for letting). Any interest the employee actually pays is relieved as normal (eg as a deduction from total income or as an expense deductible from property income). *Handwritten: $= 1,458$*

If the loan partly qualifies for tax relief (eg a loan to buy computer equipment used partly for business purposes and partly privately) the employee is taxed on the value of the interest by reference to the official rate but is then given tax relief on the qualifying part of the interest he pays and the 'benefit' interest – ie the qualifying part of interest at the official rate. [s.178]

Example 10

Anna, who is single, has an annual salary of £35,000 and a loan from her employer of £24,000 at 2% interest to buy a holiday cottage which Anna uses herself and lets to tenants. The net rents (before interest relief) are £4,500 and 15% of general expenses have been disallowed to reflect Anna's occupation.

The official rate of interest is to be taken as 6.25%.

What is Anna's tax liability for 2008/09?

4 Tax-free benefits – summary

There is a fairly long list of benefits which are *non-taxable* on *all* employees, including:

(a)   Accommodation and subsistence:

(i)   **Job-related accommodation** (see 2.3.2.)

(ii)   **Meals in a staff canteen**, provided that they are available to all employees on broadly similar terms

(iii) The first 15p per working day of luncheon vouchers

(iv)   Personal incidental expenses of up to £5 per night for employees working away from home in the UK, or £10 per night if working abroad which would otherwise be taxable (eg laundry, newspapers, telephone calls home)

However, where more than one night is spent away, the exemption works on an aggregate basis eg for four nights the overall limit is £20

(v)   Subsistence costs for 'site based employees' (see 5.2)

(b)   Travel:

(i)   **The provision of a car parking space at or near the place of work**

(ii)   **Mileage allowances for cars etc within the HMRC Authorised mileage rates** (see 2.4)

(iii) A payment for additional transport costs or the cost of overnight accommodation in a case where public transport is disrupted by industrial action

(iv)   A payment for a taxi or hired car for an employee who is occasionally required to work late (after 9pm), in circumstances where either public transport has ceased or it would be unreasonable to expect the employee to use it. If such arrangements occur frequently (more than 60 times a year) or regularly (eg every Friday), then *no* exemption is available

(v)   The reimbursement to a director or employee of costs necessarily incurred in travelling to another company in the same group of which he is a director

(vi)   **Home to site travel costs for 'site based employees'**

(vii) The provision of works buses with a seating capacity of 9 or more which are used mainly to bring employees to and from work

(viii) The payment of general subsidies to public bus services used by employees to travel to work, regardless of whether the employees pay the same fare as other members of the public or any fare at all

(ix)   The provision of bicycles and cycling safety equipment made available for employees mainly to travel between home and work

(x)   The provision of workplace parking for bicycles and motorcycles

(xi)   The provision of alternative transport to get car sharers home when exceptional circumstances, such as a domestic emergency, mean that the normal car sharing arrangements unavoidably break down

(xii) Tax free breakfasts on official 'cycle to work' days

(c) **Education and training**:

(i) Payments of up to £15,480 per academic year made by an employer to an employee for attendance at a full-time training course (including a sandwich course) at a university, college, school or similar establishment

(ii) Payments made in respect of a past or present employee for the costs of a qualifying training or retraining course – full time, day release or block release

(d) **Removal expenses**:

Up to £8,000 of removal expenses borne by the employer where the employee has to move house on first taking up the employment or on a transfer within the organisation. 'Removal expenses' include for this purpose the reimbursement of interest on a bridging loan, usual professional fees, costs of finding a new home, and replacement of curtains and carpets

(e) **Entertainment**:

(i) **The provision of a Christmas party or alternative function, provided that the cost is no more than £150 per head per annum**

(ii) The provision of entertainment by a person who is neither the employer, nor connected with them

(f) **Child care**:

(i) **Child care facilities available to all employees either on the employer's premises or on other premises where the employer is responsible for the financing and management of the facilities**

(ii) £55 per week of qualifying childcare costs paid by employers either directly to an employee, or to officially registered or approved childcare providers, including those in the employee's home (eg nannies)

(g) **Home-working**:

A tax free allowance of up to £3 per week is payable to employees to cover the additional household costs of working some or all of the time at home. No record keeping is required for the flat-rate £3 per week allowance. For payments above that figure, evidence is required that the payment is wholly in respect of additional household expenses incurred by the employee in carrying out his duties at home

(h) **Miscellaneous**:

(i) **Non-cash long service awards – for service in excess of 20 years, £50 per year of service is tax-free**

(ii) Staff uniforms

(iii) Awards under a formally constituted staff suggestion scheme

(iv) Gifts (other than cash) received by reason of the employment from someone other than the employer, provided that they amount to less than £250 in a tax year from a particular source

(v) **Overseas medical insurance or expenses incurred whilst working abroad as part of the duties of the employment**

(vi) Assets or services provided to improve an employee's personal physical security from a threat arising out of his employment

(vii) **Workplace sports or recreational facilities provided by employers for use by their staff generally**. This does not apply where the employer pays or reimburses an employee's subscription to a sports club nor where the facilities are only available to limited groups of employees

(viii) Air miles and car fuel coupons obtained in the course of business travel

(ix) Liabilities and indemnities insurance premiums for directors and employees; expenditure in discharging an employee's liabilities incurred in his capacity as employee; costs of proceedings relating to such matters (any costs paid by an employee qualify for tax relief)

(x) **Private use of one mobile phone**; other mobile phones will be a taxable benefit

(xi)   Use of shower facilities and changing room on employers' premises available to all employees

(xii) **Cheap loans under £5,000** (see 3.8)

(xiii) The provision of one health screening and one medical check-up each year per employee, provided made available to all employees or those who have been identified in a health screening as requiring a medical check up.

Exam focus point

The above list is not exhaustive, but provides a reasonably comprehensive summary of the tax free benefits of which you need to be aware. The main ones are in bold.

---

5 Allowable deductions

5.1 Introduction

Three types of expenditure made by employees are deductible from employment income.

(a)   **Contributions** (within certain limits) **to an registered occupational pension scheme,**
(b)   **Subscriptions to professional bodies**, if relevant to the duties, and
(c)   **Donations to charity** (of any amount) **under an approved payroll deduction scheme**.

Other claims for deductions are hard to obtain. When they are available, they fall into the following categories.

(a)   **Qualifying travel expenses** (see 5.2)

(b)   Other **expenses incurred** *wholly, exclusively and necessarily in* **the performance of the duties**

(c)   **Capital allowances on plant and machinery** *necessarily* **provided for use** *in* **the performance of the duties**. Note that the plant cannot include the employee's own transport as the depreciation is already factored into the HMRC Authorised mileage rates (see 2.4).

Note that the word **'necessarily'** is particularly restrictive. Trading expenses for a company, sole trader or partner have to satisfy only a 'wholly and exclusively' test and are, therefore, much more likely to be allowable. This partly explains why taxpayers prefer to be self-employed rather than employed.

5.2 Travel expenses

Expenditure 'in the performance of' duties does not include expenditure incurred in order to get into a position to perform duties. **Thus travel to work (ie commuting) is not usually allowable**.

However, a deduction for commuting costs is available to employees with no permanent workplace. This includes 'site based employees' and those intending to spend less than 24 months at a temporary workplace.

A deduction is also available for **accommodation and subsistence** if an overnight stay is necessary.

5.3 Other expenses

5.3.1 Reimbursed expenses

Where an employee incurs an expense that is reimbursed by his employer, he must include the full expense as taxable earnings and deduct any amount incurred **wholly, exclusively and necessarily** in the performance of his duties.

5.3.2 Round sum allowances

Where an employee is provided with a round sum allowance (ie a lump sum) to cover future expenses, he must include the full allowance as a taxable emolument and take a deduction for any amounts spent that would be deductible from trade profits for his employer on a **'wholly and exclusively'** basis.

Example 11

Daniel earns £50,000 pa. He is given a £1,000 round sum allowance to cover his expenses for 2008/09.

He spends it as follows:

	£
Business travel	600
Staff entertaining	180
Client entertaining	150
Unaccounted	70
	1,000

Daniel has no other taxable benefits.

What is Daniel's employment income for 2008/09?

---

6 Payments on termination of employment

6.1 General provisions

Payments on termination of employment fall into one of three categories for taxation purposes.

(a) Entirely exempt payments
(b) Partially exempt payments
(c) Entirely chargeable payments.

The **following types of payment** on termination of employment are **exempt**. [ss.406-410]

(a) A payment **on death**

(b) A payment on account of **injury or disability**

(c) A lump sum payment **from or to a registered pension scheme**

(d) **Legal costs** recovered by the employee from the employer following legal action to recover compensation for loss of employment.

Any termination payment not falling within (a) to (d) above but which is made _in return for services_ will be fully taxable under normal employment income rules. The question of whether a payment is made in return for services can be a complex one, but generally, if the **contract of employment provides for payment** to be made on termination of employment, the **payment will be in return for services**. If the contract is silent on this point but a payment is made, **it will be taken to be in return for services if there was a reasonable expectation** that such a sum would be paid. Accordingly, these payments made in return for services are taxed in full as employment income.

Other payments on termination (such as compensation for loss of office), which are not taxable under the normal employment income rules because they are not in return for services, are nevertheless brought within the employment income regime by s.402 ITEPA 2003.

Termination payments subject to s.402 are, however, partially exempt: the first £30,000 is free of income tax. [s.401]

Statutory redundancy payments are exempt but must be considered when taxing termination payments under s.402 as they use up part or all of the £30,000 exempt amount. [s.403]

The cost of outplacement (eg counselling) services incurred by the employer for the employee's benefit is exempt and does not reduce the £30,000 exempt amount.

Payments received under termination settlements are taxable in the year in which they are received or enjoyed, rather than being taxed in the year of termination.

Similarly any benefits (eg the provision of a company car) which would be assessable had the employment continued, are taxed in the year in which the benefit is received or enjoyed.

HMRC may treat termination payments made on or around the time of an employee's retirement as arising from an unapproved pension scheme and so are fully taxable with no £30,000 exemption. HMRC have indicated that a man of middle years moving on to further full-time employment is obviously not retiring but that they are likely to apply this rule to a man of older years who has no other full-time employment in prospect.

Payments made in return for the employee promising, for example, not to work in a particular area **following the termination of his employment (a 'restrictive covenant')** are always **taxable in full**.

Example 12

Paula, 37, is made redundant on 10 October 2008 and her termination package includes the following:

	£
Compensation payment	50,000
Payment to required pension scheme	5,000
Company car (market value)	12,000
Statutory redundancy	6,000
	73,000

Calculate the amount assessable as employment income in 2008/09.

6.2 Termination payments after foreign service

Payments received on termination of an employment which included an element of foreign service may be exempt from tax. Complete exemption is given where the foreign service element is 'substantial'.

For the purposes of this exemption, the employee's period of service is treated as including a substantial element of foreign service where the foreign service comprises: [s.413]

(a)   Three-quarters of the whole period of service; or

(b)   The last 10 years, where the whole period of service is in excess of 10 years; or   *20 yrs*

(c)   Half of the total period of service, including any ten out of the last 20 years, where the total period of service is in excess of 20 years.

If part of the termination payment is still taxable after all other exemptions (eg the £30,000 exemption for compensation payments) and there has been foreign service during the period of employment, a **fraction of the otherwise taxable payment may be deducted** equal to: [s.414]

$$\frac{\text{period of foreign service}}{\text{total length of service up to the relevant date}}$$

Chapter roundup

- Employment income includes: general earnings and certain other receipts. Pension and certain social security benefits are also charged to tax under ITEPA 2003.

- Earnings are assessable in the tax year in which they are received. Earnings are not only wages or salary but also certain benefits and reimbursed expenses.

- The provision of living accommodation (unless it is job-related accommodation), credit cards, cash or non-cash vouchers and mileage allowances in excess of the authorised mileage rates gives rise to an assessable benefit for *all* employees.

- The living accommodation benefit is based on the annual value of the property. An additional benefit arises where the cost of the property, or in certain circumstances the market value at the date it is first occupied, exceeds £75,000.

- Relief is given to employees for the cost of using their own vehicle or bicycle for work if any mileage allowance paid is less than the authorised rates. Any excess is taxable.

- To determine whether an employee is lower paid (ie the £8,500 threshold is exceeded) all reimbursed expenses and benefits are included, but no deduction for expenses or payments (other than pension contributions and charitable donations) are taken into account.

- A director is only treated as lower-paid if, in addition to receiving earnings of less than £8,500, he both works full-time for the company and controls 5% or less of the ordinary share capital. _employment only_

- The general rule for valuing benefits for lower-paid employees is the second-hand value, ie the amount of money into which it can be converted.

- The general rule for valuing benefits for employees earning £8,500+ and directors is the employer's cost of provision, unless special rules apply.

- The benefits that are only chargeable on employees paid £8,500+ and on directors are:

  - Expenses in connection with living accommodation
  - The provision of a company car and private fuel
  - The provision of a company van with significant private use
  - Use of assets owned by the employer and
  - Taxable cheap loans.

- Some benefits are exempt for all employees (eg workplace parking).

- Only pension contributions, subscriptions to professional bodies, charitable donations under an approved payroll deduction scheme and expenses incurred 'wholly, exclusively and necessarily' in the performance of the employee's duties can be deducted from employment income.

- Employees can only claim a deduction for commuting costs if they are site based employees or have a temporary workplace (<24 months).

- Certain payments made on the termination of employment are completely exempt, eg on death of the employee.

- The first £30,000 of non-contractual termination payments is tax-free. Statutory redundancy pay is <u>exempt</u> but uses up part/all of the £30,000 exempt amount. _eats into £_

  even if > £30,000 still exempt

1.   Describe the basis of assessment for employment income.

2.   An employee is provided with a flat by his employer (not job-related accommodation). The annual value of the flat is £400; rent paid by the employer amounts to £3,900 per annum.

   How much is included in the employee's earnings in respect of this benefit?

3.   The additional charge on 'expensive' accommodation (costing more than £75,000) applies only to employees paid £8,500+ pa and directors. True/False?

4.   Megan, an employee, received the following in 2008/09

	£
Salary	5,560
Company car (benefit)	2,310
Reimbursed expenses (of which 75% are deductible)	880

   Is Megan 'an employee paid £8,500 or more'?

5.   Buster is the Managing Director of Buster Braces Ltd and is supplied with a Bentley (3 litre, petrol engine) which cost £82,000 in 2006. It has CO_2 emissions of 195g/km. He was disqualified for dangerous driving so is supplied with a chauffeur at the company's expense (full salary costs for 2008/09 – £13,500). The car is fitted with a telephone which Buster uses both for business and privately. All running costs are borne by the company. What is the total taxable benefit? Buster did 12,000 miles in 2008/09, of which 3,000 miles were for business.

6.   A video recorder costing £500 was made available to Gordon by his employer on 6 April 2007. On 6 April 2008, Gordon bought the recorder for £150, when its market value was £325. What assessable benefit arises in 2008/09 if Gordon's salary amounts to £15,000 per annum?

7.   The first £5,000 of an interest-free loan is exempt from tax. True/False?

8.   How much of a termination payment, brought within the charge to employment income by virtue only of s.402 ITEPA 2003, is exempt from tax?

9.   Is a taxable fuel benefit reduced by any reimbursement by the employee of the cost of fuel provided for private mileage?

1. Employment income is assessed on the receipts basis, ie on amounts received during the year of assessment, regardless of when it is earned.

2. £3,900, being the higher of the annual value and rent actually paid.

3. False. Only those in occupation of 'job-related' accommodation can avoid the additional charge.

4. Yes

		£
Emoluments:	Salary	5,560
	Car benefit	2,310
	Reimbursed expenses	880
	TEST HERE (>£8,500)	8,750
	Less: allowable expenses (£880 × 75%)	(660)
	ASSESSMENT	8,090

5.

	£
Car benefit (W)	21,600
Fuel benefit (£16,900 × 27%)	4,563
Telephone benefit	nil
Chauffeur £13,500 × $\dfrac{9,000}{12,000}$	10,125
Total benefit	36,288

Working

	£
Maximum value £80,000 × 27%	21,600

$(15\% + (195 - 135) \times 1/5 = 27\%)$

6. Benefit is based on the higher of:

(a)	Current MV		£325
(b)	Original MV	£500	
	Less: already assessed (in 2007/08)		
	£500 × 20%	(100)	
			£400

ie £400

Therefore the assessable benefit after deduction of the amount paid (£150) is £250.

7. False – only if the loan does not exceed £5,000 is it exempt.

8. £30,000 (as reduced by any Statutory Redundancy payment).

9. Not unless the employer is fully reimbursed, in which case the fuel benefit is nil.

Solutions to chapter examples

Solution to Example 1

	£
2007/08	
Basic salary paid 30 April 2007 to 31 March 2008 inclusive	24,000
Bonus for six months to 30 June 2007 – determined before the end of the period of account – 'received' 31.12.07	8,000
Employment income 2007/08	32,000
2008/09	
Basic salary (30.4.08 – 31.3.09 inclusive)	24,000
Bonus for six months to 31 December 2007 – not determined until the AGM and payable subsequently therefore 'received' 30 April 2008	11,500
Employment Income 2008/09	35,500

Solution to Example 2

		£
Benefit: greater of		
– annual value	£300	
– rent paid	£3,380	3,380
Less: reimbursed to the company		(520)
Taxable benefit		2,860

Solution to Example 3

Basic charge:

	£
Annual value	1,400
Less: contribution	(1,400)
	nil

Additional charge:

	£	£
Cost including improvements £(125,000 + 8,000)	133,000	
Less:	(75,000)	
Excess	58,000	
£58,000 × 6.25%		3,625
Less: balance of contribution £(3,000 – 1,400)		(1,600)
Taxable benefit		2,025

Solution to Example 4

		£
Authorised mileage rates:	10,000 × 40p	4,000
	4,000 × 25p	1,000
		5,000

(a)	Taxable benefit: (40p × 14,000 = £5,600) – 5,000	£600
(b)	Deduction: £(14,000 × 25p = 3,500) – 5,000	£(1,500)
(c)	Deduction:	£(5,000)

TQT
Tax Qualification Training

Solution to Example 5

	£	£
Salary		12,000
Car benefit		2,990
Net earnings		14,990
Accommodation benefit:		
Annual value – exempt (job related)	nil	
Additional services:		
Electricity	250	
Gas	200	
Gardener	150	
Redecorations	1,000	
	1,600	
Restricted to 10% of £14,990	1,499	
Less: employee's contribution (12 × £50)	(600)	899
Employment income		15,889

Solution to Example 6

	£
Car benefit £22,000 × 30% (15% + (195 − 135) × 1/5 + 3%)	6,600

Note that 198 is rounded down to 195 to be exactly divisible by 5.

Solution to Example 7

	£
List price (N1)	25,000
Less: capital contributions (maximum)	(5,000)
	20,000
£20,000 × 35% (N2)	7,000
3/12 × £7,000 (N3)	1,750
Less: contribution to running costs (£100 × 3)	(300)
Car benefit	1,450

Notes

(1)   The discounted price is irrelevant
(2)   15% + (260 − 135) × 1/5 = 40% restricted to 35% max
(3)   Only available for 3 months in the year

Solution to Example 8

Car was available for 10 months.

	£
List price £15,000 × 15%	2,250
£2,250 × $^{10}/_{12}$	1,875
Less contribution (10 × £25)	(250)
	1,625
Fuel benefit £16,900 × 15% × $^{10}/_{12}$	2,112
Total taxable benefit	3,737

If the contribution of £25 per month had been towards the petrol, the benefit assessable would have been £(1,875 + 2,112) = £3,987. Conversely, if the cost of private petrol were fully reimbursed by the employee then there would have been no fuel benefit at all.

Solution to Example 9

Averaging method

	£
$6.25\% \times \dfrac{(30,000 + 10,000)}{2}$	1,250
Less: interest paid	(250)
Taxable benefit	1,000

Alternative method

	£
£30,000 $\times \dfrac{8}{12}$ (6 April 2008 – 5 December 2008) $\times$ 6.25%	1,250
£10,000 $\times \dfrac{4}{12}$ (6 December 2008 – 5 April 2009) $\times$ 6.25%	208
	1,458
Less: interest paid	(250)
Taxable benefit	1,208

Solution to Example 10

	£
Salary	35,000
Cheap taxable loan: £24,000 × (6.25 – 2 =) 4.25%	1,020
Employment Income	36,020
Property income: (4,500 – [£24,000 × (4.25 + 2)% × 85%])	3,225
	39,245
Net income	
Less: Personal allowance	(6,035)
Taxable income	33,210

Income tax

	£
£33,210 × 20%	6,642

Solution to Example 11

	£	£
Salary and round sum allowance – employment income		51,000
Less: expense deduction:		
Round sum allowance	1,000	
Less: client entertaining	(150)	
unaccounted	(70)	
		(780)
		50,220

Note. Client entertaining is never deductible as a trading expense.

Solution to Example 12

	£
Compensation payment	50,000
Payment to registered pension scheme – exempt	–
Company car	12,000
Statutory redundancy – exempt	–
	62,000
Less: exemption net of statutory redundancy pay £(30,000 – 6,000)	(24,000)
Assessable	38,000

Short Form Questions:

5.1 – 5.23 inclusive

Long Form Questions:

5.1	Mr Thomas
5.2	Alf
5.3	Mr Bjork
5.4	HiTech computers
5.5	Grovelands
5.6	Mr Morris

6

Tax efficient remuneration

- understand the tax charges for employees receiving shares directly from their employer

- calculate the tax charge for employees receiving shares under an unapproved share option scheme

- identify the various approved employee share schemes and understand when there may be a tax charge

References: ITEPA 2003 unless otherwise stated

1 Share options and incentives

1.1 Introduction

Share schemes are an important element in the remuneration package of key executives. They can provide both a reward for contributions made to the company's success and an incentive to maintain and improve its performance. The legislation provides for beneficial tax treatment for various schemes approved by HMRC.

Share schemes fall into two main categories.

(a)   **Those under which shares are allocated or transferred directly to employees or directors, and**
(b)   **Those which provide for the granting of share options.**

A share option is a right to buy shares in the future at a price fixed at the time the option is granted. Assuming that the market price of the shares either is or will in the future be above the option price, an employee will then be able to acquire shares at a discount to their full value at the time the option is exercised.

In this section, we consider in outline the tax implications of both unapproved and approved share schemes.

1.2 Shares

If an **employee or director obtains shares or securities in a former, current or prospective employer** ('Employment Related Securities') **at below their market value there will be an income tax charge at the date of acquisition based on the difference between market value and the amount paid for the shares, if any.**

1.2.1 Restricted shares

If the shares (or securities) are subject to restrictions that depress their value, such as risk of forfeiture, there will not only be a tax charge on acquisition as above (unless the restriction will cease within 5 years, in which case there is no tax on acquisition), but there will also be a charge (a post-acquisition charge) when the shares are sold or the restriction is lifted within five years.

The post acquisition charge is broadly based on the difference between the unrestricted market value (UMV) (ie the amount a third party would pay if there were no restrictions) and the actual market value (AMV) taking into account the effect of the restrictions.

The employee may jointly elect with their employer to pay any additional tax up front within fourteen days of acquisition of the restricted shares. In this case they will pay income tax on the difference between the UMV and price paid for the shares at acquisition. There will be no income tax on a future sale or when the restriction is lifted and **any future growth will be subject to capital gains tax** (CGT) (see later in this text).

If instead the employee chooses to pay at the later date income tax will be charged on the proportion of the difference between the UMV and AMV at acquisition as a percentage of the current UMV at the later date. The balance will be subject to CGT (see later in this text).

1.2.2 Conversion of convertible securities

Where securities are acquired that are convertible into other securities the value of the right to convert is disregarded at acquisition.

Instead income tax is charged on the gain arising from the conversion. So, if ordinary shares are converted into preference shares the charge is made on the difference in market value between the two types of shares at that date (not any gain arising since acquisition).

1.3 Unapproved share option schemes

Where a person is *granted* an option to buy shares, he is not taxed at the date of the grant of the option.

Where a profit is realised on the *exercise* of a share option, the specific income employment charge is the market value of the shares at the time of the exercise of the option, less both the cost of the shares and the cost of the option where applicable.

Example 1

On 1 December 2008 James exercised options under an unapproved share option scheme run by his employer and acquired 1,000 shares at the option price of £3 per share. The market value at that date was £5 per share.

Calculate the amount assessable to income tax in respect of the exercise of the options.

The base cost of the shares for capital gains tax (CGT) purposes will be the market value at the date of the exercise (see later).

1.4 Approved share schemes

1.4.1 Introduction

There are four types of approved share scheme of which you need to be aware.

(a)   Share incentive plans (SIP)
(b)   Savings-related share option schemes (Save As You Earn or 'SAYE')
(c)   Company share option plans (CSOP)
(d)   Enterprise Management Incentive schemes (EMI)

1.4.2 Share incentive plans (SIPs)

Under a share incentive plan it is possible for employees to avoid not just income tax and NIC but also capital gains tax provided certain conditions are met. It is also possible for employees to buy shares out of their pre-tax remuneration.

The scheme is operated by creating a trust ('the plan') which acquires shares in the employer company using funds from that company. The trustees then award the shares to the employees in accordance with the employer's instructions and hold the shares within the plan on behalf of the individual employees.

There are four ways in which an employee can obtain plan shares. [s.64 Part 8, Sch 2]

(a)   An employer can give up to £3,000 worth of shares (**'free shares'**) to an employee and can make the award of some or all of the shares dependent on reaching pre-set performance targets.

(b)   An employee can be allowed to buy shares (**'partnership shares'**) out of pre-tax remuneration up to a value of the lower of £1,500 per year and 10% of salary to be held within the plan.

(c)   An employer can match the partnership shares bought by the employee by giving him up to 2 free shares (**'matching shares'**) for every partnership share purchased again to be held within the plan.

(d)   An employee can use up to £1,500 of his dividends from the existing plan shares each year to reinvest in further plan shares (**'dividend shares'**).

The employer company must offer all employees (even part-time) the opportunity to participate in the scheme. The company can specify a minimum employment period before an employee is allowed to participate but this must not be greater than 12 months.

Employees must be awarded free shares on similar terms (eg based on level of remuneration or length of service). The award can be conditional on the meeting of performance targets by the employee or his team but the different targets set for different employees must be broadly comparable with a similar chance of being met. There must be no deliberate weighting of rewards in favour of directors and the more highly paid employees.

The tax advantages are summarised in the table below as follows:

	Free shares	Partnership shares	Matching shares	Dividend shares
Tax on award	None	None – tax relief for salary used to buy shares	None	None
Tax on removal of shares from plan within 3 years of award	On market value when taken out	On market value when taken out	On market value when taken out	Original dividend taxable but in year when shares taken out of plan if removed within holding period
Tax on removal between 3 and 5 year of award	On lower of: – value at award; and – value on removal	On lower of: – salary used to buy shares and – value on removal	On lower of: – value at award; and – value on removal	None
Tax on removal after 5 years	None	None	None	None

Employees are only liable to CGT on the increase in value of the shares arising after they have come out of the plan (removal). CGT is therefore avoidable by keeping the shares in the plan until just before the employee sells them.

1.4.3 Savings related share option schemes (SAYE)

An employee or director who is granted rights to acquire shares under an approved savings-related share option scheme is not charged to income tax on the receipt of that right (ie on the grant of the option), nor on the exercise of it (ie when the shares are acquired). Capital gains tax may be payable, the allowable cost being the actual amount paid on exercise (ie cost of shares and option).

Such a scheme must be linked to a contractual savings scheme (an SAYE scheme) to which the employee or director contributes a fixed amount, between £5 (company cannot set minimum at more than £10) and £250 per month for a 3 or 5 year contract. In some cases the contract will last for 7 years but no additional contributions may be made after 5 years.

At the end of the contractual period a repayment of contributions may be taken together with a tax free bonus dependent on the length of the contract. This is used to acquire the shares at the option price.

To be approved, the scheme must satisfy a number of conditions. Principal amongst these is the rule that the price at which shares may be acquired must be stated when the option is obtained and must be no less than 80% of the market value at that time.

1.4.4 Approved company share option plans (CSOP)

This scheme need not be made available to all employees.

There are no income tax charges on the grant or exercise of the CSOP option, and no charge on the growth in value of the shares.

The only charge will be to capital gains tax on the eventual disposal of the shares on the difference between the market value at sale and the exercise price paid for the shares.

There is no minimum time that the employee must hold the shares after exercising his option and before selling the shares, so that the cost of exercising the option can effectively be funded from the sale proceeds. The scheme is not linked to any SAYE scheme, and is much more flexible than the savings-related scheme (see 1.4.3 above).

The maximum value of shares any one person can have under option at any time is £30,000.

The options must not be exercisable less than 3 years from the date of grant.

The price at which the shares are acquired must not be manifestly less than their market value at the date the option is grated.

1.4.5 Enterprise Management Incentives (EMIs)

The EMI scheme enables small trading companies to attract and retain high calibre staff. There are similarities with the approved company share option plans (CSOP) (see 1.4.4 above) but the reliefs are more carefully targeted and the conditions harder to satisfy.

Under an EMI scheme a **trading company** with **gross assets not exceeding £30 million** can award **key employees** with **share options worth up to £120,000 each** at the time the option is granted. The maximum value of options which may be granted at any time under an EMI scheme is £3 million.

There will be **no tax on the grant of an option** under an EMI scheme. Additionally, there will be **no income tax or NIC charged on the employee when the options are exercised** provided that the exercise price is set at the market value of the shares at the date of grant. There will be a charge to income tax where the options were granted at a discount, on the difference between the exercise price and the market value of the shares when the options were granted. The shares will be subject to CGT when sold.

The scheme is administratively simple to operate. There is no approval procedure to follow. Instead, the company enters into a share option agreement with each employee separately and notifies the details to HMRC within 92 days.

The company must comply with certain further conditions. Principally it must be carrying on a trade which would qualify under the EIS rules (see Chapter 4).

From 6 April 2008, the schemes are restricted to companies with less than 250 full-time equivalent employees.

Chapter roundup

- Where shares are obtained in an employer company at below their market value there will usually be an income tax charge.

- There is no charge to income tax when share options are granted under an unapproved share option scheme. However, gains realised on the *exercise* of an unapproved share option are subject to income tax, based on the market value of the shares acquired less the cost of the shares and the option.

- A SIP allows employees to acquire shares in their employer company whilst avoiding income tax, NIC and capital gains tax. Employees can obtain free shares from the employer, purchase partnership shares from pre-tax salary, the employer can match the partnership shares, and dividends can be reinvested in further shares.

- An SAYE scheme must be linked to a contractual savings scheme, which is used to acquire shares on exercise of an option, and be available to all employees. The exercise price must be at least 80% of the market value of the shares at the date of grant. There is no income tax on grant or exercise but capital gains tax may be charged on a disposal of any shares acquired under such a scheme

- Under the CSOP scheme there is no charge to income tax when the options are granted nor when the options are exercised.

- Under an EMI scheme options over shares worth up to £120,000 per employee may be granted, up to a maximum of £3 million. There is no tax charge on the grant of the option, and a charge will only arise on exercise if the option price is less than the market value of the shares at the time the options were granted.

1. Emma, Fiona and Gillian all participate in their employer's approved share incentive plan. On 1 June 2006 they were each awarded free shares worth £3,000.

    Assume they withdraw their shares as follows.

	Date withdrawn	Value when withdrawn £
Emma	1 May 2009	3,500
Fiona	1 July 2009	3,650
Gillian	1 July 2011	4,000

    Which withdrawals will suffer an income tax charge and on what value? Give your reasons.

2. On 1 November 2008, Dean exercised options in a share option scheme run by his employer and acquired 2,000 shares at the exercise price of £4 per share. The market value at that date was £6 per share.

    Calculate the income tax liability as a result of the above assuming Dean is a higher rate taxpayer and

    (a) The scheme has HMRC approval, or
    (b) The scheme is unapproved.

Solutions to Quiz

1. Emma: charge on £3,500
    Withdrawal within 3 years

    Fiona: charge on £3,000 (lower of value on award and on withdrawal)
    Withdrawal 3 – 5 years

    Gillian: no charge
    Withdrawal after 5 years

2. (a) No IT due on exercise of shares in an approved scheme

    (b) Income tax on exercise

	£
MV of shares at exercise (£6 × 2,000)	12,000
Less exercise price (£4 × 2,000)	(8,000)
	4,000

    IT due @ 40% = 1,600

Solution to chapter example

Solution to Example 1

	£
Market value at exercise (£5 × 1,000)	5,000
Exercise price (£3 × 1,000)	(3,000)
Amount subject to income tax	2,000

Now try the following questions

Short Form Questions:

6.1 – 6.3 inclusive

Long Form Question:

6.1	Sue

6: Tax efficient remuneration | Part A Personal Income tax

7

Pensions

- understand the tax treatment of pensions
- calculate and explain the tax relief available for pension contributions
- understand the tax consequences of taking funds out of a pension at retirement age

References: FA 2004 unless otherwise stated

1 Introduction

1.1 Types of pension

From 6 April 2006 the same set of rules apply to all personal and employer provided pensions.

An employer may set up an occupational pension scheme for its employees. The scheme may either require contributions from employees or be 'non-contributory'. The employer may use the services of an insurance company (an insured scheme) or may set up a totally self administered pension fund.

In all other cases **any individual with or without earnings, or even without any taxable income, can pay into a personal pension**. An employee can contribute to both their employer's occupational pension scheme and a personal pension scheme, subject to the rules below.

1.2 Taxation of the pension fund

The premiums (ie contributions) go into a fund that is invested and is ultimately used to provide a pension.

Income and gains within the pension are not liable to tax. It might help to think of a pension fund as a tax-free wrapper around any investments within the fund.

1.3 State pension

Individuals can also provide for a pension by contributing to the state pension scheme through their National Insurance Contributions (NICs). The state scheme has no impact on income tax during an individual's working career.

2 Contributions

2.1 Introduction

An individual can contribute to any number of pension schemes, out of both income or capital, and to both occupational and personal schemes, so long as he stays within the contribution limits (see below).

The payments can even be made on behalf of another (eg a parent for a child, or a husband for a wife).

There are two main restrictions on the amount of contributions that can be made into a pension scheme: the annual allowance and the lifetime allowance.

2.2 Annual allowance

The '**annual allowance**' is effectively the maximum amount that can be paid into a pension tax-free each year during the pension input period. The annual allowance for 2008/09 is £235,000 and is given to you in the Association's tax tables.

The **pension input period** is normally the period of 12 months commencing on the date of the first contribution to the scheme and each anniversary thereafter. The end date of the pension input period will determine the tax year that the excess value will be tested against the annual allowance.

If more than this allowance is paid into the pension there is a tax charge of 40% on the extra that must be included on the individual's self assessment tax return.

The annual allowance charge does not apply in the year benefits are taken (see below).

2.3 Lifetime allowance

The '**lifetime allowance**' is the maximum amount that can be accumulated in a pension during lifetime. The lifetime allowance for 2008/09 is £1.65 million and is given to you in the Association's tax tables.

If this amount is exceeded there is a tax charge when benefits are taken from the fund. If the benefit is taken as a lump sum the charge on the excess is 55%, otherwise the income tax charge is 25%. The tax charge is added to the tax payer's tax liability which has been calculated on their income to arrive at their total tax liability for the year (see Chapter 1 section 9)

Individuals whose pension funds exceeded the lifetime allowance at 6 April 2006 (£1.5 million) could register a claim with HMRC on or before 5 April 2009 to protect their existing rights.

3 Tax relief

3.1 Amount of tax relief

Each year, tax relief is available to an individual for pension contributions up to the higher of:

(a)   **100 per cent of relevant earnings (salary and other earned income) subject to the 'annual allowance' (see above), and**

(b)   **£3,600.**

3.2 Obtaining tax relief *(gross)*

3.2.1 Occupational pension schemes

→ no need for expansion of basic rate as already retrieved via deducting from salary pre-tax

Occupational pension scheme contributions may be made gross. The gross amount of the contributions is deducted from employment income on the face of the income tax computation.

Employers however often operate net pay arrangements ie they deduct gross pension contributions from the employee's earnings before operating PAYE. The individual therefore obtains basic and higher rate tax relief, if appropriate at source.

Contributions paid by the employer are deductible for the employer in calculating their taxable profits. These **employer's contributions are not taxable benefits for the employee**. They are added to the employee's own contributions when determining if the annual allowance has been exceeded.

Provision can be made for a tax free lump sum to be paid on the employee's retirement or death in service.

An employee who feels that his employer's scheme is inadequate may make additional voluntary contributions (AVCs), either to the employer's scheme or to a separate scheme operated by an insurance company (freestanding AVCs). These are deductible from the employee's taxable pay, but only to the extent that they, plus any contributions by the employee to the employer's scheme, do not exceed the maximum amount that qualifies for tax relief (see above).

Freestanding AVCs are paid net of basic rate tax.

3.2.2 Personal pension schemes *(NET)*

→ relief gained by extending basic rate band

All contributions made to personal pension schemes are paid net of basic rate tax. The pension company then recovers the basic rate tax from HMRC. So, for every £80 contributed in a tax year, the government will contribute a further £20. In this way all taxpayers obtain basic rate tax relief.

Higher rate tax relief is obtained by increasing a higher rate taxpayer's basic rate tax band by the amount of the gross contribution (like we did with Gift Aid in Chapter 1 section 7.2).

Even those with no or little income can contribute up to £3,600 to a personal pension scheme each year.

Exam focus point

Do not confuse the way in which tax relief is obtained for the two different types of pensions. Personal pension scheme contributions are paid **net** and relief is given at source and by extending the basic rate band of higher rate taxpayers. Occupational pension scheme contributions are usually made **gross**, out of pre-tax salary, so relief is given immediately at the employee's highest tax rate.

Example 1

Darren has self employment earnings of £300,000 for the tax year 2008/09 and makes gross contributions of £240,000 to his registered personal pension scheme during the year.

Required

(a) State the maximum amount of gross pension contributions for which Darren will be entitled to tax relief and the actual amount he will have paid into the pension during the year.

(b) Explain how tax relief is given for pension payments and calculate his income tax liability for 2008/09.

4 Drawing a pension

4.1 Pension age

Employees can draw part of their pension from a company scheme whilst they are still working full or part time for the same employer so long as they have reached the requisite age.

From 2010 the minimum age for receiving a pension will rise from 50 to 55. For women the state pension age will rise gradually from 60 to 65 between 2010 and 2020.

4.2 Tax free lump sum

Individuals can usually take a tax-free lump sum of as much as 25% of their pension fund, subject to a maximum of 25% × the lifetime allowance.

The tax free lump sum is not available once the investor reaches age 75.

4.3 Balance of the pension fund

There are a number of alternative ways of taking the balance of the pension fund.

(a)   Take a scheme pension – secure for life
(b)   Buy an annuity – providing a regular income for life
(c)   Draw income directly from the pension (an unsecured pension) up to age 75
(d)   Draw income directly from the pension as an 'alternatively secured pension' (ASV) up to age 75

Drawing income means that regular income may be withdrawn from the pension fund while the fund remains invested.

An **Alternatively Secured Pension** (ASV) allows the investor to draw an income from the pension fund without buying a lifetime annuity. The maximum income available for withdrawal each year will be 70% of a level single-life lifetime annuity. The alternatively secured pension can be converted into a lifetime annuity at any time.

4.4 Taxation of pension income

Apart from the tax free lump sum (above) all other income taken from a pension (including the state pension) is taxed as non-savings income.

Chapter roundup

- Employees can contribute to their employer's occupational pension scheme and/ or a personal pension. Other individuals can only contribute to a personal pension.

- Income and gains within a pension are tax free. The pension is effectively a tax-free wrapper.

- Contributions can be made on behalf of another person and out of income or capital.

- The 'annual allowance' is the maximum amount that can be paid into a pension tax-free each year. In 2008/09 this is £235,000. Contributions in excess of the annual allowance are taxed on the individual tax payer at 40%.

- The 'lifetime allowance' is the maximum amount that can be accumulated in a pension during lifetime. In 2008/09 this is £1.65m.

- Tax relief for pension contributions made by individuals is given on the higher of 100% of relevant earnings and £3,600.

- Occupational pension scheme contributions are often paid gross. Tax relief, at basic and higher rates, is obtained by deducting the contributions from taxable employment income.

- Contributions paid by employers are deductible for the employer and count towards the annual and lifetime allowances.

- Additional voluntary contributions (AVCs) can be made either to the employer scheme or separate scheme.

- Basic rate tax relief on personal pension schemes is given by HMRC who add the additional 20% to the scheme as the payments are paid in net. Higher rate relief is also given to higher rate taxpayers by extending the basic rate tax band.

- When drawing a pension a lump sum of up to 25% × the fund is available. There is flexibility regarding how to take the balance of the pension.

- The pension on retirement is treated as non-savings income of the taxpayer.

Quiz

1. What is the maximum amount that can be contributed by an individual to a pension for which tax relief is available?

2. What is the lifetime allowance for 2008/09? When must a pre-6 April 2006 pension fund in excess of this be registered by to avoid a tax charge?

TQT
Tax Qualification Training

Solutions to Quiz

1. The higher of:

    £3,600 and 100% × relevant earnings.

2. £1,650,000. Register pre-6 April 2006 fund by 5 April 2009.

Solution to chapter example

Solution to Example 1

(a) As Darren's earnings are £300,000, all of the contributions of £240,000 qualify for tax relief.

    He will have paid £192,000 (£240,000 less 20%) to the pension company.

(b) Basic rate tax relief has been given at source. Higher rate tax relief will be given by extending Darren's basic rate tax band for 2008/09 to £274,800 (34,800 + 240,000).

    However, there will be tax charge at the rate of 40% on the excess of his contributions above the annual allowance of £235,000.

    His income tax liability for the tax year 2008/09 is:

	£
Trading profit	300,000
Personal allowance	(6,035)
Taxable income	293,965
Income tax:	
£274,800 at 20%	54,960
£19,165 at 40%	7,666
	62,626
Add: excess contribution charge	
£5,000 (240,000 − 235,000) at 40%	2,000
Tax liability	64,626

> Now try the following questions

Short Form Questions:

7.1 – 7.6 inclusive

Long Form Questions:

7.1	Mr Matthews (Pilot Paper)
7.2	Ed & Joan
7.3	Dwaine Pipe

8

Overseas matters

The purpose of this chapter is to help you to:

- define the terms residence, ordinary residence and domicile and explain their significance

- outline the scope and basis of assessment of overseas income

- calculate double taxation relief

References: ITTOIA 2005 unless otherwise stated

1 Residence, ordinary residence and domicile

1.1 Introduction

In Chapter 1 of this Study Text we explained that a taxpayer's *residence, ordinary residence* and *domicile* had important consequences in establishing the treatment of his UK and overseas income. The rules are now set out in detail.

Exam focus point

The broad definitions of residence, ordinary residence and domicile which follow are derived from statute, case law and HMRC practice. HMRC publish a booklet (IR20) from which the definitions below are taken. You will find extracts from IR20 in the miscellaneous section of your tax legislation.

1.2 Residence and ordinary residence

1.2.1 Residence

A person is deemed to be resident in the UK for a given tax year if, in that tax year, he is present in the UK for a total of 183 days or more. There are no exceptions to this.

It is possible to be regarded as UK resident for a tax year even if the individual spends less than 183 days in the UK.

(a) Individuals leaving the UK for short periods remain UK resident if they usually live in the UK. Non-residence would generally only be achieved by complete absence from the UK for the tax year.

(b) Individuals leaving the UK permanently are treated as remaining UK resident if visits to the UK average 91 days or more each year.

(c) **Visitors to the UK** are treated as UK resident for a tax year if visits are regular and, **after four tax years**, **visits have averaged 91 days or more pa**. Residence applies for the fifth year onwards. However, a visitor to the UK is treated as UK resident from the start of the first tax year if it is clear from the outset that the 91 days pa average of visits to the UK is intended. If a decision is made to make visits in excess of 91 days pa on average then the visitor is treated as UK resident from the start of the tax year of the decision. *— intention changes within the year the residence changes*

(d) Short term visitors coming for a period of at least two years employment in the UK are treated as UK resident *from* from the day of arrival to the day of departure. *start of year.*

For the purpose of the 91 day test above, days which are spent in the UK because of exceptional circumstances beyond the individual's control (eg illness) are excluded from the calculation.

From 2008/09, when calculating UK days for the purposes of the 183 day or 91 day tests, any days where the individual is present in the UK at midnight are counted. (There is an exception for days spent in transit between two countries outside the UK, which are not counted provided the individual does not engage in activities which are to a substantial extent unrelated to passage through the UK eg business meetings).

1.2.2 Ordinary residence

A person who is resident in the UK will be deemed to be ordinarily resident where his residence is of a habitual nature. Ordinary residence implies a greater degree of permanence than mere residence. A person, being deemed by HMRC to be ordinarily resident, may appeal to the Special Commissioners within three months of HMRC's decision. The significance of ordinary residence is principally in connection with overseas income.

1.2.3 Splitting the tax year

Strictly, each tax year must be looked at as a whole: a person is resident and/or ordinarily resident for either no part, or all, of the tax year, depending on the circumstances. Thus a person who is ordinarily resident in the UK and who goes abroad for a period which does not include a complete tax year, is regarded as remaining resident and ordinarily resident in the UK throughout. **It is the practice by concession, however, to split the tax year if the person**:

(a) Is a **new permanent resident** or comes to stay for at least three years, provided he was previously not ordinarily resident, or

(b) **Comes to the UK to take up employment for a period which is expected to be at least two years**. Again, the concessionary treatment is available only to an individual who was not ordinarily resident in the UK prior to his arrival, or

(c) Has **left the UK for permanent residence abroad**, provided that he becomes not ordinarily resident in the UK, or

(d) (i)   **Is proceeding abroad to take up employment which covers at least a whole tax year**, and

    (ii) Interim visits to the UK do not amount to 183 days or more in any one tax year or 91 days or more on average.

A spouse/civil partner's residence and ordinary residence status is quite independent of their partner's status and is determined by their own circumstances. If, for example, a husband is employed abroad full-time, and his wife goes out to join him but later returns to the UK without having been away for a complete tax year, she is regarded as remaining resident and ordinarily resident here although he may be neither resident nor ordinarily resident.

HMRC will generally decide whether an individual is full-time employed on the basis of the particular circumstances of his employment and are not prepared to issue blanket guidelines.

1.2.4 Coming to the UK

A person whose home has previously been abroad and who comes to the UK to take up permanent residence here is regarded as resident and ordinarily resident from the date of his arrival.

A person who comes to the UK to work for a period of at least two years is treated as resident here for the whole period from arrival to departure. **If he does not initially intend to stay for at least three years and does not buy accommodation or take a lease on accommodation exceeding three years, he is treated as becoming ordinarily resident from the start of the tax year following the third anniversary of his arrival**. This rule applies whether the individual comes for employment in the UK or for some other purpose.

If an individual comes to the UK and, before the point at which the above rule would impose ordinary residence, he either buys or takes a greater than three year lease on accommodation, or **changes his intention on the length of his stay in the UK, he will become ordinarily resident**:

(a)   **from the date of first arrival if the relevant event occurs in his first tax year in the UK**; or
(b)   **from the start of the tax year in which the event occurs**.

For example, if Hans arrived in the UK on 1 October 2008 intending only to stay for 30 months, he will become ordinarily resident in 2012/13 if he still remains in the UK by then. If he bought a house in the UK in December 2008 he would be ordinarily resident for 2008/09 (from 1 October 2008). However, if he delayed buying a house until July 2009 he would not become ordinarily resident until 2009/10.

1.3 Domicile

Broadly speaking, a person is domiciled in the country in which he has his permanent home. Domicile is distinct from nationality or residence. A person may be resident in more than one country, but at any given time he can only be domiciled in one. **A person acquires a *domicile of origin* at birth; this is normally the domicile of his father** and therefore not necessarily the country where he himself was born. **A person retains this domicile until he acquires a different *domicile of choice*.** A domicile of choice can be acquired only by individuals aged 16 or over.

If, before reaching that age, **the person** (ie father) **whose domicile determined the minor's own domicile, acquires a new domicile of choice**, the minor's domicile changes similarly – *domicile of dependency*.

To acquire a domicile of choice a person must sever his ties with the country of his domicile of origin and settle in another country with the clear intention of making his permanent home there. Long residence in another country is not in itself enough to prove that a person has acquired a domicile of choice there unless it can be regarded as indicating intention; there has to be evidence that he firmly intends to live there permanently.

Example 1

Cedric, who has lived in Wales all his life, is now aged 44. He plans to spend the next 20 years in France, selling his house in Wales and transferring all of his assets to France. He will then return to Wales to retire. When will he become non-UK domiciled?

1.4 Taxation of income

Generally, **a UK resident** is **liable to UK income tax on his UK and foreign income** whereas a **non-resident is liable to UK income tax only on income arising in the UK** ie income received during the tax year. Generally, UK residents enjoy personal allowances whilst usually non-residents do not (but see Chapter 1).

However for individuals who are **not resident, for the whole of the tax year, tax on UK interest income is limited to the tax deducted at source.** Where interest is received gross, e.g. NSB accounts, the interest is not taxed and where interest is received net e.g. bank interest, the tax liability is limited to the basic rate deducted at source.

Non-resident individuals who are **also not ordinarily resident** in the UK **may apply to receive bank and building society interest gross and therefore will have no UK tax liability on their UK interest.**

All gilt edged securities are automatically given FOTRA (Free of Tax to Residents Abroad) status thereby giving exemption from tax for investors who are not ordinarily resident in the UK.

A UK resident who is not domiciled in the UK can claim to be taxed on their foreign income on a *remittance basis* only – ie only to the extent that such income is brought to the UK. The remittance basis for foreign income also applies to British subjects resident but not ordinarily resident in the UK. [s.831]

1.5 Remittance basis

This section is new.

1.5.1 General provisions

The remittance basis can be claimed by persons who are:

(a) **Non-UK domiciled**, or
(b) **Not ordinarily resident**.

Individuals who make the claim are known as 'remittance basis users' (RBUs). If they do not make the claim, the arising basis applies to their foreign income. A claim for the remittance basis must be made in respect of each tax year.

A claim is not required however (ie the remittance basis applies automatically) where:

(a) **The individual is not UK domiciled or not ordinarily UK resident in the tax year and has unremitted income and gains below £2,000**, or [s.809D ITA 2007]

(b) **The individual**

   (i)   **Is not UK domiciled or not ordinarily resident**
   (ii)   **Has no UK income or gains for the tax year**
   (iii) **Does not remit any foreign income or gains in the tax year and**
   (iv)   **Either – has been resident in not more than 6 of the 9 preceding tax years or**
            – is under 18 throughout the year. [s.809E ITA 2007]

If the remittance basis applies, foreign dividends and foreign interest are not treated as savings income, ie the income is always taxed as non savings income at 20% and 40%. [s.1A(4) ICTA 1988]

1.5.2 Additional remittance basis charge

Where an individual claims the remittance basis for a tax year and the individual is:

–   aged 18 or over in the tax year and
–   has been UK resident in at least 7 of the 9 preceding tax years

They are subject to a remittance basis charge (RBC) of £30,000. The £30,000 charge is in addition to any tax due on remitted income and gains. Those individuals to which the remittance basis applies automatically (see 1.5.1) are not subject to the £30,000 RBC.

The individual must 'nominate' to which of his unremitted income (and/or gains) the charge relates. When he makes remittances in the future they will be treated as coming from un-nominated income and gains *before* nominated income and gains. When nominated income or gains are remitted to the UK in the future they are not taxed again. **[s.809G ITA 2007]**

Example 2

Sophia is UK resident but not UK domiciled. She receives overseas bank interest of £250,000 (gross) during the tax year but only remits £50,000 to the UK. She has no unremitted gains and makes a remittance basis claim for the year. She is a higher rate taxpayer and has been UK resident for the last ten years.

You are required to calculate Sophia's income tax liability. Ignore double tax relief.

1.5.3 When is income remitted to the UK?

An 'actual' remittance takes place where actual monies are brought into the UK. Remittances of capital are not taxed as income. For this reason it is essential that RBUs keep foreign income and capital in separate bank accounts, and remit only from the capital account.

A remittance can also occur in certain other situations, for example when assets representing the monies are brought into the UK. **This is known as a 'constructive' remittance.**

1.6 Summary

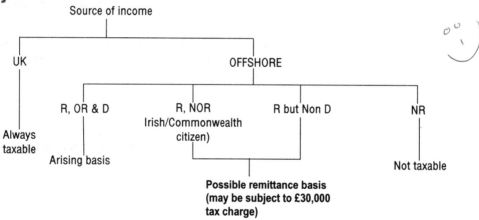

2 Overseas income

2.1 Introduction

The most common examples of overseas income, which are covered in further detail below, are:

(a)   Interest from foreign savings institutions
(b)   Dividends from overseas companies
(c)   Rent from property abroad, and
(d)   Foreign pension income.

The detail for employment income from duties carried on abroad and partnership or trade profits from a business carried on and controlled wholly outside the UK are not in the Personal Taxation syllabus.

2.2 Basis of assessment

The same basis of assessment applies for foreign income as for UK income, eg the receipts basis for foreign savings income and the accruals basis for foreign property income.

The remittance basis (ie only income brought into the UK is taxed) can be claimed by:

(a)   Persons not *domiciled* in the UK, and
(b)   British subjects not *ordinarily resident* in the UK.

This was explained in section 1.4.

If the remittance basis applies all income, including foreign dividends and interest, are treated as non-savings income in the tax computation ie taxed at the basic rate of 20% and higher rate of 40%..

2.3 Overseas savings income

The charge to income tax on foreign source savings income follows the same rules as for UK savings income. So foreign interest or dividends falling within the basic rate band are taxable at 20% or 10% respectively and foreign dividends falling in the higher rate band are taxed at 32½% (unless the remittance basis applies – see above).

Previously only UK dividends came with a 10% non-refundable tax credit. From 6 April 2008 this tax credit is also available to individuals receiving dividends from non UK resident companies where they own less than 10% of the shares.

Any foreign tax paid on foreign source income is allowed as a credit up to the amount of the UK tax due on that income (see below).

2.4 Income from overseas property

The income tax treatment of income from property situated outside the UK is computed using the same rules as for UK property income (See Chapter 3).

All income arising from overseas property – even if in different countries – is treated as derived from a single business which is separate and distinct from any UK property income. Therefore, there is no possibility of obtaining relief for a UK property loss against overseas rental income, or *vice versa*.

2.5 Foreign pensions

If a person is taxable on an arising basis only 90% of the foreign pension income arising is taxable.

If the remittance basis applies, the full amount remitted is taxable.

3 Double taxation relief (DTR)

3.1 Introduction

As we have seen, **UK tax applies to the worldwide income of UK residents and the UK income of non-residents.**

When other countries adopt the same approach it is clear that some **income may be taxed twice**:

(a)   **Firstly in the country where it arises**
(b)   **Secondly in the country where the taxpayer resides**

Double taxation relief (DTR) may avoid the problem, or at least diminish its impact.

3.2 Double taxation agreements

Typical provisions of double taxation agreements based on the OECD Model Agreement are as follows.

(a)   Total exemption from tax is given in the country where income arises in the hands of, for example:

(i)   Visiting diplomats
(ii)   Teachers on exchange programmes

(b) Preferential rates of withholding tax are applied to, for example, payments of rent, interest and dividends. The usual rate is frequently replaced by 15% or less

(c) DTR is given to taxpayers in their country of residence by way of a credit for tax suffered in the country where income arises

(d) There are exchange of information clauses so that tax evaders can be chased internationally

(e) There are rules to determine a person's residence and to prevent dual residence (tie-breaker clauses)

(f) There are clauses which render certain profits taxable in only one rather than both of the contracting states

(g) There is a non-discrimination clause so that a country does not tax foreigners more heavily than its own nationals

3.3 Unilateral relief

If no relief is available under a double taxation agreement, UK legislation provides for unilateral relief.

Foreign income must be included gross (ie inclusive of foreign tax) in the UK tax computation. A deduction is then available for the lower of:

(a) **The UK tax**
(b) **The foreign tax**

The UK tax on the foreign income is the difference between:

(a) The UK tax before DTR on all income including the foreign income
(b) The UK tax on all income except the foreign income

In both (a) and (b), we take account of tax reductions.

Exam focus point

Examiner's report – Personal Taxation

May 2007 – Part 11 Question 1

Many candidates did not appreciate the restriction on double tax relief.

Example 3

Jane is resident, ordinarily resident and domiciled in the UK. She has the following income for 2008/09.

	£
UK salary	33,312
Interest on foreign debenture (net of foreign tax at 5%)	5,700
Foreign rents (net of foreign tax at 60%)	1,500

Assuming that maximum DTR is claimed, show her UK tax liability.

3.4 Expense relief

Where there is no point in claiming credit relief as above, perhaps because trading losses have eliminated any liability to UK tax, the taxpayer may elect for expense relief instead. No credit is given against the UK tax liability for foreign tax suffered, instead only the income *after* foreign taxes is brought into the tax computation.

3.5 Other matters

If foreign taxes are not relieved in the year in which the income is taxable in the UK, no relief can be obtained in any earlier or later year.

Credit relief, whether under a treaty or unilateral, is ignored when working out the tax which remains to be reduced by tax reductions.

Taxpayers who have claimed relief against their UK tax bill for taxes paid abroad must notify HMRC in writing of any changes to the foreign liabilities if these changes result in the DTR claimed becoming excessive. This rule applies to all taxes not just income tax.

Exam focus point

Examiner's report – Personal Taxation (old syllabus)

May 2000 – Question 5

This was the least popular question to answer, and although there were a few good answers, the majority were confused over the difference living abroad would make to the UK tax liability of Mr and Mrs Little. Very few explained the basis of determining the UK residence status of an individual or the taxation of rental income for an overseas landlord. Most candidates explained the position regarding personal allowances correctly, and the taxation of foreign income on returning to the UK.

However, several candidates wasted time explaining the potential capital gains tax liability on the rental properties when this was not required by the question.

Chapter roundup

- An individual is resident the UK if:
    - he is present in the UK for 183 days or more in the tax year, or
    - he makes substantial and habitual visits to the UK which *average* 91 days or more a year for each *of four* consecutive tax years.
- Usually an individual is resident or not resident for a complete tax year, but HMRC will split a tax year in the following three cases:
    - permanent emigration
    - permanent immigration or arriving for employment lasting for at least two years
    - going abroad under a full-time contract of employment lasting a complete tax year (interim visits < 183 days/91 days on average).
- An individual becomes ordinarily resident if:
    - he has been resident for three tax years, or
    - he has just taken up residence in the UK and appears likely to remain resident in the UK for the next three years.
- An individual becomes ordinarily resident from the start of the tax year following the third anniversary of arrival or from the start of the tax year of the relevant event (eg buying a house in UK) if earlier.
- Domicile indicates one's permanent home.
    - *Domicile of origin:* an individual's father's domicile is his first domicile.
    - *Domicile of dependence:* a minor child (< 16) changes his domicile if his father changes his domicile.

- *Domicile of choice:* an adult can change his domicile if he clearly renounces his existing domicile, but this is difficult to establish.

- An individual who is UK resident, ordinarily resident and UK domiciled is liable to UK income tax on all income (UK and overseas) on an arising basis.

- An individual who is UK resident but not UK domiciled is liable to UK income tax on

  - UK income – arising basis

  - Overseas income – arising basis unless remittance basis claimed (or applies automatically)

- An individual claiming the remittance basis who has been UK resident in seven out of the preceding nine tax years will be subject to a £30,000 tax charge on unremitted foreign income and gains.

- An individual who is not UK resident is only liable to UK income tax on income arising in the UK.

- UK interest paid gross to a non resident is tax free.

- Income from overseas property is taxed using the same rules as for UK property income. Losses on UK property income cannot be set against profit on overseas property income or vice versa.

- Double tax relief (DTR) is available where income is taxed both in the UK and in another country.

Quiz

1. Meredith is domiciled in the state of New York, but resident and ordinarily resident in the UK since 2005. To what extent is Meredith charged to UK income tax on rental income from letting a property in New York?

2. Hector, who is resident, ordinarily resident and domiciled in the UK, receives a pension of £8,000 per annum from his former employer, a Canadian company based in Montreal. Hector used to work in Montreal.

    To what extent is Hector charged to UK income tax on the pension?

Solutions to Quiz

1. Meredith can make a claim for the remittance basis to supply such that only the rental income remitted to the UK is taxed. The £30,000 annual charge will not apply in 2008/09 as Meredith has not been resident in the UK for seven out of the nine years preceding 2008/09.

2. Hector is charged on an arising basis, but on only 90% (ie £7,200) of the full amount.

Solutions to chapter examples

Solution to Example 1

Cedric will not become non-UK domiciled, because he intends to return to the UK.

Solution to Example 2

Sophia is taxable on the remitted income and is also subject to the £30,000 charge. She must nominate (£30,000 ÷ 40% =) £75,000 of her unremitted income of the year for the charge. She can bring this income into the UK in the future without triggering a tax charge.

She does not receive a personal allowance because she is a remittance basis user.

	£
Tax on remitted income: £50,000 × 40%	20,000
Add: remittance basis charge	30,000

| Total income tax due | | | 50,000 |

Solution to Example 3

	Non-savings £	Savings £	Total £
Salary	33,312		
Overseas interest £5,700 × 100/95		6,000	
Overseas rents £1,500 × 100/40	3,750		
Net income	37,062	6,000	43,062
Less personal allowance	(6,035)		(6,035)
Taxable income	31,027	6,000	37,027

	£
Non-savings income	
£31,027 × 20%	6,205
Savings income	
£3,773 × 20%	755
£2,227 × 40%	891
Tax liability	7,851
Less: double taxation relief	
Rents (see below)	1,196
Interest (see below)	300
	(1,496)
Tax due	6,355

Since the rents are taxed more highly overseas, these should be regarded as the top slice of UK taxable income. Taxable income excluding the rents is £33,277 and the UK tax on this is:

	£
£33,277 × 20%	6,655

The UK tax on the rents is £1,196 (£7,851 − 6,655). Since foreign tax of £2,250 (60% of £3,750) is greater, the DTR is the smaller figure of £1,196. Foreign interest was taxed abroad at the rate of 5% (£300). Since the UK rate is clearly higher (taxed at 20%) the DTR given is limited to £300.

Now try the following questions

Short Form Questions:

8.1 – 8.4 inclusive

Long Form Question:

8.1	Ricardo Garcia

Personal Taxation

Part B:
Capital Gains Tax

- identify the basic charging provision and basis of assessment to CGT
- set out the rate of CGT
- identify chargeable persons, occasions and assets
- identify exempt assets
- outline the rules for payment of CGT
- identify the overseas aspects of CGT

References: TCGA 1992 unless otherwise stated

Outline of CGT

Finance Act 2008 made significant changes to the capital gains tax regime. The rules set out in the following CGT chapters are the current rules which apply to disposals by individuals on or after 6 April 2008.

1 The charge to tax

1.1 Basic charging provision

CGT is charged on the total amount of chargeable gains made by a chargeable person in a tax year after deducting:

(a) Any allowable losses accruing to that person in the same year of assessment, and

(b) To the extent that they have not been set off in the previous year of assessment, any allowable capital losses brought forward from earlier years.

Capital losses are dealt with further in Chapter 10.

1.2 Basis of assessment

UK resident or ordinarily resident individuals are liable to CGT on the disposal of assets situated anywhere in the world. The concepts of residence and ordinary residence have the same meaning as for income tax purposes.

1.3 Rate of CGT

For individuals there is an annual exemption for each tax year. For 2008/09 it is £9,600. The annual exemption is deducted from total chargeable gains to give the taxable gain in the tax year.

The taxable gain is then taxed at a flat rate of **18%**.

Example 1

In 2008/09, Carol has chargeable gains, before the annual exemption, of £25,000. How much CGT is payable by her on these gains.

Individuals who claim to be taxed on a remittance basis (eg because they are non-UK domiciled) will not be entitled to an annual exemption.

2 Chargeable persons, disposals and assets

2.1 Persons chargeable to CGT

The following are examples of persons chargeable to CGT:

(a) Individuals
(b) Partners (who are individually responsible for their share of partnership gains)
(c) Trustees.

The following are examples of persons exempt from CGT:

(a) Charities using gains for charitable purposes
(b) Registered pension funds
(c) Persons who are neither resident nor ordinarily resident in the UK
(d) Authorised unit and investment trusts

2.2 Disposals chargeable to CGT

A chargeable disposal includes:

(a) A sale of an asset or part of an asset
(b) A gift of all or part of an asset
(c) The receipt of insurance proceeds on the loss or destruction of an asset
(d) The receipt of a capital sum following the surrender of rights to an asset, and
(e) The appropriation of an asset to trading stock.

A chargeable disposal occurs on the date of contract, which may in some circumstances differ from the date of actual transfer. Where the contract is conditional, the date of disposal is taken as the date on which the condition is satisfied. However, when a capital sum is received under (c) or (d) above, the disposal takes place on the day the sum is *received*.

Where a disposal involves an acquisition by someone else ((a) or (b) above), the date of acquisition for the recipient of the asset is the same as the date of disposal.

The following are not treated as disposals:

(a) Passing of assets on death (the heirs inherit assets as if they bought them at death for their then market values, but there is no disposal for the deceased on the death)
(b) Transfers of assets as security for a loan or mortgage.

Gifts to charities and housing associations are generally not chargeable to CGT.

2.3 Assets chargeable to CGT

All forms of property, wherever in the world they are situated, are chargeable assets for CGT purposes unless they are specifically designated as non-chargeable by the legislation.

Gains on disposal of the following assets are exempt:

(a)   Motor vehicles suitable for private use

(b)   NS&I certificates, premium bonds and SAYE deposits

(c)   Foreign currency for private use

(d)   Betting and lottery winnings

(e)   Decorations awarded for bravery (unless purchased)

(f)   Damages for personal or professional injury

(g)   Life assurance policies (exempt in the hands of the original beneficial owner)

(h)   Works of art, scientific collections etc provided they are of national importance and are given for national purposes (breach of any conditions imposed will nullify the CGT exemption)

(i)   Principal (or main) private residence

(j)   Gilt-edged securities (ie Treasury stock) and qualifying corporate bonds (loan stock)

(k)   Wasting chattels (tangible movable property with a life of 50 years or less, eg a racehorse)

(l)   Debts other than debts on a security

(m)   Pension and annuity rights

(n)   Investments held in an individual savings account (ISA).

3 Administration of CGT

CGT is chargeable for tax years, like income tax. Any gains arising in the year from 6 April 2008 to 5 April 2009 will be charged in 2008/09.

There is one payment of CGT due on 31 January after the end of the tax year, ie 31 January 2010 for 2008/09. There are no payments on account for CGT.

It may also be possible to pay CGT in instalments (see Chapter 15).

Tax Qualification Training

4 The overseas aspects of CGT

4.1 General

Individuals are liable to CGT on the disposal of assets situated anywhere in the world if they are resident or ordinarily resident in the UK at any point in the year in which the gain is made. By concession, individuals who arrive in or leave the UK during the year may be able to split the tax year for CGT purposes ie they are charged to CGT only in respect of disposals made after the date of arrival or before the date of departure.

The concession does not apply if the individual has been resident or ordinarily resident:

(a)   at any time in the five tax years before the tax year of arrival, or

(b)   for at least four out of seven tax years prior to the year of departure.

If a person is UK resident or ordinarily resident but is not UK domiciled, they may claim the remittance basis of taxation, such that gains on the disposal of assets situated overseas (see below) are chargeable to CGT to the extent that the proceeds are *remitted* to the UK.

However, as discussed in Chapter 8, if an individual claiming the remittance basis has been UK resident for seven out of the previous nine tax years, they will be subject to a tax charge of £30,000 on their unremitted foreign income and gains. The £30,000 charge does not apply if the individual is under 18 years old or if the unremitted foreign income and gains for the tax year amount to less than £2,000.

Losses on assets situated overseas made by non-UK domiciled persons who claim the remittance basis of taxation cannot be set off against any gains.

However, a non-UK domiciled individual who does **not** claim the remittance basis (and is therefore taxed on worldwide gains on an arising basis) will from 2008/09 get relief for foreign capital losses.

Moreover, even individuals who normally claim the remittance basis will be able to elect from 2008/09 into a regime which allows them to get relief for foreign capital losses in any years where they choose to be taxed on an arising basis. The election is irrevocable and, as it requires the non-domiciled individual to disclose details of their unremitted gains, it is optional.

Example 2

Sergio is UK resident but not UK domiciled and has claimed to be taxed on the remittance basis. In 2008/09 he has the following gains and losses:

	£
Gains on sale of UK shares	10,000
Gain on sale of overseas house	10,000
Loss on sale of overseas shares	(4,000)

The proceeds of sale of the overseas house were £25,000. He remits £5,000 during the year from the proceeds.

Show Sergio's chargeable gains after the annual exemption.

4.2 Non-UK residents

Normally a disposal of assets situated in the UK is not a chargeable event if the vendor is neither resident nor ordinarily resident in the UK at the time of disposal. However, a liability to CGT may arise if the person is carrying on a trade, profession or vocation in the UK through a permanent establishment and an asset which has been used for the purpose of the permanent establishment is either disposed of or removed from the UK.

A charge will also arise if the UK trade, profession or vocation ceases. In this case, and in the case of removal of assets from the UK, there is a deemed disposal of assets at their market value.

4.3 Temporary non-residents

Temporary non-residents may be taxable on gains realised whilst they are abroad if:

(a) **They are outside the UK for less than five years between the year of departure and the year of return.**

(b) **They were UK resident or ordinarily resident for four out of the seven years immediately preceding the year of departure.**

Net gains realised in the year of departure are taxed in that year (this applies whether the absence is temporary or permanent under general principles). Subsequent gains/losses are chargeable/allowable in the year of return as if they were gains/losses of that year.

Gains on assets acquired in the non-resident period are not included in the above charge nor are gains which are already chargeable because they arise on a permanent establishment's assets (see above).

4.4 Double taxation relief (DTR)

If a gain on the disposal of an overseas asset is taxed both overseas and in the UK, DTR will be available.

The DTR applies in the same way as for income tax ie relief is given for the lower of the UK and overseas tax. However, the annual exemption is deducted pro rata from gains on different assets to give the taxable gain in each case.

Example 3

Geraldine who is UK resident and ordinarily resident, makes a gain on a UK asset of £20,000 and on a non-UK asset of £10,000 in 2008/09. She paid foreign tax of £3,000 on the non-UK asset. She has taxable income of £17,000 in the year. Calculate the DTR available.

Ignore

4.5 Location of assets

For CGT purposes assets are located as follows:

(a)	Immovable property	— where physically located
(b)	Tangible movable property (chattels)	— where physically located at time of disposal
(c)	A debt	— where the creditor is resident
(d)	Government securities	— within country of that government
(e)	Shares and securities	— in country in which registered
(f)	Goodwill of a business	— where business is carried on
(g)	Patents	— where registered

TQT
Tax Qualification Training

Chapter roundup

- CGT is charged on 'chargeable gains' that arise when a 'chargeable person' makes a 'chargeable disposal' of a 'chargeable asset'.

- Individuals are entitled to an annual exemption for each tax year.

- Capital gains are taxed at a flat rate of 18%.

- A disposal occurs not only when there is a sale of an asset but also when there is a gift or a capital sum is received (eg insurance money received when an asset is damaged or destroyed).

- Certain assets, such as cars, are exempt from CGT.

- CGT is due on 31 January following the tax year. On certain occasions the CGT may be paid by instalments.

- CGT is charged on persons who are resident or ordinarily resident in the UK and persons only temporarily abroad. A tax year may be split into resident and non-resident parts by concession but the concession is denied in certain circumstances.

- A UK resident and/or ordinarily resident person is chargeable to CGT on disposals of their worldwide assets.

- UK resident and/or ordinarily resident persons who are not UK domiciled and claim the remittance basis are taxable on UK gains on an arising basis and on foreign gains to the extent that proceeds are remitted to the UK (subject to an £30,000 tax charge on unremitted foreign gains if they have been resident for 7 of the last 9 years). Losses on overseas assets are not normally allowable. However, if the individual chooses to be taxed on an arising basis, they will get relief for losses on foreign assets.

- Double taxation relief may be available to reduce the tax liability when the same gain is taxed in two countries.

Quiz

1. Compute Martha's CGT liability for 2008/09, assuming she has:

   Chargeable gains (before AE)   £28,400

2. Which of the following constitute chargeable disposals for CGT?

   (a)   A gift of shares
   (b)   A sale of 2 acres of land out of a plot of 10 acres
   (c)   The demolition of a building

3. Which of the following are chargeable assets for CGT purposes?

   (a)   Proceeds from backing the winner of the Grand National
   (b)   Damages awarded in an action for libel
   (c)   A diamond necklace
   (d)   A vintage Rolls Royce

4. What is the *earliest* date on which CGT may become payable for 2008/09?

5. In which country are the following assets situated?

   (a)   A villa in Portugal
   (b)   Securities issued by the government of Italy, purchased through a UK agent
   (c)   Shares in a company which is UK resident for tax purposes but whose share register is maintained in Jersey, Channel Islands
   (d)   A diamond necklace owned by a UK resident but which is kept in the vaults of a French bank

Solutions to Quiz

1.

	£
Martha – 2008/09	
Chargeable gains	28,400
Less: annual exemption	(9,600)
Taxable gain	18,800
CGT thereon:	
£18,800 @ 18%	3,384

2. All of them.

3. (c) only – (a), (b) and (d) are exempt assets.

4. 31 January 2010

5.
   (a) Portugal
   (b) Italy
   (c) Jersey
   (d) France

Solutions to chapter examples

Solution to Example 1

	£
Chargeable gains	25,000
Less: Annual Exemption (AE)	(9,600)
Taxable gains	15,400
Tax: £15,400 × 18%	2,772

Solution to Example 2

Part of gain remitted is $\frac{5,000}{25,000} \times £10,000 = £2,000$

The loss on the sale of overseas shares is not available to reduce either the UK or overseas gains and neither is the annual exemption as the remittance basis is being claimed for 2008/09..

Sergio's chargeable gains are:	£
UK gains arising	10,000
Overseas gain remitted	2,000
Chargeable gains	12,000

Solution to Example 3

The annual exemption is split:

[handwritten annotations: "appropriate exemption on both assets", "what proportion of the taxable exemption she can set against her gain"]

UK asset $\frac{20,000}{30,000} \times £9,600 = £6,400$, giving a taxable gain of £13,600

[handwritten: 9,600]

Non-UK asset $\frac{10,000}{30,000} \times £9,600 = £3,200$ giving a taxable gain of £6,800

UK CGT on overseas asset is:	£
£6,800 @ 18%	1,224
DTR is the lower of £1,224 and £3,000 ie	1,224

[handwritten: only claim sufficient to cover the UK liability on the asset]

Short Form Questions:

9.1 – 9.3 inclusive

Long Form Questions:

9.1	Peter Jones
9.2	Simon James

10

Computing gains and losses

References: TCGA 1992 unless otherwise stated

The purpose of this chapter is to help you to:

- set out the basic CGT computation
- understand how to set off capital losses in the most tax efficient way
- use the valuation rules for specific assets (eg shares)
- identify connected persons and understand the consequences of transfers between them
- understand the value at which transfers take place between husband and wife/civil partners
- apply the part disposal rules
- understand the tax treatment of debts and loans

1 Basic computation

1.1 Pro forma CGT computation

A chargeable gain or allowable loss is generally calculated as follows:

	£
Disposal consideration (or market value)	X
Less: costs of disposal	(X)
Net proceeds	X
Less: allowable costs *eg. commission*	(X)
Chargeable gain (allowable loss)	X/(X)

Exam focus point

In computational CGT questions, if an individual disposes of several assets in the tax year, you will need to calculate the gain/loss on each asset individually using the above pro forma.

1.2 Disposal consideration

Normally, it is the actual consideration passing between the parties which is taken into account. However where the disposal is not a bargain at arm's length (ie a gift or sale at under value) the disposal is deemed to take place at market value.

1.3 Costs of disposal

These may include:

(a)   Valuation fees
(b)   Estate agency fees
(c)   Advertising costs
(d)   Legal costs

These costs are deducted from gross proceeds of sale.

1.4 Other allowable costs

Allowable costs include:

(a)   **Original cost of acquisition** (or market value at the date of acquisition)
(b)   **Incidental costs of acquisition**
(c)   **Capital expenditure incurred in enhancing the asset** (see below).

1.5 Enhancement expenditure

Enhancement expenditure means capital expenditure which enhances the value of the asset and is *reflected in the state or nature of the asset at the time of disposal*. Certain costs are specifically excluded from this category as follows:

(a)   Cost of repairs and maintenance
(b)   Cost of insurance
(c)   Any expenditure which is treated as a deduction for the purposes of assessing the taxpayer to income tax, and
(d)   Any expenditure transferred out of public funds eg council grants.

Example 1

Fred bought an asset on 15 February 1984 for £5,000. Enhancement expenditure of £2,000 was incurred on 10 April 1985. Fred sold the asset for £20,500 on 20 December 2008. Incidental costs of sale were £500.

You are required to calculate the chargeable gain arising.

---

2 Capital losses

gain before exemption!

Exam focus point

In a computational CGT question there is often a loss (capital or trading) arising. You will be required to show how it should be relieved.

2.1 Current year losses — *must take off losses before Annual exemption (only in current year)*

Allowable losses are deducted from chargeable gains in the tax year in which they arise.

Any loss in excess of gains in the same year is carried forward and set against gains made in future years.

TQT
Tax Qualification Training

Example 2

George has chargeable gains for 2008/09 of £10,000 and allowable losses of £6,000. How will he take relief for the losses?

2.2 Losses carried forward

Losses carried forward by an individual are set off automatically against future gains.

Brought forward losses are used only to the extent that they reduce chargeable gains down to the annual exemption. No set-off is made if net chargeable gains for the current year do not exceed the annual exemption.

Example 3

Bob has chargeable gains of £11,300 for 2008/09 and losses brought forward of £6,000. How will Bob take relief for these losses?

Example 4

Tom has chargeable gains of £5,000 for 2008/09 and losses brought forward from 2007/08 of £4,000. How will Tom take relief for these losses?

2.3 Losses in the year of death

The *only* (examinable) time that an individual may carry *back* capital losses is on death. Losses (in excess of gains) arising in the tax year in which an individual dies can be carried back to the previous three years of assessment on a **LIFO basis** (ie most recent year first). Losses are utilised so as to reduce chargeable gains for each of the years to an amount equal to the annual exemption of that year.

This will result in a repayment of CGT that has already been paid.

Example 5

Joe dies on 1 January 2009. His chargeable gains and allowable losses for recent years, before taking account of annual exemptions, have been as follows:

		Gain /(Loss)	Annual Exemption
		£	£
2008/09	Gains	2,000	9,600
	Losses	(12,000)	
2007/08	Gains	9,400	9,200
2006/07	Gains	2,200	8,800
2005/06	Gains	19,200	8,500

You are required to show how the losses arising in 2008/09 are utilised.

2.4 Trading losses set against capital gains

Where relief is claimed for trading losses under s.64 ITA 2007 against general income of a given year, the taxpayer may include a further claim to set the loss against his chargeable gains for that year. [s.261B TCGA 1992]

The trading loss must first be set against net income of the year of the claim, and only any excess loss is set against capital gains. The taxpayer cannot specify the amount to be set against capital gains, so the annual exemption may be wasted.

The amount of loss which can be relieved is the lower of:

- The 'relevant amount' = the amount of trading loss available for offset

- The 'maximum amount' = the chargeable gains in the year less current year capital losses and capital losses brought forward.

Example 6

Sibyl had the following results for 2008/09.

	£
Loss available for relief under s.64	27,000
Income (before PA)	19,500
Chargeable gains	16,000
Annual exemption for capital gains tax purposes	9,600
Current year capital losses	5,600
Capital losses brought forward	4,500

Show how the loss would be relieved against income and gains.

2.5 Share loss relief

Relief is available for losses arising on the disposal of shares in certain unquoted trading companies (broadly EIS type companies). [s.131 ITA 2007]

The capital loss is computed as normal but is instead **deducted from the taxpayer's general income in**:

    (a)   The year of assessment in which the disposal takes place; and/or

    (b)   The preceding year of assessment.

A claim must be made by the anniversary of 31 January following the end of the tax year of the loss, so by 31 January 2011 for 2008/09.

The taxpayer cannot choose the amount of loss to relieve, but can choose whether to set a loss first against the current year's income and then against the preceding year's income, or the other way round, just like a normal trading loss.

Exam focus point

Examiner's report – Personal Taxation (old syllabus)

Nov 2004 – Question 5

Many failed to notice that the loss on the shares in Wonder Fabrications could be set against income which therefore meant that for many candidates the answer produced a capital gains tax liability.

---

3 Valuation of assets

3.1 The basic rule

Where market value is used in a CGT computation, the value to be used is the price which the asset might reasonably be expected to fetch on a sale in the open market.

3.2 Shares and securities

Quoted shares and securities are valued at the **lower of two figures** as quoted in The Stock Exchange Daily Official List as follows:

(a)   'Quarter-up' rule: add a quarter of the difference between the lower and the higher quoted prices to the lower quoted price, or

(b)   'Average rule': take the **average of highest and lowest marked bargains** (ignore marked special prices).

Example 7

Shares in A plc are quoted at 100-110p. The marked bargains for that day were 99p, 102p and 110p. What value will the shares have for CGT purposes?

Unquoted shares are much harder to value than quoted shares. HMRC's special Shares Valuation division deals with the valuation of unquoted shares. **You will be given the market value in your examination**.

3.3 Negligible value claim

If an asset's value becomes negligible, a claim may be made to treat the asset as though it had been sold and then immediately reacquired at its current market value. This will give rise to an allowable loss. This 'negligible value' claim is often used for shares that have become worthless. [s.24(2)]

The claim can be backdated up to two tax years, provided that the asset had become negligible in value at that time, eg in 2008/09 a claim can be made that an asset's value became negligible in 2006/07, which crystallises an allowable loss in 2006/07.

If the asset is subsequently sold, the base cost of the asset will be the value at the time of the negligible value claim.

Example 8

Rhona owns shares in Alf Ltd which she purchased in 1983. Following a sudden change in the company's business in the summer of 2007 the shares plummet in value and the company goes into liquidation. Rhona only learnt of the liquidation in May 2008.

For which tax year(s) may a negligible value claim be made?

3.4 Probate value

Where an individual inherits an asset on the death of another person they are treated as acquiring that asset at the market value at the date of death. This is known as the 'probate value'.

4 Connected persons

4.1 Introduction

A transaction between 'connected persons' is automatically treated as not being made at arm's length. Consequently the **acquisition and disposal are treated as taking place at market value**, regardless of any actual price paid.

If a loss results, it can **only be set off against gains arising in the same or future years from transactions with the** *same* connected person *while they remain connected*.

4.2 Definition of connected persons

An individual is connected with:

(a)   His spouse or civil partner
(b)   His relatives (brothers, sisters, ancestors and lineal descendants)
(c)   The relatives of his spouse/civil partner
(d)   The spouses of his relatives and his spouse's/civil partner's relatives
(e)   Business partners, partners' spouses/civil partners and partners' relatives
(f)   Trustees of any settlement of which the individual is the settlor.

A company is connected with another person if:

(a)   That person has control of the company, or
(b)   He and persons connected with him together have control of it.

A company is connected with another company if:

(a)   The same person has control of both companies, or
(b)   One person has control of one company and persons connected with him have control of the other.

4.3 Assets disposed of in a series of transactions

A taxpayer might attempt to avoid tax by disposing of his property piecemeal to persons connected with him. For example, a majority holding of shares might be broken up into several minority holdings, each with a much lower value per share, and each of the shareholder's children could be given a minority holding.

To prevent the avoidance of tax in this way, **where a person disposes of assets to one or more persons, with whom he is connected, in a series of linked transactions, the disposal proceeds for each disposal will be a proportion of the value of the assets taken together**. Thus in the example of the shareholding, the value of the majority holding would be apportioned between the minority holdings. Transactions are linked if they occur within six years of each other.

5 Married couples

5.1 Introduction

A husband and wife (or partners in a civil partnership) are taxed as two separate people. Each has an annual exemption, and losses of one cannot be set against gains of the other.

Disposals between a husband and wife (or civil partners) living together do not give rise to chargeable gains or allowable losses. The disposal is said to be on a **'no gain/no loss' basis. The acquiring spouse/partner takes over the base cost of the disposing spouse/partner.**

Example 9

Jacob gave his wife Leah a painting in July 2005. Its market value was £50,000. He had acquired the painting in February 1999 for £10,000. Leah sold the painting in June 2008 for £75,000.

Calculate Leah's chargeable gain.

A couple are treated as living together unless they are separated under a court order or separation deed, or are in fact separated in circumstances which make permanent separation likely. A transfer in the tax year of separation will therefore be treated as a no gain/no loss transfer. The spouses/civil partners will be connected persons until divorce (see below).

Exam focus point

Examiner's report – Personal Taxation (old syllabus)

May 2006 – Question 3

This was a fairly popular question but candidates were not very clear on the consequences of the separation and divorce, many just explaining the tax position of the two individuals.

5.2 Jointly owned assets

Where an asset is jointly owned, the spouses/civil partners' actual interests determine the tax treatment, so if there is evidence that a wife's share is 60%, then 60% of any gain or loss will be attributed to her. If there is no evidence of the actual interests, HMRC accept that the asset is held in equal shares.

Where an income tax declaration has been made (see Chapter 1) stating how income from the asset is to be shared for income tax purposes, there is a presumption that the same split will apply for CGT purposes.

5.3 Tax planning issues

If a spouse who is making other substantial gains wishes to dispose of an asset standing at a gain and the other spouse has his/her CGT annual exemption available, **the asset could first be transferred, at no gain/no loss, to the spouse with the annual exemption who can then sell the asset**. The transfer must have 'no strings attached' to be effective for tax purposes.

6 Part disposals

6.1 General rules

The disposal of part of a chargeable asset is a chargeable event for CGT purposes. The chargeable gain (or allowable loss) is computed by **deducting only a fraction of the original cost of the whole asset**. The fraction is:

$$\frac{A}{A+B} = \frac{\text{value of the part disposed of}}{\text{value of the part disposed of} + \text{market value of the remainder}}$$

The balance of the cost is used when the rest of the asset is sold.

Example 10

Mr Heal possesses a set of four Chippendale chairs (treated as a single asset for CGT purposes) which originally cost him £27,000 in March 1984. He sold one of the chairs at auction in July 2008 for £20,000, before auction expenses of 10%. The market value of the three remaining chairs together is £46,000.

You are required to calculate Mr Heal's chargeable gain.

6.2 Small part disposals of land [s.242]

If the consideration on the part disposal of land is small *and* the total consideration in that tax year from all disposals of land do not exceed £20,000, the taxpayer may claim instead to deduct the 'small' sale proceeds from the base cost of the land rather than calculate the gain on the part disposal.

'Small' is defined as not more than 20% of the total market value of the land (A + B) immediately before the disposal.

Example 11

Tony sells 2 acres of land out of a plot of 20 acres for £10,000 in 2000/01 (his only disposal that tax year). The market value of the 20 acre plot was £80,000 immediately prior to the sale. The remaining 18 acres are sold in 2008/09 for £100,000.

Date of acquisition:	30 April 1983
Original cost:	£45,000
Date of part disposal:	30 April 2000
Date of final disposal:	30 August 2008

Assume a claim was made in respect of the part disposal under s.242 TCGA 1992.

You are required to show the adjustment to Tony's base cost on the sale in 2000/01 and his chargeable gain in 2008/09.

Exam focus point

Attempt the following example on your own before looking at the solution. Use the steps below:

Step 1 **Calculate the chargeable gain on each asset as a separate working**.

Step 2 Prepare a **summary table** and aggregate the gains calculated in Step 1. This should be the first page of your answer and should clearly reference in your workings from Step 1 above.

Step 3 If there are any **losses** available for offset, these **should be deducted – current year capital losses first, then capital losses brought forward**.

Step 4 **Deduct the annual exemption** to arrive at the taxable gain.

Step 5 **Calculate the CGT payable at 18%**.

Example 12

Brian made the following disposals on 2 November 2008:

(1)   Sold a warehouse used in his trade at auction for £70,000 (gross). The auction house charged him a commission of 10% on the sale. The warehouse had cost him £10,000 in May 1983.

(2)   Sold a tenanted cottage for £18,000 net of costs of sale, which amounted to £200. He had inherited the cottage, which was one of a pair, on the death of his grandfather in October 1983. They were valued as a pair for probate purposes at £14,000. The value of the cottage retained by him was estimated at £12,000 when he sold the other one.

He has losses brought forward of £3,000 at 6 April 2008.

You are required to compute his capital gains tax liability.

7 Debts and loans

7.1 Debts

7.1.1 Introduction

Debts are specifically included in the definition of chargeable assets.

7.1.2 Ordinary debts

The original creditor (ie lender) (or his personal representative or legatee) **does not have a chargeable gain or an allowable loss on a disposal of the original debt** (unless it is a debt on a security – see below).

If someone purchases the debt from the original lender and then disposes of it, he will be liable to tax on any gain or entitled to an allowable loss. The satisfaction (ie payment) of a debt is treated as a disposal.

However, if the debt was acquired from the original lender and is disposed of at a loss by someone connected with that lender, the loss is not allowable.

Illustration

Fred lends £10,000 to Tom. Fred assigns (ie sells) the debt to Harry for £9,000. Tom repays the full amount lent to Harry.

Whether or not Harry is connected with Fred, Harry has made a disposal and realised a gain of £1,000.

7.2 Debt on a security

A 'debt on a security' is not necessarily a 'secured' debt (ie its payment is not secured on another asset, for example a mortgage is secured on the property over which it is given).

To be a debt on a security it must be:

- **Capable of being held as an investment**
- **Marketable** (ie be capable of being realised at a profit)
- **From an institution** (not from an individual)
- **Evidenced in writing**
- **Loan stock** or similar.

Exam focus point

If the original lender disposes of a debt on a security there will be a chargeable gain or an allowable loss because they are generally commercial investments. In all other ways a debt on a security is treated in the same way as an ordinary loan.

7.3 Loans to traders

7.3.1 Introduction

Although usually the original lender is not entitled to an allowable loss when a debt becomes irrecoverable, relief is available for certain loans to traders, and for guarantees in respect of such loans.

The lender must claim the relief.

7.3.2 Qualifying loans

A qualifying loan must satisfy the following conditions: [s.253(1)]

(a) **The money lent is used by the borrower wholly for the purposes of a trade (not involving lending money) carried on by him**, including furnished holiday lettings, *and*

(b) **The borrower is resident in the UK,** *and*

(c) **The debt is** *not* **a debt on a security**.

The lender can make a claim for loss relief if:

- The loan capital (ie principal) has become irrecoverable, and
- He has not assigned the right to recover the amount, and
- The lender and the borrower were **not spouses** or civil partners either when, or after, the loan was made.

The date of the 'disposal' is the date of the claim, although the lender can specify an earlier time (not more than two years before the beginning of the tax year in which the claim is made) so long as the above conditions were satisfied at that earlier time.

Chapter roundup

- **CGT is a tax on the increase in value of assets between acquisition and disposal.**

- **Disposal proceeds are actual money received or market value, if the disposal is not a bargain at arm's length.**

- **Allowable expenditure includes the acquisition cost, enhancement expenditure and incidental costs of acquisition or disposal.**

- **Chargeable gains and losses arising in a tax year are netted off.**

- **Excess allowable losses must be carried forward and set against chargeable gains arising in a subsequent year to bring the chargeable gain down to the level of the annual exemption.**

- **Losses incurred in the year of death can be carried back against gains arising in the preceding three years on a LIFO basis.**

- **Individuals can elect to set trading losses against chargeable gains subject to certain conditions.**

- **Losses on unquoted shares may be set against general income.**

- **A loss arising on a transaction between connected persons may be set off in restricted circumstances.**

- **Shares are valued at the lower of the quarter-up and average bargain values.**

- **No gain/no loss disposals effectively transfer base costs between spouses and civil partners.**

- **For a part disposal, allowable expenditure is apportioned between the part disposed of and the part retained using the formula:** $\dfrac{A}{A+B} \times \text{cost}$.

- **In the case of a 'small' part disposal of land the taxpayer may elect that no part disposal takes place. Instead allowable expenditure are reduced by the 'small' disposal proceeds. 'Small' means the disposal proceeds do not exceed 20% of A + B and the proceeds from the part disposal (and from all land disposals in the tax year) do not exceed £20,000.**

- **Only the disposal of a debt on a security gives rise to a gain or loss to the original lender. Usually there is no chargeable gain or allowable loss unless the lender purchased the debt.**

- **In certain cases a taxpayer can claim an allowable capital loss for irrecoverable loans made to traders.**

1. Yvette buys a 15% shareholding in Blanche Ltd, a trading company. On 9 August 2002 for £125,000. She sells the shares on 12 December 2008 for £160,000. She has never been an employee or director of the company. Show her taxable gain after annual exemption.

2. Philip has chargeable gains of £12,700 and allowable losses of £2,300 in 2008/09. Losses brought forward at 6 April 2008 are £7,000. What amount is chargeable to CGT in 2008/09? What are the losses carried forward?

3. Losses arising in the year in which an individual dies are set first against gains arising in the year of death. Any excess losses may then be carried back and set against gains of the four preceding years, using gains of a more recent year before those of an earlier year. True/False?

4. Compute the CGT value of the following shares in quoted companies:

   (a) Z plc – quoted prices : 250p and 260p
       marked bargains : 248p, 254p and 262p

   (b) Y plc – quoted prices : 402p and 420p
       marked bargains : 380p (special), 390p and 410p

5. With which of the following persons is Joe connected for CGT purposes?

   (a) His son Eddie
   (b) His cousin Frank
   (c) A company, Joe Ltd, of which he owns 95% of the ordinary share capital and voting power
   (d) His brother Ray's wife

6. Richard sells 4 acres of land in May 2008 out of a plot of 10 acres for £38,000. Costs of disposal amount to £3,000. The 10-acre plot cost £41,500 in 1987. The market value of the 6 acres remaining is £48,000.

   Compute the chargeable gain.

Tax Qualification Training

1.

	£
Proceeds	160,000
Less: cost	(125,000)
Chargeable gain	35,000
Less: Annual exemption	(9,600)
Taxable gain	25,400

2.

	£
Gains in year	12,700
Losses in year	(2,300)
	10,400
Losses brought forward (£10,400 – 9,600)	(800)
	9,600
Annual exemption	(9,600)
Chargeable amount	£ nil

Losses carried forward at 5 April 2009
£(7,000 – 800) = £6,200.

3. False – the carry back period is three years only.

4. (a) Z plc : lower of

(i) 250p + ((260-250p)/4) = 252.5p

(ii) $\dfrac{248+262}{2}$ = 255p

ie 252.5p per share

(b) Y plc : lower of

(i) 402p + ((420 – 402p)/4) = 406.5p

(ii) $\dfrac{390+410}{2}$ = 400p

ie 400p per share

5. Joe is connected with all except (b), his cousin.

6.

	£
Proceeds	38,000
Less: costs of disposal	(3,000)
	35,000
Less: allowable cost : £41,500 × $\dfrac{38,000}{38,000+48,000}$	(18,337)
Chargeable gain	16,663

Solution to Example 1

The computation of the chargeable gain will be as follows:

	£
Disposal proceeds	20,500
Less: incidental costs of sale	(500)
Net proceeds	20,000
Less: allowable costs (5,000 + 2,000)	(7,000)
Chargeable gain	13,000

Solution to Example 2

As the losses are *current year* losses they must be fully relieved against the £10,000 of gains to produce net gains of £4,000, despite the fact that net gains are now below the annual exemption, part of which will be wasted.

Solution to Example 3

Bob's loss relief can be restricted to £1,700 so as to leave net gains of:

£(11,300 − 1,700) = £9,600;

which will be exactly covered by his annual exemption for 2008/09. The remaining £4,300 of loss relief (ie 6,000 − 1,700) is carried forward to 2009/10.

Solution to Example 4

His gains of £5,000 are covered by his annual exemption for 2008/09. He can therefore carry forward all of his losses to 2009/10.

Solution to Example 5

Loss relief is:

	£	Gains £	Losses £
2008/09			
Gains	2,000		
Less: losses	(12,000)		
Loss available for c/b			10,000
2007/08			
Gains	9,400		
Less: loss c/b	(200)	9,200	(200)
Less: AE		(9,200)	
Taxable gain		nil	
Loss available for c/b			9,800
2006/07			
Gains		2,200	
Less: AE (part)		(2,200)	
Taxable gain		nil	
2005/06			
Gains	19,200		
Less: loss c/b	(9,800)		(9,800)
		9,400	
Less: AE		(8,500)	
Taxable gain		900	
Unrelieved loss			nil

This will generate a repayment of CGT paid in the earlier years.

Solution to Example 6

	£
Income	19,500
Less: s.64 loss relief	(19,500)
Net income	0
Chargeable gains	16,000
Less: current year capital losses	(5,600)

Less: s.261B TCGA 1992 loss relief: lower of:

Loss remaining £(27,000 – 19,500) = £7,500; and

Chargeable gains less current year capital losses and all capital losses brought forward:

£(16,000 – 5,600 – 4,500) = £5,900	(5,900)
	4,500
Less: annual exemption – restricted	(4,500)
	0

A trading loss of £(7,500 – 5,900) = £1,600 is carried forward. Sibyl's personal allowance and £(9,600 – 4,500) = £5,100 of her CGT annual exemption will be wasted. Her capital losses brought forward of £4,500 would be carried forward to 2009/10.

Although we deducted the capital losses brought forward of £4,500 in working out how much trading loss to use, we do not actually need to use any of the £4,500 unless there are gains remaining after the annual exemption. Capital losses brought forward are never utilised where it would mean wasting the annual exemption.

Solution to Example 7

The valuation of the shares in A plc for CGT purposes will be the lower of:

(a) $100 + 1/4\ (110 - 100) = 102.5$; and

(b) $\dfrac{110 + 99}{2} = 104.5$

The market value for CGT will therefore be 102.5p.

Solution to Example 8

For 2007/08 or a later year until the liquidation is complete. Although Rhona discovers the information in 2008/09 and usually a negligible value claim can be backdated two years, the shares were not of negligible value in 2006/07. So 2007/08 is the earliest year for the claim.

Solution to Example 9

The transfer from Jacob to Leah is automatically at no gain no loss.

	£
The base cost for Leah is:	
Original cost to Jacob	10,000

Note. The market value of the painting at transfer is irrelevant.

When Leah sells the painting, a gain will arise:

	£
Proceeds	75,000
Cost (as above)	(10,000)
Chargeable gain	65,000

Solution to Example 10

	£
Disposal proceeds	20,000
Less: incidental costs of sale	(2,000)
Net proceeds	18,000
Less: cost (working)	(8,182)
Chargeable gain	9,818

Working

The cost of the single chair being sold is: $\dfrac{A}{A+B} \times \text{cost}$

$$\frac{20,000}{20,000 + 46,000} \times £27,000 = £8,182$$

Solution to Example 11

(a) *Part disposal*: adjustment to cost

	£
Original cost	45,000
Proceeds from part disposal (small as < 20% and < £20,000)	(10,000)
Allowable cost c/f	35,000

(b) *Subsequent disposal*

	£
Proceeds	100,000
Less: allowable cost (above)	(35,000)
Chargeable gain	65,000

Solution to Example 12

Summary

		£
Chargeable gains:	Warehouse (W1)	53,000
	Cottage (W2)	9,563
Less: loss b/f		(3,000)
Net gains		59,563
Less: annual exemption		(9,600)
Taxable gain		49,963

Tax @ 18% = £8,993

Workings

(1) *Warehouse*

	£
Proceeds (net) (70,000 – 7,000)	63,000
Cost	(10,000)
Chargeable gain	53,000

(2) *Cottage*

	£
Proceeds	18,200
Less selling costs	(200)
Net proceeds	18,000
Cost: $\dfrac{18,200}{18,200 + 12,000} \times 14,000$	(8,437)
Chargeable gain	9,563

TQT
Tax Qualification Training

Short Form Questions:

10.1 – 10.10 inclusive

Long Form Questions:

10.1	Dorrit
10.2	Kidson
10.3	Harbottle

11

Shares and securities

1 The need for special rules

Shares present special problems when computing gains or losses on their disposal. Suppose that a taxpayer buys some quoted shares in X plc on the following dates:

		Cost £
5 May 1983	100 shares	150
17 January 1985	100 shares	375
2 May 1998	100 shares	1,000

On 15 June 2008, he sells 220 of his shares for £3,300. To determine his chargeable gain, we need to be able to work out which shares out of his three original holdings were actually sold. Since one share is identical to any other, it is not possible to work this out by reference to factual evidence.

As a result, it has been necessary to devise '**matching rules**'. These allow us to **identify which shares have been sold and so work out what the allowable cost (and the gain) on disposal should be**. These rules are considered in detail below.

2 Disposals on or after 6 April 2008 by individuals

This section is significantly changed by Finance Act 2008.

For individuals, the matching of shares sold is in the following order:

(a)   Shares acquired on the **same day** (average cost)

(b)   Shares acquired in the **following thirty days** on a FIFO (first in, first out) basis

(c)   Shares from the share pool (average cost) which contains all shares acquired prior to the disposal date.

Example 1

George bought the following shares in Red plc:

Date	No.	Cost £
1.5.06	9,000	18,000
20.2.09	2,000	5,000
12.3.09	5,000	12,000

He sold 10,000 shares on 20 February 2009 for £30,000.

Show George's gain on sale.

---

3 The share pool [s.104]

The share pool may also be referred to as the 's.104 pool' or 's.104 holding' indicating where in TCGA1992 the relevant legislation can be found.

3.1 The composition of the share pool

The share pool, comprises all shares of the *same* class in the *same* company which were acquired prior to the disposal date.

3.2 The calculation of the share pool value

In order to compute the value of the share pool, **two columns are required showing**:

(a)   The **number of shares**
(b)   The aggregated **cost** of the shares

Oliver bought 1,000 shares in Judith plc for £2,750 in August 1982, another 1,000 for £3,250 in December 1984 and 2,000 more shares in July 1986 at a cost of £4,000.

On 9 July 2008 Oliver disposed of 3,000 shares for £18,000.

Compute the chargeable gain on disposal.

4 Reorganisations

4.1 Introduction

There are several circumstances where a company will reorganise its share capital including:

(a)   Bonus issues (or scrip issues): quoted and unquoted shares
(b)   Rights issues: quoted and unquoted shares
(c)   Capital distributions: quoted and unquoted shares
(d)   Reorganisations of quoted shares
(e)   Takeovers: quoted and unquoted shares

The effects of such transactions on an individual is that his existing, original holding is in some way altered. The problem so far as CGT is concerned is usually how to apportion the original base cost between the original shareholding and whatever the shareholder has after the reorganisation.

4.2 Bonus issues

Bonus shares are effectively free shares, issued at no cost, to existing shareholders. When a company (quoted or unquoted) issues bonus shares, the **size of the shareholder's original holding is increased but there is no need to adjust the original cost**.

The bonus issue shares are treated as being acquired at the date of each original acquisition of the underlying shares. The normal matching rules then apply.

Example 3

Show how the disposal of the ordinary shares of X plc would be matched assuming the following transactions had taken place:

6.4.83   Purchase of 800 shares
6.4.88   Purchase of 600 shares
6.5.99   Purchase of 1,000 shares
1.7.08   Bonus issue of 1 for 4
6.7.08   Sale of 2,200 shares.
15.7.08   Purchase of 200 shares

4.3 Rights issues

4.3.1 Effect of a rights issue

The difference between a bonus issue and a rights issue is that in a **rights issue the new shares are paid for so we must adjust the original cost**.

Example 4

Julia had the following transactions in the shares of T Ltd:

July 1983	purchased 1,500 for	£3,750
July 1988	purchased 1,000 for	£3,000
May 1999	purchased 2,000 for	£8,000
June 2000	takes up 1 for 4 rights issue at £4.20 per share	
October 2008	sells 5,625 for	£50,400

Compute the chargeable gain or allowable loss arising.

4.3.2 Sale of rights nil paid

Where the shareholder does not take up his rights to buy new shares but instead sells that right to a third party, the proceeds received from the third party are treated as a capital distribution (see below) and the **proceeds will be dealt with under the part disposal rules** where A = the proceeds received and B = the MV of the existing shareholding. However, if the proceeds are 'small' (ie less than the higher of £3,000 or 5% of the value of the shares at the time of the rights issue), the proceeds are deducted from cost.

Alternatively, if the proceeds of sale of the rights are greater than the full original cost of the shares, an election can be made to use the full cost of the shares in calculating the gain. The base cost carried forward will then be nil.

4.4 Capital distributions: quoted and unquoted shares

For CGT purposes, a capital distribution (such as a payment received on a liquidation) is a repayment of share capital. The way in which the distribution is dealt with depends on the size of the distribution.

The normal rule is that the **distribution will be treated as a part disposal of the asset and dealt with accordingly** (see Chapter 10).

If, however, the **distribution is 'small'**, defined as less than the higher of £3,000 or 5% of the value of the shares, any gain arising may be 'rolled over' by **reducing the allowable cost of the shares for a later disposal by the amount of the 'small' distribution received**.

Example 5

Barr holds 1,000 shares in Woodleigh plc for which he paid £10,000 in October 1986. The company is now in liquidation and in July 2008 the liquidator made a distribution of £4 per share.

Show how this will be treated if the market value of the shares before the distribution is either:

(a)   £65,000; or

(b)   £84,000 and in December 2008 Barr received a final distribution of £90,000.

Where the proceeds from a distribution are greater than the full original cost of the shares, the taxpayer may elect to have the **full cost** set against the part disposal proceeds. Therefore on a later disposal of the shares, allowable cost will be nil.

4.5 Reorganisation of shares

A reorganisation takes place where new shares, or a mixture of new shares and securities (debentures), are issued in exchange for the original shareholding. **A reorganisation does not in itself amount to a disposal of the original shareholding. Instead the new holding is regarded simply as having been acquired on the same date and for the same consideration as the old**. The problem is how to apportion the original cost between the different types of capital issued on reorganisation.

If the new shares and/or securities are *quoted*, then the original cost is apportioned by reference to the market values of the new types of capital on the first day of quotation after the reorganisation.

Example 6

Dan owns ordinary shares in Sullivan plc, purchased as follows:

1983	2,000	shares costing	£1,750
1985	3,000	shares costing	£13,250

In 2008 there was a reorganisation whereby each ordinary Sullivan plc share was exchanged for 2 'A' ordinary shares (quoted at £2 each) and 1 preference share (quoted at £1 each).

Show how the original costs will be apportioned.

Where the new holding comprises *unquoted* shares or securities, the original cost is again apportioned on the basis of the market value of those new shares or securities. However in this case it is the market value *at the date of a subsequent disposal* which is used. Therefore if the shares are sold a few at a time, a separate calculation is needed for every subsequent disposal.

Example 7

An unquoted company reorganises its share capital in August 1988, so that for every 10 ordinary shares, a shareholder receives:

6	'A' ordinary shares
14	5% preference shares

Samuel originally owned 10,000 ordinary shares in the company which he acquired in 1984 for £16,000. In September 2008 he sells 7,000 of his preference shares, at which time the market value of the preference shares is £1.25 each and of the 'A' ordinary shares, £3.50 each.

Compute the allowable cost to set against proceeds from the September 2008 disposal.

4.6 Takeovers

Liability to CGT does not normally arise on a 'paper for paper' takeover, ie when a company is taken over and the shareholders of the old company receive shares in the new company in exchange for their old shares. For both quoted and unquoted shares **the new holding is deemed to have been acquired on the same date and at the same cost as the original holding**.

If part of the takeover consideration is in cash, then a liability will arise on the proportion of the gain that the cash element bears to the overall consideration and the normal part disposal rules will apply. If the cash received is 'small', ie not more than the higher of £3,000 and 5% of the total value on the takeover, then the small distribution rules apply and the cash received will be deducted from cost for the purpose of further disposals.

The takeover rules apply where the company issuing the new shares (the acquiring company) takes over more than 25% of the ordinary share capital of the old company (the target company) or where the acquiring company makes a general offer to shareholders in the target company which would, if accepted, give the acquiring company control of the target company.

Example 8

Le Bon holds 10,000 £1 shares bought originally for £2 each in Duran plc, a quoted company. In 2008 the board of Duran plc agrees to a takeover bid by Spandau plc under which shareholders in Duran plc are to receive 3 Spandau plc shares plus £1.50 cash for every 4 shares held in Duran plc. Immediately following the takeover, the shares in Spandau plc are quoted at £5 each.

Show Le Bon's chargeable gain.

Note that 'paper for paper' transactions are only treated as not giving rise to any immediate CGT liability if the transactions are entered into for *bona fide* commercial reasons and not for tax avoidance motives.

5 Gilts and qualifying corporate bonds

5.1 Definition and treatment

The disposal of gilts or qualifying corporate bonds (QCBs) does not usually give rise to a chargeable gain or an allowable loss.

Gilts include Treasury Loans, Treasury Stock, Exchequer Loans, Exchequer Stock and War Loan.

A QCB is a security (or debenture, or loan note) that:

(a) Represents a '**normal commercial loan**'. This excludes any bonds which are convertible into shares, or which carry the right to excessive interest or interest which depends on the results of the issuer's business;

(b) Is **expressed in sterling** and for which no provision is made for conversion into or redemption in another currency.

Exam focus point

Assume that loan notes (or loan stock) qualify as QCBs in your exam unless told otherwise.

5.2 Reorganisations involving QCBs

Special rules apply when a reorganisation or takeover involves QCBs issued in exchange for shares.

When QCBs are issued, the chargeable gain which would have arisen if the shares had been sold for cash at their market value at the time of the reorganisation must be computed. This gain is then 'frozen' (ie not charged) until the QCB is redeemed, sold or given away.

If the disposal is a no gain/no loss disposal to a spouse/civil partner, the gain does not become chargeable until a disposal outside the marriage/partnership.

If the reorganisation is followed by the owner's death while he still owns the QCBs, the gain never becomes chargeable.

Example 9

Mr Holland bought 10,000 shares (a 25% shareholding) in Tilbrook Ltd in June 1988 for £18,000. On 19 May 2008, Tilbrook plc was taken-over by Difford Group plc and Mr Holland received:

- 20,000 ordinary shares in Difford Group plc
- £10,000 85% QCB loan stock in Difford Group plc
- £10,000 cash.

At 19 May 2008, the ordinary shares in Difford Group plc were quoted at £2.50 and the QCB Loan Stock at £1.50.

Show the gains arising as a result of the above.

Chapter roundup

- **Special matching rules apply to identify which shares an individual is selling out of a holding acquired at different times.**

- **Disposals on or after 6 April 2008 by individuals are matched with acquisitions in the following order:**
  - **same day acquisitions (average cost)**
  - **acquisitions in the next thirty days (FIFO)**
  - **the share pool (also known as the s.104 pool) (average cost)**

- **Bonus and rights issues are broadly treated as acquired at the same date as the original holding to which they relate.**

- **Where shares are converted into other shares, no disposal takes place, and the new shares take over the original shares' acquisition date and cost.**

- **On a takeover, 'paper for paper' transactions (ie shares received in exchange for other shares) are not usually chargeable disposals.**

- **If both cash and shares (or securities) are received on a takeover, there is a part disposal in respect of the cash element.**

- **Disposals of gilts and QCBs are exempt from capital gains tax. Losses are not allowable.**

- **If a QCB is exchanged for shares on a reorganisation, the gain is calculated at the date of the reorganisation but is frozen and not charged until a later disposal.**

1. Set out the order of matching for 5,000 shares sold by an individual on 7 November 2008, if acquisitions have been made as follows:

	No of shares
30 October 1983	3,000
4 April 1984	2,000
30 September 1987	2,000
10 July 1989	1,000
7 November 2008	1,000
30 November 2008	2,000

2. A capital distribution is treated as small if it amounts to less than the higher of £X and Y% of the value of the shares. What are X and Y?

3. Reggie owns 5,000 ordinary shares in Perrin plc (a quoted company) which cost him £7,000 in 1984. Perrin plc is the subject of a takeover bid by Marwell plc (also a quoted company) which offers, in exchange for each Perrin plc ordinary share:

   2 Marwell Ltd £1 ordinary shares – valued at 75p each
   £1 Marwell Ltd loan stock – valued at 80p

   Compute the base costs for any later disposal of the new shares and loan stock owned by Reggie.

1. (a) 2,000 shares acquired on 30.11.08
    (b) 1,000 shares acquired on disposal date
    (c) 2,000 (out of 8,000) shares from the share pool

2. X = 3,000, Y = 5.

3. Market value of new holdings:

			£
Ordinary shares:	5,000 × 2 × 75p		7,500
Loan stock:	5,000 × 80p		4,000
			11,500

Base cost of Perrin plc shares (£7,000) is allocated in the ratio 7,500 : 4,000, ie

Base cost of Marwell plc shares:

$$£7,000 \times \frac{7,500}{11,500} = £4,565$$

The loan stock is presumably a qualifying corporate bond and will therefore be exempt on disposal. However, 4,000/11,500 of the gain which would have arisen if the 5,000 Perrin Ltd shares had been sold (instead of taken over) will crystallise on the disposal of the loan stock instead.

Solutions to chapter examples

Solution to Example 1

Matching:

12.3.09	5,000 shares (following 30 days)
20.2.09	2,000 shares (same day)
1.5.06	(9,000) → 3,000 shares (share pool)
	10,000

Note: In this case we do not need to construct a share pool as there is only one acquisition prior to the date of disposal.

Gains

12.3.09 holding

	£	Gains £
Proceeds $\frac{5,000}{10,000}$ × £30,000	15,000	
Less: cost	(12,000)	3,000

20.2.09 holding

Proceeds $\frac{2,000}{10,000}$ × £30,000	6,000	
Less: cost	(5,000)	1,000

1.5.06 holding

Proceeds $\frac{3,000}{10,000}$ × £30,000	9,000	
Less: cost $\frac{3,000}{9,000}$ × £18,000	(6,000)	3,000
Total gains		7,000

Solution to Example 2

Share pool:

	No of shares	Cost £
August 1982	1,000	2,750
December 1984	1,000	3,250
July 1986	2,000	4,000
	4,000	10,000
Disposal: July 2008	(3,000)	
Cost: $\frac{3,000}{4,000} \times 10,000$		(7,500)
Pool c/f	1,000	2,500

	£
Proceeds	18,000
Cost	(7,500)
Chargeable gain	10,500

Solution to Example 3

Order of matching:

(i)   *Next 30 days*

		No. of shares
Purchase	15.7.08	200
Disposal	6.7.08	(200)

(ii)   *Share pool*

		No. of shares
Purchase	6.4.83	800
Purchase	6.4.88	600
Purchase	6.5.99	1,000
		2,400
Bonus issue (1 for 4)		600
		3,000
Disposal	6.7.08	(2,000)
Pool c/f		1,000

Note: The bonus issue is not treated as a separate acquisition, but is matched with previous acquisitions

Solution to Example 4

Share pool:

	No. of shares		Cost £
Purchase July 1983	1,500		3,750
Purchase July 1988	1,000		3,000
Purchase May 1999	2,000		8,000
	4,500		14,750
Rights issue (1 for 4)	1,125	× £4.20	4,725
	5,625		19,475
Disposal October 2008	(5,625)		(19,475)
	–		–

Calculate gain:

	£
Proceeds	50,400
Cost	(19,475)
Chargeable gain	30,925

Solution to Example 5

(a) The normal part disposal rules apply as not small. A equals the proceeds received. The market value of the shares before the distribution equates to A+B.

	£
Disposal proceeds	4,000
Less: cost £10,000 × $\frac{4,000}{65,000}$	(615)
Chargeable gain	3,385

(b) The first distribution is less than 5% of the value of the shares (£84,000 × 5% = £4,200). The gain is deferred until receipt of the final distribution:

	£	£
Disposal proceeds		90,000
Less: cost	10,000	
Less: small distribution	(4,000)	(6,000)
Chargeable gain		84,000

Solution to Example 6

The value of the new holding is:

	£
10,000 'A' ordinary shares at £2	20,000
5,000 preference shares at £1	5,000
	25,000

The original costs will be apportioned in the ratio of 4:1 (ie 20,000 : 5,000) as follows:

Share pool:

	No. of shares	Cost
		£
Purchase 1983	2,000	1,750
Purchase 1985	3,000	13,250
	5,000	15,000

Apportioned cost:

10,000 new ordinary shares: $\frac{20,000}{25,000} \times 15,000 = £12,000$

5,000 new preference shares: $\frac{5,000}{25,000} \times 15,000 = £3,000$

Solution to Example 7

Original cost: 10,000 ordinary shares = £16,000

Market values of new holdings in September 2008:

6,000 'A' ordinary shares @ £3.50 each = £21,000

14,000 5% preference shares @ £1.25 each = £17,500

Allowable cost of shares sold:

$\frac{7,000}{14,000} \times \frac{17,500}{17,500+21,000} \times £16,000 = £3,636$

Solution to Example 8

Total value of the takeover package due to Le Bon on the takeover:

		£
Shares	3/4 × 10,000 (= 7,500) × £5	37,500
Cash	1/4 × 10,000 × £1.50	3,750
		41,250

The share for share element of the takeover does not give rise to a CGT event. The new shares in Spandau plc simply take on the acquisition date and original cost of the old shares in Duran plc.

Since the cash (£3,750) exceeds the higher of £3,000 and 5% of £41,250, ie £3,000, it cannot be rolled over by deducting it from the acquisition cost. It is therefore a part disposal.

	£
Disposal proceeds (cash received)	3,750

Less: apportioned cost:

$$\frac{\text{Value of disposal}}{\text{Value of disposal} + \text{value of part retained}} \times \text{original cost}$$

	£
$\dfrac{3,750}{3,750 + 37,500} \times 10,000 \times £2$	(1,818)
Chargeable gain	1,932

Solution to Example 9

Value received on takeover:

	£
Ordinary shares (20,000 × £2.50)	50,000
QCB Loan Stock (£10,000 × £1.50)	15,000
Cash	10,000
Total	75,000

Original cost of Tilbrook plc shares allocated as follows:

	£

Ordinary shares in Difford Group:

	£
$\dfrac{50,000}{75,000} \times £18,000$	12,000

QCB Loan Stock in Difford Group

	£
$\dfrac{15,000}{75,000} \times £18,000$	3,600

Cash

	£
$\dfrac{10,000}{75,000} \times £18,000$	2,400
Total	18,000

Gain on receipt of cash:

	£
Proceeds	10,000
Less: cost (above)	(2,400)
Chargeable gain	7,600

Gain on receipt of QCB:

	£
Proceeds (MV of QCB)	15,000
Less: cost (above)	(3,600)
Frozen gain	11,400

This gain is frozen until the loan stock is disposed of.

New ordinary shares:

This is a 'share for share' disposal so no gain arises. The new shares in Difford Group plc are treated as having been acquired in June 1988 for £12,000.

Now try the following questions

Short Form Questions:

11.1– 11.3 inclusive

Long Form Questions:

11.1	Julie Green (Pilot Paper)
11.2	Mr Jones
11.3	Richard Price
11.4	Eric James

12

Chattels and wasting assets

- define the terms 'chattel' and 'wasting asset'
- calculate the gain or loss on the disposal of chattels
- understand the taxation of wasting assets that are not chattels
- understand and apply the rules for the taxation of leases

References: TCGA 1992 unless otherwise stated

1 Chattels

1.1 Definition

A *chattel* is tangible movable property (it can be moved, seen and touched). A *wasting asset* is an asset with an estimated life of fifty years or less.

In general, wasting chattels, eg racehorses, are exempt from CGT.

1.2 Gains

If a chattel is not a wasting asset, any gain arising will still be exempt from CGT if the gross proceeds and cost are both £6,000 or less.

If sale proceeds exceed £6,000, but the cost is less than £6,000, the gain is limited to:

$5/3 \times$ (gross proceeds – £6,000).

Example 1

Adam purchased a Chippendale chair on 1 June 1985 for £800. On 10 October 2008 he sold the chair at auction for £6,480 net of the auctioneer's 10% commission. Show the chargeable gain arising.

$$5/3 \times (6,480 - 6,000)$$

Exam focus point

Examiner's report – Personal Taxation (old syllabus)

May 2002 – Question 2

...The gain on the sale of the vase was calculated correctly in many cases but there were a few who muddled the chattel relief calculation. The vintage car was treated correctly in most cases, but there were a few who appeared to consider that because the car was 'vintage' it became chargeable. ...

1.3 Capital losses

Where a chattel is sold for less than £6,000, but cost more than £6,000, any allowable loss is restricted to that which would arise if it were sold for gross proceeds of £6,000.

Example 2

Eve purchased a manuscript on 1 July 1982 for £8,000 which she sold in October 2008 at auction for £2,800. Costs of disposal were £280. Compute the gain or loss arising.

A loss cannot be turned into a gain under this provision. If a real loss arises, but substituting £6,000 for the sale proceeds produces a theoretical gain, then there is no allowable loss or chargeable gain.

Exam focus point

The CGT treatment of non-wasting chattels may be examined in the short form or part of long form questions. The tricky bit is spotting that the asset in question is a non-wasting chattel. The trick is to look out for assets with relatively low values.

1.4 Plant and machinery

There are special rules for plant and machinery qualifying for capital allowances (CAs):

Proceeds < Cost	No allowable loss for CGT (relief already given by CAs).
Proceeds < £6,000, Cost < £6,000	Exempt.
Proceeds > £6,000, Cost < £6,000	Chargeable (regardless of expected useful life). Any CAs given will have been clawed back as a balancing charge. Apply the non wasting chattels' restriction to the gain if appropriate.

Example 3

Suppose the asset sold by Adam in example 1 was plant and machinery. How much is the chargeable gain?

2 Wasting assets (other than leases)

Special rules apply to wasting assets that are not chattels. An example of an 'intangible' wasting asset is a copyright.

The allowable expenditure in respect of a wasting asset is deemed to waste away to nothing over its predictable life on a straight line basis.

> ### Example 4
>
> Sarah acquires a copyright for £20,000 for use in her trade on 10 May 1999 when it has 15 years to run. On 9 August 2008 she sells the copyright for £17,500. What is her CGT position?

3 Leases

3.1 Introduction

A lease is the right to occupy land for a fixed period of time. **For CGT purposes a distinction is made between a long lease which has more than 50 years to run and a short lease which has 50 years or less to run.**

There are five different situations to consider:

(a)   Assignment (ie sale) of a long lease
(b)   Assignment of a short lease
(c)   Granting (ie sub-letting) of a long lease out of a freehold or out of a long head-lease
(d)   Granting a short lease out of a freehold or out of a long head-lease
(e)   Granting a short lease out of a short head-lease.

The duration of the lease is usually determined by the period specified in the lease.

> ### Exam focus point
>
> Note the importance of the distinction between assignment (sale) of a lease and grant (sub-letting) of a lease.

3.2 Assignment of a long lease   *SALE*   → normal disposal ie proceeds (less cost)

This is the simplest case, since the assignment (sale) of a long lease is the same as a **disposal of the whole asset.** Any gain on disposal will be chargeable to CGT (subject to any private residence exemption – see Chapter 13). **The gain is computed in the same way as for any other asset.**

3.3 Assignment of a short lease   *SALE*   ≤ 50 yrs = wasting asset ∴ calculate proportion of cost which is wasted ie (original yrs in lease / cost) × yrs left (portion)

A lease which has less than 50 years to run at the date of disposal is a wasting asset. As we saw above, when calculating the gain on the disposal of a wasting asset only a **certain proportion of the original cost is deductible** as the rest of it will have wasted away. In the case of short leases the proportion is determined by a table of percentages contained in Schedule 8 TCGA 1992. [para 1 Sch 8]

The allowable proportion is given by X/Y × original cost where X is the percentage relating to the number of years left for the lease to run at the date of the assignment, and Y is the percentage relating to the number of years the lease had to run when first acquired by the disposer.

The table only provides percentages for exact numbers of years. Where the duration is not an exact number of years the relevant percentage is found by **adding** one twelfth of the difference between the two years on either side of the actual duration for each extra month. Odd days of 14 or more will count as a month. These rules are also given in Schedule 8. *{ look up §*

The percentages are reproduced in the Association's Tax Tables available to you in the examination.

Example 5

Mr A acquired a 20 year lease on 1 August 1999 for £15,000. He assigned it on 1 August 2008 for £19,000.

You are required to compute the chargeable gain arising.

3.4 Grant of a long lease   _lease_ → Part disposal = $\frac{original\ cost}{proceeds + remainder}$ × amount of premium paid for the lease

If the taxpayer grants a lease out of his freehold or long lease, then this is treated as a part disposal. Where the lease is granted for 50 years or more, the gain on the part disposal is calculated using the usual part disposal rules. **The gain will be calculated by deducting the following proportion of the original cost from the proceeds**:

Original cost × $\dfrac{A}{A+B}$

where **A** is the premium paid for the lease, and **B** is the value of the remainder, in this case the value of the right to get the property back on the expiry of the lease, known as the *reversionary interest*. This will be given to you in the examination.

Example 6

Mr B acquired a freehold property for £18,000 on 1 January 1983. On 1 July 2008 he granted a ~~60~~ 30 year lease for a premium of £20,000. At the time of the grant the value of the reversion was £25,000.

You are required to compute any chargeable gain arising.

3.5 Grant of a short lease out of a freehold or long lease   _lease_

If a short lease is granted out of a freehold or long head-lease, part of the premium is assessable as property income (see Chapter 3) **and must be excluded from the CGT computation**. We do this by using the following formula:

Original cost × $\dfrac{a}{A+B}$ 2% × (n-1) × premium = proportion assessable as property income

where **a** is the capital value of the premium, **A** is the total premium, and **B** is the value of the reversionary interest.

Example 7   2% × (30-1) × 20,000

Assume the facts as in the previous example, except that the lease is for 30 years rather than 60.

3.6 Grant of a short lease out of a short lease   _lease_

If a short lease is granted out of a short head-lease, part of the premium will be assessable as property income (see Chapter 3) which must be excluded from the CGT computation.

We do this by initially using the full amount of the premium as the consideration for CGT purposes. The cost is then adjusted using the lease percentage table in Schedule 8. The allowable proportion is given by $\frac{X-Y}{Z}$ × original cost where:

- X is the percentage relating to the number of years left for the lease to run at the date of grant of the sublease
- Y is the percentage relating to the number of years left to run at the date when the sublease expires, and
- Z is the percentage relating to the number of years the lease had to run when first acquired.

After calculating the gain, the amount chargeable as property income is deducted to arrive at the chargeable gain. This deduction cannot turn a chargeable gain into an allowable loss, nor can it increase the amount of an allowable loss.

Example 8

On 1 June 2003, Amy paid a premium of £30,000 to acquire a 30 year lease on a property. On 1 June 2008, she granted a 10 year sub-lease over the whole property in return for a premium of £40,000. The rent payable under the sub-lease was the same as the rent payable under the original lease.

Calculate Amy's chargeable gain.

Chapter roundup

- Chattels are 'tangible moveable property' ie assets which can be moved, seen and touched.

- 'Wasting chattels', ie those with a predictable life of less than 50 years, are exempt from CGT unless they qualify for capital allowances (when a gain is chargeable, but a loss is not allowable).

- The following summarises the rules relating to disposals of non wasting chattels.

Proceeds	Cost	CGT implications
≤ £6,000	≤ £6,000	Exempt
> £6,000	> £6,000	Gain calculated in normal way
> £6,000	< £6,000	Gain calculated in normal way but restricted to $^5/_3 \times$ (gross proceeds − £6,000)
< £6,000	> £6,000	Loss is restricted by deeming proceeds to be £6,000

- The cost of a wasting intangible asset (eg a copyright) wastes away over time, so only the cost remaining at the date of disposal can be deducted in the CGT computation.

- When considering the tax consequences of transactions involving leases, it is essential to ascertain whether the transaction involves the assignment (sale) of an existing lease, or the sub-letting (grant) of a lease out of a freehold or a superior lease.

- An assignment involves transferring the lease from one person to another, with the transferor entirely disposing of his interest.

- The grant of a sub-lease is treated as a part disposal of the lease. Where a lease is granted for 50 years or less part of the premium received will be subject to a charge as property income, with the balance chargeable to CGT.

- The following table summarises the different ways in which leases are treated for CGT purposes.

	Type of lease	Treatment
Assignment	Lease > 50 years	Whole gain chargeable
	Lease ≤ 50 years	Gain chargeable according to percentage table
Granting of leases	Sub-lease > 50 years	Normal part disposal rules
	Sub-lease ≤ 50 years, out of freehold or headlease > 50 years	Part disposal rules with premium reduced by any premium charged to income tax
	Sub-lease ≤ 50 years, out of headlease < 50 years	Full premium used as proceeds. Adjust cost using lease percentage table. Deduct property income assessment.

Quiz

1. What is a wasting asset?

2. Robert sells his racing greyhound 'Spot' for £15,000, having bought him as a pup for £100 four years ago. What is the chargeable gain/allowable loss?

3. Micky sells his gold watch in August 2008 for £8,000, having acquired it in November 1996 for £5,800.

    Compute the chargeable gain.

4. Petra sells a diamond ring, which she inherited from her aunt, for £5,000. Probate value of the ring was £7,600. What is the allowable loss on sale?

5. State how your answer to Question 4 above would differ if the probate value of the ring had been £4,600.

6. Assignment of a lease with 40 years to run is the disposal of a wasting asset. True/False?

7. Danny assigns a lease on 30 November 2008 which he acquired on 31 May 2002, at which time it had exactly 30 years to run. If Danny paid £55,000 for the lease in May 2002, compute the allowable cost for the disposal on 30 November 2008.

8. Edward grants a 60 year sub-lease out of his 999 year head lease for a premium of £80,000. Edward's head lease was acquired by him two years ago at a cost of £105,000. If the value of the reversionary interest is agreed to be £40,000, how much of Edward's original cost is allowable against the premium received on the grant of the sub-lease?

9. Show how your answer to Question 8 above would differ, if the sub-lease had been for a duration of only 40 years instead of 60.

Solutions to Quiz

1. An asset with a predictable life of not more than 50 years.

2. Nil – a greyhound is a wasting chattel and hence exempt from CGT.

3.

	£
Proceeds	8,000
Less: cost	(5,800)
	2,200

The chargeable gain cannot exceed:

5/3 ($£8,000 - 6,000$) = £3,333

Chargeable gain (lower gain) = £2,200

4.

	£
Deemed proceeds	6,000
Less: cost (= probate value)	(7,600)
Loss	(1,600)

5. As proceeds and original cost (ie, probate value in this instance) are less than £6,000, the gain is exempt. There is therefore neither a gain nor a loss.

6. True

7. Allowable cost: $£55,000 \times \dfrac{X}{Y}$

X: % for 23 years 6 months = $78.055 + (^{6}/_{12} (79.622 - 78.055)) = 78.839$

Y: % for 30 years = 87.330

Therefore, allowable cost = $£55,000 \times \dfrac{78.839}{87.330} = £49,652$

8. Part disposal formula is used:

Allowable cost = original cost $\times \dfrac{A}{A + B}$

ie $£105,000 \times \dfrac{80,000}{80,000 + 40,000} = £70,000$

9. Part disposal formula (modified):

Allowable cost = original cost $\times \dfrac{a}{A + B}$

Where a = that part of the premium not charged to income tax as property income.

	£
Full premium	80,000
Less: 2% $\times$ (40 − 1) $\times$ £80,000	(62,400)
Property income assessment	17,600

Allowable cost: $£105,000 \times \dfrac{62,400}{80,000 + 40,000} = £54,600$

Solutions to chapter examples

Solution to Example 1

	£
Gross proceeds (£6,480 × $\frac{100}{90}$)	7,200
Less: incidental costs of sale (10%)	(720)
Net proceeds	6,480
Less: cost	(800)
	5,680

Restricted to a maximum of 5/3 × £(7,200 − 6,000) = £2,000

Solution to Example 2

Eve has a loss that must be calculated using deemed proceeds of £6,000.

	£
Deemed disposal proceeds	6,000
Less: incidental costs of disposal	(280)
	5,720
Less: cost	(8,000)
Allowable loss	(2,280)

Solution to Example 3

Chargeable gain	£2,000

Exactly the same calculation as example 1

Solution to Example 4

	£
Disposal proceeds	17,500
Less: cost	
£20,000 × $\frac{5\frac{3}{4}}{15}$	(7,667)
Chargeable gain	9,833

Note: The sale proceeds are for what is left of the copyright (ie 5.75 years) so we match this to the cost of what is left (ie 5.75 years worth of 15 years' cost). The remainder of the cost has wasted away.

Solution to Example 5

	£
Disposal proceeds	19,000
Less: cost	
£15,000 × $\frac{11 \text{ years}}{20 \text{ years}}$ ie $\frac{50.038}{72.770}$	(10,314)
Chargeable gain	8,686

50.038 = percentage for 11 years (time left on lease at disposal on 1.8.08)

72.770 = percentage for 20 years (time on lease when purchased on 1.8.99)

Solution to Example 6

	£
Disposal proceeds	20,000
Cost:	
£18,000 × $\frac{20,000}{20,000 + 25,000}$	(8,000)
Chargeable gain	12,000

Solution to Example 7

The property income assessment will be:

	£
Premium	20,000
Less: 2% × (30 − 1)× £20,000	(11,600)
Property income	8,400

	£
Capital element of premium	11,600
Less: cost:	
$£18,000 \times \dfrac{11,600\,*}{20,000\,* + 25,000}$	(4,640)
Chargeable gain	6,960

Note: the numerator (top number) of the part disposal fraction is the *capital element* of the premium, whilst the denominator (bottom number) is the total premium.

Solution to Example 8

Amy's allowable expenditure on the grant of the sub-lease is:

$£30,000 \times \dfrac{81.100 - 61.617}{87.330}$ (see working) = £6,693

The amount of the premium chargeable as property income is:

	£
Premium	40,000
Less: 2% × (10 − 1)× £40,000	(7,200)
Property income	32,800

Amy's gain is therefore:

	£
Premium	40,000
Less: allowable expenditure	(6,693)
Gain	33,307
Less: chargeable as property income	(32,800)
Chargeable gain	507

Working for percentages:

61.617 = 15 years	Life left when 10 year sublease ends
81.100 = 25 years	Life left when sublease granted 1 June 2008
87.330 = 30 years	Life when purchased on 1 June 2003

Now try the following questions

Short Form Questions:

12.1 – 12.7 inclusive

Long Form Questions:

12.1	Doug
12.2	Mr Cole
12.3	CGT Leases

The purpose of this chapter is to help you to:

- calculate the relief available on the disposal of an individual's home

- identify an individual's PPR where he owns more than one home

- calculate the further relief available where a residence is let as residential accommodation

- understand how business use of a property impacts on the availability of PPR relief

References: TCGA 1992 unless otherwise stated

1 General principles

1.1 Relief for actual/deemed occupation

A gain arising on the sale of an individual's only or main private residence (principal private residence) is exempt from CGT. Any loss is not allowable. The exemption covers a garden and grounds up to half a hectare (slightly over one acre), but it can exceed half a hectare if the house is sufficiently large to warrant it.

The exemption applies to both leasehold and freehold property.

Husband and wife (and partners in a civil partnership) are entitled to only one principal private residence between them. This applies even though they are generally taxed independently.

The basic rule is that the gain is wholly exempt where the owner has occupied the whole of the residence throughout his period of ownership. Where occupation has been for only part of the period, the proportion of the gain exempted is: [s.223]

$$\text{Total gain} \times \frac{\text{period of occupation}}{\text{total period of ownership}}$$

A further proportionate restriction is made where only part of the property has been occupied as his residence, eg where part is used exclusively for business purposes.

The last 36 months of ownership is exempt in all cases if at some time the residence has been the taxpayer's main residence. [s.223(1)]

There will be no exemption on a property that is acquired wholly or partly for the purpose of making a gain on a subsequent disposal. However, it is difficult for HMRC to prove such an intention.

The period of occupation is also deemed to include certain periods of absence, provided the individual had no other exempt residence at that time and the **period of absence was at some time both preceded by and followed by a period of actual occupation**.

The periods of *deemed occupation* are: [s.223(3)]

(a) **Any period** (or periods taken together) of absence, for any reason, **up to three years**. Where the period exceeds three years, three years out of the longer period are deemed to be a period of occupation;

(b) **Any periods** during which the owner was **required by his employment to live abroad**;

(c) **Any period** (or periods taken together) **not exceeding four years** where the owner was:

   (i) **Self-employed and forced to work away from home** (UK and abroad)

   (ii) **Employed and required to work elsewhere in the UK** (overseas employment is covered by (b) above.)

The above periods apply even if the residence is let while the owner is away.

Although exempt periods of absence must usually be preceded and followed by a period of actual occupation, the re-occupation requirement is waived by extra-statutory concession where the individual has been required to work abroad or elsewhere in the UK (paras (b) and (c) above) and is unable to return home because the terms of his employment require him to work elsewhere.

Also by HMRC concession, a house is treated as occupied as the owner's main residence for a period of up to 12 months (or longer if there is a good reason) if he was prevented from taking up residence because the house was being built or altered or because necessary steps were being taken to dispose of their previous residence.

Example 1

Mr A purchased a house in July 1982 for £50,000. He lived in the house until June 1984 and then moved to a rented apartment until June 1988. He then worked abroad for ten years before returning to the UK to live in the house again in July 1998. He stayed in the house for six months before moving out to live with friends until the house was sold on 23 December 2008 for £150,000.

Calculate any chargeable gain arising on disposal.

1.2 Disposal of a garden

Where the main residence is sold along with part of the garden, leaving the rest of the garden to be sold separately (for development purposes) at a later date, the PPR exemption will not be available on the later sale as the garden is no longer part of the individual's main residence. HMRC has indicated that this view will only be taken if the garden has development value. [Varty v Lynes (1976)]

2 More than one residence

2.1 Election for residence to be treated as main residence

Where a person has more than one residence, he may, by notice to HMRC, nominate which is his main residence. The notice must be given within two years of the second property being used as a residence. The nomination may be varied at a later date. The individual must actually reside in both residences, at least from time to time. Any period of ownership of a residence not nominated as the main residence will be a chargeable period. An election can have effect for any period beginning not more than two years prior to the date of the election.

If no election is made then HMRC can determine, based on all the facts, whether the property is or is not the taxpayer's PPR. The taxpayer may appeal to the Commissioners.

2.2 Job-related accommodation

A person lives in job-related accommodation (see Chapter 5) where:

(a)   it is necessary for the proper performance of his duties; or

(b)   it is provided for the better performance of his duties and it is one of the kinds of employment in which it is customary for employers to provide accommodation; or

(c)   there is a special threat to the employee's security and use of the accommodation is part of security arrangements.

An individual living in job-related accommodation will be treated as occupying any second house that he owns and where he intends, in due course, to occupy the house as his only or main residence. It is not necessary to establish any form of actual residency in such cases. The benefit of this rule has been extended to apply to self-employed persons living in 'job-related' accommodation (eg tenants of public houses).

2.3 Husband and wife and civil partners

Where spouses (or civil partners) live together, only one residence can qualify as the main residence for PPR relief.

By extra-statutory concession, in a case where a marriage/partnership has broken down and one partner owning or having an interest in the matrimonial home has ceased to occupy the house, the departing partner will continue to be treated as resident for CGT purposes. This is provided that the other partner has continued to reside in the home and the departing partner has not elected that some other house should be treated as his or her main residence for this period. This concession only applies where one spouse/partner disposes of his interest to the other.

3 Letting relief

Gains may also be exempt where they relate to a period while the property is let, up to a certain limit. The two main circumstances in which letting relief will apply are: [s.223(4)]

(a)   When the owner is absent and lets the property during his absence, and

(b)   When the owner lets part of the property while still occupying the rest of it. In this case the owner will get full PPR relief on the part he has occupied and letting relief on the rest of the property.

In both cases **the letting must be for _residential_ use** and the last 36 months of ownership of the property will qualify for full relief even if the whole or part of the property is let during that period.

Letting relief is restricted to the lowest of:

(a)   **The gain relating to the letting period** (and not already covered by the deemed occupation provisions);
(b)   **The gain that is already exempt under the PPR provisions**; and
(c)   **£40,000**.

Letting relief cannot turn a gain into an allowable loss, nor increase an existing loss.

Where a lodger lives as a member of the owner's family, sharing their living accommodation and eating with them, no part of the accommodation is treated as having ceased to be occupied as the owner's main residence. The question of letting relief does not therefore arise and full PPR relief would be available on disposal.

Similarly where lodgers are taken in under the 'rent-a-room' scheme – which gives income tax exemption on £4,250 of gross rental income (see Chapter 3) – it will not lead to a restriction of PPR. Again letting relief will not be relevant.

Exam focus point

PPR relief and lettings relief are regularly examined in the long form questions of Personal Taxation either computationally or in a written question. Make sure you are familiar with the deemed occupation periods and letting relief. This is all in s.223 TCGA 1992.

Example 2

Miss Coe purchased a house in May 1982 for £90,000 and used it as her main residence. She sold it on 30 September 2008 for £384,000, having let half of it from 1 January 1984 to 30 September 1988. She then lived in the whole of the property until sale.

Calculate the chargeable gain arising.

4 Business use

Where part of a residence is used exclusively for business purposes the gain attributable to that part will always be taxable.

Example 3

Mr Woof purchased a property for £35,000 on 1 December 1982 and began operating a veterinary practice from that date in one third of the house. He sold the house on 1 December 2008 for £130,000. He continued to operate the veterinary practice from new premises which he rented.

Compute the chargeable gain, if any, arising on disposal.

Chapter roundup

- **Gains arising on the disposal of a dwelling house are exempt from CGT if the house was the individual's only or main residence throughout the period of ownership.**

- **Where the house is not owner-occupied throughout the period of ownership only the proportion of the gain attributable to the period of owner-occupation is exempt.**

- **Certain 'periods of absence' are deemed to be periods of occupation. The last 36 months of ownership are always treated as a period of occupation.**

- **Although gardens of up to one half hectare (possibly more) are also covered by the private residence exemption, the disposal of part of a garden, following the disposal of the house, attracts no relief.**

- **Where an individual owns more than one residence he may, within two years of acquiring the second, nominate one as his main residence.**

- A married couple (or civil partners) **may have only one qualifying residence.**

- **Where the house or part of it is let as residential accommodation, letting relief may be available up to a maximum of £40,000.**

- **Where part of a house is *used exclusively* for business purposes, the gain attributable to the business use portion is not eligible for PPR relief.**

Quiz

1. Provided the property has at some time been the owner's principal private residence, the last .... months of ownership is always an exempt period. How many months?

2. In what circumstances is the following requirement ignored: that in order for a period of absence to be treated as deemed occupation, the taxpayer must actually occupy the property at some time *after* the period of absence?

3. Where an individual sells one of two properties which he owns, both of which he has occupied from time to time as a residence, what is the CGT position, assuming he has failed to make any election?

4. Ruth sells a house which has been partly occupied by her as her principal private residence and partly let to students as residential accommodation.

   The facts are:

   - Gain before PPR relief: £155,000.
   - Occupied solely by Ruth as her PPR from 15 July 1988 (date of purchase) to 30 June 1989
   - Occupied from 1 July 1989 to 31 December 2008 (date of sale) 20% by Ruth, 80% by students.

   Compute:

   (a) The PPR exemption, and
   (b) The chargeable gain after all exemptions and reliefs.

5. Hannah has always used one room of her house exclusively as an office – HMRC has agreed that this amounts to 10% of the whole property. If the gain on the sale of the property is £124,000, compute the chargeable gain on the assumptions that Hannah owned the property from 1 July 1987 to 30 November 2008.

1. 36

2. By concession, where the taxpayer has been absent either because he was working abroad or because he was working elsewhere in the UK, and he is prevented from re-occupying the property because the terms of his employment require him to work elsewhere.

3. HMRC will determine, based on the facts, whether the property sold is or is not the taxpayer's principal private residence. The taxpayer has a right of appeal to the Commissioners.

4. Gain before relief   £155,000

   (a)   PPR exemption:

   (i)   1.7.88 – 30.6.89: 100% exemption
   (ii)   1.7.89 – 31.12.05: 20% exemption
   (iii) 1.1.06 – 31.12.08: 100% exemption (last 36 months)

		£
(i)	1/20½ × £155,000 × 100% =	7,561
(ii)	16½/20½ × £155,000 × 20% =	24,951
(iii)	3/20½ × £155,000 × 100% =	22,683
	Exempt gain due to PPR exemption	55,195

   (b)   Chargeable gain:

	£
Gain before relief	155,000
Less: PPR exemption	(55,195)
Gain attributable to letting period	99,805
Less: s.223 TCGA 1992 relief – *lowest* of:	
– £40,000	
– £55,195 (PPR relief)	
– £99,805 (16½/20½ × £155,000 × 80%) (relates to let period)	(40,000)
Chargeable gain	59,805

5.

	£
Gain before relief	124,000
Less: PPR exemption	
£124,000 × 90%	(111,600)
Gain after PPR	12,400

Solution to Example 1

(a) Exempt and chargeable periods

		Exempt months	Chargeable months
(i)	July 1982 – June 1984	24	–
(ii)	July 1984 – June 1988	36	12
(iii)	July 1988 – June 1998	120	–
(iv)	July 1998 – December 1998	6	–
(v)	January 1999 – December 2005	–	84
(vi)	January 2006 – December 2008	36	–
		222	96

(b) *Explanations*

(i) July 1982 – June 1984

A period of owner occupation.

(ii) July 1984 – June 1988

Deemed occupation for up to '3 years of absence for any reason'. The period is both preceded and followed by owner occupation.

(iii) July 1988 – June 1998

Deemed occupation as the owner is required by his employment to live abroad. The period is both preceded and followed by a period of owner occupation.

(iv) July 1998 – December 1998

A period of owner occupation.

(v) January 1999 – December 2005

Not occupied. Deemed occupation for up to '3 years of absence for any reason' has already been used.

(vi) January 2006 – December 2008

Covered by the final 36 months exemption.

(c) *Calculation of the chargeable gain*

	£
Disposal proceeds	150,000
Less: cost	(50,000)
Gain before PPR relief	100,000
Less: exempt under PPR provisions	
$\dfrac{222}{222+96} \times £100,000$	(69,811)
Chargeable gain	30,189

In this example, had Mr A gone straight to live with friends in July 1998 instead of having six months occupation he would have lost not only the extra six months, but also the periods from July 1988 to June 1998, as these two periods of absence would lose their status as deemed occupation as the property was not occupied again by the owner prior to sale.

Solution to Example 2

	£	£
Disposal proceeds		384,000
Less: cost		(90,000)
Gain before PPR relief		294,000
Less: PPR exemption		

$$£294,000 \times \frac{260 \text{(W1)}}{317 \text{(W2)}}$$ (241,136)

$$£294,000 \times \frac{57 \text{(W3)}}{317 \text{(W2)}} \times \tfrac{1}{2}$$ (26,432)

		(267,568)
Left in charge		26,432
Less: letting relief		
lowest of:		
(a) gain relating to letting period: £26,432		(26,432)
(b) PPR relief given: £267,568		
(c) £40,000		
Chargeable gain		nil

Workings:

		Months
(W1) Period not let and fully occupied as PPR: 1.5.82 – 31.12.83		20
	1.10.88 – 30.9.08	240
		260

(W2)   Period of ownership: 1.5.82 – 30.9.08   = 317 months

(W3)   Period let: 1.1.84 – 30.9.88   = 57 months

Note. Miss Coe cannot claim exemption for part of the period of letting under the 3-year absence rule since during this time she has a main residence which qualifies for relief (ie the rest of the house).

Solution to Example 3

	£
Disposal proceeds	130,000
Less: cost	(35,000)
Gain before PPR relief	95,000
Less: PPR exemption £95,000 × $^2/_3$	(63,333)
Chargeable gain	31,667

PPR exemption is lost on one third owing to use of that part exclusively for business purposes. Note that the exemption is restricted for business use for the *whole* period of ownership, including the last 36 months.

Now try the following questions

Short Form Questions:

13.1 – 13.3 inclusive

Long Form Questions:

13.1	Owning two homes (Pilot paper)
13.2	Peter Stamp

14

Other CGT reliefs

- understand and apply the gift relief rules in appropriate situations

- understand and apply the rules for EIS deferral relief

- understand the tax treatment when insurance money (ie compensation) is received when an asset is damaged or destroyed

References: TCGA 1992 unless otherwise stated

1 Introduction to CGT reliefs

In this section we consider CGT reliefs that are available to either reduce or defer gains arising on the disposal of certain assets.

We have already considered Principal Private Residence relief, which exempted or reduced the gain arising on the sale of a taxpayer's main residence. In this chapter we consider the circumstances in which a chargeable gain may be deferred. When a gain is deferred it is transferred, usually to another asset, until some later date.

In this chapter we consider gift relief, EIS deferral relief and the CGT position when compensation is received when an asset is damaged or destroyed.

In all cases the gain on disposal of the asset is calculated in the normal way and then the appropriate relief is applied to reduce/defer the gain.

2 Gift relief

2.1 General principle

If an individual makes a gift to another individual (who is resident or ordinarily resident in the UK) gift relief may be available.

The transferor's gain calculated (using proceeds equal to market value) is reduced by the relief and the transferee acquires the asset at that market value less the transferor's deferred gain. [s.165]

A partial claim is not allowed, for example, to ensure sufficient gains remain to be covered by losses or the annual exemption.

The transferor and transferee must make a joint claim for the relief within five years from 31 January following the tax year of disposal (ie within approximately 5 years and 10 months of the end of the tax year of the gift).

2.2 Assets attracting gift relief

The relief only applies if the gifted property is: [s.165 (2)]

(a)   An **asset used in a trade**, profession of vocation carried on by:

    (i)   The transferor, or

    (ii)   The transferor's personal company (a company in which 5% or more of the voting rights are controlled by the individual in question), or

    (iii)   A trading company owned by a holding company which is his personal company

or

(b)   **Shares or securities of a trading company** (or the holding company of a trading group) where:

    (i)   The shares are **not quoted** on a recognised stock exchange, or

    (ii)   The **company** (or holding company) **is the transferor's personal company** (ie transferor can exercise at least 5% of the voting rights).

    (The fraction CBA/CA must be used to calculate the eligible gain – see below.)

Gift relief is also available where *any* asset is gifted to a trust (other than to a disabled person's trust) as there is also an Inheritance Tax charge. [s.260(2)]

Trusts are outside the scope of the Personal Taxation syllabus and so are not covered further.

2.3 Gifts of shares

Where shares in a personal company are disposed of, the gain on these shares is first calculated using original cost. Only one asset is being sold, the shares, and hence a single gain is calculated. Only the gain relating to the proportion of the chargeable business assets of the company qualifies for gift relief. This rule relates to gains on the disposal of shares only.

Therefore it is necessary to apportion the gain in the ratio of total chargeable business assets (CBAs) to total chargeable assets (CAs) (ie the fraction $^{CBA}/_{CA}$) using the market value of those assets at the date of disposal of the shares (often given in the form of a balance sheet extract).

A CA is any asset chargeable to capital gains tax. Assets that are exempt from CGT (eg cash, stock, debtors, motor cars and items of plant and machinery with cost and value of less than £6,000) are ignored.

A CBA is a chargeable asset used in the trade or the business. This excludes shares and other assets held as investments, such as rental property.

The gain attributable to the value of chargeable non-business assets will not attract gift relief so this element always remains chargeable.

If the shares are in a holding company, the apportionment is made by reference to the chargeable assets of the whole trading group.

Example 1

On 6 August 2008 Henry gifts his 8% shareholding in a trading company to his brother resulting in a gain of £60,000. The market value of the shares was £150,000. Total chargeable assets at the time of the sale amounted to £40,000 of which total chargeable business assets amounted to £30,000.

You are required to calculate the chargeable gain arising to Henry and the base cost of the shares for his brother, assuming all available reliefs are claimed.

Example 2

Mr McGregor owns 10% of the shares of an unquoted trading company. On 1 January 2009, the company's net assets were:

	£
Plant*	50,000
Factory	1,050,000
Investments	500,000
Net current assets	300,000
	1,900,000

* made up of items with a market value of more than £6,000 each.

Mr McGregor bought the shares in 1983 for £200,000 and gifted them to his son on 1 January 2009 when their market value was £950,000.

You are required to calculate the chargeable gain arising.

Gift relief is not available on gifts of **shares to companies**.

2.4 Gifts of business assets with non-business use

In the case of a gift of a business asset, the amount of the gain that can be deferred is reduced if the asset has not been used in the transferor's trade (or that of his personal company) **throughout his period of ownership**. The reduction is pro rata on a time basis.

If the asset is a building, part of which was used for a non business purpose during the period of ownership, a 'just and reasonable' restriction will apply.

Example 3

Keith gives a factory to his son realising a chargeable gain of £50,000. He has owned the factory for 8 years and has used it in his trade for 5 years. For the other 3 years it was let as a warehouse.

You are required to calculate what part of the gain is eligible for gift relief and what part is immediately chargeable.

Remember, in the case of a gift of shares (see above), the deferred gain is restricted if the company owns non-business chargeable assets at the date of the gift.

2.5 Sales at an undervalue

If the disposal involves actual consideration which is less than the market value (ie a sale at an undervalue rather than an outright gift), then **the gain that can be held-over is the gain** *less* **the excess of the actual consideration over allowable costs.** This excess is immediately taxable.

> ### Exam focus point
>
> Gift relief is an extremely examinable topic both computationally and in written questions. Make sure you know which assets qualify for the relief (s.165) and how much gain can be deferred in both the case of an outright gift and a sale at undervalue.

Example 4

On 1 August 2008 Angelo sold shares in his personal trading company valued at £200,000 to his son Michael for £50,000. Angelo had originally purchased the shares in July 1982 for £30,000. Michael sold the shares for £195,000 in October 2009. Angelo and Michael jointly elect for relief under s.165 TCGA 1992.

You are required to compute any chargeable gains arising assuming the rates for 2008/09 continue to apply for later years.

2.6 Relief before FA 1989

Gift relief was available for the transfer of *all* assets before 14 March 1989. So, paintings, quoted shares and non business property assets generally could qualify for gift relief.

It is important to know that gift relief applied generally before 14 March 1989 as the recipient of such a gift will still have to use a base cost reduced by the deferred gain when calculating a gain on a future disposal.

2.7 Anti-avoidance: the emigrating donee

Consider the situation where a gift relief claim is made but then the recipient emigrates. When they eventually sell the asset there will be no UK CGT, as they are not resident or ordinarily resident, so the deferred gain never becomes chargeable.

Anti-avoidance rules apply to ensure that this deferred gain will eventually crystallise so **where the recipient becomes not resident and not ordinarily resident in the UK, the deferred gain will be assessed on them immediately before they become not resident and not ordinarily resident**. This rule only applies if the recipient leaves the UK within 6 tax years of the end of the year of the gift.

The deferred gain will not crystallise if the recipient disposes of the asset before ceasing to be resident and ordinarily resident. A disposal to the recipient's spouse/civil partner does not count unless the spouse/civil partner then disposes of the asset to a third party.

If the tax payable by the recipient has not been paid within a year of the due date, HMRC may assess the transferor instead. The transferor has the right to recover the tax from the recipient.

If the recipient ceases to be resident because he takes up full-time employment abroad, then, provided residence in the UK is resumed within three years and the asset is not disposed of in the meantime, the deferred gain will not be assessed in the way described above.

3 EIS CGT deferral relief

3.1 General provisions

If an individual makes a gain on the disposal of *any* asset, the gain may be deferred (ie delayed) if the individual subscribes for Enterprise Investment Scheme (EIS) shares. [Sch 5B]

The EIS shares do not need to qualify for the EIS income tax reduction for this deferral relief to be available. So the investor can be 'connected' with the company (ie he can own more than 30% of the shares and can be an employee or director) and he can invest more than the maximum allowed under the income tax rules (£500,000 for 2008/09). [Sch 5B Para. 2(1)]

3.2 Amount of relief

For every £1 invested in EIS shares, the investor can defer £1 of gain.

He can defer up to the full amount he subscribes for his shares, although he can specify a lower amount in his claim to take into account the availability of losses and the annual exemption.

The gain is deferred and is 'frozen' until, usually, the EIS shares are sold (see 3.4 below).

Example 5

Robert made a gain of £196,000 on the disposal of a holiday cottage in 2008/09. He subscribed for some shares in a company which qualified under the EIS rules. How much should Robert claim to defer if:

(a)   The shares cost £200,000 and Robert wants to take the maximum deferral relief possible?
(b)   The shares cost £170,000 and Robert wants to take the maximum deferral relief possible?
(c)   The shares cost £200,000 and Robert has no other chargeable gains?

3.3 Conditions

3.3.1 The gain to be deferred

The gain must either arise on the disposal of an asset or on a gain, 'frozen' under these rules, crystallising (ie coming back into charge) [Sch. 5B Para. 1]

3.3.2 The investor

The investor must be: [Sch. 5B Para. 17]

(a)   **An individual, (or the trustees of a trust for an individual)**
(b)   **UK resident or ordinarily resident when he makes the gain and also when he subscribes for the EIS shares**

3.3.3 The company

The company must be a qualifying company under the EIS income tax rules (broadly an unlisted company carrying on a qualifying trade) (see Chapter 4).

3.3.4 The shares

The investor must subscribe for the shares wholly in cash.

The shares must: [Sch 5B para 1A]

(a)   Be new ordinary shares, fully paid up
(b)   Not be redeemable before the termination date (generally three years after their issue)

(c)   Not have preferential rights to dividends or assets on a winding up within that period.

(d)   Be subscribed and issued for genuine commercial purposes (not for the avoidance of tax)

(e)   Be issued to raise money for a qualifying business activity

Deferral relief will be withdrawn if the money raised is not used for the qualifying business activity within a certain time (usually 80% within twelve months from the issue of the shares and the remaining amount by twenty four months from the issue of the shares).

3.3.5 Time for investment

The shares must be subscribe for the shares within the period of one year before and three years after the gain to be deferred accrues.

3.3.6 The claim

The claim must be made by 31 January nearly six years after the end of the tax year in which the deferred gain arose (ie by 31 January 2015 for 2008/09 gains). [Sch. 5B Para. 6]

3.4 Taxing the deferred gain

3.4.1 Chargeable events

The deferred gain will crystallise (ie come back into charge) if:

(a)   **The investor disposes of the shares to anyone, except to his spouse or civil partner**

(b)   **The investor's spouse or civil partner disposes of the shares, and they had acquired the shares from the investor**

(c)   **The investor becomes non resident within the three years following issue of the shares (the 'relevant period'),** unless he is employed full time abroad for up to three years and keeps the shares until he returns to the UK

(d)   **The investor's spouse or civil partner becomes non resident** within the relevant period (except as in (c) above), if they acquired the shares from the investor

(e)   **The shares cease being 'eligible shares',** eg the company ceases to be a qualifying company, the money subscribed is not used for a qualifying business activity. However, if a company becomes listed this does not result in the gain coming back in charge unless there were arrangements in place at the outset for it to become listed.

The deferred gain becomes chargeable in the year of the event , not the year when it originally arose (if different). The gains is charged on the person holding the shares at that date, whether the investor or his spouse or civil partner if the shares have been passed to them. [Sch 5B Paras. 4, 5]

4 Compensation and insurance monies

4.1 Destroyed assets

If an asset is destroyed or lost (and not merely damaged) **any insurance monies (ie compensation) received will be chargeable to CGT. However, if the proceeds are used to replace the asset within twelve months any gain can be deducted from the cost of the replacement asset.** If only part of the proceeds are used, the gain immediately chargeable is limited to the amount not spent. The rest of the gain is then deducted from the cost of the replacement. [s.23(4)]

Example 6

Alison bought a painting in January 1987 for £10,000. It was destroyed in a fire in August 2008 and she received £80,000 from the insurance company two months later. In March 2009 she bought another painting for £75,000 and made a claim under s.23(4) TCGA 1992.

Show Alison's CGT position in respect of the above.

4.2 Damaged assets

If an asset is damaged and insurance money (compensation) is received as a result, there is a part disposal, with the insurance money as the proceeds. The taxpayer can avoid a part disposal computation by electing for the insurance money to be deducted from the cost of the asset ('rolled over') so long as the asset is non-wasting and:

(a)   Not more than the higher of £3,000 or 5% of the insurance money is *not* used in restoring the asset; or

(b)   The insurance money is less than the higher of £3,000 or 5% of the value of the asset (ie is 'small').

If (a) and (b) do not apply there will be a part disposal calculation, although the taxpayer can elect for this to apply only to the part of the proceeds not used in the restoration. The allowable cost will include the costs of restoration.

Example 7

Mr Jones bought a building which cost £40,000 on 15 August 1990. On 10 September 2008 it was damaged in a fire and, as a result, £33,000 insurance proceeds were received. Of this £20,000 was used to restore the building; the market value of the building immediately after restoration was £62,000.

You are required to calculate the chargeable gain arising on disposal and the base cost of the building for future computations.

5,000

30,000

(·

TQT
Tax Qualification Training

Chapter roundup

- Gift relief applies to gifts and sales at an under value of business assets, including certain shares.

- The transferor's gain is effectively transferred to the donee because the base cost of the asset for the donee is reduced by the deferred gain (ie the gift relief claimed).

- For a sale at an undervalue the deferred gain is the gain less any actual consideration received in excess of allowable cost.

- Gift relief is restricted where there has been non-business use of an asset or where shares are gifted and there are non-business chargeable assets held by the company.

- The emigration of the recipient of the gift within six years will result in the crystallisation of the chargeable gain. An exception is made for individuals employed abroad on a temporary basis.

- A gain on disposal of any asset may be deferred if the individual reinvests the amount of the gain in shares in a qualifying EIS company.

- Relief is given on a £1 for £1 basis (although it is possible to specify a smaller amount in the claim to preserve losses or the annual exemption)

- There are detailed conditions to be satisfied regarding the shares and EIS company.

- If an asset is destroyed or lost a gain is calculated when insurance money is received, unless the money is spent replacing the asset within 12 months.

- If an asset is damaged there is a part disposal when insurance money is received, unless the money is spent restoring the asset. If only part of the money is spent the gain can be deferred.

Quiz

1. The gift relief election for gifts between individuals must be made jointly by the transferor and the transferee. True/False?

2. In what circumstances may the gain on a gift of a business asset between individuals be *fully* (as opposed to only partially) deferred?

3. On 15 May 2008 Philippa makes a gain on the sale of a painting of £60,000. She invests £75,000 in shares of a qualifying EIS company on 22 December 2008. Philippa makes no other disposals during 2008/09 and has capital losses brought forward of £12,000. What is the optimum claim she should make for EIS deferral relief?

4. Where an asset is completely destroyed there is a part disposal of the asset. True/False?

1. True

2. (a) There is no actual consideration, or there is a sale at an undervalue and the actual consideration is less than the transferor's base cost; and

    (b) The whole of the asset has been used throughout the transferor's period of ownership in the transferor's (or his personal company's) trade.

3. In order to utilise her losses and annual exemption, Philippa should claim EIS deferral relief of:

    £60,000 – 12,000 – 9,600 = £38,400.

    This will allow her 2008/09 taxable gains to be reduced to nil as follows:

	£
Gain before relief	60,000
Less: EIS deferral relief	(38,400)
	21,600
Less; capital losses b/f	(12,000)
	9,600
Less: AE	(9,600)
Taxable gain	–

4. False. If the asset is only damaged there is a part disposal.

Solutions to chapter examples

Solution to Example 1

Total gain (on shares)	£60,000

Proportion relating to chargeable business assets eligible for relief:

$$£60,000 \times \frac{30,000}{40,000} = £45,000$$

	£
Less: gift relief	(45,000)
Chargeable gain relating to other chargeable non-business assets	15,000

Base cost of shares for Henry's brother:

	£
Market value at date of gift	150,000
Less: gain deferred by gift relief	(45,000)
Cost c/f	105,000

Solution to Example 2

Total chargeable business assets are:	£
Plant	50,000
Factory	1,050,000
	1,100,000

Total chargeable assets are:	£
Plant	50,000
Factory	1,050,000
Investments	500,000
	1,600,000

Gain on sale of shares

	£
Disposal proceeds (use market value)	950,000
Less: cost	(200,000)
Gain before gift relief	750,000

Eligible for relief:

$$£750,000 \times \frac{1,100,000}{1,600,000} = £515,625$$

	£
Less: gift relief	(515,625)
Chargeable gain	234,375

Solution to Example 3

	£
Total gain	50,000
Less: $3/8$ of £50,000 for letting	(18,750)
Gain eligible for gift relief	31,250
Chargeable gain £(50,000 − 31,250)	£18,750

Solution to Example 4

(a) *Angelo's CGT position*:

	£
Disposal proceeds (market value)	200,000
Less: cost	(30,000)
Gain before relief	170,000
Less: gain held over:	
Gain less: actual proceeds *less* cost (remains chargeable now)	
£170,000 − £(50,000 − 30,000)	(150,000)
Chargeable gain	20,000

(b) *Michael's CGT position*:

	£
Disposal proceeds	195,000
Less: base cost = MV at gift *less* gain held-over	
£(200,000 − 150,000)	(50,000)
Chargeable gain	145,000

Solution to Example 5

(a) £196,000. The cost of the shares exceeds the gain, so the whole gain can be deferred.

(b) £170,000. The cost of the shares is less than the gain, so the claim is restricted to the amount subscribed for the shares. The rest of the gain (£26,000) is chargeable (unless he subscribes for more EIS shares)

(c) Robert should claim to defer £186,400. This is calculated as follows (*hint*: work backwards!):

	£
Gain before relief	196,000
Less: EIS reinvestment relief	(186,400)
Chargeable gain	9,600
Less: annual exemption	(9,600)
Taxable gain	nil

Solution to Example 6

	£
Gain on destruction of original painting ('disposal' date is October 2008)	
Proceeds	80,000
Less: cost	(10,000)
	70,000
Less: gain deferred (balancing figure)	(65,000)
Chargeable gain*	5,000

* Equal to proceeds not reinvested (ie £80,000 − £75,000)

TQT
Tax Qualification Training

Base cost of new painting:	£
Price paid	75,000
Less: gain deferred	(65,000)
Revised base cost c/f	10,000

Solution to Example 7

Chargeable gain	£
Compensation received	33,000
Less: used in restoration	(20,000)
Consideration for part disposal	13,000
Allowable cost:	

$$(40,000 + 20,000) \times \frac{13,000}{13,000 + 62,000}$$ (10,400)

Chargeable gain	2,600

Base cost of restored building	£	£
Original cost		40,000
Cost of restoration		20,000
		60,000
Less: insurance money not used in part disposal computation	20,000	
cost used in part disposal computation	10,400	
		(30,400)
Base cost c/f		29,600

Now try the following questions

Short Form Questions:

14.1 – 14.8 inclusive

Long Form Questions:

14.1	Fran & Anna
14.2	Joe Bloggs
14.3	P J Laval
14.4	Simon
14.5	Emily
14.6	Mr Richman
14.7	Peter
14.8	Sarah Stone

Personal Taxation

Part C:
Administration

15

The purpose of this chapter is to help you to:

- understand when an individual must notify HMRC of their liability to income tax and capital gains tax

- understand the tax return, penalties for late filing and the need to retain records

- outline the way reliefs are claimed

- explain how an individual pays his income tax and CGT liabilities including the right to pay CGT by instalments

- set out HMRC's powers to enquire into returns and make determinations and discovery assessments

- understandable the penalties for making incorrect returns

References: TMA 1970 unless otherwise stated

Administration of income tax and CGT

1 Introduction

Personal tax compliance for income tax and capital gains tax (CGT) is administered through the self-assessment system. The major burden is placed on the taxpayer and his advisers.

References in this section to income tax include (where appropriate) Class 4 NIC.

2 Notification of liability to income tax and CGT

Individuals who are chargeable to income tax or CGT for any tax year and **who have not received a notice to file a tax return must notify their chargeability** to HMRC **within six months from the end of the tax year** ie by 5 October 2009 for 2008/09. [s.7(1) & (2) TMA 1970]

If a person has no chargeable gains and is not liable to higher rate tax they do not need to notify HMRC if all his income: [s.7(3)-(7)]

(a)   Is subject to PAYE
(b)   Has had (or is treated as having had) income tax deducted at source, or
(c)   Is UK dividend income.

The maximum penalty for not notifying HMRC in time is 100% × the tax still unpaid by 31 January next following the tax year, ie by 31 January 2010 for 2008/09. There is no penalty if all tax is paid by the due date. [s.7(8)]

3 Tax returns and keeping records

3.1 Tax returns for individuals

The tax return comprises a Tax Form, together with supplementary pages for particular sources of income. Taxpayers receive the supplementary pages they need depending on their known sources of income, together with a Tax Return Guide and various notes relating to the supplementary pages. Taxpayers with new sources of income may have to ask the order line for further supplementary pages.

Where a taxpayer filed their previous year's return electronically, or used a computer generated substitute form, the taxpayer may be sent a notice to file a return, rather than the official HMRC return form. This is intended to reduce unnecessary waste of paper.

The Tax Form is broken down into 24 question areas:

The tax return is broken down into five parts:

Part 1 This establishes whether or not the taxpayer has the following types of income or gains. If so the taxpayer will need to complete the appropriate colour coded supplementary pages.

(i)   Employment income
(ii)   Self employment
(iii)   Partnership income
(iv)   Income from land and property in the UK
(v)   Foreign income and gains
(vi)   Income from trusts and settlements
(vii)   Capital gains
(viii) Non-residence and non-domicile
(ix)   Other

Part 2 Details of student loan repayments.

Part 3 Other income: Details of income and tax credits for sources not covered in the supplementary pages – eg interest, dividends and taxable Social Security benefits such as the State Retirement Pension.

Part 4 Tax reliefs: Claims for relief for the year just ended – eg for pension contributions, gift aid payments, married couple's allowance and blind person's allowance.

Part 5 If the return is submitted on paper by 31 October 2008 or online, HMRC will calculate the tax due. If the taxpayer opts to calculate the tax himself he then completes the Tax Calculation summary pages.

The Calculation Guide involves taking figures for income, gains, allowances and credits appearing earlier on the main tax return or on the Supplementary pages and following step by step instructions. The steps are designed for those with no tax knowledge, in fact tax specialists could be at a disadvantage if they try to work out what the steps are achieving! The Calculation Guide does not have to be submitted but taxpayers are advised to keep it in case HMRC 'need to see it'.

This part also requires the following information.

Section 1   Details of tax refunds from the Tax Office for the year just ended and, if so, how much.

Section 2   If not enough tax has been paid, up to £2,000 can be coded into an employee's PAYE code.

Section 3   Where a repayment of tax is due a choice between receiving a repayment or giving it to charity is given.

Section 4   Other information – to provide details of your tax adviser and any other additional information the taxpayer wishes to supply.

Section 5   This is the declaration that the information provided is correct and complete.

Individuals, trustees and personal representatives do not need to complete the CGT pages of the return if their chargeable gains do not exceed the annual exemption, except where the sale proceeds exceed four times the annual exempt amount or they have allowable losses.

3.2 Short tax return

Certain individuals with simple tax affairs can submit a 'short tax return', which is four pages long with supplementary capital gains pages if required. HMRC automatically issues the return based on the previous year's return.

It can be used by the following:

(a)   Employees (other than directors)

(b)   Pensioners.

The individual must have only standard investment income, and/or a little income from property.

Tax does not have to be calculated on the form, although a simple calculation is available for the taxpayer's own information.

3.3 Time limit for submission of tax returns

The time limit for making a return depends on how it is filed. [s.8]

Taxpayers and their advisers may either file electronically or complete the return by hand. From 6 April 2007 substitute returns are not acceptable.

Type of return	Filing date
Paper return	Later of 31 October following the end of the tax year (ie for 2008/09 this will be 31 October 2009) and 3 months after date of issue.
Electronic return	Later of 31 January following the end of the tax year (ie for 2008/09 this will be 31 January 2010) and 3 months after the date of issue.

Where an individual or trustees wish HMRC to calculate the tax due on their behalf the following deadlines apply:

*   31 October following the tax year to which the return relates or
*   if later, within 2 months after the notice to make the return was issued.

These deadlines are not relevant to individuals who submit electronic tax returns as the online filing system automatically calculates and therefore self assesses the taxpayer's tax liability.

For the small number of taxpayers who do not have access to facilities allowing them to file online HMRC will allow extra time (until the 31 January deadline) for them to file paper returns.

3.4 Penalties for late filing

Automatic penalties are charged for the late delivery of a tax return. [s.93(1)]

The maximum penalties for late delivery of a tax return are:

(a)	Return **less than six months** late:	£100 [s.93(2)]
(b)	Return **more than six months but not more than 12 months** late:	£200 [s.93(4)]
(c)	Return **more than 12 months** late:	**£200 + 100% of the tax liability** shown in the return [s.93(5)]

In addition, the General or Special Commissioners can issue a notice of direction imposing a maximum penalty of **£60 per day**. In this case the additional £100 penalty imposed under (b) if the return is more than six months late is not charged. [s.93(2)]

[handwritten margin note: is that from the date they impose it or backdated]

The fixed penalties of £100/£200 can be set aside by the Commissioners if they are satisfied that the taxpayer had a **reasonable excuse** for not delivering the return. If the **tax liability shown on the return is less than the fixed penalties of £100/£200**, the fixed penalty will be **reduced** to the amount of the tax liability. The tax geared penalty is **mitigable** by HMRC or the Commissioners. [s.93(7)]

Where a return is filed electronically, **supporting documents may be sent separately** (eg by post). Provided they are **submitted within one month** of the return and have been referred to in the return HMRC will accept that they 'accompany' the return for the purpose of making a discovery assessment within s.29 TMA 1970. [SP1/97]

3.5 Standard accounting information

3.5.1 Three line accounts

Owners of small businesses, including property letting businesses, may include simplified **'three line' accounts** (ie income *less* expenses = net profit) on their tax return. **The turnover of the business, or gross rents from property, must be less than £30,000 pa.** The taxpayer must keep records (see below) whether producing detailed or three line accounts. Where a business's turnover falls below £30,000 for several years, HMRC may start an enquiry (see below) to ensure that turnover has been correctly stated.

3.5.2 Submission of accounts

The tax return requires trading results to be presented in a standard format. In many cases the expense categories required by HMRC are different from those the taxpayer uses, and they will produce separate accounts. There is no requirement to submit these accounts with the tax return. However, the advantage of filing such accounts is the ability of HMRC to raise a discovery assessment (see below) is restricted.

3.6 Keeping records

Taxpayers must keep all records used in making and delivering a correct tax return. The time period depends on whether or not the taxpayer is in business. [s.12B] [IR booklet SA/BK3]

Records must be kept until the later of:

(a) (i) **5 years after the 31 January** following the year of assessment where the taxpayer is **in business** (as a sole trader or partner, or property letting), or

(ii) **1 year after the 31 January** following the year of assessment **otherwise**, or

(b) provided notice to deliver a return is given before the date in (a):

(i) the time after which enquiries by HMRC into the return can no longer be started, or
(ii) the date any such enquiries have been completed.

Where a person receives a notice to deliver a tax return after the normal record keeping period has expired, he must keep all records in his possession at that time until no enquiries can be raised in respect of the return or until such enquiries have been completed. [s.12B(2A)]

The maximum penalty for each failure to keep and retain records is £3,000 per tax year/accounting period. [s.12B(5)]

Taxpayers can usually keep copies of original documents except where the documents show domestic or foreign tax deducted or creditable. In this case the originals (eg dividend or interest certificates and vouchers issued under the sub-contractor's scheme) must be kept. [ss.12B(4) & (4A)]

Similar rules require records to be kept in respect of a 'stand-alone' claim (see below). [Sch 1A para 2]

4 Amendments and claims for reliefs

4.1 Corrections and amendments

HMRC can amend a taxpayer's return to correct any obvious errors or mistakes in the return within nine months of receiving the tax return. [s.9ZB]

The taxpayer can amend his tax return within 12 months of the 31 January filing deadline whether he has filed a paper return or online. Such amendments are not confined to the correction of obvious errors. [s.9ZA]

Amendments may be made by the taxpayer whilst an enquiry is in progress, although they will not take effect until the end of the enquiry. The contents of the amendment may be taken into account in the enquiry. [s.9B]

4.2 Claims for reliefs

Generally any claims and elections that can be made in a tax return must be made in this way if HMRC issues a return. Claims for any relief, allowance or repayment of tax must be quantified at the time the claim is made. [s.42]

Certain claims have a time limit that is longer than the time limit for filing or amending a tax return. **A claim may be made after the time limit for amending the tax return has expired.** Claims not made on the tax return are referred to as **'stand alone' claims.**

The time limit for making a claim is 5 years from 31 January following the year of assessment, unless a different limit is specifically set for the claim. [s.43]

Many reliefs have a shorter time limit of one year from the 31 January following the end of the year of assessment, ie 22 months after the end of the year of assessment.

A certain amount of formality in the claims procedure is needed as a taxpayer needs to be able to calculate his or her tax liability. For example, **capital losses are only allowable if notified to HMRC and notification is treated as a claim for relief for the year in which the loss arises.** Therefore, notification of such losses must be made within 5 years from 31 January next following the year of assessment in which they arise. [s.16(2A) TCGA 1992]

4.3 Error or mistake claims

An error or mistake claim may be made for errors in a return where tax would otherwise be over charged. The time limit is 5 years from 31 January following the tax year. The claim cannot be made where the tax liability was calculated in accordance with practice prevailing at the time the return was made. [s.33 & 33A]

In considering the claim, HMRC may take into account the taxpayer's liabilities for other years. If the claim leads to an overpayment of tax for one or more years, but an underpayment in others, only the net amount will be repaid.

An error or mistake claim may not be made in respect of any claim. **If a taxpayer has made an error or mistake in a claim (whether included on the return or a stand alone claim), the taxpayer may make a supplementary claim within the time limits allowed for the original claim.**

The taxpayer may appeal to the Special Commissioners against any refusal of an error or mistake claim.

TQT
Tax Qualification Training

5 Payment of income tax and capital gains tax

5.1 Introduction

In general, taxpayers make three payments of income tax and (where appropriate) one payment of capital gains tax for each year of assessment. The pattern of payments is usually:

31 January in the year of assessment: **1st payment on account of income tax**

31 July after the year of assessment: **2nd payment on account of income tax**

31 January after the year of assessment: **Final payment to settle the income tax liability for the year; and Payment of any CGT liability**

HMRC will issue payslips/demand notes in a credit card type 'Statement of Account' format, but there is no statutory obligation for them to do so and the onus is on the taxpayer to pay the correct amount of tax on the due date.

Statements of account are normally issued shortly before a payment is due, when a payment is made, and at intervals so long as any tax remains outstanding. Copies of statements of account are normally only issued to agents in June and December, unless the client authorises all statements to be sent to the agent.

5.2 Payments on account

Payments on account (POAs) are usually required where the taxpayer's tax (and Class 4 NICs but not Class 2 NICs) due for the previous year exceeded the amount of income tax deducted at source (including PAYE deductions and tax credits on dividends). **This excess is known as 'the relevant amount'.**

Student loan repayments are not included in the relevant amount, and payments on account of student loan repayments are not required. [s.59A(1) & (8)]

The POAs are each equal to 50% of the relevant amount for the previous year, and are due by 31 January in the tax year and the following 31 July. [s.59A(2)]

Example 1

Gordon is a self employed builder who paid tax for 2008/09 as follows:

		£
Total amount of income tax liability		9,200
This included:	Tax deducted by contractors on under the Construction Industry scheme	1,700
	Tax deducted on savings income	1,500
He also paid:	Class 4 NIC	2,206
	Class 2 NIC	109
	Capital gains tax	4,800

How much are the payments on account for 2009/10?

POAs are not required if the relevant amount falls below £500 or if the relevant amount is less than 20% of the total liability. [s.59A(1)]

5.3 Claims to reduce payments on account

Where a taxpayer's liability in the year is expected to be lower than in the previous year (for example if he has sold a rental property) **he can claim to reduce his POAs:**

(a)   **To a stated amount, or** [s.59A(4)]

(b)   **To nil.** [s.59A(3)]

The claim must state the reason why the taxpayer believes his tax liability will be lower, or nil.

If the taxpayer's eventual liability is higher than that estimated he will have reduced the POA too far. Although the POA will not be adjusted, there will be an interest charge on underpayment (see below).

There may be a penalty based on the difference between the expected and actual POAs if the claim was made fraudulently or negligently. It is likely that this penalty will only be charged if there are repeated excessive claims. [s.59A(6)]

5.4 Payment of income tax and capital gains tax

The balance of any income tax due for a year of assessment (after deducting POAs and tax deducted at source), together with any capital gains tax liability for that year, is payable on the 31 January following the year of assessment. [s.59B(1), (2) & (4)]

Example 2

Giles had made payments on account for 2008/09 of £6,500 each on 31 January 2009 and 31 July 2009, based on his 2007/08 liability. He then calculates his total income tax and Class 4 NIC liability for 2008/09 at £18,000 of which £2,750 had been deducted at source. In addition he calculates that his CGT liability for disposals in 2008/09 is £5,120.

What is the final payment due for 2008/09?

5.5 Surcharges on unpaid tax

The following surcharges are imposed in respect of late paid income tax and capital gains tax: [s.59C(1)-(3)]

(a)	**Tax paid less than 28 days late:**	none
(b)	**Tax paid more than 28 days but not more than six months late:**	5% ← _up to 6 months after Feb_
(c)	**Tax paid more than six months late:**	10% ← _After 6 months_

The surcharge broadly applies to the balancing payment of income tax and capital gains tax.

Exam focus point

Note that the surcharge rules do not apply to late payments on account of income tax.

5.6 Interest

5.6.1 Interest on overdue tax

Interest is chargeable by HMRC on the late payment of both POAs of income tax (under s.59A TMA 1970) **and payments of income tax and capital gains tax** (under s.59B TMA 1970). In both cases **interest runs from the due date until the day before the actual date of payment.** You will be given the interest rate applicable in the exam. [s.86(1)-(3)]

5.6.2 Repayment of tax and repayment supplement

Interest will be received from HMRC on overpayments of: [s.824(1) ICTA 1988]

(a)   **POAs**
(b)   **Payments of income tax and capital gains tax, including tax deducted at source or tax credits on dividends, and**
(c)   **Penalties and surcharges**.

Repayment supplement runs from the original date of payment (even if this was prior to the due date), **until the day before the date the repayment is made**. Income tax deducted at source for a year of assessment and tax credits are treated as if they were paid on the 31 January following the year of assessment. [s.824(3)(a), (b) ICTA 1988]

Tax repaid is identified with tax payments in the following order: [s.824(4) ICTA 1988]

(a)   Final balancing payment

(b)   Equally to the payments on account

(c)   Income tax deducted at source/tax credits

(d)   In so far as it is attributable to tax paid in instalments, to a later instalment in priority to an earlier one.

The rate of repayment supplement will be given in the exam.

5.7 Payment of CGT by instalments

If the proceeds for a disposal are received in instalments, the general rule is that the whole gain is chargeable up front as normal. However, if the proceeds are receivable in instalments over a period exceeding eighteen months, the taxpayer may elect for the CGT to be spread over the *shorter* of: [s.280 TCGA 1992]

(a)   The period of instalments; and

(b)   Eight years.

There is also an instalment option for CGT due on gifts which do not qualify for gift relief (see Chapter 14) where the gifted assets are: [s.281 TCGA 1992]

(a)   **Land**

(b)   **Shares or securities (quoted or unquoted) out of a controlling holding, or**

(c)   **Unquoted shares or securities**.

The CGT is then payable in ten equal yearly instalments where the taxpayer elects in writing. The first instalment is due on the normal due date. No time limit for the election is specified so the normal limit of five years from 31 January following the year of assessment given by s.43 TMA 1970 applies. In practice, however, the election should be made before the first payment is due.

Interest will normally be chargeable on the outstanding balance.

The taxpayer may pay off the outstanding instalments (plus accrued interest) at any time. The outstanding balance and accrued interest become immediately payable if the asset gifted is sold.

6 Enquiries, determinations and discovery assessments

6.1 Enquiries into returns

6.1.1 Raising the enquiry

HMRC can enquire into a return filed on time within 12 months of receiving it. [s.9A]

If the return is filed after the due filing date, HMRC has until the quarter day following the first anniversary of the actual filing date. The quarter days are 31 January, 30 April, 31 July and 31 October.

If the taxpayer has amended the return after the due filing date for the return, the enquiry 'window' extends to the quarter day following the first anniversary of the date the amendment was filed. Where the enquiry was not raised within the limit which would have applied had no amendment been filed, the enquiry will be restricted to matters contained in the amendment.

The officer does not have to have, or give, any reason for raising an enquiry. In particular the taxpayer will not be advised whether he has been selected at random for an audit. Enquiries may be full enquiries, or may be limited to a particular 'aspect' of the return.

6.1.2 During the enquiry

In the course of the enquiry HMRC **may require the taxpayer to produce documents, accounts or any other information required**. The taxpayer has the right to appeal to the Commissioners. [s.19A] [paras 6, 6A] [Sch 1A]

During the course of his enquiries the officer may amend a self-assessment if it appears that insufficient tax has been charged and an immediate amendment is necessary to prevent a loss of tax to the Crown. This might apply if, for example, there was a possibility that the taxpayer might emigrate, or bankruptcy proceedings be commenced. [s.9C]

Amendments may be made by the taxpayer whilst an enquiry is in progress, although they will not take effect until the end of the enquiry. The contents of the amendment may be taken into account in the enquiry.

If a return is under enquiry HMRC may postpone any repayment due as shown in the return until the enquiry is complete. HMRC has discretion to make a provisional repayment but there is no facility to appeal if the repayment is withheld. [s.9B] [s.59B(4A)]

6.1.3 Completion of the enquiry

An enquiry is not complete until HMRC issues a closure notice. The notice must either state that the return needs no amendment, or must amend the return.

Once an enquiry is complete, HMRC cannot make further enquiries. HMRC may, in limited circumstances, raise a discovery assessment if they are of the opinion that there has been a loss of tax (see below). [s.9A(3) & s.12AC(4)] [para 5(3) Sch 1A]

6.2 Determinations ◁— if no submission of ITR, determines tax due as not able to raise an enquiry

HMRC may only raise enquiries if a return has been submitted.

If a taxpayer has not submitted a return by the due filing date, HMRC may make a 'determination' of the amounts liable to income tax and capital gains tax and of the tax due. This determination is treated as if it were a self-assessment. This enables the officer to seek payment of tax, including payments on account for the following year and to charge interest. [s.28C]

The determination must be made within the period ending 5 years after 31 January following the year of assessment. It may be superseded by a self-assessment made within the same period or, if later, within 12 months of the date of the determination.

6.3 Discovery assessments

If HMRC discovers that profits have been left out of a return, that any assessment has become insufficient, or that any relief given is excessive, a 'discovery' assessment may be raised to recover the tax lost. Conditions limit the circumstances in which a discovery assessment may be made. [s.29]

If the tax lost results from an error in the taxpayer's return but the return was made in accordance with prevailing practice at the time, no discovery assessment may be made. [s.29(2)]

A discovery assessment may only be raised where a return has been made if:

(a)   The taxpayer or his agent has been **fraudulent or negligent**, or [s.29(4)]

(b)   **HMRC did not have information made available to him to make him aware of the loss of tax** at the time that enquiries into the return were completed. [s.29(5)]

Information is considered to be 'made available' to HMRC if it could be reasonably inferred by the officer or if it is contained in:

(i)   the return for the relevant tax year (or preceding two tax years),
(ii)   any claim submitted for the relevant tax year (or preceding two tax years), or
(iii)   accounts, statements or documents accompanying the return or claim or produced in the course of the enquiry.

Tax charged on a discovery assessment is due thirty days after the issue of the assessment. [s.59B(6)]

TQT
Tax Qualification Training

6.4 Appeals

6.4.1 Notice of appeal

A taxpayer may appeal against an amendment to a self-assessment, or an amendment to or disallowance of a claim, following an enquiry, or against an assessment which is not a self-assessment, such as a discovery assessment. [s.31(1), para 9(1) Sch. 1A]

The appeal must be made within 30 days of the amendment or self-assessment, except that the time limit for appeals relating to personal allowances for non-residents, and for questions of domicile, residence and ordinary residence is three months.

The notice of appeal (usually given on form 64-7 (New)) must state the *grounds* of appeal, which may be stated in general terms. At the hearing the Commissioners may allow the appellant to put forward grounds not stated in his notice if they are satisfied that his omission was not wilful or unreasonable. [s.31A(5)]

In some cases it may be possible to agree the point at issue by negotiation with HMRC, in which case the appeal may be settled by agreement. This is less likely for amendments to self-assessments following enquiries, as it is likely that the point at issue will have been considered during the course of the enquiry.

If the appeal cannot be agreed, it will be heard by the General or Special Commissioners.

(From April 2009 the Special and General Commissioners and VAT Tribunals will be replaced with a single unified tribunal called the Tax Chamber of the First-tier Tribunal.)

6.4.2 Postponement of payment of tax

A taxpayer must still pay their tax on time even where a notice of appeal has been issued unless he obtains a 'determination of the Commissioners, or the agreement of HMRC, that he **can postpone paying some or all of the tax pending the determination of the appeal**. [s.55(2)]

If the taxpayer has grounds for believing that he has been overcharged he may apply to the Commissioners for a determination. His application must be in writing, specifying the amount by which he believes he is overcharged and giving his reasons for that belief. It is separate from the notice of appeal although normally made at the same time since the time limit is the same. [s.55(3)]

The taxpayer must apply to the Commissioners within 30 days of the issue of the amendment or of the assessment. He can make an application at a later stage if there has been a change in the circumstances of the case. [s.55(3A)]

If the Commissioners deal with the matter there will be a formal hearing. It is more usual however for the taxpayer to reach an agreement, made or confirmed in writing, with HMRC on the postponement of payment of a specified sum. As regards the amount not postponed, the determination or the agreement has the same effect as if an amendment or assessment had been issued on the date of the determination or the agreement (hence the tax is due 30 days later, if that is later than the normal due date). [s.55(5)] [s.55(7) & (8)]

When the appeal itself has been determined, if the Commissioners find that any part of the postponed tax is due HMRC issues a notice of the amount payable. That amount is then due for payment 30 days after the issue of the notice as if it had been an amendment or assessment. [s.55(9)]

Interest however is still payable from the normal due date. [s.86]

7 Penalties for incorrect returns (Sch 24 FA07)

This section is new.

Following the merger of the Inland Revenue and HM Customs and Excise the Finance Acts 2007 and 2008 have introduced a number of changes to the tax administration and penalty regimes in order to standardise the powers available to HMRC across **all** taxes.

Changes to the penalty regime where an incorrect return is submitted to HMRC, as set out below, comes into effect for **income tax, VAT and corporation tax** for **returns submitted after April 2009**. The new regime therefore **applies for example to the 2008/09 income tax return**.

The new system applies to the **submission of inaccurate returns or documents and the failure to notify HMRC where an under assessment is made.**

The level of the penalty is a **percentage of the revenue lost** as a result of the inaccuracy or under assessment and **depends on the behaviour of the taxpayer** as follows:

- Mistake   No penalty
- Failure to take reasonable care   30% of revenue lost
- Deliberate understatement   70% of revenue lost
- Deliberate understatement with concealment   100% of revenue lost

The above penalties may be reduced depending on whether the taxpayer makes an <u>unprompted disclosure</u> as follows. An unprompted disclosure is where the taxpayer makes disclosure when he has no reason to believe that HMRC have or are about to discover the inaccuracy.

Penalty	Minimum penalty	
	Unprompted	Prompted
30% penalty (reasonable care)	0%	15%
70% penalty (deliberate understatement)	20%	35%
100% penalty (concealed deliberate understatement)	30%	50%

For returns submitted prior to April 2009 a tax geared penalty of up to 100% of the tax underpaid applies where a person **fraudulently or negligently** submits an incorrect return, statement or declaration to HMRC. The penalties could be mitigated depending on the extent of disclosure (up to 20% abatement), cooperation (up to 40% abatement) and the gravity of the error (up to 40% abatement).

Chapter roundup

- Self-assessment is the system under which taxpayers are required to complete returns and self-assess their tax liabilities. Each return has working sheets to enable the taxpayer to calculate his own income tax and CGT liability.

- An individual must advise HMRC within 6 months of the end of the tax year if he is chargeable to income tax or CGT and he has not already received a tax return.

- The taxpayer makes two POAs and then a third payment to finalise his income tax liability. The POAs are due on 31 January in the year of assessment and 31 July immediately following. The final payment is due on 31 January following the end of the year of assessment.

- Only one CGT payment is due on 31 January after the end of the tax year.

- Self-assessment is enforced through a system of automatic penalties and surcharges, together with strict rules for interest on late paid tax. Random enquiries, or 'audits', are used to ensure that taxpayers are complying correctly with their obligations. Additional penalties may be imposed in cases of fraud or neglect.

- There are strict procedural rules for raising and carrying out enquiries into tax returns, so that when the date for commencing enquiries passes, or enquiries are completed, the taxpayer may be certain that his tax affairs are final. The only exception is where a loss of tax is 'discovered'.

- Penalties apply for the submission of the incorrect returns. For returns submitted after April 2009 the penalty is a percentage of the revenue lost and depends on the behaviour of the taxpayer.

Quiz

1. When must an individual notify HMRC of a new source of income for 2008/09?

2. Brenda was issued with her 2008/09 tax return on 15 April 2009. By which date must Brenda submit the completed form?

3. John is self employed. For how long must he retain his 2008/09 business records?

4. Which taxes are subject to payment on account for an individual?

5. An individual may not reduce a payment on account to £nil.

   True or False?

6. Only CGT on gifts subject to gift relief quality for CGT instalments.

   True or False?

1. By 5 October 2009.

2. If Brenda submits the return online then it is due by 31 January 2010. If Brenda submits a paper return it must be submitted by 31 October 2009.

3. Until 31 January 2015 (ie 5 years after 31 January 2010).

4. Income Tax and Class 4 NIC.

5. False.

6. False.

Solutions to chapter examples

Solution to Example 1

The relevant amount is:

	£
Income tax:	
Total income tax liability for 2008/09	9,200
Less: tax deducted for 2008/09 £(1,700 + 1,500)	(3,200)
	6,000
Class 4 NIC	2,206
	8,206

Payments on account for 2009/10:

31 January 2010	× ½	£4,103
31 July 2010	As before	£4,103

There is no requirement to make payments on account of capital gains tax (nor Class 2 NIC).

Solution to Example 2

Income tax and Class 4 NIC: £18,000 − £2,750 − £6,500 − £6,500 = £2,250. CGT = £5,120.

Total payment due on 31 January 2010 (excluding the first payment on account for 2009/10) £2,250 + £5,120 = £7,370

Now try the following questions

Short Form Questions:

15.1 – 15.3 inclusive

16

Other aspects
of the syllabus

1 Introduction

Apart from taxation there are other key areas of the syllabus for candidates to study.

Throughout this text you will have seen icons highlighting law. These icons refer candidates to specific areas within the Essential Law for the Tax Adviser manual.

Exam focus point

The syllabus for law is contained at the front of the law manual 'Essential Law for the Taxation Technician'. You should look at this and ensure that you read through any areas you have not yet studied.

There are other essential publications that must be studied:

- ATT Professional Rules and Practice Guidelines (2006 version)
- Money Laundering Guidelines (December 2007 including supplementary guidance dated 21 April 2008)
- Professional Conduct in Relation to Taxation

If you visit the official ATT website at www.att.org.uk you will find these publications plus much more valuable information for students.

Exam focus point

The above three publications require knowledge at the 'principles' level of the syllabus. Candidates are expected to have an awareness that a provision exists and its main thrust without necessarily knowing the details of the provision.

Throughout your studies you **must** refer to these publications whenever possible.

Now try the following questions

Short Form Questions:

16.1 – 16.11 inclusive

Personal Taxation

Question and Answer Bank

Short form questions

1.1 Mary, a single woman aged 67, has net income of £22,580. What are the total allowances available to Mary for 2008/09?

1.2 Darren aged 70 is registered blind. His wife Edna is aged 74. Calculate the maximum allowances that Darren may deduct from his net income in 2008/09.

1.3 In 2008/09 James has a salary of £42,540 (PAYE £7,000). He makes a Gift Aid donation to the RNLI of £560.

 What is his tax payable?

1.4 Joe is aged 90 and has net income of £30,800. He is married to Jean. What allowances and tax reductions is Joe entitled to in 2008/09?

1.5 Martin Keynes is aged 16 and is at school.   *has to be 18 to be assessed*

 He has the following income in 2008/09:

 £2,000 (gross)   from his Barclays bank account where he pays in earnings from his newspaper round
 £375 (gross)   interest from building society account set up in his name by his mother
   not i assessible on mother
 What is his net income for 2008/09?

1.6 William was born on 6 March 1930 and is single. In the year ended 5 April 2009 he had income of £23,500 and paid £500 (gross) under Gift Aid to the NSPCC, a registered charity. What are William's personal allowances for 2008/09?   *expands adjusted Net income (ie like basic rate band)*

1.7 John is an unmarried student. In the year to 5 April 2009 he received the following:

	Gross £	Tax deducted £
Scholarship from a charity — *exempt*	1,935	–
Legacy from late grandfather — *not taxable as taxed at source from the estate*	12,000	–
Earnings from employment	3,700	740
Building society interest	300	60

 What is the maximum tax repayment he can claim?

Exam focus point

Question 1.8 below is taken from the Pilot Paper for the Personal Taxation Certificate paper.

1.8 Simon is 14 and in full-time education. During 2008/09 he received £6,000 (net) from a discretionary trust. He has no other source of income. Calculate Simon's tax position for 2008/09.

1.9 Bert Harvey, born on 8 June 1945, and his wife Betty, born on 18 June 1934, have the following income in 2008/09:

		£
Bert	Earnings	10,214
Betty	State Pension	2,340
	Occupational Pension	5,200

 What is Bert's tax liability for 2008/09?

1.10 Nicholas, a 72-year-old retired journalist, received the following income during the year ended 5 April 2009:

	£
Income from writing and lecturing	7,700
Net income distributed from his grandfather's discretionary trust	1,650

 Nicholas entered into a civil partnership with Paul on 1 March 2009. He is 59 years old and has net income of £5,000. Calculate Nicholas's tax payable/repayable for 2008/09.

1.11 Richard Key gifted some shares to his twin daughters, Donna and Dawn, age 17. Donna is married and presently working. Dawn is unmarried and at college. Each daughter received a dividend of £1,500 in 2008/09.

Explain who will be taxed on the dividend income received by Donna and Dawn.

1.12 Simon has a full time salary of £34,500. His wife Sarah works part-time earning £14,500 pa. They have a daughter aged 6, she is cared for by her grandmother when Sarah is working. What child tax credit for 2008/09 can they claim assuming their income was the same in 2007/08.

Exam focus point

Question 1.13 below is taken from the Pilot Paper for the Personal Taxation Certificate paper.

1.13 Anthea, aged 34, is a single parent with a daughter, Chloe, aged 7. Anthea works 20 hours a week (during school hours) as an administrator earning £17,000 in 2008/09. She has no other income. Calculate Anthea's entitlement to tax credits for 2008/09.

1.14 Gilbert, aged 5, receives £75 each year in interest income from a deposit account set up for him as a gift from his father. If he has no other income how will this be taxed? Explain your answer.

1.15 Debbie is a single parent with a child aged 5 and she works less than 30 hours a week. Her income for 2007/08 was £8,000 and for 2008/09 is £8,200. What tax credits can she claim for 2008/09?

1.16 Debbie and Johnny are married and have 3 children aged 10, 14 and 18. The eldest child is in full time education. In 2007/08 Johnny had a salary of £21,500 from his full time job. It has not changed in 2008/09. Debbie has no income. What tax credits are available for 2008/09?

1.17 Tanya, age 17, has been unable to work for the past five days due to illness. She earns an annual salary of £15,000. How much weekly statutory sick pay is she entitled to and why?

1.18 Alan is a single man, aged 73. He has income from pensions of £50,000 in 2008/09 and makes the following payments:

   (a)   Mortgage interest of £5,040 on a loan of £56,000 taken out to purchase his main residence.

   (b)   Interest of £2,610 on a loan taken out to make a loan to a close company in which he owns 10% of the ordinary share capital.

   (c)   Maintenance payments to his first wife of £3,000 pa under a court order dated 1 July 1995.

Calculate Alan's tax liability for 2008/09.

2.1 Ian has a salary of £27,040 and building society interest received (gross) of £15,000. Calculate Ian's tax liability for 2008/09.

2.2 Neil and Jenny have held a joint NatEast Bank account for many years. Jenny has only ever put £100 into the account. During 2008/09 interest received on the account amounted to £300. How much of the interest should be taxed on Jenny?

2.3 Christopher has received the following amounts of interest on his NS&I products:

	Year ended 5 April 2009 £
Easy Access Savings account	276
NS&I Certificates	125

He also received a tax repayment for 2007/08 to which the Collector of Taxes added interest of £89.

What is the total amount assessable as interest income for the year ended 5 April 2009?

2.4 Julian made a five-year loan to Roch Ltd and a five-year loan to his next door neighbour, Bob. During 2008/09 he received interest on both of the loans.

Will the interest receipts be received gross or net? Explain your answer.

TQT
Tax Qualification Training

2.5 Pamela owns 1,000 £1 ordinary shares in Esher plc. The following dividends were declared:

8p per share for the year ended 31 March 2007, paid 1 June 2008
4p per share for the year ended 31 March 2008, paid 1 June 2009

What amount will Pamela enter into her tax computation for 2008/09?

2.6 Lucy received the following income in 2008/09:

			£
1.	Lloyds Bank		
	Oxford Street branch		8,680
	Guernsey branch		640
2.	Interest on government stock issued in May 2004		5,000

What is her taxable income for 2008/09?

2.7 Sharon has the following income credited to her current account in 2008/09:

	£
Bank deposit interest	1,960
Building society interest	1,600
UK dividends	2,000
	5,560

She has no other sources of income. What is the total amount of tax repayable to Sharon?

2.8 In 2008/09 Sandra has net earnings of £3,929. She also received bank interest of £2,500 and dividends of £34,000. What is her tax payable assuming she has suffered PAYE of £800?

Exam focus point

Questions 3.1 to 3.3 below are taken from the Pilot Paper for the Personal Taxation Certificate paper.

3.1 Ben owns a house which he lets out furnished to earn extra income.

In 2008/09 the property was let for the whole year at a rate of £1,500 per month (although he only received rental income of £16,500 as one month was paid late).

He incurred the following expenses

	£
Agent's fee (6 April 2008 – 5 April 2009)	1,800
Mortgage interest	4,200
Water rates	120
Cost of building new porch	2,500
Insurance	500

Calculate Ben's taxable property income.

3.2 Property is anything that can be owned. Although the term is often used to refer to land, it is a much wider concept and includes all assets both tangible and intangible. Explain the difference in legal terms between ownership and possession of property.

3.3 An owner of land may agree to sell it in a number of different ways. Explain the four ways in which a sale of land may take place.

3.4 Harry owns a property which is let for the ten weeks from 1 July 2008 at a rent of £160 per week. The tenants leave at the end of this period having paid only £1,300 of the total amount due. Harry writes off the outstanding debt.

The property is re-let to new tenants on 1 March 2009 for a rent of £400 per month payable in arrears. He received the first payment on 10 April.

He pays interest of £700 during the year ended 5 April 2009 on a loan to purchase the property.

What is his property income assessment for 2008/09?

3.5   John owns two properties:

Whitehouse – let at a rental of £4,000 per annum, payable quarterly in advance. The tenant was late in paying the last quarter's rent for the quarter to 5 April 2009 and John did not receive payment until 25 April 2009.

Blackhouse – let at a rent of £2,000 per annum payable quarterly in advance. Blackhouse was unlet throughout 2007/08; however, a tenant moved in on 24 June 2008.

What is John's property income assessment for 2008/09?

3.6   Henry owns a property which he lets for the first time on 1 July 2008 at a rent of £4,000 per annum payable monthly in advance.

The first tenants left without notice on 28 February 2009 and the property was re-let to new tenants on 4 April 2009 at a rent of £5,000 per annum payable yearly in advance.

Henry's allowable expenditure was £1,000 in the year. What is his property income assessment for 2008/09?

3.7   Polly lets out a furnished property for £8,000 per annum. She pays insurance of £300 per annum and water rates of £400 per annum. What is the amount assessable as property income?

3.8   Brian rents out a room in his main residence for £5,000 per annum, allowable expenses relating to the rental were £600. What is Brian's property income assessment for 2008/09? Explain your answer.

3.9   State four of the conditions for a property to qualify as a furnished holiday let.

3.10   Personal property under English law can be divided into 'choses in action' and 'choses in possession'.

Explain what is meant by the underlined terms.

4.1   What is the maximum amount of cash and shares that an individual can invest in an ISA in 2008/09?

4.2   What are the main income tax benefits of an ISA?

4.3   Bert, a single man, has taxable non-savings income of £56,840 in 2008/09 (all earnings). He invests £580,000 of cash he inherited in qualifying Enterprise Investment Scheme shares in November 2008. What is the tax reduction available to him?

4.4   Gemma has invested the following amounts in qualifying VCTs during 2008/09:

| 10 June 2008 | VCT 1 | £150,000 |
| 5 September 2008 | VCT 2 | £60,000 |

She receives dividends in 2008/09 as follows:
| VCT 1 | £3,000 |
| VCT 2 | £3,400 |

What amount of net dividends (if any) must be included in her taxable income?

Explain your answer.

Exam focus point

Question 5.1 below is taken from the Pilot Paper for the Personal Taxation Certificate paper.

5.1   Daisy, a full time employee, was made redundant by her employer in June 2008. She received the following redundancy package:

	£
Statutory redundancy pay *exempt*	3,800
Ex gratia cash payment ✓	25,000
Market value of company car – ownership transferred to Daisy ✓	12,000
Outplacement counselling *exempt*	4,500

What amount, if any, will be taxable on Daisy?

5.2 Janet is a director of Dragon Ltd. The company accounts show the following remuneration:

Year ended	Salary £	Bonus £
31 December 2008	9,000	2,400
31 December 2009	10,000	4,200

The bonus is paid on 28 February following the year end. The salary is paid evenly over the year.

What is the amount of Janet's income assessable to tax for 2008/09?

5.3 Tina commenced employment with Harrison Electrics Ltd on 1 November 2008. She was paid a salary of £1,000 per month and from 1 January 2009, was given the use of a new Ford Escort 1400cc which has a list price of £15,000 with all private petrol paid for by the company. The emission rate is 170g/km. What are her total earnings from Harrison Electrics Ltd for 2008/09?

5.4 In 2007 Whitegate plc bought a new 3-litre car which has a list price of £14,000 for the sole use of James, one of its directors. The emission rate is 198g/km. The company pays car expenses including all the petrol but James repays to the company a nominal £0.02 per mile for petrol consumed in private motoring. What is James's assessable benefit for 2008/09?

5.5 In 2007/08 Jim, a director of a wine importing company, is paid £10,000 per annum and is given the use of a new 2-litre car which has a list price of £16,000 and an emission rate of 200g/km, plus wine which cost the company £1,000. Jim's 20-year old student daughter, Jane, also works for the company on Saturdays, is paid £15 per day and has the use of a new 1,150cc car which has a list price of £12,000 and an emission rate of 163g/km. Jim uses £600 of the wine promoting the company's products. No private petrol is paid for by the company.

What are Jim's earnings for 2008/09?

5.6 Albert, who has been employed by Roberts Tools Ltd as a salesman for several years, earned a salary of £14,800 in 2008/09 and had the use of a 2-year old Ford Escort 1100, which has a list price of £12,000. The emission rate is 155g/km. No private diesel was paid for.

Albert is also given an expense allowance of £80 each month to cover incidental costs of travelling. At the end of the tax year, he calculated that, of this, £750 would be allowable for tax purposes.

What is the amount to be entered on Albert's form P11D in respect of benefits for 2008/09?

5.7 Grasshopper Ltd has a dispensation from HMRC in respect of travel and subsistence expenses directly reimbursed to its employees.

Mr Adams commenced employment with Grasshopper Ltd on 1 January 2009 and was paid £1,000 per month. His expenses were paid as

1st Jan 1st Mar
1st Feb 1st Apr

(1) a round sum allowance of £100 per month payable on the 1st of the month, plus
(2) reimbursement of specific travel and subsistence expenses of £250 up to 5 April 2009.

Calculate the amounts to be entered on the P11D for Mr Adams for 2008/09.

5.8 Sue earns £15,000 working for Redbridge Ltd and uses the crèche provided by the company for her child. The cost to the employer is £3,000 per year.

Tara earns £12,000 working for Bluefield Ltd. Her employer pays her registered childminder's fees of £3,200 per annum.

What amounts, if any, are assessable in respect of childcare for 2008/09?

5.9 Daphne is an employee of Surbiton Ltd. The company provided her with a credit card, and during the year paid the following amounts on her behalf:

	£
Annual fee	30
Daphne's private purchases	257
Interest charge for late payment	46
	333

What is Daphne's assessable benefit for 2008/09?

5.10 Joshua is an employee of Mumbles plc, earning £12,000 per annum. He received the following benefits in the year ended 5 April 2009.

	£
Work place parking estimated value	720
Luncheon vouchers (£1 a day for 240 days a year)	240
Credit card expenditure: goods purchased for business use	272

What are Joshua's taxable benefits in 2008/09?

5.11 A company throws a staff party which cost £200 per head. How much may the company deduct in arriving at its profit, and what amount is the tax position for the employee?

5.12 Finlay, a chartered accountant, is the Finance Director of Globe Ltd, a company which is based in Derbyshire. He personally incurs the following expenses in 2008/09:

(1)   Subscription to the Chartered Institute of Taxation of £220

(2)   Subscription to local golf club of £250, as required by Globe Ltd in order to promote the firm's business contacts

(3)   Subscription to the Naval Club in London of £200 in order to have somewhere to stay overnight when his duties necessitate an overnight stay in London.

What amount is he able to deduct from his assessable income for 2008/09?

5.13 Bert earns £18,000 pa and lives in job related accommodation provided by his employer. The company pays £2,000 rent and £3,100 for household expenses in the year ended 5 April 2009. What are Bert's taxable earnings for 2008/09?

5.14 Paul was provided with two mobile phones costing £250 each and a laptop computer costing £5,000 by his employer on 5 April 2008. During 2008/09 he used his mobile phone 40% of the time for personal calls (the other was used by his daughter) and the laptop 60% of the time for non business purposes. What are Paul's assessable benefits for 2008/09?

5.15 John has a salary of £30,000 pa. He drives his own 1.5l engine car to work taking his 2 year old daughter to a crèche on the way. John's employer pays the cost of the crèche which is £200 per week. John is provided with a designated parking space at his employer's premises. This costs the employer £1,000 pa. Sometimes John has to drive to clients and his employer reimburses him for his business mileage at 60p per mile. In 2008/09 John did 5,000 business miles. Calculate John's earnings for 2008/09.

5.16 Ruth is an employee of Benson Ltd and earns a salary of £45,000 pa. Benson Ltd have loaned her £20,000 so she can redecorate her house. As at 5 April 2008 there was an outstanding balance of £15,000. On 5 January 2009 Ruth repaid a further £5,000. Ruth pays Benson Ltd interest at 3% pa on the loan. The official rate of interest throughout 2008/09 is 6.25%. What is Ruth's taxable benefit for 2008/09?

5.17 Jason is an employee of Saranson Ltd. The company provide him with a house near their office. Saranson Ltd bought the house in 1981 at a cost of £80,000. Jason moved in 1991 when the market value of the house was £130,000. At 6 April 2008 the market value of the house was £250,000 and the gross annual value is £5,000. Jason pays Saranson Ltd rent of £3,000 pa. Calculate Jason's assessable benefit for 2008/09 assuming the official rate of interest is 6.25%.

5.18 Natalie is a receptionist at Hospitality Hotel. She was provided with the use of a dinner set by the hotel on 6 October 2007. Its market value at that date was £2,000. On 6 October 2008 the hotel agreed to sell the dinner set to Natalie for £1,000, its market value at that date was £1,500. Calculate the assessable benefit on Natalie for 2008/09.

5.19 Judy is an employee of Markham Ltd. She earns £25,750 pa and is provided with a company owned flat. The flat cost the company £60,000 when it was bought in 1992. Judy moved in 1999 when the flat had a market value of £100,000. The annual value of the flat is £3,000. Markham Ltd also pays for Judy's heating and lighting bills, this costs the company £400 pa. Judy is also provided with furniture for use in her flat. The market value of the furniture was £2,500 in 1999. Calculate Judy's assessable benefit for 2008/09 assuming the official rate of interest is 6.25%.

TQT
Tax Qualification Training

5.20 George was unexpectedly made redundant on 15 August 2008. His redundancy package was as follows:

	£
Payment in lieu of notice	8,000
Ex-gratia payment	40,000
Statutory redundancy pay	5,000

The £40,000 payment was not contractual and George did not expect it. How much of the package is taxable?

5.21 Alan receives a non-contractual termination payment of £51,000 from Duxton Ltd. He has spent 10 years out of his 30 years service with the company working abroad, his last 2 years of service being spent in the UK. How much of the termination payment will be exempt from income tax.

5.22 Charles Prosser is a company director and occupies a house owned by the company. The house was purchased in May 2002 for £400,000 and an extension was added in September 2008 at a cost of £30,000. The gross annual value of the house for rating purposes was £2,225. During 2008/09 Charles paid £2,725 as rent to the company. Assume that the official rate of interest for 2008/09 was 6.25%.

Calculate the amount assessable on Charles Prosser for 2008/09 as a benefit in respect of the provision of accommodation.

5.23 List six items that you would expect to see covered in a typical contract for consultancy services provided by an independent contractor.

Exam focus point

Question 6.1 below is taken from the Pilot Paper for the Personal Taxation Certificate paper.

6.1 Ray was granted an Enterprise Management Incentive option in July 2005 to acquire 10,000 shares for £1.50 each in Ex Ltd, his employing company. The shares were worth £2 each at the date of grant. He exercised the option in July 2008 when the share price was £4.75.

Explain the income tax consequences of the grant and exercise, assuming all the conditions for a qualifying EMI option are met.

6.2 What is the maximum value of 'free shares' and 'partnership shares' that can be allocated to an employee per annum under an all-employee share incentive plan (SIP)?

6.3 George exercises his option over 10,000 shares which he received from an unapproved share option plan. The exercise price was £11.50 each and the shares were worth £15.00 each at the date of exercise. He is a higher rate taxpayer. What is the income tax payable on exercise?

7.1 George has the following income:

	£
Profits from his publishing business	28,000
Dividend income from shares	5,400

What is the maximum amount George can pay into his personal pension on which he is entitled to tax relief?

7.2 Norma is a housewife. She is 52 years old. Her only taxable income in 2008/09 is a dividend of £5,000.

Norma wants to take out a pension. Explain the maximum contribution that she can make in respect of 2008/09 on which tax relief is available?

7.3 Daniel aged 30 is an employee of Smithson Ltd. His salary for 2008/09 is £48,000 (PAYE £8,500). The company does not have an occupational pension scheme so Daniel pays contributions into his personal pension.

In 2008/09 Daniel pays £5,000 into his pension. What is Daniel's higher rate tax exposure for 2008/09?

7.4 Jeremy has earnings of £400,000 in 2008/09. Advise him of the maximum contribution he can make to a pension in the year and obtain tax relief and the tax consequences of contributing this amount.

7.5 Cindy plans to start drawing her pension in 2008/09. Her personal pension fund is worth £65,000. How much can Cindy take as a tax free lump sum?

 TQT
Tax Qualification Training

7.6 Maxine has taxable earnings of £50,000 in 2008/09. Her employer deducts a contribution into the company's registered occupational pension scheme of £9,000 from these earnings before operating PAYE. She has no other taxable income.

Show Maxine's tax liability for 2008/09.

Question 8.1 below is taken from the Pilot Paper for the Personal Taxation Certificate paper.

8.1 Marco, an Italian citizen, arrived in the UK on 5 August 2007 to work for the UK branch of his Italian employer for 2 years.

In 2008/09 he received the following income:

	£
Salary – paid in UK	60,000
– paid in Italy	15,000
Company car benefit (UK)	5,200
Bank interest – UK (net)	35
– Italy (gross)	500

No element of the income received in Italy was remitted to the UK. 20% of Marco's working time was spent in Italy. Calculate Marco's taxable income for 2008/09.

8.2 Wayne is domiciled in America but has lived in London for 15 years. In 2008/09 he remits £10,000 of foreign dividends during the tax year and has a further £400,000 of foreign dividends which he does not remit. The dividends arse in respect of a 25% shareholding in a company resident in America. He is a higher rate taxpayer and has made a claim under s.809B ITA2007 for the remittance basis to apply. How much is his tax liability on his foreign dividends?

SHOW SHAUN!

8.3 Egbert is UK resident and ordinarily resident. He worked in Germany many years ago and now receives a German pension of £10,000 each year. How much of the pension is taxable in 2008/09?

8.4 Ronald (a British citizen) goes abroad for full time employment.

State the conditions which must be satisfied for him to be treated as not resident and not ordinarily resident from the date of his departure until the date of his return.

Exam focus point

Question 9.1 below is taken from the Pilot Paper for the Personal Taxation Certificate paper.

9.1 Jenny sold a painting in 2008/09 realising a chargeable gain of £18,000. Calculate Jenny's capital gains tax liability for 2008/09.

9.2 What is the minimum residency requirement for an individual to be within the charge to capital gains tax?

9.3 Which of the following assets are exempt for capital gains tax purposes?

- a diamond brooch
- a thoroughbred racehorse — *wasting chattel*
- a lease with an unexpired term of 25 years
- a micro-computer used in a business
- a limousine used by a car hire company
  exempt

Exam focus point

Questions 10.1 and 10.2 below are taken from the Pilot Paper for the Personal Taxation Certificate paper.

10.1 David was left a painting in June 1989 on the death of his great aunt. Records showed she had purchased it in May 1985 for £7,200 and it was worth £11,200 on her death in 1989. David decided to sell the painting in May 2008 when it was worth £31,250. Calculate the chargeable gain on the sale of the painting.

10.2 Toby bought a plot of land in July 2001 for investment purposes for £18,000. In June 2008 a local developer offered him £125,000 for the plot. Toby decided however to keep a quarter of the plot and sold the remaining site to the developer for £85,000. The plot that Toby retained was valued at £30,000. Calculate the chargeable gain arising in 2008/09.

10.3 Edwin has chargeable gains of £9,000 and allowable losses of £5,000 in 2008/09. He has allowable losses brought forward of £6,000. What are the allowable losses carried forward to 2009/10?

10.4 James has the following chargeable gains and losses arising from disposals of assets:

Tax year	2006/07	2007/08	2008/09
	£	£	£
Gains	2,000	4,000	12,000
Losses	(5,000)	(2,000)	(2,000)

All assets had been owned for many years. What is the maximum allowable loss carried forward to 2009/10?

10.5 Paul invites the following people to a celebration dinner:

(1) his wife
(2) his mother-in-law
(3) his business partner
(4) the ex-wife of his business partner
(5) his uncle
(6) his step-father
(7) his band manager

Who is connected with Paul for CGT purposes?

10.6 Callum bought a freehold shop for use in his business on 13 July 2002 for £120,000. On 12 March 2005, when the shop was worth £150,000, he transferred the shop to his wife, Grace, who also used the shop in her business. On 12 May 2008, Grace sold the shop for £170,000. What is Grace's chargeable gain on the shop?

10.7 James sold assets to the following individuals, creating chargeable gains and allowable losses as shown below:

	Date of sale	Chargeable gain/ (allowable loss)
		£
Charles, his brother	1 March 2008	10,000
	15 June 2008	(8,200)
	29 September 2009	14,000
Sarah, his sister	2 August 2008	21,500
	1 July 2009	8,000
Mr Smith (not connected with James)	22 December 2008	9,000

Which gain will the allowable loss be set off against? Explain your reasoning.

10.8 Mr Cairns has net income for 2008/09 of £5,000. He has a current year trading loss of £40,000.

Chargeable gains for the year amount to £19,000 and capital losses for the year £1,000. Capital losses brought forward at the beginning of 2008/09 are £2,000.

How much trading loss will be available to carry forward at the end of 2008/09 if maximum loss relief for trading losses is taken?

10.9 Julie owned a field which she purchased on 13 August 1987 for £8,000. On 10 September 2008, she sold a quarter of the field for development for £30,000. The remainder of the field was then worth £10,000. What is Julie's chargeable gain?

10.10 Mattheus made gains of £16,900 (all on business assets owned for many years) and losses of £7,000 in 2008/09. He has losses brought forward of £5,000.

You are required to calculate the losses to carry forward to 2009/10.

Exam focus point

Question 11.1 below is taken from the Pilot Paper for the Personal Taxation Certificate paper.

11.1   Andrew bought 2,000 shares in X plc for £18,000 in August 2006 and a further 1,000 shares for £10,000 in September 2006. He sold 1,500 shares for £22,500 in January 2009. Calculate his chargeable gain.

11.2   Amber had the following transactions in the shares of Zingo Ltd:

		£
19.2.83	Purchased 2,000 shares, cost	10,000
20.9.90	Purchased 1,000 shares, cost	8,000
15.11.08	Sold 1,500 shares, proceeds	22,000

What is Amber's chargeable gain for 2008/09?

11.3   Mr Smith acquired 5,000 shares in S plc in April 1985 for £5,605. In July 1999 S plc made a bonus issue of one ordinary share for every five held. In December 2008 Mr Smith sold 3,500 of his shares for £6,250. What is the chargeable gain?

12.1   Lionel purchased a Victoria Cross medal in May 1983 for £3,000 and a vintage car in June 1985 for £4,000. He sold them both to a collector in April 2008 for £14,780 and £15,500 respectively.

What, if any, are his chargeable gains for 2008/09?

12.2   Giles purchased a picture in July 1991 for £4,500 and sold it in September 2008 for £7,500 before incurring £300 expenses of sale. What is Giles' chargeable gain?

12.3   Gail sold a painting for £90 in December 2008 which had cost £6,260 in January 1983. What is Gail's allowable loss for 2008/09?

12.4   On 1 April 1990 Mr Laycole acquired a painting on the death of his father at a probate value of £3,000. He sold the painting at auction for £7,200 on 30 October 2008 incurring costs of £350. Compute the chargeable gain.

12.5   In August 2008 Miranda, a sole trader whose business is ongoing, disposed of two assets on which capital allowances have been claimed.

	Purchase Price	Disposal Proceeds
	£	£
Motor car	8,000	4,000
Machinery	5,500	7,500

Both assets were purchased in October 2005. Calculate Miranda's chargeable gain or allowable loss.

12.6   Adrienne acquired a 90-year lease on 31 March 1983 for £40,000. On 31 March 2009 she granted a sublease of 55 years for £30,000. The reversionary interest is valued at £82,500. What is Adrienne's chargeable gain?

12.7   Jerome acquired a freehold property for £30,000 in March 1991. In November 2008 he granted an 11-year lease for a premium of £10,000 at which time the reversionary interest was valued at £50,000. What is Jerome's chargeable gain?

13.1   Neil sold a house on 30 June 2008. He realised an £80,000 gain before taking account of any PPR relief. The house was originally purchased on 1 October 1982 and was occupied by Neil until 30 June 1985 at which date he purchased and moved into another residence, letting the original house until the date of sale.

What is his chargeable gain?

13.2   Robert owned a property with three storeys of equal value in Sheffield. He bought it on 30 June 1985 for £20,000. He used the top two storeys as his main residence. The ground floor was rented out to students. The ground floor has a separate access door. On 30 November 2008 Robert sold the whole property for £200,000. What is his chargeable gain?

13.3   Give two examples of periods of absence from a property which are deemed periods of occupation for the CGT principal private residence exemption.

Exam focus point

Question 14.1 below is taken from the Pilot Paper for the Personal Taxation Certificate paper.

14.1 Jeremy Brett, who had run a manufacturing business for many years, decided to reduce the size of the operation in 2008/09. He therefore gave one of the factories (which had always been used for his business) to his son John although John persuaded his father to accept £50,000 in return.

The factory had been acquired on 2 January 1983 for £42,000. It was worth £225,974 and standing at a gain of £110,000 when it was passed to John in August 2008.

Calculate Jeremy's chargeable gain, if any, for 2008/09 and state the base cost for John, on the assumption that gift relief is claimed.

14.2 On 1 January 2009 Arthur sold a qualifying asset to his son, Hugo, for £12,000. At that time the market value of the asset was £22,000. Arthur had purchased the asset in July 1985 for £4,000.

Gift relief is claimed on the disposal. Who needs to make the claim and what is the deadline for the claim?

14.3 On 1 January 2009 Adam sold a business asset to his son, Bernard, for £12,000. At that time the market value of the asset was £22,000. Adam had purchased the asset in July 1985 for £4,000.

In 2010/11 Bernard permanently ceased to be resident in the UK. At the time he left the UK the asset had a market value of £25,000.

What chargeable gain arises as a result (assuming a joint claim for holdover relief had been made in respect of the January 2009 disposal), on whom is this chargeable and in what tax year?

14.4 Robert bought an 80% holding in an unquoted trading company on 10 July 2004 for £160,000. He gave the holding to his daughter, Lauren, on 13 December 2008, when it was worth £300,000. At that date, the assets of the company were:

	£
Factory	300,000
Quoted investments	50,000
Net current assets	25,000
	375,000

What is the gain chargeable on Robert before the annual exemption?

14.5 In July 2008 Phil sold an asset of his farming business to his daughter Shula for £63,000 when its open market value was £95,000. Phil had bought the asset in May 1995 for £44,000. How much gift relief can be claimed by Phil and Shula?

14.6 In March 2008 Keith Pringle purchased an antique tea set for £24,000. In September 2008 the teapot was broken and he received £4,000 from the insurance company as compensation. The remaining tea set was valued at £16,000. Calculate the gain/loss arising.

14.7 Patrice makes a gain of £600,000 in July 2008 on the sale of a flat in Brighton (not her main residence). In November 2007 she had subscribed £800,000 for shares in a qualifying EIS company and makes the maximum possible claim for EIS deferral relief. In August 2009 Patrice emigrates to Switzerland.

What chargeable gains will arise in 2008/09 and/or 2009/10?

14.8 In 1999 John invested £50,000 to acquire a 10% shareholding in Silvanus Ltd. In July 2008 he sold all his shares in this company for £800,000. He invested £650,000 in a qualifying EIS company in March 2009. John has £150,000 of capital losses brought forward as at 6 April 2008 and made no other disposals in 2008/09.

What is the optimum amount of EIS deferral relief which John should claim, assuming that he makes all beneficial claims?

Exam focus point

Question 15.1 below is taken from the Pilot Paper for the Personal Taxation Certificate paper.

15.1   A landlord is allowed to submit a simplified return in respect of rental income provided the appropriate condition is satisfied. What is the condition and what needs to be recorded on the return?

15.2   Thomas Apple received his 2008/09 tax return on 19 May 2009. Outline Thomas's options for filing this tax return.

15.3   John's income tax and CGT position for 2007/08 is as follows:

	£
Income tax liability	10,250
Tax deducted at source	(5,000)
	5,250
Class 4 NIC	1,000
CGT liability	8,200
Payments on account made re 2007/08	(5,000)
	9,450

Calculate John's payments on account for 2008/09 stating the due dates.

16.1   One of your clients, Martin Edwards, pays his pension scheme contributions through you as broker and the insurance company have just sent you commission thereon of £500. What steps should you take under the ATT Professional Rules and Practice Guidelines 2006?

16.2   A prospective client has contacted you to take over from his existing adviser. He alleges that the previous adviser was incompetent and insists that you do not contact him. What should you do?

16.3   Sheila and Ken Walters, each a client of many years standing, have decided to divorce 'amicably'. They have effectively lived apart under the same roof for some time. Ken is only interested in his garden and Sheila has made the golf club her second home so they feel they should formally separate with an intention to divorce. They are both insistent that you should continue to act for them. What should you do?

16.4   What are a member's usual responsibilities in respect of due dates and interest on tax where a member undertakes tax compliance work for a client?

16.5   If a member is engaged in a fee dispute with a client he may call for arbitration from the ATT. True/ False.

16.6   Which type of fee arrangement is specifically considered within the regime for disclosure of tax avoidance schemes?

16.7   Robbie's firm is holding £20,000 of a client's money. How long can they hold the money before they should open a designated interest bearing client account?

16.8   What are the three ways in which land can be legally held?

16.9   What is the maximum number of legal owners of land?

16.10   In the case of registered land at what point does the legal title pass from the seller to the buyer?

16.11   Sara has been unfairly dismissed. What orders may the employment tribunal make in her favour?

1.1 **Mr Daphnis**

Mr Daphnis (aged 69) is married to Chloë (aged 76) and is registered blind.

Mr Daphnis's net income for 2008/09 was £22,980, made up of rental income (£12,980) and savings interest (£10,000). Chloë's only income is her pension of £4,500.

You are required to calculate Mr and Mrs Daphnis's allowances and tax reductions for 2008/09. Also give brief advice on how they could improve their joint tax position.

1.2 **Mr Rich**

Mr Rich earned £58,000 from his employment in 2008/09. He paid tax of £13,800 under PAYE.

He paid £12,000 (net) to Oxfam via Gift Aid in the year.

You are required to calculate his tax due/ owed.

The following question is taken from the Pilot Paper for the Personal Taxation Certificate paper.

1.3 **Tax Credits**

You have recently received the following letter from one of your clients:

21 Avon Avenue
Avonbury
Bucks

T Adviser
Corton & Co
West Street
Anytown

Dear Tom

Thank you for preparing our tax returns, which we have signed and are returning to you for submission.

On another matter, as you may know, my husband and I are expecting a baby this June. I have heard a lot on TV about child and working tax credits and wondered whether I would be entitled to any when the baby is born, particularly as I will only be working part time going forward.

I have done some research and am familiar with the rates of the allowances together with the conditions that need to be met to be entitled to them eg age, working hours etc. However, the one thing I cannot work out is how to calculate income to compare to the income limit of £6,420.

Can you explain to me how my income would be calculated for tax credit purposes or is it simply the same as taxable income for income tax purposes?

I look forward to hearing from you.

Best regards

Julie Smythe

Julie Smythe is an employee who received the following income in 2008/09.

	£
Salary	22,000
Car benefit	2,150
Medical insurance	540
Use of home entertainment system (benefit amount)	1,200

She paid her own subscription to the Institute of Personnel and Development of £150.

Her husband is a self-employed designer who, after several loss-making years, made a profit in 2008/09 of £13,500 as adjusted for tax purposes and after loss relief.

They received bank interest on their joint savings account of £45 (net) and paid £10 per month to the RSPCA under the Gift Aid scheme.

You are required to write a reply to Julie Smythe addressing the definition of income for tax credit purposes.

You are NOT required to provide any calculations. **(10 marks)**

2.1 Mr Poor

Mr Poor took early retirement in 2002 when he was 55. He now works part-time. In 2008/09 his gross earnings were £5,600 and he paid tax under PAYE of £250. He received £900 in dividends and £800 of building society interest. He received interest on his Midwest Savings Bank account totalling £80.

You are required to calculate his tax payable/repayable.

2.2 Jonty

Jonty, aged 38, is a married man whose wife has no income. The following information is relevant for the year ended 5 April 2009:

(1) His salary was £42,000 (PAYE deducted £8,200)

(2) His other income was:

	£
Building society interest received	80
Dividends received	63

(3) In March 2009 Jonty closed down his NS&I investment account which he had kept for many years. Interest of £142 was credited.

(4) He made a donation of £396 (net of basic rate tax) to Oxfam in May 2008 under Gift Aid.

(5) Jonty won £100 on the Grand National.

(6) He has one child aged 4 whom his wife looks after. Jonty works over 30 hours per week.

You are required to compute the tax payable by/ repayable to Jonty for 2008/09. You are also required to calculate any Credit/Working Tax Credit available.

2.3 Fred

Fred (72) is married to Wilma (61). Fred received the following income in 2008/09:

	£
Rental income	16,200
Building society interest	4,400
UK Treasury Stock interest	290
UK company dividends	7,000

Wilma has no income.

You are required to calculate Fred's tax payable for 2008/09.

2.4 Fiona

Fiona, who is 35, lives on her own. She has been running her own business for many years. She has agreed with HMRC that her profits for 2008/09 are £32,000.

During 2008/09 she received the following investment income:

	£
UK dividends	8,000
Jersey bank interest	4,300
Premium bond winnings	13,000
Child benefit in respect of her 6 year old twins for whom she has sole custody	1,630

Fiona borrowed £24,000 in March 2007 to invest in shares in a close company. She pays interest at 4% per annum. She repaid £10,000 of the loan when she received her Premium Bond winnings on 5 December 2008. She subscribed for £3,000 of shares in an EIS company with the remainder.

She pays an annual donation to charity of £1,600.

You are required to calculate Fiona's tax payable for 2008/09.

2.5 Jane Bradbury

Jane Bradbury is in her 30s. Her husband died last year leaving her to bring up their child now aged 2. The child attends a registered nursery for 3 days a week at a cost of £20 per day. Jane works 20 hours per week.

Jane is a partner in a small firm making children's clothes. Her profit share for 2008/09 has been agreed at £7,140.

Jane pays interest of £4,800 each year on a loan she took out in 2000 to buy into the partnership.

Jane has an investment portfolio which generated dividends of £4,950 in 2008/09. Her only other income is bank interest received on a bank account of £200.

Calculate Jane's tax repayable for 2008/09. Calculate any Child Tax Credit/Working Tax Credit due.

2.6 George and Mildred Roper

George Roper (aged 73) married Mildred (age 76) on 10 February 2009. Both have been married before. George pays his ex-wife Liz £250 each month by way of maintenance after their divorce in 1997. Mildred's former husband Brian died in May 2005.

George's income for 2008/09 is as follows:

	£
Earnings from part time consultancy work (PAYE deducted £1,000)	11,000
Pension from former employer (PAYE deducted £570)	2,600
State pension (£87 per week)	4,524
UK Treasury stock interest	180
Rental income from holiday home	4,000
UK dividends received	2,115

George pays interest at 10% per annum on a loan which he had taken out to buy shares in Hi Tek Ltd. £10,000 of the loan is outstanding and interest relief is claimed under s.392 ITA 2007.

Mildred's income for 2008/09 is as follows:

	£
State pension (£84 per week)	4,368
Building society interest received	8,400
Distribution from discretionary trust	4,000
Interest from bank account in Guernsey	950
Premium Bond winnings	400
UK dividends received	720

Mildred pays £500 each year to the NSPCC (a registered charity) under Gift Aid.

Calculate George and Mildred's tax payable/repayable for 2008/09.

3.1 Randall

Randall owns three properties which are let on the following terms, all rents being payable quarterly in advance on (31 March, 30 June, 30 September and 31 December). Randall is responsible for repairs on all properties; the rents on properties A, B and C are full rents.

A   Let at £620 a year on a 20-year lease which commenced in 1990.

B   Let at £348 a year on a lease which expired on 30 September 2008, then empty until 31 December 2008 when let at £440 a year.

C   Let at £100 a year throughout the year.

TQT
Tax Qualification Training

Expenditure by Randall on these properties in the year was as follows:

	A £	B £	C £
Agent's commission	20		
Advertising for tenants		76	
Repairs: while let	142		119
while empty		255	

You are required to:

(1) **Calculate the property income assessment for Randall for 2008/09.**

(2) **Explain the income tax implications of paying a premium on granting a lease.**

3.2 **Corelli**

Corelli, aged 41, owns three properties:

A   5 Arnhem Avenue
B   17 Blenheim Road
C   27 Cannae Road.

All are let out unfurnished.

A   This was let until 24 June 2008 at an annual rental of £1,200. On 29 September 2008, it was let out to a new tenant on a 10-year lease agreement. The annual rental is £800. The tenant paid a premium of £5,000 on 29 September 2008.

B   This was let throughout 2008/09. The annual rental was £3,100. The rental due on 25 March 2009 was not received until 12 April 2009.

C   This was let from 24 June 2008 at an annual rental of £600.

All the rents are payable quarterly in advance on the normal quarter days and are sufficient normally to cover the landlord's outgoings.

Properties A and B were acquired in 1981; property C was purchased on 15 April 2008.

Expenditure in connection with the properties was as follows:

	A £	B £	C £
Agent's commission 1 May 2008	25	35	10
1 November 2008	25	35	10
Repairs (note)	–	100	1,800
Advertising for new tenants 10 July 2008	50	–	–

Note. The repairs in respect of property C are analysed as follows:

	£
Installation of new kitchen equipment	300
Retiling part of the roof after damage in May 2008	1,500
	1,800

Corelli's other income during 2008/09 was as follows:

	£
Dividends received	15,300
Salary (PAYE £2,210)	16,450

(i)   **You are required to compute Corelli's income tax payable for 2008/09.**   (7 marks)

(ii)   **You are required to explain the difference between freehold and leasehold land.**   (5 marks)

(Total: 12 marks)

4.1 **Enterprise investment Scheme**

You are required to describe the income tax relief and capital gains tax exemption in respect of an investment in shares qualifying under the Enterprise Investment Scheme.

Your answer should cover the main points in brief outline only.

5.1 **Mr Thomas**

Mr Thomas is a director of a private company; his remuneration for 2008/09 was £30,000.

During the year ended 5 April 2009, the following benefits were provided to him:

(1) Accommodation in a four bedroom house, owned by the company.

	£
Original cost 1993	80,000
Cost of extension 1997	25,000
Annual value	750

Mr Thomas moved in on 1 March 2002, at which time the house was valued at £125,000.

Expenses paid directly by company 2008/09:	£
Council tax	1,400
Electricity	750
Gas	250
Telephone	350
Redecoration (internal)	700
Gardener	1,500

(2) Interest-free loan for a non-qualifying purpose – first advance 6 June 2008

		£
6.6.08	advance	10,000
6.8.08	advance	5,000
6.12.08	repaid	7,500
6.2.09	advance	4,000
6.3.09	repaid	2,500

(3) Car – Mercedes, list price £21,500, purchased 1 June 2005. The emission rate is 150g/km.

— 1,600 cc Escort, list price £10,000, purchased 5 August 2008, used by Mrs Thomas. The emission rate is 165g/km.

No petrol was provided for either vehicle.

You are required to calculate the benefits assessable on Mr Thomas for 2008/09.

Assume that the official rate of interest charged throughout 2008/09 was 6.25%.

5.2 **Alf**

You have been consulted by Alf, one of the directors of your company, who has no shareholding in the company, concerning the taxability of emoluments and benefits received. The following information is provided for the tax year 2008/09.

(1) Alf's salary is £32,600 (PAYE £5,755).

(2) An expenses allowance of £2,500 for 2008/09 spent as follows:

	£
Business travelling	1,800
Entertainment:	
Overseas customers	400
Overseas suppliers	100
United Kingdom customers	200

(3) Benefits for the year were as follows:

(i) The company purchased hi-fi equipment for Alf's personal use at a cost of £800. The company retained ownership of the equipment.

(ii) Alf had exclusive use of a new 2.5 litre petrol engined car with a list price of £15,000. The emission rate is 180g/km. No petrol was provided for private motoring.

(iii) Medical insurance was provided for £300. Alf would have had to pay £450 to take out the insurance personally.

(iv) Alf visited Saville Row for 5 tailored shirts, which were paid for by the company, on Alf's behalf at cost of £400.

(v) Alf's other income for 2008/09 is as follows:

	£
Bank interest received	5,440
Dividends received	4,000

(vi) He pays £1,600 each year to charity under Gift Aid.

You are required to calculate the tax due by Alf for 2008/09, giving brief explanatory notes on the treatment of his benefits and expenses.

5.3 Mr Bjork

Mr Bjork is chairman and chief executive of Peepop Ltd.

He receives a salary of £46,000 per annum and during the income tax year 2008/09 he is provided with the following benefits:

The company provided him with the use of a 2,100 cc petrol Jaguar motor car with a list price of £20,000 from 6 April 2008. The emission rate is 220g/km.

On 31 July 2008 he was involved in a serious road accident and the car was written off. He was charged with dangerous driving and the company met his legal costs of £2,000.

While he had use of the Jaguar, he contributed 50% of the cost of his private fuel.

When he resumed work on 1 October 2008, he was provided with a Mercedes car with a list price of £30,000 and the use of a chauffeur. This car is used solely for business purposes. The emission rate is 190g/km.

Throughout the year, his wife, who is not employed by the company, has been provided with the use of a 2 litre BMW car with a list price of £15,000 four years ago; the company meets all running costs and petrol bills. The emission rate is 240g/km.

He is provided with the use of video equipment which had been purchased by the company at a cost of £800.

He is given a computer by Peepop Ltd on 6 October 2008, when it has a market value of £200. He has had use of that computer since 6 October 2005 when its market value was £6,000.

You are required to compute the total amount of benefits assessable on Mr Bjork for 2008/09.

5.4 HiTech Computers

Giles has worked for HiTech Computers Plc for many years and he has recently been promoted to sales manager, receiving a £5,000 pay rise from 1 July 2008. His revised salary is £36,000. He has continued to pay contributions into his registered occupational pension of 5% of his salary and bonus. He has received sales commission as follows:

Year ended 31 December 2007	£3,000 received 28 February 2008
Year ended 31 December 2008	£4,000 received 28 February 2009

As a result of his promotion, he has been provided with a flat in London, due to being required to spend increasing amounts of time in London. The company pays £5,000 annual rent on the property, which has an annual value of £2,400. He is required to contribute £100 per month towards this.

Giles still has an interest free loan from the company for the purchase of his private car. The amount outstanding was £15,000 on 6 April 2008 and £10,000 on 5 April 2009. He has a car parking space provided in London under the HiTech Computers Plc building that costs the company £1,200 per annum.

Other perks that Giles receives are as follows:

(1)   Free medical insurance – the cost to the company is £385 per annum although if Giles had taken this out privately, he would have to pay £525 to cover both him and his wife.

(2)   £100 per month payment towards the provision of crèche facilities for his child who attends a registered private nursery.

(3)   A newspaper allowance of £20 per month.

You are required to calculate Giles's earnings for 2008/09, giving explanations of your treatment of the benefits.

Assume that the official rate of interest is 6.25% for the whole year.

5.5 Grovelands

Grovelands Ltd, an electrical company, was taken over in 2008. Freddie, a senior executive in charge of business sales did not get along with new management and his employment was terminated on 31 December 2008. The company provided him with an ex-gratia payment of £84,974, of which £72,487 was paid on 31 December 2008 and £12,487 in May 2009.

Freddie's salary from Grovelands Ltd for the year to 31 December 2008 had been £29,333. He subsequently took a part-time consultancy post with another company for £8,400 per annum. The salary was to be paid in equal monthly instalments in arrears. This new job started on 1 February 2009.

Grovelands Ltd had allowed Freddie the use of a home entertainment system, which was worth £5,000 when loaned to him on 1 July 2007. On his departure from the company, Freddie bought the system (now worth £1,000) for £150.

Freddie's other income and charges for the year 2008/09 were as follows:
Benefits:

	£
Company car (2500 cc; list price in 2007 was £22,300; approved CO_2 emissions figure 214 g/km).	
BUPA subscription	200
London Transport season ticket	2,641
UK dividends – amount received	2,754
Bank interest received	1,386
Gift aid payment (net)	800

Freddie drove his company car on business for 1,200 miles (out of a total of 10,000 miles) during 2008/09. Grovelands Ltd paid directly for all the car's running expenses including petrol which amounted to £3,200 up to 31 December 2008, at which date it was returned to the company.

(i)   **You are required to compute Freddie's total income tax liability for 2008/09.**   **(15 marks)**
(ii)   **You are required to explain the meaning of summary dismissal and constructive dismissal. (5 marks)**

(Total: 20 marks)

5.6 Mr Morris

Mr Morris, aged 41, joined William and Sons Limited in March 2007. He negotiated a package comprising a basic annual salary of £25,450, a two litre company car (list price £14,665; CO_2 emissions 187g/km) with all private petrol provided and also health insurance costing £340 paid on his behalf by the company.

PAYE of £6,234 was deducted from his salary in 2008/09.

Mr Morris received the following amounts from his investments in 2008/09:

	£
Building society account interest	312
UK dividends	738

He also held a joint account with his wife at Burford Bank which had been credited with £256 worth of interest in 2008/09.

Mr Morris inherited a house in Devon from his father 15 years ago. This property (which is furnished) is let out by Mr Morris, who employs a letting agent to deal with the rental. The details for 2008/09 are as follows:

6.4.08 – 31.8.08

Let to the Adams family
Gross rent per annum £8,000 payable quarterly in arrears

	£
Agents fees	267
Repairs and maintenance	400
Gardener	100
Council Tax (for 2008/09)	590
Water rates	85

1.10.08 – 5.4.09
Let to the Potter family
Gross rent per annum £12,000 payable quarterly in arrears

Agents fees	600
Repairs and maintenance	1,500
(including £1,000 incurred in September 2008)	
Gardener	200
Water rates	100
Cost and installation of new gas fire	435

Note: The rent due on 31 March was not actually paid until 15 April 2009.

Mr Morris also pays £156 each year to Oxfam under the gift aid scheme (no election to carry back the payment to 2007/08 will be made).

You are required to calculate Mr Morris's outstanding income tax payable for 2008/09.   **(10 marks)**

6.1   **Sue**

Sue has been a director of Porchester Ltd for three years. In order to reward her performance to the company on 1 January 2009, she was granted 5,000 ordinary share options under an approved scheme to buy shares at £4.00 at any time in the next 10 years. The market value of the shares at January 2009 was £3.96. She is planning to buy the shares in 8 years time when she estimates that the share price will have risen to £10.00. She plans to sell them shortly afterwards (assume share price at date of sale = £10.40).

You are required to:

(a)   **Explain the tax consequences of the granting of the share options and the subsequent sale by Sue.**

(b)   **Explain how your answer would change if the scheme was unapproved and the exercise price was £3.00.**

The following question is taken from the Pilot Paper for the Personal Taxation Certificate paper.

7.1   **Mr Matthews**

Mr Matthews, an architect, changed employers at the beginning of April 2008. He was sent a tax return form for the first time in respect of 2008/09. He has therefore approached the partner that you work for to help him with his tax affairs. Although it is already mid February 2010 he has just sent in his tax return, which he has started to complete himself, for review. He has calculated his total income as follows:

Source of income

	Total income £	Tax suffered £
Salary (from P60)	48,750	11,754
Medical insurance (from P11D)	375	
Allowance for business miles (own calculation)	111	
Parking in car park next to office (paid for by employer, figure from parking receipts retained and reimbursed)	720	
Building Society Interest received (from passbook)	320	80
Income from Discretionary Trust (from R185)	2,000	800
Total income	52,276	12,634

He has sent in his P60, P11D and the form R185 which agree with the above figures.

He has entered the following information on your firm's tax return questionnaire:

Date of birth: 1.10.1973

Business Mileage

Drove 925 miles on business in 2008/09. Reimbursed by employer 12p per mile.

Subscriptions

Member of the Institute of Architects

Subscriptions paid by Mr Matthews: £285 paid 1.1.08; £295 paid 1.1.09

Charitable donations

£10 per month paid to Dogs Trust
£15 per month paid to English Heritage

Can I get relief for these payment and if so how does it work?

Also – can you explain how a charity can benefit if I have overpaid tax?

Pension Contributions

No pension provision at present

You are required to:

(1) **Review Mr Matthews' calculation of income and tax suffered and produce an amended version, explaining any changes that you have made.** **(6 marks)**

(2) **Produce notes for the partner to enable him to explain to Mr Matthews how he may be able to get relief for the charitable donations he has made, how the relief would be given and how a charity could benefit if he has overpaid tax.** **(5 marks)**

(3) **Calculate Mr Matthews' tax payable/repayable based on your calculation of total income giving relief for the charitable donations.** **(3 marks)**

(4) **Produce a statement outlining the tax rules concerning payments to a personal pension plan including how much Mr Matthews could contribute to a personal pension plan (based on his 2008/09 income), the tax saving that he would achieve and whether a claim can be made for relief against 2008/09 income.** **(6 marks)**

(Total: 20 marks)

7.2 **Ed & Joan**

Ed Tommy and Joan Ball are in partnership running a design studio, with profits being shared in the ratio 4:1. They both wish to start saving for their retirement and would like to make maximum contributions to a pension. The partnership's trading profit for 2008/09 is £175,000. Neither Ed or Joan has any other income.

(a) **Advise Ed and Joan of the maximum amount they can each contribute to a pension for 2007/08 and 2008/09.**

(b) **Explain the method by which Ed and Joan will be given tax relief for their pension contributions and show their income tax liability.**

(c) **Explain how they will be able to continue to contribute to their pensions if the partnership ceases trading on 5 April 2009 and they no longer have earnings.**

7.3 **Dwaine Pipe**

Dwaine is the sales director of a small central heating and plumbing company based in the Midlands. The company draws up accounts to 31 December each year.

Dwaine's salary (paid monthly) for the year ended 31 December 2008 was set at £20,000 per annum. This was raised to £22,000 at the Board meeting on 20 January 2009. PAYE deducted in 2008/09 came to £6,000.

Dwaine also receives half yearly bonuses dependent on the performance of his sales team. These have been as follows:

Bonus period	Bonus	Awarded	Received
6 m/e 31.12.07	£3,000	31.3.08	30.4.08
6 m/e 30.6.08	£3,850	30.9.08	31.10.08
6 m/e 31.12.08	£4,250	31.3.09	30.4.09

In addition to his salary and bonus, Dwaine receives the following benefits:

1. **Company cars**

   Vauxhall Cavalier 1.6, list price £10,629, first registered on 1 March 2003. He returned the car at the end of October 2008. The emission rate is 145g/km. He was required to pay £40 per month for the private use of the Vauxhall. All diesel for business use was paid by the company.

   On 1 November 2008 he exchanged the Vauxhall for a brand new Audi A6, list price £18,500. A CD player was added at Dwaine's request at a cost of £400. The emission rate is 200g/km. Again the company paid for all petrol for business mileage.

   Dwaine was involved in an accident on Christmas Day which left the Audi in the garage until 15 January 2009. He was provided with a replacement vehicle (another Audi) which he used until his own car was returned.

2. **Mobile phone**

   As Dwaine needs to be in contact with the office, he was provided with a mobile phone. The company reimbursed all Dwaine's calls at a cost of £2,400 in the year. Dwaine estimates that only 10% of these were for private reasons.

3. **Interest free home loan**

   The company lent Dwaine £75,000 on 1 June 2008 to buy his flat in Birmingham. Dwaine repaid £15,000 of the loan on 1 January 2009.

4. **Nursery fees**

   Dwaine's son Wayne has a place at a local approved nursery for which the company have agreed to meet the costs. These amounted to £45 per week in 2008/09.

5. **Personal pension**

   The company does not have an occupational pension scheme and has therefore agreed to make contributions into Dwaine's personal pension plan. Dwaine makes payments of £150 per month – the company add an extra £100 per month.

6. **Central heating system**

Dwaine's new flat came without central heating. The company provided the materials free of charge and Dwaine fitted the system himself. The materials cost the company £800 and usually retail at £1,200 to customers.

7. **Staff suggestion scheme**

Dwaine won second prize in the scheme being a crate of champagne costing £150. His suggestion will save the company around £3,000 in costs.

8. **Round sum allowance**

Dwaine is given a general allowance of £1,000 each year. In 2008/09 he spent this as follows:

	£
Hotel bills while away on business	710
Entertaining customers	160
	870

He was unable to account for the remainder.

His other income for the year was as follows:

Interest on ISA account	£1,000
Interest received on Halifax account (joint with his wife)	£14,000
Premium bond winnings	£120

Dwaine also made a donation to Oxfam of £400 under Gift Aid.

You are required to calculate the income tax payable/(repayable) by Dwaine for the year ended 5 April 2009.

Assume an official interest rate of 6.25% throughout.

8.1 **Ricardo Garcia**

Ricardo Garcia is resident and domiciled in Spain.

He has recently married a British woman and will be coming to live permanently in London when he retires; he has advised you that he will continue to return to Spain for holidays.

He has a large pension from the Spanish company that he used to work for, which he will need to bring into the UK for living expenses. He will keep his Spanish bank account and his large portfolio of Spanish investments.

The house which he presently owns in Spain will be rented out.

Mr Garcia has requested that you write to him explaining the basis of assessment in the UK on his worldwide income. He does not require any calculations at this stage.

You are required to draft a letter to Mr Garcia as requested.

9.1 **Peter Jones**

Peter Jones' income and chargeable gains for 2008/09 were as follows:

	£
Building society income (net)	3,200
Dividends (net)	800
Rental income	5,289
Chargeable gains (before annual exemption)	40,000

You are required to:

(1) **Calculate the excess of income tax paid over the income tax liability and the income tax repayment due to Peter Jones for 2008/09.**

(2) **Calculate the capital gains tax due for 2008/09.**

9.2 Simon James

Simon James wrote to you on 3 March 2009 on various matters, including the following in relation to capital gains tax:

'I recently read an article in the financial columns of a newspaper which explained the meaning of residence, ordinary residence and domicile. Unfortunately, that article did not consider the relevance of these concepts in determining taxation liabilities. I am particularly concerned with the capital gains tax implications and I should be grateful if you would explain the significance of those terms in relation to that tax.'

You are required to write a letter explaining the relevance of residence, ordinary residence and domicile in determining an individual's liability to capital gains tax.

10.1 Dorrit

Dorrit has been trading for many years and has produced the following recent results:

Year ended	£
31 December 2008	15,000 profit
31 December 2009	(28,000) loss

He has UK property income of £3,000 per annum and in 2008/09 realised a chargeable gain of £16,000 on a painting which was originally acquired on 2 May 1998.

You are required to compute Dorrit's revised net income and chargeable gains, before the annual exemption for 2008/09 assuming earliest possible relief is sought for the loss.

10.2 Kidson

Kidson purchased a plot of land on 1 January 1983 for £8,000. On 31 August 2008, he sold part of the land for £45,000 but declined an offer of £50,000 for the rest.

You are required to calculate the taxable gain arising on the sale assuming this is the only capital transaction Kidson has in 2008/09.

10.3 Harbottle

The following information relates to your clients Fred and Iris Harbottle, both aged 30, who have been married for five years.

Fred is employed full time by a firm of chartered accountants at a salary of £35,000.

Iris is not currently working as she is staying at home to look after their two young children, aged 4 and 6. She leaves them with registered childminders one afternoon a week for which she pays £20 a week.

They have each inherited a portfolio of investments, details of which are as follows:

Fred has approximately £100,000 invested in shares currently yielding £7,000 gross income.

Iris has approximately £30,000 invested in shares which yield £1,200 gross.

They intend to make disposals of their investments during 2008/09 resulting in chargeable gains of £10,700 for Fred and £2,500 for Iris.

They also have an Investment Account with National Savings Bank in joint names which yields £2,000 each year.

You are required to:

(a) **Calculate the income tax and capital gains tax liabilities of the couple for 2008/09; and** (5 marks)

(b) **State what planning action the couple may take in order to reduce their 2008/09 income tax and capital gains tax liabilities.** (5 marks)

(c) **Calculate the amount of Child Tax Credit and Working Tax Credit that Fred and Iris are entitled to in respect of 2008/09.** (5 marks)

(Total: 15 marks)

11.1 Julie Green

You are currently preparing the tax return of Julie Green, who runs her own marketing company. You have completed all of her return apart from the capital gains tax pages. As well as selling a painting that she had been left by her great aunt for proceeds of £25,000 (chargeable gain £12,000), she had a number of transactions in respect of her holding of Target plc shares.

The gains in respect of the Target plc shares have been calculated by your firm's new capital gains software, but as part of the review process you are required to check the calculations.

Julie Green's file records the following transactions:

Date	Event	Cost/proceeds £
1 June 1993	Purchase 50 shares	1,000
18 September 1996	Purchase 50 shares	3,800
21 May 1997	Purchase 100 shares	9,300
10 December 1997	Bonus issue 1:2	N/A
15 January 2002	Purchase 100 shares	8,200
29 June 2008	Sale 75 shares	10,150

From her tax return questionnaire you establish that on 16 August 2008 she also sold 75 shares for £8,500.

Her holding represents less than 1% of the issued share capital of the company and she has never worked for Target plc.

You are required to calculate the gains arising in 2008/09 in respect of the Target plc shares, producing a complete working sheet to place on the file.

11.2 Mr Jones

Mr Jones purchased 5,000 shares in XYZ plc in August 1982 for £6,250. He subsequently carried out the following transactions.

Date	Number of shares bought/(sold)	Cost (proceeds) £
September 1982	2,000	3,000
November 1985	5,000	9,500
October 1987	(3,000)	(6,500)
May 2001	1,000	3,000
July 2008	(7,000)	(31,500)

The company has 100,000 shares in issue.

You are required to calculate the chargeable gains for Mr Jones for 2008/09.

11.3 Richard Price

Richard Price works for PB plc, a large UK quoted trading company. He has acquired shares in PB plc via a company share option plan in recent years as follows:

Date	Shares Acquired	Cost £
15.3.1990	2,000	2,000
17.12.1996	4,000	10,000

In May 1998 there was a 1:5 rights issue at £5 per share which Richard took up in full.

On 4 October 2008, Richard sold 1,800 shares at £7.50 each.

He still works for the company and his holding comprises less than 1% of the shares in issue.

Calculate the chargeable gain on the disposal.

11.4 Eric James

On 3 March 2009 Eric James sold 2,000 ordinary shares (4% shareholding) in Toucan Play plc for £9,100. These shares had been acquired as a result of a takeover on 4 June 2000 of Parrot Games plc in which Eric had held 1,000 shares. These had been acquired in January 1999 for £4,000.

The terms of the takeover were 2 ordinary shares and 4 preference shares in Toucan Play plc for every share held in Parrot Games plc. Immediately following the takeover the ordinary shares and preference shares in Toucan Play plc were valued at £4.20 and £2 respectively.

You are required to calculate the chargeable gain arising from the above transaction.

12.1 Doug

Doug sold the following items on 1 August 2008:

(1) A Ming vase bought in January 1984 for £2,000. The sales proceeds were £8,000.

(2) A Leonardo cartoon bought in March 1984 for £7,200 and sold for £5,500.

(3) A lathe bought for use in his business in March 1985 which cost £4,300. The sales proceeds were £9,500. Doug had claimed capital allowances on this asset.

You are required to calculate Doug's taxable gain for 2008/09 assuming he made no other disposals in the year.

12.2 Mr Cole

Mr Cole made the following disposals in 2008/09:

1. On 2 June 2008 he sold his 1952 vintage Ford motor car for £7,200. He had bought the car in June 2005 for £3,600 and had incurred restoration costs of £500.

2. On 2 September 2008 he sold 5 acres of land out of a 40 acre plot for £38,000. He had acquired the whole plot (for investment purposes) for £32,000 in July 1989. The value of the remaining 35 acres was £82,000 in September 2008.

3. On 1 November 2008 he sold an antique chest for £7,000. He had bought this in June 1999 for £4,000.

4. On 3 December 2008 he sold a painting for £11,500, incurring costs of sale of £150. He had been left the painting by his grandfather who had paid £2,000 for it in June 1985. It was worth £4,700 when his grandfather died in August 1989.

5. On 15 January 2009 he sold a vase for £900. He had paid £7,500 for this in August 1997 believing it to be a Shelley vase but in fact it was a reproduction.

You are required to calculate the capital gains tax payable by Mr Cole for 2008/09. **(10 marks)**

12.3 CGT Leases

(1) Joe acquired an 80 year lease on a property for £38,000 on 29 July 1982. He assigned the lease on 29 July 2008 for £79,000.

(2) As (1) except that it was a 57 year lease when it was acquired.

(3) Harold acquired the freehold of a property for £25,000 on 1 May 1990. On 1 October 2008 he granted a 60 year lease on the premises for a premium of £30,000, the value of the reversion being £7,500.

(4) As (3) except that the lease granted was a 20 year lease, the premium received £20,000 and the value of the reversion £17,000.

(5) Ebury, a trader who has been in business for many years making up accounts annually to 31 January, was granted a 25 year lease of business premises on 1 September 2008 at a premium of £12,000 and an annual rent of £3,000 payable monthly in advance.

You are required to calculate the chargeable gains arising in (1) to (4) above and show the deductions to be made in respect of the lease in Ebury's accounts ((5) above) to 31 January 2009.

13.1 Owning two homes

Your managing partner has asked you to write an article to be published on your firm's website. There have been a number of queries submitted recently concerning the Capital Gains Tax implications of owning two homes and she feels that this would be a good topic to have an article on.

She has supplied you with a case study of a typical family to refer to in the article.

Case Study

Family	Mr and Mrs Hammond; two children aged 4 and 2.		
	Current family home:	Bought 15 August 1997	
		Cost	£150,000
	Occupied throughout period of ownership by Mr and Mrs Hammond		
	To be sold May 2008	Proceeds	£560,000
New acquisitions May 2008	House in country	Cost	£400,000
	Flat in town	Cost	£175,000

Plans   Mr Hammond to reside in flat in town Monday night – Thursday night; weekends in country house

Mrs Hammond to reside in country house.

Flat in town either:

(a)   to be sold after five years when Mr Hammond will live full time in country, or

(b)   to be let after five years and sold five years later

House to be family home until children leave home.

You are required to draft an article:

(a)   **Explaining the key Capital Gains Tax implications arising from the above, broken down in to sections as follows:**

(i)   **The Capital Gains Tax implications of selling the current family home.**   **(2 marks)**

(ii)   **The Capital Gains Tax implications for Mr and Mrs Hammond of residing in two homes and any action that they should consider.**   **(5 marks)**

(iii)   **The advice that you would give Mr and Mrs Hammond based on their circumstances and the resulting Capital Gains Tax consequences of the flat either being sold after five years or being sold after ten years, having been let for five years.**   **(7 marks)**

(iv)   **The Capital Gains Tax consequences of the sale of the house in 20 years.**   **(1 mark)**

(b)   **Answering a frequent question from couples – what is the difference between owning our house as joint tenants or owning it as tenants in common? (Under Scottish Law – what is the difference between joint property and common property?)**   **(5 marks)**

You should assume that the facts of the case study will be reproduced on the website.

(Total: 20 marks)

13.2 Peter Stamp

On 2 May 1982 Peter Stamp, a retired solicitor, bought a private dwelling-house for £70,000, which he sold for £270,000 under a contract dated 3 July 2008. The house was situated in grounds of one half of a hectare.

He lived in this house as his only residence until 1 February 1986. It was then let for residential purposes until 1 December 1995. From that date until the date of sale the property was unoccupied.

You are required to compute the chargeable gain arising on the sale of the house.

14.1 Fran and Anna

Fran sold a factory worth £500,000 to her friend Anna for £100,000 on 1 June 2008 and moved her business to new premises. Fran had bought the factory on 1 January 1993 for £75,000. On 1 July 2010 Anna sold the factory for £520,000.

Both Fran and Anna have elected for gift relief to apply and have used the factory for the purposes of their respective sole trades.

You are required to calculate the chargeable gains for Fran and Anna. Assume that 2008/09 tax rates and legislation continue to apply throughout.

14.2 Joe Bloggs

Joe Bloggs had the following transactions in December 2008:

(1) He sold his flat for £700,000, which he had purchased in July 1982 for £200,000. He has always used his spare bedroom, which is approximately one quarter of the total floor space, as an office and property expenses have always been apportioned accordingly.

(2) Joe sold unquoted trading company shares to his daughter for £375,000. The shares had recently been valued at £450,000. The company had no investments. He had purchased the shares for £75,000 in September 1989.

You are required to calculate the amount subject to capital gains tax for 2008/09 on the disposals in (1) and (2) above assuming all available reliefs are claimed.

14.3 P J Laval

P J Laval had the following transactions in assets during the year 2008/09.

(1) Sold his house, 'Chez Nous', for £99,000 on 14 May 2008, having bought this for £37,000 on 6 April 1982, incurring expenditure of £2,000 on additions on 6 May 1983. The house has never been used as his only or main residence.

(2) Sold 1,400 shares in Vic plc, a quoted company, for £8,710 on 18 July 2008 having purchased 1,400 shares on 10 February 1983 at a cost of £3,500.

There was a bonus issue of 1:4 on 10 March 1984.

(3) On 31 March 2009, Laval gifted his entire holding of shares in Lavaling Ltd, his personal trading company, to his son. If he had sold his shares on that date to a third party he would have realised a capital gain of £80,000. At that date, the company's assets consisted of:

	Book value at 31.3.09 £	Market value at 31.3.09 £
Freehold property	20,000	130,000
Quoted securities	8,000	30,000
Stocks	70,000	70,000
Debtors	35,000	35,000
Cash and bank balances	21,000	21,000
	154,000	286,000

Laval has never worked for the company.

(i) **You are required to compute the amount of capital gains tax payable by Laval for the year 2008/09, assuming he claims all available reliefs.** (13 marks)

(ii) **Briefly describe the three legal estates in land: freehold, leasehold, and common hold.** (5 marks)

(Total: 18 marks)

14.4 **Simon**

You have received the following memorandum from a partner in your firm:

'To: Frances Ackland
From: Simon Evans
Date: 3 December 2008
Subject: Deferral of gains

I have just disposed of some shares in Blue plc, a quoted company. I need some advice on how I can defer the gains arising from this sale. I remember reading something in the Tax Department's newsletter about a special relief to enable me to do this. Can you give me some details?

You may like to know that I acquired the Blue plc shares in September 1988 as a gift from my father. He had originally acquired them in 1983 and we elected to defer the gain arising. You will find the details in my personal tax affairs file. I sold the Blue shares for £200,000 on 30 November 2008. I have no other assets for CGT purposes and no other spare cash other than the proceeds of the Blue shares.

I would like to use some the proceeds of the sale to invest in a house in France, probably about £100,000. My wife and I intend to move to France in the next couple of years to restore the house'.

You ascertain that the held over gain on the Blue shares was £15,000 and that they were worth £65,000 in September 1988.

You are required to write a memorandum in reply. (10 marks)

14.5 **Emily**

Emily made the following disposals in 2008/09:

(1) **Factory**

   Acquired 1 July 2003 for £150,000. Emily let out the factory rent free to her partnership business. The factory was sold for £225,000 on 10 July 2008.

(2) **Painting**

   This had been acquired by Emily's husband Arthur on 1 March 1996 for £50,000. Arthur had given the painting to Emily on 1 July 2001 when it was worth £60,000. Emily sold the painting for £73,000 on 2 May 2008.

(3) **Vase**

   Emily had acquired this asset on 10 August 1988 for £40,000. She sold it on 1 December 2008 for £19,000.

You are required to calculate Emily's CGT liability for 2008/09 assuming she claims all available reliefs.

14.6 **Mr Richman**

White Cottage
Plumsted
Yorkshire
4 May 2009

Dear Mr Jones,

I have recently (on 4 April 2009) sold a house, 'Red Bricks', for £370,000. The house was originally purchased on 6 April 1982 for £90,000 and was used as my principal residence until 5 April 1987. From 6 April 1987 until 5 April 1994 the house was empty while I was working abroad. I am an architect and have always been treated as self-employed from when I started to practise in 1973.

On my return to the UK in April 1994 I moved back into the house. In April 1995 the house was converted (at a cost of £20,000) to a flat upstairs (which I used as my residence) and offices downstairs from which I ran my practice. I moved out of the flat at Red Bricks on 5 October 2006 and the flat was empty until the whole property was sold on 4 April 2009. The flat occupied exactly half of the property and I believe this has been agreed with HM Revenue & Customs. I continued to use the offices for my practice until shortly before the sale.

I should be grateful if you would write to me setting out how any Capital Gains Tax liability will be calculated, taking into account any reliefs due and when the tax will be payable. I have no other capital gains for 2008/09.

Yours sincerely

A Richman.

You are required to draft a letter as requested.

14.7 **Peter**

Peter made the following disposals in 2008/09:

(a)   He purchased a building for £200,000 on 1 January 1983 which he let commercially as offices. On 10 April 2008 he sold the building for £600,000.

(b)   He held 20,000 shares (1% shareholding) in Forum Follies plc which he purchased in May 1986 for £50,000. In March 2009, Exciting Enterprises plc acquired all the share capital of Forum Follies plc. Under the terms of the take-over for every two shares previously held in Forum Follies plc shareholders received three ordinary shares in Exciting Enterprises plc plus £1 cash. Immediately after the take-over the ordinary shares in Exciting Enterprises plc were quoted at £3 each.

(c)   Peter purchased shares in Dassau plc, a quoted company, as follows.

	No of shares	Cost
		£
December 1984	1,000	2,000
April 1987 1 for 2 rights issue		£2 per share

In November 2008 he sold 1,200 shares for £9,500.

Peter had capital losses brought forward from 2007/08 of £6,400.

You are required to calculate the CGT payable by Peter for 2008/09 and state the due date for payment.

14.8 Sarah Stone

Sarah had the following transactions in 2008/09.

April 2008:

She sold all her shares in Peterson Ltd for £150,000. She had acquired the shares as follows:

Date	No	Cost £	Notes
1/3/86	50,000	25,000	Probate value from father
1/8/99	5,000	10,000	Purchased
1/10/00	1:5 rights issue	£3 per share	

June 2008:

She sold a grandfather clock which she had purchased in September 1994 for £5,800. She received £8,000 after selling costs of £250.

September 2008:

She sold her stamp collection for £3,100. She had purchased it for £7,000 in June 1987.

January 2009:

She sold a house which she had bought as an investment property in January 1983 for £28,000. She added a loft bedroom at a cost of £10,000 in February 1984. She sold it for £75,000.

Sarah had capital losses brought forward of £15,000.

Calculate Sarah's CGT payable.

1.1   Allowances

	£
PAA Age > 65	9,030
Less: restriction (W)	(390)
	8,640

(W) Restriction = ½ £(22,580 − 21,800) = 390

1.2

	£
PAA	9,030
BPA	1,800
	10,830

The MCA does not reduce net income. It is a tax reduction. He would still get an MCA due to the fact that at least one of the couple was over 73 at 5 April 2008.

1.3

	£
Earnings/ net income	42,540
Less: PA	(6,035)
Taxable income	36,505

£	
35,500 × 20% (W)	7,100
1,005 × 40%	402
Tax liability	7,502
Less tax suffered: PAYE	(7,000)
Tax payable	502

Working

Basic rate band extended to 34,800 + (560 × 100/80) = 35,500

1.4

	£
Personal allowance	
PAA (> 75)	9,180
Less: ½ £(30,800 − 21,800)	(4,500)
	4,680
Restrict to basic PA	6,035
MCA − tax reduction	6,625
Less: excess restriction £(6,035 − 4,680)	(1,355)
	5,270
@ 10%	527

1.5   £2,000

Interest from building society account will be assessed on his mother.

1.6

	£
Age 75 or over in the tax year	
Age allowance	9,180
Less: ½ (23,500 − 500 − 21,800)	(600)
	8,580

Age allowance is restricted where net income exceeds £21,800 but also remember to reduce it by Gift Aid donations.

1.7

	£
Earnings	3,700
Interest income	300
Net income	4,000
Less: PA	(6,035)
Taxable income	–
IT repayable:	
Earnings – PAYE	740
Interest – 20% tax credit	60
	800

Scholarship received by a <u>full-time</u> student is not taxable. Legacy is a capital receipt and not subject to income tax.

1.8

	£
Trust income (£6,000 × 100/60)	10,000
Less: PA	(6,035)
	3,965
Income tax:	
3,965 @ 20%	793
Tax deducted:	
Trust: £10,000 @ 40%	(4,000)
Tax repayable	(3,207)

1.9

	£
Bert	
Net income	10,214
PA (Bert not over 65)	(6,035)
Taxable income	4,179
Tax	
£4,179 × 20%	835
Less: tax reduction – MCAA	
£6,535 × 10%	(654)
Tax liability	181

MCA is given to Bert as his wife is born before 6 April 1935

1.10

	£
Trade profits	7,700
Discretionary trust income (£1,650 × 100/60)	2,750
	10,450
Less: PA	(9,030)
Taxable income	1,420
Tax @ 20%	284
Less: MCA (£6,535 × 2/12 × 10%)	(109)
Tax liability	175
Less: tax deducted (£2,750 × 40%)	(1,100)
Repayable	(925)

Income from a discretionary trust comes with 40% tax credit.

1.11 Income of minor unmarried children (ie Dawn) is taxed in the hands of the parent if it derives from a parental settlement. Therefore, Richard is taxed on Dawn's income. As Donna is married, the dividend is treated as her own income.

1.12

	£
2007/08 joint income £(34,500 + 14,500)	49,000
Less: threshold	(15,575)
	33,425
Restriction × 39%	13,035

So per child credit of £2,085 is withdrawn.

As joint income < £50,000, Sarah is entitled to family element of CTC ie £545.

1.13

	£
Child Tax Credit	
Family entitlement	545
Child element	2,085
Working Tax Credit	
Basic element	1,800
Lone parent element	1,770
	6,200
Less: restriction	
(17,000 − 6,420) × 39%	(4,126)
Total credits	2,074

1.14 Investment income of a child arising out of a gift by his parent is aggregated with the income of that parent. However where the income does not exceed £100 (gross) pa it is treated as the income of the child.

Therefore, this income would be taxed on Gilbert and would be covered by his personal allowance.

1.15

		£
WTC:	Basic	1,800
	Lone parent	1,770
CTC:	Family	545
	Child	2,085
		6,200
Less: 39% of excess income (W)		(616)
Total credits		5,584
Working		
07/08 income		8,000
Threshold		(6,420)
		1,580
@ 39%		616

1.16

		£
WTC:	Basic	1,800
	Couples	1,770
	> 30 hrs	735
CTC:	Child £(2,085 × 3)	6,255
	Family	545
		11,105
Less: (W)		(5,881)
Credit		5,224
Working		
Income		21,500
Threshold		(6,420)
		15,080
× 39%		5,881

1.17 As Tanya is over 16, earns more than £90 per week and has been sick for more than four consecutive days she is entitled to SSP of £75.40 per week.

1.18

Alan – 2008/09

		£
Income		50,000
Less:	Reliefs:	
	Loan interest	(2,610)
		47,390
Less:	PA	(6,035)
Taxable income		41,355

Tax thereon:

	£
£34,800 @ 20%	6,960
£6,555 @ 40%	2,622
	9,582
Less: Maintenance payment (£2,540 × 10%)	(254)
Tax liability	9,328

2.1

	Non Savings £	Savings £
Earnings	27,040	
BSI		15,000
Less: PA	(6,035)	
Taxable income	21,005	15,000
Tax:		
21,005 @ 20%		4,201
13,795 @ 20% [34,800 - 21,005] (savings)		2,759
1,205 @ 40% (15,000 – 13,795)		482
36,005		7,442

Note that 'tax liability' is **before** deducting tax suffered at source.

2.2 $\frac{1}{2} \times £300 \times \dfrac{100}{80} = £188$

There is a presumption that spouses hold jointly held assets equally.

2.3

	£
Savings a/c (received gross)	276
Interest income	276

Interest on NS&I Savings Certificates and HMRC repayment supplement are tax free.

2.4 Interest from loans made by an individual to an individual are received gross.

Interest paid by a company to an individual is paid under deduction of 20% income tax.

2.5 1,000 × 8p = £80 × 100/90 = £89

Dividends taxed on receipts basis.

2.6

	£
UK bank interest (£8,680 × 100/80)	10,850
Guernsey interest	640
Interest on government stock (paid gross)	5,000
Net income	16,490
Less: PA	(6,035)
Taxable income	10,455

2.7

	Savings income £	Dividend income £
BDI (£1,960 × 100/80)	2,450	
BSI (£1,600 × 100/80)	2,000	
Dividends (£2,000 × 100/90)		2,222
Net income	4,450	2,222
PA	(4,450)	(1,585)
Taxable income	–	637
Tax @ 10%		64
Tax credit on dividends (£637 @ 10% **taxable** dividend)		(64)
Tax due		Nil
Less tax deducted at source on bank interest £(490 + 400)		(890)
Tax repayable		(890)

2.8

	Non-Savings £	Savings £	Dividends £
Earnings	3,929	3,125	
Bank interest £2,500 × $\frac{100}{80}$			
Dividend £34,000 × $\frac{100}{90}$			37,778
Net income	3,929	3,125	37,778
Less: PA	(3,929)	(2,106)	
Taxable income	–	1,019	37,778

Tax £1,019 @ 10 % (savings)		102
£33,781 @10% (dividends)		3378
£3997 @ 32½% (37,778 – 33,781) (dividends)		1,299
Tax liability		4,779
Less: dividend credit 10% × £37,778 (taxable dividend)		(3,778)
		1,001
Less: PAYE		(800)
Tax payable		201

3.1

	£
Gross rents (£1,500 × 12) (accruals basis)	18,000
Less: Agent's fees	1,800
Interest	4,200
Water rates	120
Insurance	500
Wear and tear allowance ((18,000 – 120) × 10%)	1,788
Property income	9,592

3.2 In legal terms, ownership is the most extensive possessory right conferred by the law.

Owners can do with their property what they wish eg use it, sell it, give it away or use it as security for a loan.

Possession is the exercise (or power of exercising) physical control over property.

3.3 Unconditional sale – the contract is not subject to conditions precedent or subsequent.
Conditional sale – the contract is subject to something occurring eg grant of planning permission.
By option – the contract can be triggered by the service of a notice.
By pre-emption – if the seller wants to sell he must first offer it to the person who has the pre-emption right.

3.4

	£
Rent receivable (10 × £160) + £400	2,000
Less: bad debt £(1,600 – 1,300)	(300)
Interest	(700)
Property income	1,000

3.5

	£
Whitehouse: rent accrued in the year	4,000
Blackhouse: (9/12 × £2,000)	1,500
	5,500

No bad debt relief as payment was actually received.

3.6

	£
Rents receivable (£4,000 × 8/12)	2,667
Expenses paid	(1,000)
	1,667

Note. The rent receivable from the new tenants will begin to be assessed in 2009/10.

3.7

	£
Income	8,000
Less: insurance	(300)
water rates	(400)
wear and tear allowance: 10% × £(8,000 – 400)	(760)
Property income	6,540

Remember the wear and tear allowance for furnished lettings.

3.8 Brian should elect to assess rents received over £4,250 ie £(5,000 – 4,250) = £750 under the rent-a-room scheme, otherwise property income of £4,400 (£5,000 – £600) would be assessable. No deduction is then available for expenses.

3.9 Four from:

- Available for 140 days a year
- Actually let for 70
- Not more than 155 days in a year are periods of longer term occupation (ie let to same tenant for more than 31 continuous days).
- Situated in the UK
- Furnished
- Let with a view to a profit

3.10 Personal property is divided into choses in action (property such as debts, shares, negotiable instruments and all forms of intellectual property) and choses in possession (leasehold land and buildings and personal chattels such as furniture and machinery).

4.1 Maximum overall investment – £7,200.
Maximum cash investment –£3,600

4.2 There is no income tax on interest or dividends.

4.3 Tax on taxable income

£	£
34,800 × 20%	6,960
22,040 × 40%	8,816
	15,776
Less: EIS income tax reduction: £500,000 × 20% (restricted)	(15,776)
	0

It is not possible to have a tax reduction in excess of the tax on taxable income.

4.4 The first £200,000 worth of VCT investments made in a tax year will give rise to tax free dividends.

Taxable net dividends

$$\frac{10,000}{60,000} \times £3,400 = \underline{£567}$$

5.1 Daisy

	£
Statutory redundancy pay (exempt)	–
Cash	25,000
Value of car	12,000
Outplacement counselling (exempt)	–
	37,000
Less: exemption £(30,000 – 3,800)	(26,200)
Taxable	10,800

5.2 Salary

	£	£
9/12 × £9,000	6,750	
3/12 × £10,000	2,500	9,250
Bonus received in 2008/09 (28.2.09)		2,400
		11,650

5.3

	£
Salary (5 × £1,000)	5,000
Car benefit (£15,000 × 22% × 3/12)*	825
Fuel benefit (£16,900 × 22% × 3/12)*	929
	6,754

$$* \frac{(170-135)}{5} = 7\%$$

Percentage: 15% + 7% = 22%

5.4

	£
Car (£14,000 × 27%)*	3,780
Petrol (£16,900 × 27%)	4,563
	8,343

There is no reduction in the assessable benefit for contributions made by an employee towards the cost of private petrol. Only made for full refunds (in which case the benefit would be nil).

$$* \frac{195-135}{5} = 12\% \text{ (round down the emissions so it is divisible by 5)}$$

15% + 12% = 27%

5.5 Earnings:

	£
Salary	10,000
Car (£16,000 × 28%)*	4,480
Second car (£12,000 × 20%)**	2,400
Cost of wine	1,000
Earnings	17,880
Less: expenses	(600)
	17,280

The second car is assessed on Jim because his daughter receives it by virtue of *his* employment, not hers (would you expect a company car if you just worked on Saturdays?)

$$* \frac{200-135}{5} = 13\% \qquad 15\% + 13\% = 28\%$$

$$** \frac{160-135}{5} = 5\% \qquad 15\% + 5\% = 20\% \text{ (}Note.\text{ Round down)}$$

5.6 Form P11D:

	£
Car (£12,000 × 22%)*	2,640
Expenses allowances (12 × £80)	960
	3,600

The amount spent by Albert on allowable expenses would be claimed separately by him on his tax return.

The company must report the full allowance.

* $\dfrac{155 - 135}{5}$ = 4% + 18% = 22% (*Note*. For cars running on diesel, the minimum percentage is 18%)

5.7

	£
Round sum allowance (£100 × 4) (not covered by dispensation)	400
Specific reimbursement – covered by dispensation	–
	400

A dispensation means that the item covered by it does not have to be reported on the P11D.

5.8   Sue: Nil
Tara: £340 (£3,200 – (52 × £55 exempt)

No taxable benefit for onsite work place nursery. First £55 of all other qualifying childcare costs are a tax free benefit. – on tax tables!

5.9   Private purchases £257 only. She will only ever be assessed on the goods/services bought with the card.

5.10   £204 (240 × £0.85) Workplace parking is not taxable.

5.11   Company can deduct full amount ie £200 per head so long as this is 'reasonable' (assume so).

Staff entertaining becomes a taxable benefit to employees if it cost the employer > £150 per head.

Each employee here has a £200 benefit (note that the employer may settle tax for them (PSA)).

5.12

	£
Professional subscriptions allowed	220
Subscription for accommodation allowable	200
	420

Golf club subscription disallowed

5.13

	£
Salary	18,000
Accommodation – not taxable as job related	–
Household expenses £3,100	
limited to 10% × £18,000	1,800
Earnings	19,800

5.14

	£	£
Mobile phone for employee – not taxable	–	
Mobile phone for family member: 20% × £250	50	
		50
Laptop – 20% × £5,000	1,000	
Less: 40% re business use	(400)	600
		650

Note. If private use of laptop had been merely <u>incidental</u> there would be no taxable benefit.

5.15

	£	£
Salary		30,000
Benefits: crèche		
$((200 - 55) \times 52)$	7,540	
parking space	–	
business miles		
$(5,000 \times 60p)$	3,000	
Less: authorised mileage rates $(5,000 \times 40p)$	(2,000)	
Earnings		8,540
		38,540

5.16

	£
Average method: $\dfrac{15,000 + 10,000}{2} \times 6.25\%$	781
Less: interest paid 5/4/08 – 31/12/08: £15,000 × 3% × 9/12	(338)
1/1/09 – 5/4/09: £10,000 × 3% × 3/12	(75)
	368

Strict basis:	
5/4/08 – 5/1/09: £15,000 × (6.25% – 3%) × 9/12	365
6/1/09 – 5/4/09: £10,000 × (6.25% – 3%) × 3/12	81
	446

HMRC have the option to assess Ruth using the strict basis.

5.17

	£
Gross annual value	5,000
less rent paid by Jason	(3,000)
	2,000
Additional charge (use MV as moved in > 6 yrs after purchase)	
£(130,000 – 75,000) × 6.25%	3,438
	5,438

5.18   Assessable benefit is the greater of

(a)

	£
Market value at acquisition	1,500
less price paid	(1,000)
	500

(b)

	£
Original market value	2,000
less assessed in respect of use (07/08)	
$^6/_{12} \times 20\% \times £2,000$	(200)
less assessed in respect of use (08/09) $^6/_{12} \times 20\% \times £2,000$	(200)
less price paid	(1,000)
	600

∴ Benefit is £600

5.19

	£
Flat: Annual value	3,000
Household expenses	400
Furniture (20% × £2,500)	500
	3,900

Note. There is no additional charge for the accommodation as the original cost was less than £75,000.

5.20

	£	£
Payment in lieu of notice		8,000
Ex-gratia payment		40,000
Exemption	30,000	
Less: statutory redundancy pay	(5,000)	
		(25,000)
		23,000

5.21 First £30,000 will be exempt + 10/30 of the excess

ie £30,000 + 10/30 × £(51,000 – 30,000) = £37,000

5.22

		£
S105	Annual value	2,225
	Less: rent paid	(2,225)
		NIL
S106	£(400,000 – 75,000) × 6.25%	20,312
	Less: excess rent paid £2,725 – 2,225)	(500)
Net benefit		19,812

The calculation is based on expenditure incurred by the company *before* the year of assessment in question.

5.23 Any six from:

- names of client and consultant
- commencement date of contract
- description of services
- fees
- expenses
- confidentiality
- non-exclusivity
- termination

6.1 There are no income tax consequences at the date of grant.

When the option was exercised there would not normally be an income tax charge. However, as the option was granted at a discount there will be an income tax charge at the date of exercise. The amount of the discount will be charged to income tax, giving chargeable income of £5,000 (£10,000 × (£2.00 – £1.50)).

6.2 'Free shares' are the shares an employer can give to an employee – maximum £3,000 per annum.

'Partnership shares' are the shares the employee is allowed to purchase from pre-tax salary to be held in the plan – maximum is the lower of £1,500 per annum and 10% of salary.

6.3

	£
10,000 × £(15 – 11.50) =	35,000
@ 40%	14,000

7.1 Higher of: (i) 100% × earnings ie £28,000
      (ii) £3,600

ie £28,000. (*Note.* Dividends are not relevant earnings for pension contribution purposes)

7.2 Norma has no relevant earnings. She may make a maximum contribution of £3,600 (gross) into a personal pension.

7.3

	£
Earnings	48,000
less PA	(6,035)
Taxable income	41,965
BRB extended to 34,800 + (5,000 × $\frac{100}{80}$)	(41,050)
	915
Tax @ 40%	366

7.4 Jeremy can pay up to £400,000 into a pension in the year and obtain tax relief. He would pay 80% directly to the pension (£320,000) and the fund would reclaim the 20% (£80,000) from HMRC. However, as he would be paying more than the 2008/09 annual allowance of £235,000 into his pension, he will have to pay 40% tax on the excess (40% × £165,000 = £66,000).

7.5 Maximum tax free lump sum: 25% × £65,000 = £16,250

7.6

	£
Earnings	50,000
Less pension contribution	(9,000)
Net income	41,000
Less PA	(6,035)
Taxable income	34,965

Tax

	£
£34,800 × 20%	6,960
£165 × 40%	66
34,965	7,026

8.1

	£
Total employment earnings	£80,200
Amount relating to UK duties (80%)	£64,160
Amount enjoyed in UK: £(60,000 + 5,200)	£65,200
Income from employment	65,200
Interest (£35 × 100/80)	44
	65,244
Less PA	(6,035)
Taxable income	£59,209

8.2 As Wayne is taxable on the remittance basis the dividends will be treated as non-savings income, rather than dividend income. He will pay tax at 40% (and not the dividend rate of 32.5%) as he is a higher rate taxpayer.

£10,000 @ 40%   £4,000

In addition, as he has been UK resident for 7 years of the preceding 9 tax years, Wayne will be subject to an extra £30,000 income tax charge on his unremitted foreign dividends. Hence, his total tax liability will be £34,000.

8.3 As Egbert is UK resident and ordinarily resident he is taxable on his worldwide income on an arising basis. However, only 90% of foreign pensions are taxable so he will be taxed on £9,000 (90% × £10,000).

8.4 ESC A11

(a) Absence for employment purposes must span a complete tax year; and

(b) Interim visits to the UK do not amount to 183 days or more in any one tax year or 91 days or more on average.

9.1

	£
Chargeable gain	18,000
Less: annual exemption	(9,600)
	8,400
£8,400 @ 18%	1,512

9.2 The person needs to be resident **or** ordinarily resident in the UK.

9.3 A racehorse, as wasting chattels are exempt from CGT.

The limousine, as all cars are exempt from CGT.

10.1

	£
Sale proceeds	31,250
Less probate value	(11,200)
Chargeable gain	20,050

10.2

	£
Sale proceeds	85,000
Less: cost $\dfrac{85,000}{85,000+30,000} \times 18,000$	(13,304)
Chargeable gain	£71,696

10.3

	£
Gains	9,000
Current year losses (must be set against current year gains)	(5,000)
	4,000
AE	(9,600)
	–
Losses c/f (*Note.* Losses b/f reduce chargeable gains to AE level only)	6,000

10.4

	2006/07 £	2007/08 £	2008/09 £	
Gains	2,000	4,000	12,000	
Losses	(5,000)	(2,000)	(2,000)	
	(3,000)	2,000	10,000	
c/f	3,000		(400)	c/f £2,600
			9,600	

Explanation: Losses b/f reduce gains down to AE level only.

10.5 The persons connected (for CGT purposes) to Paul are his:
- wife
- mother-in-law
- business partner
- step-father

10.6

	£
Proceeds	170,000
Less: cost	(120,000)
Gain	50,000

Explanation: Transfer between spouses is on no-gain/no-loss basis so base cost for Grace is £120,000.

10.7 As losses from a sale to a connected person can only be set against gains to the same connected person, the loss of £8,200 will be carried forward and set against the gain of £14,000 arising on the sale to Charles on 29 September 2009.

Note. Carry back of the loss is not allowed.

10.8

	£
Loss memo	40,000
s.64 v net income	(5,000)
	35,000
Against capital gains (max)	
(19,000 – 1,000 – 2,000)	(16,000)
Loss c/f	19,000

10.9

	£
Proceeds	30,000
Less: cost	
$\dfrac{30,000}{30,000+10,000} \times £8,000$	(6,000)
Chargeable gain	24,000

10.10

	£
Gains	16,900
Losses	(7,000)
	9,900
Losses b/f (9,900 – 9,600)	(300)
	9,600
Less: annual exemption	(9,600)
Taxable gain	Nil

Losses c/f (5,000 – 300) = £4,700

11.1 Share pool:

	No. of shares	Cost
		£
Purchase Aug 06	2,000	18,000
Purchase Sept 06	1,000	10,000
	3,000	28,000
Sale Jan 09	(1,500)	(14,000)
c/f	1,500	14,000

Calculate gain:

	£
Proceeds	22,500
Cost	(14,000)
Chargeable gain	8,500

11.2 Share pool

	No. of shares	Cost
		£
Purchase 19.2.83	2,000	10,000
Purchase 20.9.90	1,000	8,000
	3,000	18,000
Sale 15.11.08	(1,500)	(9,000)
c/f	1,500	9,000

Calculate gain:

	£
Proceeds	22,000
Cost	(9,000)
Chargeable gain	13,000

11.3 Share pool:

	No. of shares	Cost
		£
Purchase April 85	5,000	5,605
Bonus issue (1 for 5)	1,000	–
	6,000	5,605
Sale Dec 08	(3,500)	(3,270)
c/f	2,500	2,335

Calculate gain:

	£
Proceeds	6,250
Cost	(3,270)
Chargeable gain	2,980

12.1

	£
Victoria Cross: Proceeds	14,780
Less: cost	(3,000)
	11,780

Chargeable gain not to exceed 5/3 × £(14,780 − 6,000) = £14,633

∴ Gain = £11,780

Vintage car: Exempt

Note. Medals are only exempt if awarded for bravery or inherited.

12.2

	£
Proceeds	7,500
Selling costs	(300)
	7,200
Less: cost	(4,500)
Gain	2,700

Chargeable gain not to exceed 5/3 × £(7,500 − 6,000) = £2,500

Hence, gain is £2,500.

12.3

	Cost £
Gross proceeds (deemed)	6,000
Cost	(6,260)
Allowable loss	(260)

12.4

	£
Gross proceeds	7,200
Less: Incidental costs	(350)
	6,850
Less: Acquisition cost (probate value)	(3,000)
Chargeable gain	3,850
Limited to 5/3 × £(7,200 − 6,000)	2,000

12.5 Motor car: exempt

	£
Machinery:	
Proceeds	7,500
Less: cost	(5,500)
	2,000

Restrict to 5/3 × £(7,500 − 6,000) = £2,500

Chargeable gain = £2,000

Note. There is never a capital loss on an item on which capital allowances have been claimed as a balancing allowance would be given instead through the capital allowances computation.

TQT
Tax Qualification Training

12.6 *Grant of long lease:*

	£
Proceeds	30,000
Less cost	
$£40,000 \times \dfrac{30,000}{30,000+82,500}$	(10,667)
	19,333

12.7 *Grant of short lease:*

	£
Proceeds (capital element of premium)*	2,000
Cost $£30,000 \times \dfrac{2,000}{10,000+50,000}$	(1,000)
Chargeable gain	1,000

*	Premium	10,000
	Less: $2\% \times (11-1) \times £10,000$	(2,000)
	Assessed as property income	8,000

13.1

		£
Gain		80,000
Exempt:		
1.10.82 – 30.6.85	33 months	
1.7.05 – 30.6.08	36 months	
	69 months	
Total period		
1.10.82 – 30.6.08	309 months	
PPR relief $\dfrac{69}{309} \times £80,000$		(17,864)
Gain attributable to letting		62,136
Less: letting relief		
Lowest of (i)	£40,000	
(ii)	PPR relief: £17,864	
(iii)	letting gain (1.7.85 – 30.6.05 = 240m): £61,136	(17,864)
Chargeable gain		44,272

13.2

	£
Proceeds	200,000
Less: cost	(20,000)
	180,000
Less PPR exemption £180,000 × 2/3	(120,000)
Chargeable gain	60,000

Note. As the students occupy separate self-contained accommodation, the ground floor is treated as a separate residence, the gain on which is fully chargeable to CGT.

13.3 Any **two** of:

(a) Any period employed outside the UK

(b) Periods of up to four years working (employed or self-employed) elsewhere

(c) Up to three years for any reason

(d) The last three years of ownership where the property has been the principal private residence at some time

Note. (a) – (c) must be preceded and followed by a period of actual occupation.

14.1 *Gain chargeable on Jeremy*

	£
Excess proceeds over cost (50,000 − 42,000)	8,000

	£
Base cost for John	
MV in August 2008	225,974
Less deferred gain (£110,000 − £8,000)	(102,000)
	123,974

14.2 The claim must be made jointly by Arthur and Hugo on or before 31 January 2015 (ie 5 years from 31 January following the year of disposal).

14.3

	£
Deemed proceeds (MV)	22,000
Less: Cost	(4,000)
Gain before gift relief	18,000
Chargeable on Adam	
£(12,000 − 4,000)	(8,000)
Deferred by gift relief	10,000

The held-over gain (£10,000) is taxed on Bernard in the year he becomes non-resident (ie 2010/11).

14.4

	£
Proceeds (MV)	300,000
Less: cost	(160,000)
Gain	140,000
Gift relief (CBA/CA)	
$\dfrac{300}{300+50} \times £140,000$	(120,000)
Chargeable gain	20,000

14.5

	£
MV	95,000
Cost	(44,000)
Gain	51,000
Chargeable now £(63,000 − 44,000)	(19,000)
Gift relief	32,000

14.6

	£
Proceeds	4,000
Less cost: $24,000 \times \dfrac{4,000}{4,000+16,000}$	(4,800)
Loss	(800)

14.7 *2008/09*

Patrice can claim to defer the entire gain. (There is no upper limit for EIS deferral relief).

	£
Gain	600,000
Less EIS deferral relief	(600,000)
Chargeable gain	−

2009/10

As Patrice emigrates within 3 years, the chargeable gain of £600,000 will crystallise.

14.8 Gain on sale of Silvanus Ltd shares:

	£
Proceeds	800,000
Cost	(50,000)
Gain before EIS relief	750,000

Therefore, John's optimum claim for EIS deferral relief will be:

	£
£(750,000 − 150,000 − 9,600) =	590,400

15.1 Landlords can submit simplified returns for rental income when the total annual gross income from property is under £30,000.

They are required to record three lines:

- Gross property income
- Total allowable expenses
- Net income

15.2 If Thomas files online the return must be filed and the tax due paid by 31 January 2010. If he submits a paper return he must file by 31 October 2009. Any tax due should be paid by 31 January 2010.

15.3 POA

	£
Income tax liability	10,250
Class 4 NIC	1,000
Less: tax deducted at source	(5,000)
	6,250

POAs of £3,125 are due on 31 January 2009 and 31 July 2009. Any balancing payment is due 31 January 2010.

16.1 You should disclose this to the client. Practitioners may have a variety of financial arrangements with the client. For example, there may be an informal understanding that any commission is 'taken into account' when billing the client for services. Perhaps the fairest approach is to pay over the pension contribution on a 'no commission' basis and bill the client for the time taken in selecting and arranging his pension contract etc. Although the client then sees exactly what it is costing him he is not necessarily pleased to be billed for the work involved even though this should usually be less than the commission snipped off his pension contribution. Practitioners may also argue that higher charge-out rates would be needed if they didn't keep the commissions. The key point, however, is disclosure.

16.2 Unless the prospective client agrees to your contacting the previous adviser, you should decline to act for him. There may be exceptional circumstances where this normal rule can be overridden.

16.3 Quite possibly an amicable divorce settlement can be reached. If you believe this is likely you can continue to act for each party. It should be made clear to both spouses, however, that if a conflict of interest subsequently arises you will have to cease acting for at least one of them and this could be detrimental to both of them and to yourself.

16.4 Where a member undertakes tax compliance work for a client this will normally include responsibility for keeping the client informed of the amount of tax due for payment, the due date for payment and drawing the client's attention to the fact that interest accrues from that date.

16.5 False. The ATT will not arbitrate between a member and his client upon the amount of a disputed fee.

16.6 Contingent fees are specifically considered within the regime for disclosure of tax avoidance schemes.

16.7 It is recommended that they open an account if they hold, or expect to hold, the money for more than 30 days.

16.8 Land can be held either (i) freehold, (ii) leasehold, or (iii) commonhold.

16.9 The maximum number of legal owners of land is four.

16.10 Legal title passes from seller to buyer when contracts are exchanged.

16.11 An employment tribunal can make an order for reinstatement, re-engagement or awards of basic and/or compensatory compensation.

Solutions to long form questions

1.1   Mr Daphnis

MR DAPHNIS

	£
Allowances:	
Personal allowance (65 or over)	9,030
Restricted : ½ × (22,980 – 21,800)	(590)
PA	8,440
Blind person's allowance	1,800
Tax reductions:	
Married couple's allowance (75 or over, given based on age of older spouse)	6,625
(relief restricted to 10%)	
MRS DAPHNIS	
PA (>75)	9,180

Some of this is being wasted as Mrs Daphnis has income of only £4,500.

Mr Daphnis's allowances have been restricted due to high net income. In order to maximise the benefit of allowances the interest generating bank account could be held in joint names, leading to a 50:50 split of interest for tax purposes.

The revised position would be:

	Mr	Mrs
Current net income	22,980	4,500
(Less) / plus 50% interest	(5,000)	5,000
Revised net income	17,980	9,500

There is now no need to restrict Mr Daphnis' allowances and Mrs Daphnis does not waste her personal allowance.

1.2   Mr Rich

MR RICH
INCOME TAX COMPUTATION 2008/09

	Non-savings income £
Earnings	58,000
Less: PA	(6,035)
Taxable income	51,965
Tax thereon:	

£		£
34,800 @ 20%		6,960
15,000 @ 20% (W)		3,000
2,165 @ 40%		866
Tax liability		10,826
Tax suffered at source (PAYE)		(13,800)
Tax repayable		(2,974)

Working: Basic rate band extended by gross donation, ie (£12,000 × 100/80) = £15,000

Address
Address
Date

Dear Julie

Thank you for your letter and congratulations on your news.

The definition of income for tax credit purposes differs in a number of ways from the definition of taxable income for income tax purposes.

Firstly however, you need to be aware that you and your husband would have to make a joint claim for tax credits, as you are living together. Therefore, when calculating your entitlement to tax credits, you would need to take into account your joint income.

By following the steps that I have set out below you will be able to calculate your joint income:

(1) Calculate your gross income from savings, investments, pensions and property.

If, as in your case in 2008/09, this amounts to £300 or less it is ignored. If it exceeds £300 then only the excess over £300 is included in the calculation.

(2) Next, include your employment income.

This is basically the same as employment income for tax purposes and will include your salary and the taxable value of any benefits that you receive such as the company car and medical insurance. However, certain taxable benefits are excluded from the definition of employment income for tax credit purposes eg living accommodation and more importantly in your case use of assets (other than cars). This means that the benefit in respect of the use of the home entertainment system can be excluded.

In addition a deduction can be taken in respect of allowable employment expenses, which means that you can deduct the amount of the subscription that you paid to the Institute of Personnel and Development.

(3) The next stage is to include your husband's income from self-employment, which is simply his profits as adjusted for tax purposes.

If in any year your husband makes a loss then this will be deducted from the total of your income as calculated above. If the amount of the loss exceeds your other income then the amount of the excess will be carried forward for tax credit purposes – you are not able to carry a loss back when calculating income for tax credit.

(4) Finally, you can deduct the gross amount of any pension contributions that you make and also the gross amount of any Gift Aid payments, which means that your donation to the RSPCA can be deducted.

You will note that there is no deduction for a personal allowance when calculating income for tax credit purposes.

Please let me know if you have any other questions.

Your sincerely

T Adviser

Marking scheme

	Marks
Joint income	1
Gross savings, pensions and property income	½
£300 excess	1
Employment income – salary and benefits	1
Excluded benefits	½
Applied to home entertainment system	1
Deducted for subscription	1
Self-employment income (adjusted profits)	½
Deduct loss	½
Excess loss carried forward	1
Deduct pension contributions (gross)	½
Deduct gift aid payments (gross)	½
No personal allowance deducted	1
Presentation	1
Maximum	10

2.1 Mr Poor

MR POOR
INCOME TAX COMPUTATION 2008/09

		Non-savings income £	Savings income £	Dividend income £
Earnings		5,600		
Dividends received	$(£900 \times \frac{100}{90})$			1,000
Building society interest	$(£800 \times \frac{100}{80})$		1,000	
Bank deposit interest	$(£80 \times \frac{100}{80})$		100	
Net income		5,600	1,100	1,000
Less: PA		(5,600)	(435)	
Taxable income		nil	665	1,000

	£
Tax:	
£665 @ 10%	66
£1,000 @ 10%	100
Tax liability	166
Less: notional credit on dividend	(100)
	66
Less: Tax suffered at source	
Interest (£1,100 @ 20%)	(220)
PAYE	(250)
Tax repayable	(404)

Notes:

The personal allowance is set off against non-savings income first, then against savings income.

Dividend income should be taxed last because if there is no tax payable on dividends the notional tax credit is lost. The tax credit on the dividends can be deducted before other tax credits so as to maximise the repayment.

2.2 Jonty

JONTY
INCOME TAX COMPUTATION 2008/09

	Non-savings income £	Savings income £	Dividend income £
Earnings	42,000		
Building society interest £$(80 \times \frac{100}{80})$		100	
Dividends £$(63 \times \frac{100}{90})$			70
NS&I interest		142	
Net income	42,000	242	70
Less: PA	(6,035)		
Taxable income	35,965	242	70

Tax:	£
£	
34,800 @ 20%	6,960
495 @ 20% (W)	99
912 @ 40%	365
70 @ 32.5%	23
Tax liability	7,447
Less: notional credit on dividend	(7)
Less: tax suffered at source £(20 + 8,200)	(8,220)
Tax repayable	(780)

Workings

Basic rate threshold extended by gross donation ie (£396 × 100/80) = £495

Note. Betting income is exempt.

CTC/WTC

	£
CTC	
Family element	545
Child element	2,085
WTC	
Basic element	1,800
Couple's element	1,770
30 hour element	735
Maximum available credit	6,935

	£
Annual income £42,000 + (£242 + £70 − £300) − £495	41,517
Less: threshold	(6,420)
Excess Income	35,097
Maximum tax credit	6,935
Less: 39% of excess income	(13,687)
	Nil

∴ Will only receive the family element of £545 as income < £50,000 and the rest is reduced to nil.

TQT
Tax Qualification Training

2.3 Fred

(a)

	Non-savings income £	Savings income £	Dividend income £
Property income	16,200		
Interest (£4,400 × 100/80)		5,500	
Gilt interest		290	
Dividends (£7,000 × 100/90)			7,778
Net income	16,200	5,790	7,778 Total = £29,768
Less: PAA (W1)	(6,035)		
Taxable income	10,165	5,790	7,778

		£
Tax	£15,955 @ 20%	3,191
	£7,778 @ 10%	778
		3,969
Less: Married couples' allowance (W)		(555)
Tax liability		3,414
Less: Tax deducted:		
Dividends		(778)
Interest		(1,100)
Tax payable		1,536

Working

	£
PAA (>65)	9,030
Less: ½ £(29,768 − 21,800) = £3,984	
Max 'restriction' £(9,030 − 6,035)	(2,995)
Allowance given	6,035
Unused restriction (£3,984 − 2,995)	989
MCAA (under 75)	6,535
Less: unused restriction	(989)
	5,546

Tax reducer @ 10% = <u>555</u>

2.4 Fiona

	Non-savings income £	Savings income £	Dividend income £
Trade profits	32,000		
UK dividends (£8,000 × 100/90)			8,889
Jersey bank interest		4,300	
Total income	32,000	4,300	8,889
Less: interest relief (W1)	(827)		
Net income	31,173	4,300	8,889
Less: personal allowance	(6,035)		
Taxable income	25,138	4,300	8,889

TQT
Tax Qualification Training

Tax

	£
(25,138 + 4,300) @ 20%	6,007
£5,362 @ 10% (34,800 – 25,138 – 4,300)	536
£2,000 @ 10%(W2)	200
£1,527 @ 32½ % (8,889 – 2,000 – 5,362)	496
	7,120
Less: EIS relief (£3,000 @ 20%)	(600)
Tax liability	6,520
Less: tax deducted on dividends	(889)
Tax due	5,631

Workings

1   Loan interest relief

	£
£24,000 × 4% × 8/12	640
£14,000 × 4% × 4/12	187
	827

2   Basic rate band extension:

Gross gift aid donation £1,600 × 100/80 = £2,000

Notes:

(1)   Premium Bond winnings are tax free.

(2)   No tax is deducted at source on the Jersey bank interest.

(3)   Child benefit is tax free.

(4)   The loan interest is deductible under s.392 ITA 2007.

(5)   A 20% tax reducer is available on subscription for shares in a qualifying EIS company (up to a maximum subscription of £500,000).

2.5   **Jane Bradbury**

	Non-savings income £	Savings income £	Dividend income £
Trade profits	7,140		
Bank interest (£200 × 100/80)		250	
Dividends (£4,950 × 100/90)			5,500
Less: Deductible payments:			
Interest relief (Notes 1 & 3)	(4,800)		
Net income	2,340	250	5,500
Less: personal allowance	(2,340)	(250)	(3,445)
Taxable income	nil	nil	2,055

	£
Tax £2,055 @ 10%	205
Less: Tax credits:	
Dividends (Note 2) (£2,055 × 10%)	(205)
Interest	(50)
Tax repayable	(50)

TQT
Tax Qualification Training

CTC/WTC

	£
Child Tax Credit	
Family Element	545
Child Element	2,085
Working Tax Credit	
Basic element	1,800
Lone parent element	1,770
Childcare element (£60 × 52 × 80%)	2,496
Maximum credits	8,696

	£
Annual income £(7,140 + 5,750 − 300) Note 3	12,590
Less: threshold	(6,420)
Excess income	6,170

	£
Maximum tax credit	8,696
Less: 39% of excess income	(2,406)
	6,290

Award = £6,290 or £120.96 pw

Notes

(1) The loan to purchase an interest in a partnership is deductible under s.388 ITA 2007.

(2) The tax credit available on the dividend is 10% of the *taxable* dividend (ie the amount left after offsetting allowances).

(3) The interest relief of £4,800 is not deductible for CTC/WTC purposes.

2.6 George and Mildred Roper

GEORGE ROPER

TAX COMPUTATION 2008/09

	Non-savings income	Savings income	Dividend income
	£	£	£
Earnings	11,000		
Pension income	2,600		
State pension	4,524		
Rental income	4,000		
Gilt interest		180	
UK dividends (£2,115 × 100/90)			2,350
Total income	22,124	180	2,350
Less: interest relief (£10,000 × 10%)	(1,000)		
Net income	21,124	180	2,350 = £23,654
Less: PAA (W1)	(8,103)		
Taxable income	13,021	180	2,350

	£
Tax £13,021 + 180 @ 20% (Note)	2,640
£2,350 @ 10%	235
	2,875
Less: Tax reductions:	
Maintenance relief (W2)	(254)
MCAA (W1)	(110)
Tax liability	2,511
Less: tax deducted:	
tax on dividends	(235)
PAYE £(1,000 + 570)	(1,570)
Tax payable	706

Note. As non-savings income exceeds £2,320 the 10 % starting rate band is not available to the savings income.

TQT
Tax Qualification Training

Workings

		£
1	Personal Age Allowance:	
	PAA (>65)	9,030
	Less: ½ (£23,654 – £21,800)	(927)
	Allowance given	8,103
	Married Couples Age Allowance:	
	MCAA (≥75)	6,625
	Tax reducer @ 10% × $\frac{2}{12}$ =	110

Note. MCA given to George as his net income is higher than Mildred's.

		£
2	Maintenance payment £250 × 12	3,000
	Relief restricted to	2,540
	Tax reduction @ 10%	254

MILDRED ROPER
TAX COMPUTATION 2008/09

	Non-savings income £	Savings income £	Dividend income £
State pension	4,368		
Building society interest (£8,400 × 100/80)		10,500	
Discretionary trust (£4,000 × 100/60)	6,667		
Guernsey bank interest		950	
Dividends (£720 × 100/90)			800
Net income	11,035	11,450	800 Total = £23,285
Less: PAA (W1)	(8,750)		
Taxable income	2,285	11,450	800

	£
Tax: £2,285 @ 20 % (non-savings)	457
£35 @10% (2,320 – 2,285) (savings)	3
£(11,450 – 35) @ 20%	2,283
£800 @ 10%	80
Tax liability	2,823
Less: tax deducted:	
Dividends	(80)
Interest	(2,100)
Trust income	(2,667)
Tax repayable	(2,024)

Note. Premium Bond winnings are exempt from income tax.

Workings

1 *Personal age allowance*

	£
PAA (>75)	9,180
Less: ½ £(22,660 – 21,800) (W2)	(430)
PAA given	8,750

2 *Adjusted net income*

	£
Actual net income	23,285
Less: gross donation to charity (£500 × 100/80)	(625)
Adjusted net income for age allowance purposes	22,660

Note. Do not need to extend the basic rate band as Mildred is not a higher rate taxpayer.

3.1 Randall

(1)

	A £	Property B £	C £
Rent	620	284 (W)	100
Agent's commission	(20)		
Advertising for tenants		(76)	
Repairs	(142)	(255)	(119)
Profit/(loss)	458	(47)	(19)

	£
Profit on A	458
Less loss on B and C	(66)
Property income assessment	392

Working

	£
April – Sept ($\frac{6}{12} \times £348$)	174
Dec – March ($\frac{3}{12} \times £440$)	110
	284

(2) When a premium or similar consideration is received on the *grant* (that is, by a landlord to a tenant) of a short lease (50 years or less), part of the premium is treated as rent and is thus taxed as property income in the year of grant. A lease is considered to end on the date when it is most likely to terminate.

A formula is used to identify the amount of the premium that is taxable as property income

	A
Premium	
Less: 2% × (n – 1) × A	(a)
Taxable as rent	X

where n = number of years on the lease

3.2 Corelli

TAX COMPUTATION 2008/09

(i)

	Non-savings income £	Dividend income £
Earnings	16,450	
Dividends (£15,300 × $\frac{100}{90}$)		17,000
Property income (W)	6,560	
Net income	23,010	17,000
Less: PA	(6,035)	
Taxable income	16,975	17,000

		£
Tax:	£16,975 @ 20%	3,395
	£17,000 @ 10%	1,700
Tax liability		5,095
Less: notional credit on dividend		(1,700)
Less: PAYE		(2,210)
Tax payable		1,185

Working

Property income:

	A £	B £	C £
Income (3/12 × £1,200 + 6/12 × £800)	700		
		3,100	
(9/12 × £600)			450
Expenditure:			
Agent's commission:			
1.5.08	(25)	(35)	(10)
1.11.08	(25)	(35)	(10)
Repairs	–	(100)	(1,500)
Advertising	(50)	–	–
	600	2,930	(1,070)

Net rents   £2,460

Note. Installation of new kitchen equipment is a capital *not* a revenue expense.

Lease premium:

	£
Premium	5,000
Less: 2% × (10 − 1) × £5,000	(900)
Taxed as rent	4,100

Total property income assessment £2,460 + £4,100 = £6,560

(ii) Freehold is an <u>absolute interest</u> in land, which allows the freeholder to do as he wishes (subject to general law eg planning) with his land.

Leasehold is a <u>qualified interest</u> in land, which is limited in time. The lease normally contains a range of <u>covenants</u> binding on the tenant and his successors and the lease may be forfeitable if these conditions are not complied with.

Marking scheme

		Marks
(i)	Dividends	½
	Personal allowance	½
	Tax calculation	1
	Tax credits	½
	Property income	1½
	Commission	½
	Repairs	½
	Advertising	½
	Exclude capital expenditure	½
	Premium 'income'	1
		7
(ii)	Freehold – absolute interest	1
	– freedom of use	1
	Leasehold – qualified interest	1
	– covenants	1
	– forfeitable	1
		5

4.1 Enterprise Investment Scheme

The EIS is intended to encourage investment in the ordinary shares of unquoted companies. When a qualifying individual subscribes for eligible shares in a qualifying company, the amount subscribed is a tax reducer, saving tax at 20%. Relief must be claimed within 12 months of HMRC authorising the company to issue a certificate to the investor that the share issue qualifies for relief.

A *qualifying individual* is one who is not connected with the company at any time in the period from two years before the issue (or from incorporation if later) to five years after the issue. An individual is connected with the company if his shareholding exceeds 30%, if he is a partner of the company or if he is an employee or a non-qualifying director of the company.

A *qualifying director* is one who does not receive payment from the company apart from reasonable remuneration.

Eligible shares are newly issued ordinary shares which carry no preferential rights to dividends, assets or redemption in the five years from the date of issue.

A *qualifying company* is (broadly) an unquoted trading company. Certain trades are excluded. The company must be unquoted when the shares are issued.

The maximum total investment that can qualify in a tax year is £500,000 per individual. If an investment is less than £500 no relief is available (unless subscription is made by an approved EIS fund that pools the contributions of several investors).

Generally speaking, relief is given on an actual basis: a 2008/09 investment will attract relief against 2008/09 tax. However, a taxpayer can claim to treat up to half of his EIS investments made between 6 April and 5 October in a tax year as made in the previous tax year, subject to a maximum carry back from any one year of £50,000.

If an individual disposes of shares (or receives value from the company, for example by taking a loan from the company) within three years of their issue, the tax reduction obtained may be wholly or partly withdrawn.

If the shares are given away or sold otherwise than at arm's length within the three years, all of the tax reduction is withdrawn.

On an arm's length sale or a receipt of value within the three years, the tax reduction to be withdrawn is:

$$\text{Consideration obtained} \times \frac{\text{Tax reduction obtained on issue}}{\text{Issue price of shares}}$$

However, the withdrawal cannot exceed the tax reduction originally obtained (which may have been less than 20% of the issue price, for example because the individual did not have enough tax to reduce).

A transfer of shares between spouses/partners in a civil partnership does not give rise to a withdrawal of the tax reduction. The reduction obtained remains associated with the shares, and if the recipient partner disposes of the shares outside the marriage/partnership within three years of their issue, it is withdrawn by an assessment on the recipient partner.

The death of a shareholder is not treated as a disposal.

If shares are disposed of after three years from issue, the following consequences ensue.

(a)   The tax reduction is not withdrawn (although earlier partial withdrawals stand).
(b)   If there is a gain for CGT purposes and EIS relief has not already been wholly withdrawn, the gain is exempt.

On a disposal before or after the expiry of the three year period, any loss for CGT purposes is restricted by reducing the issue price (but not so as to create a gain). The reduction is the tax reduction obtained and not withdrawn.

When shares issued under the EIS are sold at arm's length at a loss at any time (within or outside the first three years), and the EIS relief is not wholly withdrawn, the loss may be relieved in the same way as a trading loss.

> **Tutorial note**. The detail can be found in ss.156-257 ITA 2007.

5.1 Mr Thomas

BENEFITS ASSESSABLE ON MR THOMAS – 2008/09

	£
Accommodation (W1)	3,875
Related expenses (W1)	4,950
Loan interest (W2)	495
Car 1 (W3)	3,870
Car 2 (W3)	1,400
	14,590

Workings

1 Accommodation

	£
Annual value	750
Additional charge: $6.25\% \times £(125,000 - 75,000)$	3,125
	3,875

Mr Thomas occupied the property for the first time more than 6 years after it was purchased in 1993, therefore the additional charge is based on the market value of the property when first occupied, not on cost plus alterations carried out prior to occupation.

Related expenses

	£
Household bills – light, heat, telephone £(750 + 250 + 350)	1,350
Council tax	1,400
Redecoration	700
Gardener	1,500
	4,950

2 *Cheap taxable loan*

	£
Average basis: $\dfrac{(10,000 + 9,000)}{2} \times \dfrac{10}{12} \times 6.25\% =$	£495

		£
Strict basis:	$£10,000 \times 2/12 \times 6.25\%$	104
	$£15,000 \times 4/12 \times 6.25\%$	313
	$£7,500 \times 2/12 \times 6.25\%$	78
	$£11,500 \times 1/12 \times 6.25\%$	60
	$£9,000 \times 1/12 \times 6.25\%$	47
		602

HMRC may insist on the strict basis, although in practice the difference might be considered insignificant.

3 *Cars*

Mercedes: $£21,500 \times 18\% = £3,870 \left(\dfrac{150 - 135}{5}\right) = 3 + 15 = 18\%$

Escort: $£10,000 \times 21\% \times 8/12 = £1,400 \left(\dfrac{165 - 135}{5}\right) = 6 + 15 = 21\%$

5.2 Alf

	Non-savings income £	Savings income £	Dividend income £
Earnings (W1)	37,760		
Interest (£5,440 × 100/80)		6,800	
Dividends (£4,000 × 100/90)			4,444
Less: personal allowance	(6,035)		
Taxable income	31,725	6,800	4,444

		£
Tax:	£34,800 @ 20%	6,960
	£2,000 @ 20% (W2)	400
	£1,725 @ 40%	690
	£4,444 @ 32½%	1,444
Tax liability		9,494
Less: tax credits:		
	Dividends	(444)
	PAYE	(5,755)
	Interest	(1,360)
Tax due		1,935

Workings

1   Earnings

	£	£
Salary		32,600
Expenses allowance:		
Gross allowance (N1)	2,500	
Less business travel	(1,800)	
		700
		33,300
Benefits:		
Hi-fi equipment £(800 × 20%) (N2)	160	
Car £(15,000 × 24%) (N3)	3,600	
Medical insurance (N4)	300	
Clothing (N4)	400	
		4,460
Amount chargeable as earnings		37,760

Notes

(1)   The expenses allowance is taxable, but Alf can claim the cost of business travel as an allowable deduction. Entertainment of clients is not deductible as this would not have been deductible for his employer.

(2)   The annual value of the hi-fi equipment subject to tax is 20% of its cost.

(3)   The emission rate is 45g/km greater than 135g/km. The percentage is 15% + 45/5% = 24%.

(4)   The taxable value of the medical insurance and clothing is the cost to the company of providing the benefits.

2   Basic rate band extended by gross gift aid donation: £1,600 × 100/80 = £2,000

5.3   Mr Bjork

Mr Bjork's benefits

		£	£
Jaguar:	car (£20,000 × 32% × ⁴/₁₂) (W1)		2,133
	petrol (£16,900 × 32% × ⁴/₁₂) (W1)		1,803
Mercedes:	no private use (all business use)		
BMW:	car (£15,000 × 35%) (W2)		5,250
	petrol (£16,900 × 35%) (W2)		5,915
Legal costs			2,000
Use of video equipment £800 × 20%			160
Use of computer £6,000 × 20% × 6/12		600	
Less exemption		(500)	
			100
Gift of computer (market value – see note)			200
Total benefits			17,561

Workings

1 $\left(\dfrac{220-135}{5}\right) = 17 + 15 = 32\%$

2 $\left(\dfrac{240-135}{5}\right) = 21 + 15 = 36\%$ (35% Cap)

Note. Gifts of computers (provided before 6 April 2006) and bicycles which have previously been used by the employees are subject to a tax charge based only on market value. Computers provided before 6 April 2006 continue to benefit from a £500 exemption. Computers provided after that date no longer attract the exemption.

5.4 Hitech Computers

EARNINGS FOR 2008/09

	£	£
Salary:		
April – June ($^3/_{12} \times$ £31,000)	7,750	
July – March ($^9/_{12} \times$ £36,000)	27,000	
		34,750
Bonus – paid in year		4,000
		38,750
Accommodation:		
Higher of (i) Rent paid £5,000 × $^9/_{12}$ = £3,750	3,750	
(ii) Annual value 2,400 × $^9/_{12}$ = £1,800		
Less contribution (£100 × 9 months)	(900)	
		2,850
Loan interest $\dfrac{15,000+10,000}{2} \times 6.25\%$		781
Car parking space (not taxable as near to place of work)		–
Medical insurance (cost to employer)		385
Crèche facilities (note 1)		–
Newspaper allowance £20 × 12		240
		43,006
Less: pension contribution (covered in Chapter 7) (5% × £38,750)		(1,938)
Earnings		41,068

Note. Employers' contributions of up to £55 per week towards childcare provision are tax free therefore the £100 monthly payment is not taxable.

5.5 Grovelands

(i) INCOME TAX LIABILITY 2008/09

	Non-savings Income £	Savings Income £	Dividend Income £
Employment Income – Grovelands (W1)	80,248		
Employment Income – new post (2/12 x 8,400)	1,400		
Bank interest (1,386 × $\dfrac{100}{80}$)		1,732	
Dividends (2,754 × $\dfrac{100}{90}$)			3,060
Total Income	81,648	1,732	3,060
Less: PA	(6,035)		
TAXABLE INCOME	75,613	1,732	3,060

TAX PAYABLE

Non-savings income (excluding compensation) £33,126

	£
£33,126 @ 20%	6,625
Savings income £1,733	
£1,733 @ 20%	347
Dividends £3,060	
£941 @ 10% (W4)	94
£2,119 @ 32.5%	689
Compensation £42,487	
£42,487 @ 40%	16,995
INCOME TAX LIABILITY	24,750

Workings

(1) *Employment income – Grovelands Ltd*

The 2008/09 assessable amount is computed as follows:

	£	£
Salary (£29,333 × 9/12)		22,000
Benefits:		
Motor car (22,300 × 30% * × 9/12)	5,018	
Car fuel (16,900 × 30% × 9/12)	3,802	
BUPA	200	
Season ticket	2,641	
Entertainment System (W2)	4,100	
		15,761
		37,761
Termination payment (W3)	72,487	
Less: Exempt under *S403 ITEPA 2003*	(30,000)	
		42,487
		80,248

* The appropriate percentage for the emissions figure of 214g/km rounded down to 210g/km.

(2) *Entertainment system*

	£	£
6.04.08 – 31.12.08		
£5,000 @ 20% × 9/12 =		750
Transfer higher of		
(i) MV @ transfer	1,000	
or		
(ii) MV when 1st available	5,000	
Less		
– assessed 07/08		
£5,000 @ 20% × 9/12	(750)	
– assessed 08/09	(750)	
	3,500	3,500
Less: price paid		(150)
		4,100

(3) *Termination payment*

The compensation for loss of office payment is assessed on a receipts basis and not by reference to the year in which the employment ceased.

Termination payments are treated as the top slice of income when calculating income tax.

(4)   *Gift aid payment*

£34,800 + (800 × 100/80) =   £35,800.

Higher rate relief is obtained by extending the basic rate band by the gross amount of the payment.

(ii)   Summary dismissal occurs where an employer dismisses an employee without notice or without waiting for a fixed term contract to expire. Provided that the employee has committed an act of gross misconduct, the employer incurs no liability for breach of conduct. The employee is only entitled to receive contractual salary and benefits up to the date of termination of the employment.

Constructive dismissal arises where an employee resigns as a result of the employer breaching some essential term of the employment contract without the employee's consent. The employer in this case is liable for breach of contract.

Marking scheme

		Marks	
(i)	Employment income – new post	½	
	Bank interest	1	
	Dividends	1	
	Personal allowance	½	
	Tax calculation	3	
	Grovelands employment income:		
	– Salary	½	
	– Car	1½	
	– Fuel	1	
	– BUPA	½	
	– Season ticket	½	
	– Entertainment system	2½	
	– Termination payment and £30k exemption	1½	
Gift aid		1	
			15
(ii)	Summary dismissal – definition	1	
	– no breach	1	
	– employee entitlement	1	
	Constructive dismissal – definition	1	
	– breach	1	
			5
			20

5.6   Mr Morris

MR MORRIS – INCOME TAX PAYABLE FOR 2008/09

	Non Savings Income £	Savings Income £	Dividend Income £
Employment Income (W1)	33,681		
Building society interest (312 × $\frac{100}{80}$)		390	
Bank interest (256 × 1/2 × $\frac{100}{80}$)		160	
Dividends (738 × $\frac{100}{90}$)			820
Property Income (W2)	4,635		
Total Income	38,316	550	820
Less: PA	(6,035)		
TAXABLE INCOME	32,281	550	820

TAX LIABILITY

		£	£
32,281 @ 20%			6,456
550 @ 20%			110
820 @ 10%			82
INCOME TAX LIABILITY			6,648
Less:	PAYE	6,234	
	BSI	78	
	Bank interest	32	
	UK dividends	82	
			(6,426)
INCOME TAX PAYABLE			222

Note: As Mr Morris is a basic rate taxpayer no further relief is due for the charitable donation which therefore does not impact on the tax calculation.

Workings

1   *Employment income*

	£
Salary	25,450
Car (14,665 × 25%)*	3,666
Fuel (16,900 × 25%)*	4,225
Health Insurance	340
	33,681

* Percentage for emissions figure of 187g/km rounded down to 185g/km.

2   *Property income*

	£	£
Gross rental income		
(5/12 × 8,000 + 6/12 × 12,000)		9,333
Less:		
Agents fees (267 + 600)	867	
Repairs (400 + 1,500)	1,900	
Gardener (100 + 200)	300	
Council Tax	590	
Water Rates (85 + 100)	185	
Wear and Tear Allowance	856	
((9,333 − 590 − 185) @ 10%)		(4,698)
		£4,635

Marking scheme

	Marks
Building society interest	½
Bank interest	½
Dividends	½
Personal allowance	½
Tax calculation	1
Tax credits	1
Salary	½
Car	1
Fuel	1
Health insurance	½
Rent	1
Expenses	1½
Wear and tear allowance	1
Maximum	10

TQT
Tax Qualification Training

6.1 Sue

(a) If the scheme has been approved then there are no tax consequences on the grant or exercise of the options.

When Sue comes to sell the shares she will have a chargeable gain and annual exemption as follows: (covered in the Capital Gains Tax section of the Text).

	£
Sale proceeds = 5,000 × £10.40	52,000
Cost = 5,000 × £4.00	(20,000)
Gain	32,000

(b) As the scheme is unapproved, an employment income charge will arise on the exercise of the option as follows:

	£
Market value at date of exercise	10.00
Less exercise price	(3.00)
	7.00 per share

£7.00 × 5,000 shares = £35,000

Sale of shares (covered later in the text)

	£
Sale proceeds	52,000
Cost = MV at date of exercise (5,000 × £10)	(50,000)
Gain	2,000

Tutorial note

In general terms, there is little difference between an approved and an unapproved scheme if the shares are to be sold. The approved scheme gives rise to a capital gain. The unapproved scheme results in an employment income charge but a much smaller capital gain.

However, most taxpayers would rather have profits taxed under the approved scheme rules (ie making their profit chargeable to CGT rather than income tax) as the CGT annual exemption of £9,600 is available and the rate of CGT is 18% compared to 40% for a tax payer paying income tax at the higher rate.

You should revisit this question after you have covered the Capital Gains Tax section of this Study Text.

7.1 Mr Matthews

(1) REVIEW OF CALCULATION OF TAXABLE INCOME

	Total income £	Tax suffered £
Earned Income		
Salary	48,750	11,754
Medical insurance	375	
Car parking space (Note 1)	–	
Less:		
Deduction for business mileage (Note 2)	(259)	
Subscriptions (Note 3)	(295)	
	48,571	
Unearned Income		
Bank interest (Note 4)	400	80
Trust income	2,000	800
Net income	50,971	12,634

Notes

(1) Provision of a car parking space at or near the place of work in an exempt benefit and therefore the reimbursement of the parking expenses does not form part of taxable income.

(2) Payments received for business mileage are not taxable provided they do not exceed HMRC's Authorised Mileage Rates. Where an employee is reimbursed for business mileage at a rate less than the authorised rates then a claim can be made for the shortfall as a deduction from income.

	£
Amount due under authorised rates (925 × 40p)	370
Amount actually received	(111)
Amount to claim	259

(3) Payments of a subscription to an approved HMRC body that relates to the individual's employment is allowable as a deduction from employment income under S344 ITEPA 2003. Relief is given for the amount paid in the tax year.

(4) The gross amount of the building society interest must be included in the computation of income. The tax deducted is £80, which means £320 is the net amount and gross income of £400 must be included. (Tax of 20% of the gross income is deducted at source from building society interest).

(2) Tax relief is available for donations made to charities if Gift Aid is claimed. The gift is deemed to be made net of basic rate tax, which the charity can claim from HMRC. If the donor is a higher rate taxpayer, higher rate tax relief is obtained by extending the basic rate band by the gross amount of the payment.

For example, Mr Matthews donates £120 per tax year to the Dogs Trust. Mr Matthews' basic rate band will be extended by £150 (£120 × 100/80) which means a further £150 of income will be taxed at the basic rate of tax rather than the higher rate.

The above relief is available provided that the donor made a Gift Aid declaration. Such a declaration must contain the name and address of the donor, the name of the charity and a statement that the donor has paid sufficient income or capital gains tax to cover the basic tax relief due to the charity in respect of the gift.

In addition, the donor must not receive any significant benefit from the charity as a result of the gift – although an exception to this rules applies if the benefit is simply free entry to a charity's properties.

If Mr Matthews is in a repayment position for 2008/09 he can indicate on his tax return form that he would like the repayment to be donated to a charity of his choice. He can also indicate for Gift Aid to apply to this donation and therefore will be able to claim tax relief in respect of it for next year.

(3) CALCULATION OF TAX PAYABLE/(REPAYABLE)

	£
Net income	50,971
Less: Personal allowance	(6,035)
Taxable income	44,936
£34,800 @ 20%	6,960
£375 (W) @ 20%	75
£9,761 @ 40%	3,904
Tax liability	10,939
Less tax deducted at source	(12,634)
Tax repayable	(1,695)

Working

	£
Donation to Dogs Trust (£10 × 12)	120
Donation to English Heritage (£15 × 12)	180
	300
Extension to basic rate band (£300 × 100/80)	£375

(4)   Contributions to a personal pension plan are made net of basic rate income tax.

If the taxpayer is a higher rate taxpayer higher rate tax relief is obtained by extending the basic rate band by the gross amount of the payment.

The maximum gross allowable contribution is based on the higher of:

(i)   £3,600 and
(ii) 100% × the taxpayer's relevant earnings.

Relevant earnings consist of his employment income (including benefits) less allowable expenses ie:

	£
Salary	48,750
Medical Insurance	375
Car parking space	–
Less:	
Deduction for business mileage	(259)
Subscription	(295)
Relevant earnings	48,571

Mr Matthews can therefore contribute up to £48,571 and obtain tax relief. It is unlikely he would wish to contribute this entire amount to a pension and should therefore choose an amount that will leave him with sufficient income to maintain his current lifestyle.

For example if he chose to contribute £8,500 (gross), this would result in a tax saving of £1,700, as a further £8,500 of income would be taxed at 20% rather than 40%. He would pay £6,800 (£8,500 × 80%) into the fund and HMRC would transfer £1,700 (£8,500 × 20%) into the pension fund.

Pension contributions must be paid in the current pension input period. Accordingly, it is not possible for Mr Matthews to claim relief against his 2008/09 income, as it is now mid February 2010.

Marking scheme

		Marks
(1)	Insurance	½
	Car space	1
	Business mileage	2
	Subscriptions	1
	Interest	1
	Trust income	½
		6
(2)	Paid net of basic rate tax	1
	Basic rate band extension	1
	Illustration	1
	Declaration	1
	No benefits	1
	Repayment to charity	1
	Repayment under gift aid	1
	Maximum	5
(3)	Personal allowance	½
	Tax calculation	1
	Tax credit	½
	Donations	1
		3

		Marks
(4)	Payment net of basic rate tax	½
	Extension of basic rate band	1
	Maximum contribution	2
	Relevant earnings	1
	Apply to Mr Matthews	2
	Relevant tax year	1
	Maximum	6
		20

7.2 Ed & Joan

(a) Maximum contributions

Ed and Joan can contribute any amount to their pension regardless of the level of their earnings. However tax relief will only be given for contributions up to their earnings for the tax year.

The partnership profits for 2008/09 of £175,000 split 4:1 gives Ed £140,000 profit and Joan £35,000. Therefore Ed could contribute a maximum of £140,000 and Joan £35,000 and receive tax relief on their contributions.

They cannot obtain relief for 2007/08 as contributions must be made in the current pension input period.

(b) Tax relief

Basic rate tax relief is given through the pension holder paying contributions net of 20%. This means that they pay only 80% of the gross payment into the pension. HMRC pays the extra 20% on their behalf to the pension provider.

Ed will pay £112,000 (£140,000 × 80%) and Joan will pay £28,000 (£35,000 × 80%).

In addition Ed will be entitled to higher rate relief. This is given by extending the basic rate band for the year by the amount of the gross contribution.

Joan's tax liability

	£
Trading profit	35,000
Personal allowance	(6,035)
Taxable income	28,965
Tax liability	
£28,965 @ 20%	5,793

Ed's tax liability

	£
Trading profit	140,000
Personal allowance	(6,035)
Taxable income	133,965
Tax liability:	
£133,965 at 20% (Note)	26,793

Note. Higher rate tax relief will be given by extending Ed's basic rate tax band for 2008/09 to £174,800 (34,800 + 140,000).

(c) No earnings

There is no need for the individual to have earnings. A contribution of up to £3,600 gross per tax year may be made into a pension regardless of the level of earnings.

7.3 Dwaine Pipe

INCOME TAX COMPUTATION 2008/09

	Non-savings income £	Savings income £
Earnings (W1)	36,371	
Interest on ISA		Exempt
Halifax interest £$(14,000 \times \frac{100}{80}) \times 50\%$		8,750
Premium bond winnings		Exempt
Net income	36,371	8,750
Less: Personal allowance	(6,035)	–
Taxable income	30,336	8,750

		£
Tax thereon:		
£34,800 @ 20%		6,960
£2,750 @ 20% (W7)		550
£1,536 @ 40%		614
Tax liability		8124
Less: tax deducted:		
PAYE		(6,000)
Interest (£8,750 @ 20%)		(1,750)
Tax payable		374

Workings

1 Earnings

	£
Salary	
(£20,000 × ⁹/₁₂)	15,000
(£22,000 × ³/₁₂)	5,500
	20,500
Bonuses (note 1)	
Awarded 30.9.08	3,850
Awarded 31.3.09	4,250
	28,600
Company cars:	
Vauxhall Cavalier (W2 + W3)	960
Audi A6 (W4 + W5)	2,205
	31,765
Mobile phone	Exempt
Interest free loan (W6)	3,516
Nursery fees (note 2)	Exempt
Pension contributions by employer	Exempt
Central heating (cost to employer)	800
Staff suggestion scheme	Exempt
Round sum allowance	1,000
	37,081
Less: allowable expenses	
Hotel bills	(710)
Total	36,371

2 Vauxhall Cavalier

	£
£10,629 @ 20% × 7/12 (W3)	1,240
Less employee contributions (7 × £40)	(280)
Car benefit	960

No fuel benefit as no private diesel provided.

3 $\left(\dfrac{145-135}{5}\right)$ = 2% + 18% (diesel) = 20%

4 *Audi A6*

(£18,500 + £400) @ 28% × 5/12 = £2,205

No reduction of benefit for time car in garage as unavailable for < 30 consecutive days.

No fuel benefit as no private petrol provided.

5 $\left(\dfrac{200-135}{5}\right)$ = 13% + 15% = 28%

6 *Interest-free loan*
Average

$\dfrac{75,000 + 60,000}{2}$ × 10/12 × 6.25% = £3,516

	£
Strict basis	
£75,000 × 7/12 × 6.25%	2,734
£60,000 × 3/12 × 6.25%	938
	3,672

HMRC may elect for strict basis; unlikely in practice.

7 *Personal pension contributions*

Dwaine pays £150 × 12	£1,800
× $\dfrac{100}{80}$	£2,250

Basic rate threshold extended by £500 (£400 × 100/80 Gift Aid) + 2,250 = £2,750

Notes

(1) Bonus becomes taxable in the year in which a director is *entitled* to the payment (even if this is before actual receipt).

(2) First £55 per week of childcare costs paid by employer for approved childcare are tax-free.

8.1 Ricardo Garcia

Our address

Your address

Date

Dear Mr Garcia

UK taxation on moving to this country

Thank you for your recent letter informing me of your proposed move. I set out below the main points of UK taxation on income which would be relevant to you.

Domicile and residence

The tax treatment of individuals in the UK depends on three concepts – domicile, residence and ordinary residence.

'Domicile' is a person's 'permanent home country'. It is normally a 'domicile of origin', being the domicile of one's father, and so you are presumably domiciled in Spain at present. However, it can be changed to a 'domicile of choice'. This is not done merely by the act of emigrating: it requires very positive cutting off of ties in the previous domicile, to show that there is no intention to return.

If you were unwilling to cut such ties, you would retain your domicile in Spain. In fact, this may be to your advantage, as there are certain bases of assessment to UK tax which are favourable to foreign domiciliaries.

'Residence' is established by 183 days presence in the UK in a year of assessment, but if you come here to live permanently you will be treated as resident and also ordinarily resident in the UK from the date you arrive. This is the main factor which affects your assessment to UK taxation.

Remittance basis of taxation

As a foreign domiciled individual, you can make a claim to have your overseas sources of income taxed only if remitted to (ie brought into) the UK. This will initially at least have a cash flow advantage as you are only taxed when you bring the income into the UK. However there are certain disadvantages depending on the type of income remitted. These are explained where appropriate below.

Allowances

Normally, as an EU resident, you would expect to be entitled to a personal allowance deducted from your income. However, if you claim to be taxed on the remittance basis, you will lose your entitlement to personal allowances.

Income

From the details given, you appear to have three main sources of income:

(1) **The pension**

On the basis that you retain your foreign domicile and claim for the remittance basis to apply, the pension income will be taxable only when remitted to (ie brought into) the UK. However, if you do not make a claim, or become UK domiciled, only 90% of the income from your Spanish pension will be taxable in the UK.

As it appears that you are planning to bring all of the pension income into the UK, you may decide not to make the claim for the remittance basis so that you are only taxed on 90% of the income. In this case, the income will be taxed at 20% and 40%.

(2) **Investment income**

Assuming the pension income takes you over the basic rate threshold, without a claim for the remittance basis your Spanish bank interest will be taxable at 40% and any dividend income from your portfolio will be taxable at 32.5% on an arising basis.

If you make a claim for the remittance basis to apply you will only be taxable when you bring the funds into the UK. However, if and when it is remitted, it will be taxed as non-savings income, so even the dividends will be taxed at 40%.

This will need to be weighed against the position for your pension income before deciding whether or not to make the remittance basis claim.

(3) **The rent**

Your foreign rental income is taxable in the UK on an arising basis at 40% (assuming you are a higher rate taxpayer) unless you make the remittance basis claim, in which case you will only be taxed on the amounts remitted to the UK. If rent does not cover expenses, there may be nothing to remit and thus no assessment. Expenses of letting are deductible in arriving at the amount assessable to UK income tax.

Impact of long-term residence

Once you have been resident in the UK for seven tax years, from year eight onwards if you claim the remittance basis you will be subject to a £30,000 per annum tax charge in respect of any unremitted foreign income and gains. Once you reach that stage, however, you can make a decision each tax year whether it is more beneficial to claim the remittance basis (and pay the £30,000 tax charge) or to be taxed on worldwide income and gains for that year on an arising basis.

Remittance planning

Assuming you retain your foreign domicile and would like to make a claim for the remittance basis to apply to your overseas income, I would advise you to have these amounts paid into a bank account in Spain separate from your savings; you can then spend that money when you visit Spain and not be charged to UK tax on it. If you bring across money from a different bank account (ie your previous savings) it cannot be assessed as it does not represent income arising while resident in the UK.

Note, however, that a 'constructive remittance' is taxable. If you take out a loan in Spain, bring the money to the UK, and use the Spanish income and gains to pay off the loan, you are held to have remitted the income and gains to the UK.

Conclusion

I hope that the above comments are of use to you. If you wish to discuss these or any other matters further, please do not hesitate to contact me. I suggest that we have a meeting when you next come to the UK so that we can discuss your taxation affairs in more detail.

I look forward to meeting you.

Yours sincerely,

A Adviser

9.1 **Peter Jones**

(1) INCOME TAX REPAYMENT – 2008/09

	Non-savings income £	Savings income £	Dividend income £
Building society interest × 100/80		4,000	
Dividends × 100/90			889
Rental income	5,289		
Net income	5,289	4,000	889
Less: personal allowance	(5,289)	(746)	
Taxable income	–	3,254	889

Tax:		
Savings income: £2,320 × 10%		232
£934 × 20%		187
Dividend income: £889 × 10%		89
Tax liability		508
Less: tax deducted at source:		
Credit on dividend		
(does not give rise to refund)		(89)
Building society interest		
£4,000 × 20%		(800)
Repayment due		(381)

(2) CAPITAL GAINS TAX – 2008/09

	£
Chargeable gains for the year	40,000
Less: annual exemption	(9,600)
Taxable gain	30,400
Tax:	
£30,400 @ 18%	5,472

9.2 **Simon James**

Your address

10 March 2009

Dear Mr James

Relevance of residence, ordinary residence and domicile

Thank you for your letter of 3 March in which you refer to certain capital gains tax matters.

I assume you are aware of the meaning of these terms and are concerned with just the capital gains tax implications.

In order to be liable to UK capital gains tax on gains arising in a year of assessment the person to whom the gain accrues must be either resident or ordinarily resident in the UK at some time in the tax year.

If you cease to be UK resident and have been resident or ordinarily resident for four out of the last seven tax years, you remain within the scope of UK capital gains tax unless your absence covers at least five tax years. If you return within five years, any gains made during the period of non residence will be taxable in the year of return (if the assets were acquired prior to leaving the UK).

An extra statutory concession applies for persons becoming resident part of the way through a tax year. Provided a new arrival has been non resident for the five years preceding his arrival in the UK, gains accruing in the part of the year of assessment before he became resident will not be chargeable. Similarly, a person becoming non resident part of the way through a tax year does not have to wait until the following tax year for his gains to be exempt, although this only applies to individuals who have not been resident or ordinarily resident for at least four out of seven tax years immediately before the year of departure.

Domicile status is of importance where gains are realised on overseas assets. A person domiciled in the UK is liable on gains arising on his assets wherever located. A person with a non UK domicile can make a claim to be only chargeable on overseas gains if the proceeds are remitted to the UK. This does not, however, make gains realised prior to becoming resident, chargeable. If a foreign domiciled person wishes to bring funds into the UK it is advisable that he does not remit from sources which are chargeable to capital gains tax (or income tax) on a remittance basis. Thus proceeds giving rise to gains on a remittance basis should be paid into a separate overseas bank account and remittances to the UK should be made from past savings held in another account.

It should be noted however that if an individual has been UK resident for seven out of the preceding nine tax years, he will be subject to a £30,000 per annum tax charge on unremitted foreign income and gains if that individual claims to be taxed on the remittance basis. It is necessary therefore to consider each tax year whether it is in fact advantageous to claim the remittance basis in respect of overseas income and gains.

Losses on overseas assets incurred by a non domiciled person cannot be set off against his chargeable gains, unless he does not claim the remittance basis for that year.

It is necessary to make an irrevocable election to opt for a regime which will allow overseas losses to be claimed in years when the individual is taxed on the arising basis.

If you require any further clarification on this matter please do not hesitate to contact me.

Yours sincerely

A Adviser

10.1 Dorrit

	2008/09 £
Trade profits (y/e 31.12.08)	15,000
Property income	3,000
Original net income	18,000
s.64 loss relief	(18,000)
Revised net income	nil
Chargeable gains	16,000
s.261B TCGA 1992 loss relief (W)	(10,000)
Revised gains (covered by AE)	6,000

Loss memo

Loss incurred in 2009/10	28,000
s.64 against net income of 2008/09	(18,000)
	10,000
Relief against chargeable gain of 2008/09	(10,000)
	–

Working

Maximum offset of trading loss against chargeable gains:

Lower of: £

	(i)	trading loss remaining after s.64	10,000
and	(ii)	net gains less any capital losses b/f	16,000
			∴ £10,000

10.2 Kidson

	£
Proceeds	45,000
Cost £8,000 × $\dfrac{45,000}{45,000+50,000}$	(3,789)
Chargeable gain	41,211
Less: AE	(9,600)
Taxable gain	31,611

Note. No claim is available for a 'small part' disposal as proceeds > £20,000 and > 20% of MV of land.

10.3 Harbottle

(a) 2008/09 INCOME TAX LIABILITIES

(i) Fred

	Non Savings Income £	Savings Income £	Dividend Income £
Employment Income	35,000		
NSB Interest (1/2 share)		1,000	
Dividends			7,000
Total Income	35,000	1,000	7,000
Less: PA	(6,035)		
TAXABLE INCOME	28,965	1,000	7,000

TAX LIABILITY

£	£
28,965 @ 20%	5,793
1,000 @ 20% (savings)	200
4,835 @ 10% (dividends)	483
34,800	
2,165 @ 32½% (dividends)	704
36,965	£7,180

(ii)   *Iris*

	Savings Income £	Dividend Income £
NSB Interest (1/2 share)	1,000	
Dividends		1,200
Total Income	1,000	1,200
Less: PA	(1,000)	(1,200)
TAXABLE INCOME	Nil	Nil
INCOME TAX LIABILITY		Nil

2008/09 CAPITAL GAINS TAX LIABILITIES

(i)   *Fred*

	£
Gains	10,700
Less: Annual exempt amount	(9,600)
	1,100
Capital gains tax at 18%	198

(ii)   *Iris*

	£
Gains	2,500
Less: Annual exempt amount	(9,600)
	NIL
Capital gains tax	£NIL

SUMMARY

	Fred £	Iris £	Total £
Income tax liability	7,180	NIL	7,180
Capital gains tax liability	198	NIL	198
	7,378	NIL	7,378

(b)   PLANNING ACTION

Currently, as the computations in (a) above show, Iris is not fully using her personal allowance of £6,035 nor her capital gains tax exempt amount of £9,600. The following action should be taken:

(i)   Ensure that Iris fully uses her 2008/09 personal allowance by the transfer of investments from Fred and/or the transfer of the NSB investment account from joint names into her sole name. The effect of this would be to increase Iris's income and decrease Fred's income. To achieve the desired effect there must be an outright gift so that Iris is beneficially entitled; Fred must no longer participate in the income from the investments gifted.

(ii)   The value of assets transferred into Iris's name must be at least sufficient to yield £3,835 additional income (£6,035 − £2,200).

Ideally Fred's savings income should be reduced by £2,165 so that he is not a higher rate taxpayer in 2008/09. All of his share portfolio should be transferred to Iris (currently yielding £7,000 of income (gross)) to give the best possible result. As Iris has no non-savings income the first £2,320 of her taxable income will be taxable at 10% rather than at 20% if it is taxed on Fred.

(iii)   Fred and Iris should also make their maximum investment in an ISA – they could invest £7,200 each per annum in an ISA shares account. The dividends received on these shares will be exempt from tax.

(iv)   Assuming the couple continue to realise capital gains of £13,200 each tax year the gains should be shared such that each spouse may take advantage of their £9,600 annual exemption.

Investments may be transferred between spouses at no gain/no loss and this should be done before disposal of assets to third parties.

(c) Fred and Iris are entitled to the following tax credits in 2008/09.

	£	£
CTC		
Family element	545	
Child element: 2 x £2,085	4,170	
		4,715
WTC		
Basic element	1,800	
Couple element	1,770	
30 hour element (Fred works full time)	735	
Child care (not available as Iris does not work)	–	
		4,305
Maximum WTC & CTC before excess income restriction		9,020
Restriction for excess income:		
Employment income	35,000	
Investment income (£8,000 + £2,200 - £300)	9,900	
	44,900	
WTC and CTC (excluding family element)	9,020	
Income reduction ((£44,900 - £6,420) × 39%) restricted	(9,020)	
		–
CTC family element (no reduction as income does not exceed £50,000)		545

Fred and Iris are entitled to the family element of the CTC of £545. This will be paid to Iris, by HMRC either weekly or four weekly.

TQT
Tax Qualification Training

11.1 Julie Green

Share pool:

	No of shares	Cost £
Purchase 1.6.93	50	1,000
Purchase 18.9.96	50	3,800
Purchase 21.5.97	100	9,300
	200	14,100
Bonus issue (1 for 2)	100	–
Purchase 15.1.02	100	8,200
	400	22,300
Sale 29.6.08	(75)	(4,181)
	325	18,119
Sale 16.8.08	(75)	(4,181)
c/f	250	13,938

Calculate gains:

	£
Disposal 29.6.08:	
Proceeds	10,150
Cost	(4,181)
Chargeable gain	5,969
Disposal 16.8.08	
Proceeds	8,500
Cost	(4,181)
Chargeable gain	4,319
Total chargeable gains	10,288

11.2 Mr Jones

Share pool:

	No. of shares	Cost £
Purchase Aug 82	5,000	6,250
Purchase Sept 82	2,000	3,000
Purchase Nov 85	5,000	9,500
	12,000	18,750
Sale Oct 87	(3,000)	(4,687)
	9,000	14,063
Purchase May 01	1,000	3,000
	10,000	17,063
Sale July 08	(7,000)	(11,944)
c/f	3,000	5,119

Calculate gain:

	£
Proceeds	31,500
Cost	(11,944)
Chargeable gain	19,556

11.3 Richard Price

Share pool:

	No. of shares	Cost £
Purchase 15.3.90	2,000	2,000
Purchase 17.12.96	4,000	10,000
	6,000	12,000
RI (1 for 5)	1,200	6,000
	7,200	18,000
Sale 4.10.08	(1,800)	(4,500)
c/f	5,400	13,500

Calculate gain:

	£
Proceeds (1,800 × £7.50)	13,500
Cost	(4,500)
Chargeable gain	9,000

11.4 Eric James

Sale of shares in Toucan Play plc

	£
Proceeds	9,100
Less: Cost (working)	(2,049)
Chargeable gain	7,051

Working

Total consideration received on takeover:	£
2000 ordinary shares [2000 × £4.20]	8,400
4000 Preference shares (4000 × £2)	8,000
Allowable cost of shares sold:	
$\dfrac{8,400}{16,400} \times £4,000$	2,049

12.1 Doug

Summary

	£
Gains (W1 and W3)	8,533
Less: current year loss (W2)	(1,200)
	7,333
Less: AE	(9,600)
Taxable gain	–

Workings

1	Ming vase:	£
	Proceeds	8,000
	Allowable cost	(2,000)
		6,000

Gain cannot exceed 5/3 × £(8,000 – 6,000) = £3,333

∴ Chargeable gain 3,333

2	Leonardo cartoon:	£
	Proceeds (deemed)	6,000
	Allowable cost	(7,200)
	Allowable loss	(1,200)

3	Lathe:	£
	Proceeds	9,500
	Allowable cost	(4,300)
		5,200

Restrict to $\dfrac{5}{3} \times £(9,500 - 6,000) = £5,833$ ∴ restriction does not apply.

12.2 Mr Cole

Summary

	£
Car	–
Land	27,867
Chest	1,667
Painting	6,650
	36,184
Less: current year loss	(1,500)
Net chargeable gains	34,684
Less: Annual exemption	(9,600)
Taxable gain	25,084
CGT payable:	
£25,084 @ 18%	£4,515

Workings

(1) Vintage Car

Disposal of a motor vehicle is exempt for CGT purposes.

(2)

Land	£
Sale proceeds	38,000

$$\text{Less:} \quad \text{Cost} \times \frac{A}{A+B}$$

$$£32,000 \times \frac{38,000}{38,000 + 82,000} \qquad (10,133)$$

	£
Chargeable gain	27,867

(3)

Antique Chest	£
Sale proceeds	7,000
Less: Cost	(4,000)
	£3,000

Compared to
$5/3 \times (7,000 - 6,000) =$ £1,667
Lower gain taken

(4) *Painting*

	£
Proceeds	11,500
Less: Costs of sale	(150)
	11,350
Less: Probate value	(4,700)
Chargeable gain	6,650

(5) *Vase*

	£
Deemed proceeds	6,000
Less: Cost	(7,500)
Loss	(1,500)

12.3 CGT Leases

(1) Assignment of long lease

	£
Proceeds	79,000
Cost	(38,000)
	41,000

(2) Assignment of short lease

	£
Proceeds	79,000
Cost: $£38,000 \times \dfrac{88.371}{100.000} \quad \dfrac{31 \text{ years}}{57 \text{ years}}$	(33,581)
Chargeable gain	45,419

(3) Grant of long lease – CGT part disposal

	£
Proceeds	30,000
Cost: $£25,000 \times \dfrac{30,000}{30,000 + 7,500}$	(20,000)
Chargeable gain	10,000

(4) Grant of short lease out of freehold

	£
Proceeds: capital element of premium = $(2\% \times (20 - 1) \times £20,000)$	7,600
Cost: $£25,000 \times \dfrac{7,600}{20,000 + 17,000}$	(5,135)
Chargeable gain	2,465

(5) Assessable on landlord: $£12,000 - [2\% \times (25 - 1) \times £12,000] = £6,240$

∴ allowable to Ebury £6,240/25 yrs = £250 pa

In year to 31.1.09:

	£
Deduction for lease premium £250 × 5/12	104
Rent payable 5/12 × £3,000	1,250
	1,354

13.1 Owning two homes (Pilot Paper)

A Tale of Two Properties!

(a) It is becoming increasingly common for a family to have not one but two homes that are occupied as residences. The purpose of this article is to set out the key capital gains tax implications of such a situation, using the case study of Mr and Mrs Hammond.

    (i) On the sale of the current family home there will be no capital gains tax implications and the capital gains tax pages of the tax return do not need to be completed. This is due to the valuable relief known as principal private residence (PPR) relief which ensures that the sale of a property which has been the taxpayer's only or main residence is exempt from capital gains tax ie no gain chargeable (and no loss allowable).

    (ii) However, where a taxpayer owns two properties, even if he actually resides in both, PPR relief can only apply to one property. It is worth noting at this point that a husband and wife living together such as Mr and Mrs Hammond can only have one PPR between them ie it is not possible for the flat to be Mr Hammonds' PPR and for the house to be Mrs Hammond's.

    Instead, Mr and Mrs Hammond should elect which of the house and flat they wish to have treated as their main residence for the purposes of PPR relief. The election should be made within two years of residing in the two properties, in this case by May 2010. (If the election is not made then HMRC will make the decision for you!)

    Mr and Mrs Hammond do have a right to vary the election by a further written notice which can take effect for any period starting not more than two years before the date of the second notice.

    (iii) In this situation I would advise Mr and Mrs Hammond to elect for the flat to be treated as their main residence.

    Although the country house is likely to be the property that has the largest gain on sale, we must also take into account their long term plans. Whilst the house is likely to be owned for the next 16 years, the flat is likely to be sold within five years and therefore a gain will arise on this property first.

    If the election is made for the flat to be treated as the main residence, and it is sold after five years, any gains will be exempt from capital gains tax.

    If the flat is let out after five years, it will cease to be the couple's main residence. However, as it has been their main residence at some point during their period of ownership, then on the subsequent sale of the property not only will the gain relating to the five years of residence be exempt, but also the gain relating to the last three years of ownership. The gain relating to the remaining two years of ownership is also likely to be completely exempt due to an additional relief known as letting relief.

    This applies where a property which has been the taxpayer's main residence is then let out – the gain relating to this period is exempt up to the lower of:

    – The gain already exempt under the PPR relief rules
    – The gain relating to the let period
    – £40,000

    (iv) Finally, on the sale of the country house, the gain relating to the period when the flat was the main residence will be chargeable to capital gains tax, but the balance of the gain will be covered by the PPR relief rules

(b) On a related point, I am often asked by couples – what is the difference between owning a property as joint tenants or tenants in common.

Under joint tenancy, the husband and wife own the property but each holds 100% of the property. If the husband and wife (as co-owners) wish to sell the property they must both agree to do so. It also means that on the death of one of the spouses, the ownership of the entire property is vested automatically in the surviving spouse.

However, as tenants in common each owner owns a share of the whole property eg Jane owns 60% and Paul owns 40% of the whole house, not a particular area which represents a percentage of the building. Each owner can dispose of their interest to whomever they want and do not need to seek the other owner's agreement.

On death the property passes according to the terms of the deceased's will (or under the rules of intestacy).

Scottish Law

Under Scottish Law where property is held jointly the owners have no separate estates but each holds 100% of the property. If co-owners wish to sell the property then must all agree to do so. It also means that on the death of one of the owners, the ownership of the entire property passes automatically to the surviving spouse.

In the case of common property each owner has a title to his own share which he may dispose of as he wishes and on death it will pass according to the terms of his will, legal rights or intestacy. However, this is the way that husbands and wives own property in Scotland as the owners can use a special destination to ensure that the property passes to the survivor.

Marking scheme

				Marks
(a)	(i)	No CGT on sale of home	½	
		PPR relief	½	
		Explanation	1	
				2
	(ii)	One property eligible for PPR	1	
		Husband and wife – one PPR	1	
		Election	1	
		Time limit	1	
		May 2010	½	
		Consequence of no election	½	
		Varying election	1	
		Maximum		5
	(iii)	Elect for flat	½	
		Bigger gain on country house	½	
		Flat sold earlier	1	
		Effect of election	1	
		Effect of letting	1	
		5 years' exemption	½	
		Last 3 years exempt	1	
		Letting relief	1	
		Amount of letting relief	1	
		Maximum		7
	(iv)	Part chargeable/part exempt	1	
				1
(b)		Joint tenancy:		
		Each has interest in 100% of property	1	
		Joint decision to sell	½	
		Treatment on death	1	
		Tenants in common:		
		Each has % share	1	
		No consent needed to sell	½	
		Position on death	1	
				5
				20

13.2 Peter Stamp

COMPUTATION OF CHARGEABLE GAIN ON SALE OF HOUSE

Period	Explanation	Occupation or deemed occupation (months)	Non occupation (months)
2.5.82 – 1.2.86	Actual occupation	45	
2.2.86 – 1.12.95	Letting		118
2.12.95 – 3.7.05	Absence		115
4.7.05 – 3.7.08	Last three years deemed occupation	36	
		81	233

Total ownership period = 314 months

	£
Proceeds (3.7.08)	270,000
Less: cost	(70,000)
Gain before PPR relief	200,000
Less: Exemption for main residence $\dfrac{81}{314} \times £200,000$	(51,592)
	148,408
Less: letting exemption: lowest of	
£51,592 (gain exempted by private residence relief)	
£75,159 (chargeable gain attributable to letting) (W)	
£40,000 (maximum relief available for lettings)	(40,000)
Chargeable gain	108,408

Working

Gain in let period: $\dfrac{118}{314} \times £200,000 = £75,159$

14.1 Fran and Anna

(1) *Fran's gain:*

	£
Proceeds (MV) June 2008	500,000
Allowable cost	(75,000)
	425,000
Excess of actual consideration over cost: £100,000 – £75,000	(25,000)
Gain deferred	400,000
Gain chargeable in June 2008	£25,000

(2) *Anna's gain:*

	£	£
Proceeds July 2010		520,000
Cost (MV)	500,000	
Less: gain deferred (from part 1)	(400,000)	
Base cost		(100,000)
Chargeable gain		420,000

14.2 Joe Bloggs

MR BLOGGS – CHARGEABLE GAINS 2008/09

	£
Chargeable gains (W1 + W2)	425,000
Less: annual exemption	(9,600)
Taxable gain	415,400

Workings

1   *Sale of flat*

	£
Sale proceeds	700,000
Less: cost	(200,000)
	500,000
Less: PPR relief (75% × 500,000)	(375,000)
	125,000

2   *Sale of shares*:

	£
Proceeds (market value)	450,000
Less: cost	(75,000)
	375,000

Part of the gain of £375,000 may be subject to a gift relief claim under s.165 TCGA 1992:

	£	£
Gain before relief		375,000
Less: excess actual proceeds:		
Actual proceeds	375,000	
Less: cost	(75,000)	
		(300,000)
Gain eligible for gift relief		75,000
Gain taxed now		£300,000

14.3 P J Laval

(i)   CAPITAL GAINS TAX PAYABLE 2008/09

	£
House (W1)	60,000
Vic plc shares (W2)	5,910
Lavaling Ltd (W3)	15,000
Total gains	80,910
Less: Annual exemption	(9,600)
	71,310

Tax	
£71,310 @ 18%	12,836

Workings

(W1)   House 'Chez Nous' – 14 May 2008

	£	£
Proceeds		99,000
Less:		
Enhancement – 1983	2,000	
Cost	37,000	
		(39,000)
Chargeable gain		60,000

(W2) Vic plc shares – 18 July 2008

Share pool:

	No. of shares	Cost £
Purchase 10.2.83	1,400	3,500
Bonus issue (1 for 4)	350	–
	1,750	3,500
Sale 18.7.08	(1,400)	(2,800)
c/f	350	700

Calculate gain:

	£
Proceeds	8,710
Cost	(2,800)
Chargeable gain	5,910

(W3) Lavaling Ltd shares

At the time of disposal, the market value of Lavaling Ltd's chargeable assets were:

CHARGEABLE BUSINESS ASSETS	
Freehold property	130,000
OTHER CHARGEABLE ASSETS	
Quoted securities	30,000
	160,000

The proportion of the gain of £80,000 which is eligible for gift relief is found by applying the fraction:

$$\frac{\text{Market value of chargeable business assets}}{\text{Market value of chargeable assets}} = \frac{130,000}{160,000}$$

$$£80,000 \times \frac{130,000}{160,000} = £65,000$$

	£
Overall gain	80,000
Less: Gift relief	(65,000)
Chargeable gain	15,000

(iii) Freehold is an absolute interest in land. Subject to general law the freeholder can do as he wishes with the land.

A leasehold interest is qualified. The term is limited in time and the lease normally contains a range of covenants which are binding on the tenant.

Commonhold property must originally be freehold and must be owned by a commonhold association. Individual parts (commonhold units) are held as freehold by the unit holders. The commonhold is managed by the commonhold association which hold the common parts. Only the unit holders can be members of the commonhold association.

Marking scheme

(i) **CGT summary**:

	Marks
Gains	1
AE	1
Tax @ 18%	1
House 'Chez Nous'	
Enhancement expenditure	1
Gain calculation	1
Vic plc shares	
Purchase 10.2.80	1
Bonus issue	1
Disposal from pool	1
Gain calculation	1
Lavaling Ltd shares	
Identify CAs and CBAs	1
CBA/CA fraction	1
Proportion of gain eligible for gift relief	1
Chargeable gain	1
Maximum	13
(ii) Freehold – absolute interest	1
Can do as wish with	1
Leasehold – qualified interest	1
Limited in time	½
Limited by covenants	½
Commonhold – originally freehold	1
Ownership	1
Management association	1
Maximum	5
	18

14.4 Simon

To: Simon Evans
From: Frances Ackland
Date: 5 December 2008
Subject: Deferral of gains

Thank you for your memorandum of 3 December.

First of all, I have calculated that the gain on the disposal of the Blue plc shares is £150,000 (see Appendix).

The relief you refer to is deferral relief related to the Enterprise Investment Scheme. Briefly, you can obtain the relief if you subscribe for new fully paid up ordinary shares in an unlisted trading company provided it is not carrying on certain non qualifying trades such as farming or property development. The acquisition must be made within one year before your disposal (but I presume this is not the case here) and three years after the disposal (ie by 29 November 2011). At the time of the acquisition, you must be resident or ordinarily resident in the United Kingdom. You must make a claim by 31 January 2015. However, you may wish to make a claim sooner in order to avoid having to pay tax on the gain.

In order to defer the gain of £150,000 you would need to invest at least an amount equal to this gain. Since you wish to invest about £100,000 of the proceeds in the French house, this will leave you with only £100,000 of proceeds to invest in the shares. In this case, the remainder of the gain of £50,000 would remain chargeable to CGT. From this an annual exemption of £9,600 is deducted leaving £40,400 chargeable to tax. Tax at 18% would amount to £7,272.

One other point to note is that if you become non-resident and non-ordinarily resident in the UK broadly within three years of the acquisition of the shares, the gain you have deferred will be treated as becoming chargeable immediately before this time. This is obviously a danger since you wish to move to France.

Please let me know if you require any further details.

Appendix

	£	£
Proceeds		200,000
Less: cost	65,000	
less: held over gain	(15,000)	(50,000)
Gain before EIS deferral relief		150,000

14.5 Emily

Computation of taxable gains:

	£
Factory (W1)	75,000
Painting (W2)	23,000
Less: current year loss relief (W3)	(21,000)
Net chargeable gains	77,000
Less: annual exemption	(9,600)
Taxable gains	67,400

CGT:

	£
£67,400 @ 18%	12,132

Workings

1 Factory

	£
Proceeds	225,000
Less: cost	(150,000)
Chargeable gain	75,000

2 Painting

Transfer to Emily on 1.7.01 on no gain/no loss basis

Sale by Emily

	£
Proceeds	73,000
Less: cost (= cost to Arthur)	(50,000)
Chargeable gain	23,000

3 Vase

	£
Proceeds	19,000
Less: cost	(40,000)
Loss	(21,000)

14.6 Mr Richman

(Our address)

(Your address)

9 May 2009

Dear Mr Richman

SALE OF 'RED BRICKS'

Thank you for your letter of 4 May regarding the sale of your property 'Red Bricks'. As requested I have set out below how the capital gains tax liability will be calculated, taking into account all possible reliefs.

Principal Private Residence Exemption

On the sale of a property which has at some time been used as your principal private residence (PPR) some of the gain arising will be exempt from Capital Gains Tax.

The amount of this exemption is calculated as:

$$\text{Total gains} \times \frac{\text{Period of occupation as PPR}}{\text{Period of ownership}}$$

In addition to any actual periods of occupation you are allowed to include certain deemed periods of occupation, whilst you were absent from the property.

Deemed Periods of Occupation

The following can be included as periods of occupation:

(1)   The last three years of ownership, since the property has at some time been used as your PPR; and

(2)   Four years of your period of absence whilst working abroad, since you used the property as your PPR both before and after the absence, and there was no other exempt residence during your period abroad (see below as regards the restriction due to use as offices); and

(3)   Up to three years for any reason whatsoever.

You will therefore see, from the appendix attached, that you are deemed to have occupied the house as your principal residence for 21½ of the 27 years of ownership.

Business Use

During the period whilst part of the house was used exclusively as offices, the gain attributable to that part of the property will not be exempt as you are not occupying it as your PPR.

The last three years of ownership of both parts of the house will qualify as deemed occupation as you had occupied the whole of the property as a private residence at some point beforehand.

Capital Gains Tax Payable

Accordingly, I calculate that a gain of £52,963 (see appendix) will arise after all reliefs. £9,600 of this is covered by your annual exemption and the balance will be chargeable at 18%.

Thus tax of £7,805 will be payable on 31 January 2010.

I trust the above answers your query, but if you require any further assistance please do not hesitate to contact me.

Yours sincerely

A. Jones

Appendix

1. *Calculation of chargeable gain*

	£
Proceeds	370,000
Less: cost	(90,000)
Enhancement expenditure	(20,000)
Gain before PPR relief	260,000
Less: PPR relief (£260,000 × 21.5/27)	(207,037)
Chargeable gain	52,963

2. *PPR exemption*

	Occupation	Non-occupation	Total
6.4.82 – 5.4.87 (actual)	5		5
6.4.87 – 5.4.94			
(deemed 4 years)	4	–	4
(3 years for any reason)	3	–	3
6.4.94 – 5.4.95 (occupation)	1	–	1
6.4.95 – 5.4.06			
(11 years joint use)	5.5	5.5	11
6.4.06 – 4.4.09			
(final 3 years deemed occupation)	3		3
	21.5	5.5	27

14.7 Peter

Summary of gains:

	£
Building (W1)	400,000
Forum Follies plc (W2)	5,000
Dassau plc (W3)	7,100
	412,100
Less: losses b/f	(6,400)
Chargeable gains	405,700
Less: annual exemption	(9,600)
Taxable gain	396,100

	£
£396,100 @ 18%	71,298

CGT due 31.1.2010

Workings

1 *Building*

	£
Proceeds	600,000
Less: cost	(200,000)
Chargeable gain	400,000

2 *The takeover of Forum Follies plc*

The elements in the takeover consideration have the following values:	£
Ordinary shares (30,000 × £3.00)	90,000
Cash	10,000
Total consideration received	100,000

A gain only arises on the date of the takeover in respect of the cash element.

	£
Cash received (above)	10,000
Cost 50,000 × $\frac{10,000}{100,000}$	(5,000)
Chargeable gain	5,000

3   *Dassau plc shares*

    (i)   Share pool

	No. of shares	*Cost*
		£
Purchase: Dec 84	1,000	2,000
Rights issue (1 or 2)	500	1,000
	1,500	3,000
Disposal: Nov 08	(1,200)	(2,400)
c/f	300	600

	£
Proceeds	9,500
Less cost	(2,400)
Chargeable gain	7,100

14.8 Sarah Stone

Summary

	£
Peterson Ltd (W1)	82,000
Grandfather clock (W2)	2,200
House (W4)	37,000
Stamp collection (W3)	(1,000)
	120,200
Less: capital losses b/f	(15,000)
Net chargeable gain	105,200
Less: annual exemption	(9,600)
Taxable gain	95,600
∴ CGT @ 18%	17,208

Workings

1   *Shares*

Share pool:

	No. of shares	*Cost*
		£
Acquisition 1.3.86	50,000	25,000
Purchase 1.8.99	5,000	10,000
	55,000	35,000
Rights issue (1 for 5)	11,000	33,000
	66,000	68,000
Sale: April 2008	(66,000)	(68,000)
	–	–

Calculate gain:

	£
Proceeds	150,000
Less: cost:	(68,000)
Chargeable gain	82,000

2   *Grandfather clock*

	£
Net proceeds (£8,250 – £250)	8,000
Less: cost	(5,800)
Chargeable gain	2,200

Limited to: $^{5}/_{3} \times (8,250 - 6,000) = 3,750$ (does not apply)

3   *Stamp collection*

	£
Proceeds (deemed)	6,000 (replace actual proceeds)
Less: cost	7,000
Allowable loss	(1,000)

4   *House*

	£	£
Proceeds		75,000
Less: cost	28,000	
Enhancement	10,000	
		(38,000)
Chargeable gain		37,000

Personal Taxation

Index

TQT
Tax Qualification Training

TQT
Tax Qualification Training

TQT
Tax Qualification Training

REVIEW FORM & FREE PRIZE DRAW

All original review forms from the entire TQT range, completed with genuine comments, will be entered into a draw on 31 July 2009 and 31 January 2010. The names on the first four forms picked out will be sent a cheque for £50.

Name: _____   Address: _____

_____

How have you used this Text?
(Tick one box only)

☐ Home study (book only)

☐ On a course_____

☐ Other _____

Why did you decide to purchase this Text?
(Tick one box only)

☐ Have used TQT Texts in the past

☐ Recommendation by friend/colleague

☐ Recommendation by a lecturer

☐ Saw advertising

☐ Other _____

During the past six months do you recall seeing/receiving either of the following?
(Tick as many boxes as are relevant)

☐ Our advertisement in *Tax Adviser*

☐ Our Publishing Catalogue

Which (if any) aspects of our advertising do you think are useful?
(Tick as many boxes as are relevant)

☐ Prices and publication dates of new editions

☐ Information on Text content

☐ Facility to order books off-the-page

☐ None of the above

Your ratings, comments and suggestions would be appreciated on the following areas of this Text.

	Very useful	Useful	Not useful
Introductory section	☐	☐	☐
Quality of explanations	☐	☐	☐
Examples	☐	☐	☐
Chapter roundups	☐	☐	☐
Exam focus points / Examiner comments	☐	☐	☐
Legislative references	☐	☐	☐
Question bank	☐	☐	☐
Answer bank	☐	☐	☐
Index	☐	☐	☐

	Excellent	Good	Adequate	Poor
Overall opinion of this Text	☐	☐	☐	☐

Do you intend to continue using TQT Products?   ☐ Yes   ☐ No

Please note any further comments and suggestions/errors on the reverse of this page. The TQT author of this edition can be e-mailed at: suedexter@bpp.com

Please return to: Sue Dexter, Tax Publishing Director, BPP Learning Media Ltd, FREEPOST, London, W12 8BR. BPP Learning Media Ltd is a member of the TQT joint venture.

REVIEW FORM & FREE PRIZE DRAW (continued)

TELL US WHAT YOU THINK

Please note any further comments and suggestions/errors below.

FREE PRIZE DRAW RULES

1 Closing date for 31 July 2009 draw is 30 June 2009. Closing date for 31 January 2010 draw is 30 December 2009.

2 No purchase necessary. Entry forms are available upon request from TQT Professional Education. No more than one entry per title, per person. Draw restricted to persons aged 16 and over.

3 Winners will be notified by post and receive their cheques not later than 6 weeks after the draw date.

4 The decision of the promoter in all matters is final and binding. No correspondence will be entered into.